'Aidan Hehir and Robert W. Murray have chosen an innovative strategy for surmounting the entrenched divide between scholars who believe in human rights, come what may, and commentators fatalistically resigned to the rights' worthlessness on the ground. Instead of reflexively taking sides, the two collaborators present essays by international relations experts offering many alternative perspectives. This has freed the discourse from a straightjacket of dichotomous thinking and initiated a more generative process for finding consensus on how to move the human rights agenda forward.'

– *Susan H. Bitensky, Michigan State University College of Law, USA*

'There is a trend among atrocity prevention norm entrepreneurs to gather in like-minded groups, extol their virtues and control narratives to avoid criticism. This timely volume adopts a more inclusive and reflective approach; motivated by a determination to "get atrocity prevention right", the contributions here will help practitioners to examine our motives, our policy inconsistencies, and the gaps in our analysis and practice.'

– *Robert Zuber, Director, Global Action to Prevent War and Armed Conflict*

'Refusing to be deluded by wishful thinking, the authors of this volume undertake a clear-eyed, critical analysis of R2P's successes and failures. Steering between fatalism and denial, they concede that our awareness of atrocity and the protection of civilians has been enhanced by R2P but that its time has passed. In thinking about what comes next, there is no better place to start than this provocative and highly insightful book.'

– *Stephen Hopgood, SOAS, University of London, UK*

PROTECTING HUMAN RIGHTS IN THE 21ST CENTURY

This book contributes to current debates on the protection of human rights in the 21st century.

With the global economic collapse, the rise of the BRICS, the post-intervention chaos in Libya, the migration crisis in Europe, and the regional conflagration sparked by the conflict in Syria, the need to protect human rights has arguably never been greater. In light of the precipitous decline in global respect for human rights and the eruption or escalation of intra-state crises across the world, this book asks 'what is the future of human rights protection?' Seeking to avoid both denial and fatalism, this book thus aims to:

- examine the principles at the very foundation of the debate on human rights;
- diagnose the causes of the decline of liberal internationalism so as to offer guiding lessons for future initiatives;
- identify those practices and developments that can, and should, be preserved in the new era;
- question the parameters of the contemporary debate and advance perspectives that aim to identify the contours of future ideas and practices that may offer a way forward.

This book will be of much interest to students of humanitarian intervention, Responsibility to Protect, international organisations, human rights and security studies.

Aidan Hehir is Reader in International Relations at the University of Westminster, UK. He is the author/editor of numerous titles, including *Humanitarian Intervention: An Introduction* (2nd edn, 2013) and *The Responsibility to Protect: Rhetoric, Reality and the Future of Humanitarian Intervention* (2012).

Robert W. Murray is Managing Director of Dentons Canada LLP's Government Affairs and Public Policy Practice Group and Research Fellow at the Centre for Military, Security and Strategic Studies, University of Calgary, Canada. He is the author/editor of numerous titles, including *Multilateralism as State Strategy* (2016) and *International Relations and the Arctic* (2014).

Routledge Studies in Intervention and Statebuilding
Series Editors: Aidan Hehir and Nicolas Lemay-Hébert
Founding Editor: David Chandler

A full list of titles in this series is available at: www.routledge.com/Routledge-Studies-in-Intervention-and-Statebuilding/book-series/RSIS.

Recently published titles:

International Intervention and Statemaking
How exception became the norm
Selver B. Sahin

Rethinking Democracy Promotion in International Relations
The rise of the social
Jessica Schmidt

The Politics of International Intervention
The tyranny of peace
Edited by Mandy Turner and Florian P. Kühn

The Practice of Humanitarian Intervention
Aid workers, agencies and institutions in the Democratic Republic of the Congo
Kai Koddenbrock

Peace Figuration after International Intervention
Intentions, events and consequences of liberal peacebuilding
Gëzim Visoka

Regional Intervention Politics in Africa
Crisis, hegemony, and the transformation of subjectivity
Stefanie Wodrig

Protecting Human Rights in the 21st Century
Edited by Aidan Hehir and Robert W. Murray

The Contentious Politics of Statebuilding
Strategies and dynamics
Outi Keränen

PROTECTING HUMAN RIGHTS IN THE 21ST CENTURY

Edited by
Aidan Hehir and Robert W. Murray

LONDON AND NEW YORK

First published 2017
by Routledge
2 Park Square, Milton Park, Abingdon, Oxon OX14 4RN

and by Routledge
711 Third Avenue, New York, NY 10017

Routledge is an imprint of the Taylor & Francis Group, an informa business

© 2017 selection and editorial material, Aidan Hehir and Robert W. Murray; individual chapters, the contributors

The right of the editor to be identified as the author of the editorial material, and of the authors for their individual chapters, has been asserted in accordance with sections 77 and 78 of the Copyright, Designs and Patents Act 1988.

All rights reserved. No part of this book may be reprinted or reproduced or utilised in any form or by any electronic, mechanical, or other means, now known or hereafter invented, including photocopying and recording, or in any information storage or retrieval system, without permission in writing from the publishers.

Trademark notice: Product or corporate names may be trademarks or registered trademarks, and are used only for identification and explanation without intent to infringe.

British Library Cataloguing-in-Publication Data
A catalogue record for this book is available from the British Library

Library of Congress Cataloging-in-Publication Data
Names: Hehir, Aidan, 1977– | Hehir, Aidan, editor. | Murray, Robert W., editor.
Title: Protecting human rights in the 21st century / edited by Aidan Hehir and Robert W. Murray.
Description: Milton Park, Abingdon, Oxon ; New York, NY : Routledge, 2017. | Includes bibliographical references and index.
Identifiers: LCCN 2016046370| ISBN 9781138218925 (hardback) | ISBN 9781138218932 (pbk.) | ISBN 9781315436692 (ebook)
Subjects: LCSH: Human rights. | Humanitarian intervention.
Classification: LCC JC571 .P789 2017 | DDC 323—dc23
LC record available at https://lccn.loc.gov/2016046370

ISBN: 978-1-138-21892-5 (hbk)
ISBN: 978-1-138-21893-2 (pbk)
ISBN: 978-1-315-43669-2 (ebk)

Typeset in Bembo and Stone Sans
by Florence Production Ltd, Stoodleigh, Devon, UK

Aidan would like to dedicate this book to Sarah, Esmé, Elsie and Iris.

Bob would like to dedicate this book to Brady.

CONTENTS

Contributors	xi
Acknowledgements	xv
Introduction: denial, fatalism and the protection of human rights Aidan Hehir	1

PART I
Rethinking fundamental principles — 17

1. Global constituent power: protests and human rights — 19
   Anthony F. Lang, Jr.

2. A critical examination of 'humanity' — 34
   Samuel Jarvis

3. Failed interventions and the inherent contradictions of liberal internationalism — 51
   Eric A. Heinze

4. Humanitarian intervention in post-American international society — 71
   Robert W. Murray

PART II
'Protection' and peacekeeping — 89

5. The uncertainties of international protection — 91
   Kelly Staples

6 UN peacekeeping and the protection of civilians' norm   110
    Tom Keating

 7 From showpiece interventions to day-to-day civilian
    protection: Western humanitarian intervention
    and UN peacekeeping   126
    Jonathan Gilmore and David Curran

 8 The responsibility to protect or the protection of
    civilians: which policy brand is more 'successful'?   143
    Catherine Jones

PART III
The responsibility to protect and beyond   **163**

 9 Norm complexity and contestation: unpacking the R2P   165
    Alan Bloomfield

10 'Why is it that we keep failing?' The responsibility to
    protect as a hollow norm   184
    Aidan Hehir

11 Guns vs troops: the ethics of supplying arms   201
    James Pattison

12 The limits of R2P and the case for pacifism   215
    Jeremy Moses

13 The responsibility to protect: a long view   231
    Justin Morris

    Conclusion: The future of human rights protection   249
    Robert W. Murray

Index   259

CONTRIBUTORS

Alan Bloomfield is a Research Fellow at the University of New South Wales. He is best known in the global norm dynamics research agenda for introducing the concept of the 'norm antipreneur' in a 2015 *Review of International Studies* article. A book co-edited with Shirley Scott, *Norm Antipreneurs and the Politics of Resistance to Global Normative Change* (Routledge), tests the utility of the norm antipreneur concept in 12 issue-areas, and he is currently leading an Australian-German collaborative project examining how resistance affects norms' strength and content. Empirically, he researches resistance to new humanitarian norms, primarily the responsibility to protect norm and humanitarian access and individual criminal accountability norms. He also researches Indian and Australian foreign policy. His first book, *India and the Responsibility to Protect* was published by Ashgate, and a second book, provisionally titled *Australia's Strategic Culture in the Age of the Rising Asian Giants*, will be published by Palgrave. He has also published in journals such as *The Pacific Review*, the *Australian Journal of Politics and History* and *South Asia*.

David Curran is a Research Fellow at the Centre for Trust, Peace and Social Relations, at Coventry University, specializing in Peacekeeping, Peacebuilding, and Conflict Resolution. David's primary research investigates the role of conflict resolution in training programmes for military peacekeepers, which is the topic of his forthcoming monograph to be released in 2017. Additionally, David is currently working on the impact that Protection of Civilians has had on UN peacekeeping, as well as undertaking research into the United Kingdom's relationship with UN peacekeeping. David's recent publications include: *Perspectives on Peacekeeping and Atrocity Prevention: Expanding Stakeholders and Regional Arrangements* (co-editor, 2015); 'Resonating, Rejecting, Reinterpreting: Mapping the stabilisation discourse in the United Nations Security Council, 2000–2014' (with Paul Holtom, *Stability Journal*, 2015) 'Training for Peacekeeping: Towards increased understanding of conflict resolution' (*International Peacekeeping*, 2013); 'The "Bradford model" and the contribution of conflict resolution to the field of international peacekeeping and peacebuilding' (UOC *Journal of Conflictology*, 2012); 'Cosmopolitan peacekeeping and peacebuilding in Sierra Leone: What can Africa contribute?' (with Tom Woodhouse, *International Affairs*, 2007).

Jonathan Gilmore is a Senior Lecturer in Politics and International Relations at Kingston University. His research centres on the connections between international ethics, foreign policy rhetoric and the practice of security, with particular reference to peace operations and humanitarian intervention. His previous work has been published in *Security Dialogue, European Journal of International Relations, British Journal of Politics and International Relations* and *International Affairs*. His book *The Cosmopolitan Military* was published in 2015.

Aidan Hehir is a Reader in International Relations at the University of Westminster. He is the author/editor of numerous titles, including *Humanitarian Intervention: An Introduction* (2nd edition, 2013) and *The Responsibility to Protect: Rhetoric, Reality and the Future of Humanitarian Intervention* (2012).

Eric A. Heinze is Associate Professor and Associate Chair in the Department of International Studies at the University of Oklahoma, USA, where he teaches courses on international relations, international law and international ethics. Trained as a political scientist, his research focuses on the law and ethics of armed conflict, especially pertaining to non-state actors; humanitarian intervention and R2P; and genocide and mass atrocity. He is the author of *Waging Humanitarian War: The Ethics, Law and Politics of Humanitarian Intervention* (2009); *Global Violence: Ethical and Political Issues* (2016); and is currently co-editing (with Brent Steele) the *Routledge Handbook of Ethics and International Relations*.

Samuel Jarvis is a PhD candidate at the University of Sheffield. He holds a Masters and BA in International Relations, both from the University of Leeds. His PhD research is titled 'Moral Progress and its Political Limits: "Common humanity" as a driver of state behaviour' and is funded by an ESRC White Rose Network Scholarship. The project explores the complex relationship between the concept of humanity and the R2P, assessing the normative strengths and weaknesses of humanity as a motivational force, as well as tracing the role humanity has played in the theoretical development of the R2P. His research interests broadly cover the fields of International Relations, Political Theory and International Criminal Justice.

Catherine Jones is a Research Fellow in the Department of Politics and International Studies at the University of Warwick. In March/April 2016 she was a visiting research fellow at the Ralph Bunche Centre at City University of New York. Her research primarily focuses on normative change and particularly the engagement of Asian states with global norms of intervention within institutional settings. She has published in *The Pacific Review*, *International Politics* and *Pacific Focus*, and is currently working on a monograph based on her PhD.

Tom Keating is a Professor Emeritus and former Chair of the Department of Political Science at the University of Alberta. He is the author of *Canada and World Order* (2013) and also of *Global Politics, Emerging Networks, Trends, and Challenges* co-authored with Andy Knight (2010).

Anthony F. Lang Jr. is a Professor of International Political Theory in the School of International Relations at the University of St Andrews. His research and teaching focus on the intersection of law, ethics and politics at the global level, with a focus on the use of force. His work is interdisciplinary, drawing on political science, political theory, moral philosophy and legal theory. He has published three single authored books and edited or co-edited eight other books. He has published numerous articles in peer reviewed journals and chapters in edited volumes. His current work focuses on global constitutionalism, broadly defined.

Justin Morris is a Senior Lecturer in the School of Law and Politics at the University of Hull, UK. He was Head of the (then) Department from 2007–13. His primary research interests include: the Great Powers and the notion of Great Power responsibility, the United Nations Security Council, and the Responsibility to Protect (specifically in relation to forcible intervention), topics on which he has authored a number of articles. He is co-author (with the late Professor Hilaire McCoubrey) of *Regional Peacekeeping in the Post-Cold War Era* and co-editor (with Dr Richard Burchill and Professor Nigel White) of *International Conflict and Security Law: Essays in Memory of Hilaire McCoubrey*.

Jeremy Moses is a Senior Lecturer in the Department of Political Science and International Relations at the University of Canterbury, Christchurch, New Zealand. His research interests are in the ethics of war and intervention, with a particular focus on realism, pacifism, and the Responsibility to Protect. He has published a monograph entitled *Sovereignty and Responsibility: Power, Norms and Intervention in International Relations* (2014) and has previously published articles in *Review of International Studies*, *International Politics*, *Journal of Intervention and Statebuilding* and *Global Change, Peace and Security*. The research for this chapter was supported by a grant from the Royal Society of New Zealand's Marsden Fund (UOO1421).

Robert W. Murray is the Managing Director of Dentons Canada LLP's Government Affairs and Public Policy Practice Group. He holds a Senior Research Fellowship at the Atlantic Institute for Market Studies, and Research Fellowships at the University of Calgary's Centre for Military, Security and Strategic Studies and the University of Alberta's European Union Centre for Excellence. His recent publications include *Seeking Order in Anarchy: Multilateralism as State Strategy* (2016), *System, Society and the World: Exploring the English School of International Relations* (2nd edn, 2015), *International Relations and the Arctic: Understanding Policy and Governance* with Anita Dey-Nuttall (2014) and *Libya, the Responsibility to Protect and the Future of Humanitarian Intervention* (2013) with Aidan Hehir.

James Pattison is a Professor of Politics at the University of Manchester. His work focuses on the ethical issues surrounding conflict. His first book, *Humanitarian Intervention and the Responsibility to Protect: Who Should Intervene?* (2010) was awarded a 'Notable Book Award' in 2011 by the International Studies Association (International Ethics Section). His second book, *The Morality of Private War: The Challenge of Private Military and Security Companies* (2014) considers the ethical problems raised by the privatisation of war. He is currently writing a third book, provisionally entitled *Just and Unjust Alternatives to War*. This considers the ethics of the alternatives to direct military intervention, including diplomacy, naming and shaming, economic sanctions, arming rebel groups, and inducements.

Kelly Staples, is a Lecturer in International Politics at the University of Leicester. She was awarded her PhD by the University of Manchester in 2008 for a thesis on statelessness and political theory, the starting point for her 2012 book, *Retheorising Statelessness: Towards a Background Theory of Membership*. She has also published articles on recognition, statelessness and migration. Her current research is on subjectivity in international relations in general, and the meaning of international protection in particular.

ACKNOWLEDGEMENTS

We would like to thank all those at Routledge who have helped this book come to fruition, in particular Andrew Humphrys, Hannah Ferguson and Nicholas Lemay-Hebert. We would also like to thank the anonymous reviewers whose comments, in very different ways, encouraged us to complete this project. Special thanks to our contributors for their insights, and for responding to all our requests in a timely fashion.

Aidan would like to thank his wife Sarah and daughters Esmé, Elsie and Iris for all their love, support and inspiration. Special thanks to all the great people I've met over the past two years working to help those suffering in the migrant camps in Calais; people for whom the protection of human rights is a daily vocation rather than an academic curiosity.

Bob would like to thank Brianna Heinrichs for her work in helping to bring this volume to fruition, and Tom Keating for his thoughtful comments throughout this process.

INTRODUCTION

Denial, fatalism and the protection of human rights

Aidan Hehir

In recent years, the dramatic deterioration in respect for human rights across the globe has led to a proliferation of denial and fatalism. The impetus behind this edited collection is a determination to reject both. Debates on the protection of human rights have tended to be dominated by, on one side, those determined to celebrate 'progress' in the midst of calamity and, on the other, adherents to a bleak worldview who portray the protection of human rights as a naïve, peripheral and doomed venture. Though clearly both camps are diametrically opposed, there are certain commonalities; in particular both tend towards a polarising discursive stance that limits scope for productive debate. Dissenters are invariably portrayed by adherents to each position as simply wrong, and an intellectual chasm thus yawns.

This book is, therefore, an attempt to move beyond this impasse; contributors here are consciously *not* like-minded proponents of a particular worldview or loyal adherents to a distinct international relations (IR) theory or framework. The unifying ethos here is a desire to answer a particular question, rather than, in various ways, advance a particular answer. Contributors were presented with a summary of our understanding of the contemporary state of both human rights globally and the related academic debates, and asked to focus their analysis on one of the following three themes:

- diagnosis of the causes of the decline of liberal internationalism so as to offer guiding lessons for future initiatives;
- identification of those practices and developments that can, and should, be preserved in the new era;
- questioning of the parameters of the contemporary debate and advancing perspectives that aim to identify the contours of future ideas and practices that may offer a way forward.

In this sense, the hope is that this collection will serve as a catalyst; clearly this book alone cannot re-orientate the present debate, but hopefully it will make a modest contribution towards this goal by highlighting and encouraging potentially fruitful research streams that at present receive insufficient attention. Before discussing the nature of these streams, I outline the global context that gave rise to the denial and fatalism this collection challenges.

'A new era for the human rights movement'?

In its *World Report 2000*, Human Rights Watch presented a highly optimistic analysis of the trajectory of human rights protection. Pointing in particular to the international response to both Kosovo and East Timor in 1999, the report commended what it described as the 'new willingness' to act in defence of the oppressed and heralded 'a new era for the human rights movement' (Human Rights Watch 2000). This positive prediction was certainly not unique; after the end of the Cold War many had forecast the dawn of a more human-centred world order freed from the constraints imposed by the old bipolar system (Berdal 2003, p. 9; Barnett 2010, p. 21; Chesterman 2011, p. 2). A new understanding of 'relative' sovereignty was championed as the successor to 'old-fashioned' notions of sovereign inviolability, and greater respect for 'human security' was widely vaunted as a central component in the irresistible march of liberal democracy and globalisation (Chopra and Weiss 1992; Deng *et al.* 1996, Annan 1999). Proponents of this view argued that while international law had increased in both scope and depth during the Cold War, the paralysis caused by the bipolar standoff had rendered these legal developments impotent; now, however, with the ascent of the West, these laws could be implemented and thus we were, so it was claimed, entering 'the age of enforcement' (Robertson 2002, p. xvii).

Such sentiments are rarely heard today. Indeed, while 2015 was the ten-year anniversary of the recognition of R2P at the 2005 World Summit, throughout the year human rights organisations published a series of reports lamenting the precipitous decline in global respect for human rights. In Human Rights Watch's *World Report 2015* the organisation's Executive Director Ken Roth reflected, 'The world has not seen this much tumult for a generation ... Sometimes it can seem as if the world is unravelling' (Human Rights Watch 2015, p. 1). Echoing these sentiments, Jean-Marie Guéhenno, President of the International Crisis Group, stated that 2015 had witnessed 'the unravelling of the international order' and stated, 'let's admit that when confronted with conflict and change, there is no such thing as an "international community"' (Guéhenno 2015). Amnesty International's *2015 World Report* likewise noted, 'This has been a devastating year for those seeking to stand up for human rights and those suffering in war zones' (Amnesty International 2015). At a joint press conference with UN Secretary General Ban Ki-moon, Peter Maurer, President of the International Committee of the Red Cross, stated:

> Rarely before have we witnessed so many people on the move, so much instability, so much suffering. In armed conflicts in Afghanistan, Iraq, Nigeria,

South Sudan, Syria, Yemen, and elsewhere, combatants are defying humanity's most fundamental norms. Every day, we hear of civilians being killed and wounded in violation of the basic rules of international humanitarian law, and with total impunity. Instability is spreading. Suffering is growing. No country can remain untouched.

(International Committee of the Red Cross 2015)

Similarly, a report by the UN High Commissioner for Refugees (UNHCR), warned that the 'rapid acceleration' of 'spiralling crises' suggested the world was enduring an evolving 'paradigm change' characterised by 'an unchecked slide' into a new era of violence and human suffering (UNHCR 2015, pp. 3–5). High Commissioner António Guterres noted, 'It is terrifying that on the one hand there is more and more impunity for those starting conflicts' and lamented the 'utter inability of the international community to work together to stop wars and build and preserve peace' (Jones 2015). Sadly, this trend continued into 2016; indicatively, Freedom House's report *Freedom in the World 2016* recorded a decline in respect for global freedom for a tenth consecutive year (Freedom House 2016) and in his eighth report on R2P Ban Ki-moon accepted that the international community had 'fallen woefully short' in protecting human rights, noting that the 'frequency and scale of atrocity crimes have increased' (2016, pp. 2–3).

These broader trends have been illustrated in horrific detail by two crises that have come to dominate contemporary debates on human rights protection; the conflict in Syria and the refugee crisis in Europe. Syria has, since the crisis began in 2011, been a source of open divisions between the Permanent Five Members of the Security Council (P5), rendering them incapable of implementing a coordinated remedial strategy; as UN Secretary General Ban Ki-moon declared, 'conflict-related deaths increased dramatically' as a consequence of these divisions (2016, p. 5). The desultory response naturally led to widespread criticism of the UN – particularly the Security Council – and doubts about R2P's effectiveness (Gallagher 2015; Lombardo 2015; Morris 2016). The response to Syria, some argued, was evidence that, 'R2P has tragically fallen short' and that 'the front lines of international debate seem to have not moved at all, or snapped back to where they were 15 years ago with regard to Kosovo' (Rotmann *et al.* 2014, p. 370).

The conflict in Syria additionally contributed to an unprecedented refugee crisis in Europe; for the past two years the international media has been dominated by horrific tales of the refugee's travails and yet, European states have often appeared unable, and at times actively unwilling, to help (Čulík 2015; Osborne 2015; Council of Europe 2015; Mills 2015; Ralph 2015). Indeed, in October 2015 the UN High Commissioner for Human Rights accused some European states of committing 'systemic violations of human rights' in their treatment of refugees (Calamur 2015).

There has, therefore, been a precipitous decline in respect for human rights, an increase in mass atrocity crimes, and a greater unwillingness on the part of those with the capacity to help to actually do so. While attributing this reluctance to respond to human suffering overseas to the fallout from the 2008 financial crisis, the rise of populism, and scepticism about the very efficacy of intervention and statebuilding, Ban Ki-moon also noted that the broader geopolitical context – namely the growing power of Russia and China – had impeded international efforts to respond collectively and effectively to the myriad crises that had recently erupted (2016, pp. 4–5). Given that the 'unipolar moment' appears to have been definitively replaced by a new multipolarity comprising emerging powers with obviously little appetite for prioritising human rights protection above state sovereignty, not only does the contemporary state of human rights protection look bleak, so too does its future (Hehir and Murray 2012; Newman 2016).

Denial and fatalism

Unsurprisingly then, the optimism characteristic of the 'happy nineties' has dissipated (Kaldor 2003, p. 149). It has been replaced by what Ban Ki-moon described as 'a growing defeatism about promoting ambitious agendas like protection' (2016, p. 4). And yet, while this 'defeatism' is indeed readily evident, some have, quite conversely, responded by maintaining a narrative of 'progress' and 'success'.

In the years following R2P's recognition at the 2005 World Summit many lauded the revolutionary nature of R2P in often remarkably enthusiastic terms; R2P was variously hailed as 'the most significant adjustment to sovereignty in 360 years' (Axworthy and Rock 2009, p. 69), 'an enormous normative step forward, akin to an international Magna Carta' (Slaughter 2011) and 'a brand new international norm of really quite fundamental importance and novelty . . . that is unquestionably a major breakthrough' (Evans 2009, p. 16). This initial enthusiasm for R2P can perhaps be attributed to both post-World Summit excitement and the initial delight at the intervention in Libya, but some have continued to advance such sentiments even in the face of the calamitous events of the past two years. Indicatively, Simon Adams, Director of the Global Centre for the Responsibility to Protect, declared that R2P has made 'tremendous progress' (Adams 2015b) and claimed that proponents of R2P 'have won the battle of ideas' (Adams 2015a). Likewise Gareth Evans acclaimed the 'many grounds for optimism about the future of R2P over the next decade and beyond' (Evans 2015), while perhaps most effusively, Alex Bellamy, Director of the Asia-Pacific Centre for the Responsibility to Protect, asserted, 'R2P has begun to change the world' (2015, p. 111). Such optimism in the face of widespread global tragedy could be seen by some as brave, or simply naïve; the nature of the rhetoric has led others, however, to criticise purveyors of these views for their lack of humility (Hobson 2016), their overt 'hubris' (Kersten 2015), and for irresponsibly raising expectations (Gallagher 2015).

Evidence to support these claims regarding R2P's impact and future potential tend to evidence two characteristics; first, a focus on highlighting numerical support for the concept. This takes the form of counting Security Council

Resolutions that mention R2P, and tallying the number of states who have joined R2P related groups. While these figures are certainly impressive, the mere fact that states use the term or issue a support statement can hardly be deemed in itself to constitute a meaningful endorsement of R2P; after all, states such as Bahrain, Qatar, Sudan and North Korea have affirmed R2P while continuing to engage in widespread oppression domestically. Additionally, the manner in which the Security Council has employed R2P actually suggests the concept is being consciously used to evade taking remedial action (Hehir 2016).

This strain of R2P advocacy was perhaps best captured by Simon Adams' statement at the '2016 UN General Assembly Informal Interactive Dialogue on the Responsibility to Protect'. Speaking to a near empty hall, Adams declared that the consensus on R2P 'is as strong as it is undeniable' before once again reciting a list of figures relating to invocations of R2P and the number of states in various R2P organisations. During the speech Adams challenged the audience:

> [W]ho here believes that governments should simply ignore genocide occurring within sovereign borders? That states should be permitted to commit war crimes if they deem it militarily necessary? That there should be no accountability for crimes against humanity? Or that the international community should remain silent and compliant when civilians are deliberately targeted with cluster munitions, hospitals and schools are bombed, and humanitarian aid is withheld in order to use starvation as a weapon of war?
> (Adams 2016)

Unsurprisingly, none of those in attendance raised their hands; this unwillingness to publicly support indifference to genocide, etc. was, of course, interpreted as some form of meaningful commitment.

The second characteristic of those arguments championing R2P's transformative impact relates to the nature of the 'successes' attributed to R2P. It has been claimed that R2P demonstrated its real-world influence in cases such as the Côte d'Ivoire (Evans 2016, p. 3), Kenya (Adams 2015a), Kyrgyzstan (Luck 2015, p. 4), Libya (Bellamy 2015, p. 94), and the Central African Republic (Weiss 2014, p. 7). Yet, while it may well be the case that these were successful cases of external mediation/intervention – though of course post-2011 events in Libya suggest otherwise – the evidence to support the claim that R2P played a causal role is invariably lacking or manifestly tenuous (Morris 2013; Hehir 2013; Hehir 2015).

Yet, while the zealotry of some of R2P's more effusive advocates is often polarising, the fact that R2P has, by any objective measure, failed to have the impact many hoped it would can hardly be a cause for rejoicing. As Adrian Gallagher has noted, many critics of R2P are best described not as opponents of the concept but rather as 'sceptics'; people who would like to see R2P 'change the world' but simply don't think it has or can (Gallagher 2012). While recent global events appear to have proved the sceptics right, they will have found no reason to celebrate this, given the humanitarian costs associated with R2P's failure. There are others, however, who advance a different view, one that is actively hostile to the ethos underpinning R2P. For some, the very idea of the international regulation and protection of human rights – particularly one that permits humanitarian intervention – is problematic (Crawford and Kuperman 2006; Valentino 2011; Kissinger 2012). Sovereignty must, they argue, be absolute and there should be little – if indeed any – scope for the trans-state enforcement of human rights (Luttwack 1999; Gray 2001; Bickerton et al. 2006). This view pre-dates R2P and while it is naturally heavily associated with IR 'realists' – though many have pointed out that realism actually has considerable normative underpinnings that are often obscured by more recent 'doctrinal' purveyors of the theory (Booth 1991, p. 537; see also, Leblow 2003; Molloy 2006; Williams 2007; Cozette 2008) – the idea can be found to find favour with English School pluralists (Jackson 2000) and indeed traditional 'liberals' who echo John Stuart Mill's caution against intervention (Walzer 2011).

In response to the perceived excesses of liberal internationalism – and indeed neo-conservativism – as well as the obvious failures of the interventions in Iraq and Libya, many have thus advocated the return to a more insular, state-centric world order with a far less ambitious agenda for human rights protection (Pape 2012; Posen 2015; Cunliffe 2016). The rise of the BRICS has naturally been routinely cited as further reason to jettison notions of 'relative sovereignty' and the basis for heralding the end of global human rights protection (Lowenkron and Reiss 2016). In a world where Russia and China are increasingly willing to flex their muscles, the argument goes, the focus must return to achieving a balance of power, and thus the priority should be preserving a narrowly conceived notion of order, even if this means adopting a disinterested stance towards flagrant human rights abuses (Gjozo 2016).

There are many reasons why adopting such a disposition is attractive; R2P advocacy is often unpalatable, the record of intervention and statebuilding is certainly mixed (to say the least), and a new, more dangerous systemic alignment is clearly evolving. And yet, the undeniable fact is that prioritising order in the way suggested has catastrophic consequences for millions of people. While avoiding taking action on the basis of divisive and sensitive issues such as human rights protection *may* increase order among states, it *will* facilitate the commission of heinous crimes against myriad individuals within many states. To put it succinctly, therefore, while R2P may have failed to 'change the world', it is surely better to seek alternatives rather than abandon all hope.

Charting a way forward

What then, can those disinclined to either doggedly perpetuate the notion that R2P is viable or solemnly advocate a return to order-orientated geopolitics, do? The collection seeks to make the case for alternative approaches to the duality of the current debate by addressing the questions noted earlier. The agenda is, therefore, threefold: to interrogate some of the underlying assumptions related to humanitarian intervention and the notion of liberal internationalism through which the protection of human rights has been understood and practised since the end of the Cold War; to examine the idea of 'protection' and in particular explore the 'Protection of Civilians' concept, increasingly advanced as a more viable and palatable form of intervention; to critically analyse R2P so as to understand the nature of its failings and advance alternatives. Each is reflected in the tri-partite structure of the book and summarised below.

Re-thinking fundamental principles

If they ever truly existed, both the 'unipolar moment' and the 'age of enforcement' have ended. In the face of an increasingly volatile, uncertain and seemingly callous world, it seems a new 'paradigm' for human rights truly has begun. As noted earlier, we can choose to deny this, and continue to promulgate the old ideas previously dominant, or proclaim the death of human rights protection and the ascendancy of order-orientated power-politics. Those who recoil from each, however, will naturally seek to chart an alternative course; to do so, logically, necessitates (re)examining the fundamental principles that underpinned the assumptions previously prevalent. This is the focus of Part I.

In Chapter 1, Anthony Lang advocates an approach to the protection of human rights that challenges the notion that the interpretation of, and guardianship over, legal texts related to human rights resides with formal agents of the law. Exploring foundational principles central to constitutionalism – curiously side-lined in most of the pre-existing literature on human rights protection – Lang engages with the work of James Wilson to advance prescriptions related to mobilizing 'global constituent power'. Though not dismissive of the importance of legal texts, or the inter-state forums in which these are discussed, Lang argues that there is also a pressing need for 'spaces' that facilitate a more inclusive, representative and – crucially – constitutive debate. Lang's prescriptions echo the ideas about the power of global civil society as advanced in the 1990s but differ with respect to his engagement with, and advocacy of, constitutionalism. Though – as Lang accepts – existing forms of such global constituent power are imperfect and very much underdeveloped, the prescriptions he advances clearly challenge both the state-centric account of human rights protection and regulation, and Western-centric conceptions of 'activism'.

In Chapter 2, Samuel Jarvis engages with the concept of humanity; as he notes appeals to 'common humanity' have been central to R2P advocacy since its emergence in 2001 and are repeatedly invoked in speeches and academic debates. Yet, as Jarvis observes, surprisingly little attention has been paid to determining the precise nature of 'humanity' and specifically its efficacy as a rallying cry for international responses to intra-state mass atrocities. Jarvis argues that the repeated invocation of any ambiguous or contested term invariably causes both confusion and at times hostility. Thus, far from being 'an uncontested moral principle' that serves to unify and enable collective action, appealing to 'humanity' can actually impede consensus. Jarvis thus challenges us to refocus our attention on this 'under-theorised' concept in the hope that doing so will sharpen its contours and enable it to become the binding higher principle its current proponents mistakenly believe it to already be.

In Chapter 3, Eric Heinze critically analyses liberal internationalism and the practice of liberal interventionism. Heinze notes that while intervention in the post-Cold War era came to be routinely presented as 'liberal' in nature, the manner in which these actions were conducted, and the results they produced, were in contradiction to what one might consider normative liberal principles. Heinze argues, however, that rather than seeing these interventions as somehow illiberal – with the public 'liberal' justifications being merely a rhetorical facade masking the genuine 'realist' motivations – they in fact expose liberalism's inherent contradictions. Heinze argues that while liberalism projects an image orientated around the principles of tolerance, pluralism and equality, at its core it is based on 'power politics and even oppression'. This critique has, of course, clearly profound implications for the practice of human rights protection and, in the context of the evolving systemic alignment, ultimately serves as a caution against reifying the period of Western hegemony.

This theme of systemic change is directly addressed in Chapter 4 where Robert Murray assesses the prospects for human rights protection – and specifically humanitarian intervention – in what he terms 'post-American international society'. Murray highlights the fact that a new systemic distribution of power is underway; this is clearly, he notes, of major significance and one that must be considered when thinking about the future of human rights protection. The future, Murray argues, looks 'bleak' and, to a large extent, this is because of one 'major failure', namely 'international order was never successfully renegotiated after the Cold War to allow for a shift from a Westphalian view of sovereignty to one articulated through R2P'. Murray argues, therefore, that while some operated under the assumption that there existed a 'consensus around liberal values' this was never in fact the case; as the distribution of power changed and Western dominance diminished, this lack of consensus was exposed, leaving us in the current mire. Yet, rather than merely diagnose failure, Murray argues that English School pluralism constitutes a viable means by which to negotiate the current multipolarity and better understand the nature and efficacy of norms, so that a more genuine – albeit more modest – consensus on human rights can be established as a foundation upon which to potentially build a different legal order.

'Protection' and peacekeeping

To support the idea of 'protecting' human rights necessitates an understanding of both the theory and practice of 'protection'. In recent years the UN has launched an increasing number of peacekeeping missions with a mandate to engage in the 'protection of civilians' (POC). So prevalent and important have POC operations become, that, as Tom Keating notes in his chapter, the UN Secretary General Ban Ki-moon described POC as 'the defining principle' of the UN. Unlike R2P, POC has a ready-made institutional home within the UN – the Department of

Peacekeeping Operations – and a military infrastructure through which to operationalise the idea. While the BRICS are hostile to the idea of intervention without host state consent, there is evidence that they are willing to countenance UN Peacekeeping missions; China, indeed, has greatly increased its contribution to UN Peacekeeping in recent years to the point that today it contributes more troops than any of the other P5 states (Fung 2016). Given the evolving systemic change underway, it is likely that POC within UN Peacekeeping will be the primary – if not the exclusive – means by which collective international responses to intra-state humanitarian crises are operationalised. Part II, therefore, analyses the emergence and efficacy of this increasingly important practice.

Kelly Staples examines the nature of 'protection' as it relates to international law and the challenges faced by POC missions in Chapter 5. The very idea of 'protection' is, she notes, 'contested' and 'ambiguous'; though clearly this is in itself potentially problematic, Staples argues that this should not obscure broader issues that have a greater negative impact on civilian protection. These relate, she notes, to the willingness of states to violate international human rights law in part because of its inherently weak enforcement and regulatory mechanisms. The nature of these mechanism, she argues, works against advancing 'rule-like prescriptions' with respect to human rights protection; however, the lack of a concrete legal definition of protection actually enables a degree of flexibility with respect to POC mandates in UN Peacekeeping. This flexibility, therefore, imbues UN POC operations with a capacity to adapt to a variety of contexts by virtue of facilitating ad hoc tailored responses that are more effective than potentially divisive top-down legalistic strictures.

In Chapter 6, Tom Keating advances a positive analysis of the efficacy of UN POC operations but also, perhaps more importantly, the future trajectory suggested by the increased deployment of such missions. Keating notes that the 'emerging powers' are openly hostile to the diminution of state sovereignty and particularly the practice of non-consensual military intervention, but, crucially, have demonstrated a willingness to support POC operations. Describing this as a 'significant level of consensus among members of the Council that could be cultivated' Keating thus advances an analysis that challenges the fatalism regarding human rights protection prevalent in recent years. Keating notes, however, that a number of issues remain problematic, in particular 'the failure to adequately realise POC in conflict situations' and the perennially insufficient resources allocated to these missions by UN member states.

In Chapter 7, Jonathan Gilmore and David Curran compare and contrast what they term as 'showpiece' and 'subtle' forms of intervention. Attributing the latter to the modus operandi of Western states since the end of the Cold War, they note that these interventions are characterised by agents 'prioritising the speed in which the intervention can take place and maintaining physical distance from the conflict environment'. Though invariably more spectacular, in practice these interventions have been consistently hamstrung by a shallow 'depth of commitment' that has both endangered those suffering on the ground ostensibly being 'saved', and the long-term efficacy of the mission. The sorry fate of Libya naturally looms large in their analysis. By contrast, Gilmore and Curran note that UN Peacekeeping missions with POC mandates have evolved in a steady fashion since the 1990s to the point that they now exercise significant traction despite the fact that many of these missions fail to make headlines. Gilmore and Curran note that while Western states have been the loudest champions of human rights protection, their contribution to UN Peacekeeping missions has been quite modest: aside from the troubling contrast between words and deeds this highlights, in practical terms this is problematic as Western states have military capabilities the UN could sorely do with utilising. They suggest, therefore, that more should be done to 'channel the desire of Western states to "do something" about mass atrocity crimes, into higher levels of involvement in UN peacekeeping'.

In Chapter 8, Catherine Jones argues that while R2P and POC have increasingly been treated as synonymous, they are in fact quite distinct. While R2P's advocates have been noticeably more vocal, and many ostensibly R2P-type interventions have attracted great publicity, Jones argues that the POC initiative is more influential and has produced more tangible results. Engaging with the idea of 'branding', Jones argues that the R2P 'brand' is 'stronger, and clearer, and ironically more toxic' than POC. This paradox, she notes, manifests as loud – and often polarising – advocacy from within the R2P 'bubble' in New York, obscuring the more truly global acceptance of POC. Yet, Jones notes, R2P's prominence actually has potentially beneficial consequences for POC; by virtue of its proliferation, R2P opens 'spaces' for discussing issues related to the protection of human rights within which consensus around POC often emerges as a counter to the 'toxic' R2P narrative. In this sense, Jones notes 'R2P may create audiences more willing to engage with POC because of their aversion to R2P as a discourse'. Though clearly not the role envisioned for R2P by its champions, this has potentially beneficial consequences for the global protection of human rights.

The responsibility to protect and beyond

Whatever one's opinion of the efficacy of R2P, there can be no denying its prominence in international politics. Few concepts can have moved so quickly from the pages of an independent commission's report to the centre of high-level international political debate. As, by some distance, the pre-eminent framework for discussing the relationship between human rights, the state and the international community, R2P thus demands analysis. This book's underlying ethos – as discussed earlier – is that R2P has not had the impact its proponents claim, nor does its evolution suggest it is likely to play a significant role going forward. Given this, it is naturally important to both assess the nature of R2P's failings, and think about viable alternatives.

Alan Bloomfield argues in Chapter 9 that, while R2P's ascendency to the centre of international political debates 'has contributed to the steady advance of the broader anti-atrocity agenda', both the actual influence exercised by R2P to date, and its future efficacy are limited. Through an engagement with the literature on norms – specifically how norms meaningfully influence state behaviour – Bloomfield argues that R2P ultimately suffers from a lack of teeth; while states may have increasingly affirmed R2P, and indeed at times taken measures to implement some of its less contentious elements, ultimately, when it really counts, 'the cost of non-compliance will be insufficient to induce the sort of widespread compliance that R2P's advocates seek'. Owing to the existing institutional legal and political architecture, Bloomfield argues, 'it is difficult to *consistently* impose punishments of the sort which compel compliance with emerging norms'. Unless this is addressed – or states voluntarily change their behaviour to cohere with R2P – the concept, he suggests will remain 'a well-meaning but only weakly and indirectly effective statement of intent'. In conclusion, Bloomfield argues that the 'very scope and content of R2P' must be rethought and through an inclusive, less Western-centric, process.

In Chapter 10, I challenge the conflation of R2P's widespread invocation with its purported efficacy. While I acknowledge that R2P has many of the attributes associated with a 'norm', its widespread affirmation and invocation cannot in itself be heralded as evidence of genuine, meaningful support for the concept nor of its necessarily positive efficacy. Literature on the nature and influence of norms – particularly that literature that challenges the linear 'life-cycle' model – suggests that norms, once established, can suffer co-optation, and thus be invoked for purposes other than that intended by their architects. I argue that R2P's 'hollow nature and malleability' meant it was particularly vulnerable to this process and that this hollowness best explains the popularity of the concept among states today. Ultimately, I suggest that given that R2P does not involve or envision any legal or institutional reform, and as a result is today popular but largely impotent, it is necessary to rethink the presumption that a transformative improvement in human rights protection can be achieved while the system remains unchanged.

In Chapter 11, James Pattison notes that the appetite for humanitarian intervention among Western states has rapidly declined; though Pattison cautions that this is by no means the only method of defending human rights – or acting in accordance with R2P – the likelihood is that situations *will* arise that call for action taken without the consent of the host state. Pattison notes, however, that 'alternatives to direct military intervention have not been sufficiently explored' by those assessing the ethics of humanitarian intervention. Yet, he observers an increasing propensity among Western states to supply arms to rebels groups at war with oppressive regimes as a substitute for overt military action. Assessing the ethics of this emerging practice from the perspective of the just war tradition, Pattison argues that, though widely practised, arming rebels is 'even more dangerous than engaging in direct military intervention, and offers potentially fewer countervailing benefits'. He additionally asserts, however, that 'the current international laws on providing arms *are* unfair to rebels'; rather than support legalising the supply of arms to rebels, Pattison recommends tighter restrictions on the sale of arms to states likely to commit violations of international humanitarian law.

12   Aidan Hehir

In Chapter 12, Jeremy Moses challenges the very idea of regulating 'humanitarian intervention'. He argues that whatever the intention, using military force 'cannot ever be adequately encapsulated in a normative framework' and thus initiatives such as R2P are ultimately doomed to, in practice, precipitate human suffering as 'violence necessarily takes place in an exceptional condition in which "normality" has already been suspended'. Though Moses accepts that it is conceivable that situations can arise where the use of force is legitimate, it is the manner in which such force is necessarily employed that is problematic. Drawing in particular on the intervention in Libya, Moses cautions that calls for the use of military force to protect those suffering can only ever be acted upon by states with their own set of interests and priorities. As such, he claims, 'R2P is far more likely to act as an enabling device in the interests of the greatest powers within international politics than it is to promote effective protection of civilians or restraint in the use of force'. Moses concludes, therefore, by calling for proponents of humanitarian intervention to rethink their position on the use of force, suggesting instead the 'exploration of non-violent alternatives'.

In Chapter 13, Justin Morris argues that to understand the role R2P plays within the UN today, we must appreciate the organisations original aims. By engaging with the thinking behind the establishment of the UN – and the debates that took place at the time – Morris argues that the UN is fundamentally 'a creature largely of the Great Powers' consciously designed to serve as an 'arena' for managing their interactions. Given its *raison d'être*, it is hardly surprising, Morris argues, that initiatives such as R2P are implemented selectively and prey to the whims of the powerful. The UN's narrow remit, Morris argues, should not be deemed devoid of normative merit; given the scale of the human suffering wrought by the two world wars that preceded the foundation of the UN and the likelihood that any future wars between the Great Powers would be considerably more destructive, facilitating the peaceful – if at times clearly uneasy – coexistence among the Great Powers is in itself of considerable normative worth. But, to fully appreciate the limited power of R2P demands an understanding of this preference for facilitating the interests of the Great Powers. Thus, Morris argues that while the 2005 World Summit, to some extent, made it more difficult for states – including the P5 – to openly support the right of states to treat their people *however* they please, R2P was ultimately recognised in 2005 because 'the concept leaves intact the fundamentals of the UN as understood and agreed in 1945'.

Conclusion

Soon after the 2005 World Summit, Alex Bellamy described R2P as 'the only show in town for those serious about preventing future Kosovos and future Rwandas' (2006, p. 15). Thankfully – given the widespread consensus that R2P has ultimately failed – Bellamy's stark pronouncement is simply not true. If R2P is (or was) 'the only show in town' then of course we would, reflecting on contemporary global events and R2P's evident impotence, be forced to abandon hope that the protection of human rights – even at the very least the prevention of mass atrocities – could ever be central to International Politics.

Throughout this collection, the contributors advance a variety of analyses and prescriptions that range from the theoretical to the empirical, with the ultimate aim being to positively contribute to thinking around the best way to protect human rights in the twenty-first century, in what one might call 'the post-R2P world'. It seems highly unlikely of course that R2P will disappear anytime soon, but as various contributors here note, its influence on the behaviour of states will likely continue to be minimal. The key question then for those who seek to steer clear of both denial and fatalism is 'what might work better?' Hopefully, this collection will facilitate discussions among those seeking a viable answer.

References

Adams, S 2015a, 'R2P at Ten', *E-International Relations*, 29 March. Available from: www.e-ir.info/2015/03/29/r2p-at-10/. [06 December 2016].

Adams, S 2015b, 'The Responsibility to Protect: Ten Years On', *OpenCanada*, 8 May. Available from: www.opencanada.org/features/the-responsibility-to-protect-10-years-on/. [06 December 2016].

Adams, S 2016, 'Statement of the Global Centre for the Responsibility to Protect at the 2016 UN General Assembly Informal Interactive Dialogue on the Responsibility to Protect', 6 September. Available from: www.globalr2p.org/media/files/2016-gcr2p-r2p-interactive-dialogue-statement.pdf. [06 December 2016].

Annan, K 1999, 'Two Concepts of Sovereignty', *The Economist*, 18 September, pp. 49–50.

Amnesty International 2015, 'Annual Report 2014/2015'. Available from: www.amnesty.org/en/latest/research/2015/02/annual-report-201415/. [06 December 2016].

Axworthy, L and Rock, A 2009, 'R2P: A New and Unfinished Agenda', *Global Responsibility to Protect*, vol. 1, no. 1, pp. 54–69.

Barnett, M 2010, *The International Humanitarian Order*, Routledge, London.

Bellamy, A (2006) 'The Responsibility to Protect after the 2005 World Summit', Policy Brief No. 1, Carnegie Council on Ethics and International Affairs, Avalable from: https://static1.squarespace.com/static/522cc5b4e4b0a015e8d59b21/t/522d28fbe4b074119b22da42/1378691323340/Bellamy_PreventingFutureKosovos.pdf, [06 December 2016].

Bellamy, A 2015, *The Responsibility to Protect: A Defence*, Oxford University Press, Oxford.

Berdal, M 2003, 'The UN Security Council: Ineffective but Indispensable', *Survival*, vol. 45, no. 2, pp. 7–30.

Bickerton, C, Cunliffe, P and Gourevitch, A (eds) 2006, *Politics Without Sovereignty: A Critique of Contemporary International Relations*, Routledge, London.

Booth, K 1991, 'Security in Anarchy: Utopian Realism in Theory and Practice', *International Affairs*, vol. 67, no. 3, pp. 527–545.

Calamur, K 2015, 'European Refugee Crisis: A "Systematic" Violation of Human Rights', *The Atlantic*, 22 October. Available from: www.theatlantic.com/international/archive/2015/10/czech-republic-un-human-rights-refugees/411862/. [06 December 2016].

Chesterman, S 2011, 'The Outlook for UN Reform', New York University School of Law, Public Law and Legal Theory Research Paper Series, Working Paper, August. Available from: http://ssrn.com/abstract=1885229. [06 December 2016].

Chopra, J and Weiss, T 1992, 'Sovereignty is no Longer Sacrosanct', *Ethics and International Affairs*, vol. 6, pp. 95–117.

Council of Europe 2015, 'Statement: European Countries' Migration and Asylum Policies Have Been Disastrous', 10 December. Available from: www.coe.int/en/web/commissioner/-/european-countries-migration-and-asylum-policies-have-been-disastrous?redirect=www.coe.int/en/web/commissioner/home?p_p_id=101_INSTANCE_iFWYWFoeqhvQ&p_p_lifecycle=0&p_p_state=normal&p_p_mode=view&p_p_col_id=column-1&p_p_col_count=4. [06 December 2016].

Cozette, M 2008, 'Reclaiming the Critical Dimension of Realism', *Review of International Studies*, vol. 34, no. 1, pp. 5–27.

Crawford, T and Kuperman, A (eds), 2006, *Gambling on Humanitarian Intervention*, Routledge, London.

Čulík, J 2015, 'Czech People Little Moved by Refugees' Plight', *Europe's World*, 26 October. Available from: http://europesworld.org/2015/10/26/czech-public-little-moved-by-refugees-plight/#.Vi9ch7fhDIUn. [06 December 2016].

Cunliffe, P 2016, 'From ISIS to ICISS: A Critical Return to the Responsibility to Protect Report', *Cooperation and Conflict*, vol. 51, no. 2, 233–247.

Deng, F, Kimaro, S, Lyons, T, Rothchild, D, and Zartman, W 1996, *Sovereignty as Responsibility: Conflict Management in Africa*, The Brookings Institution, Washington DC.

Evans, G 2009, 'From an Idea to an International Norm' in R Cooper and J Kohler, (eds), *Responsibility to Protect: The Global Moral Compact for the 21st Century*, pp. 15–30. Palgrave Macmillan, Hampshire and New York.

Evans, G 2015, 'R2P: Looking Back, Looking Forward', Keynote Address, Phnom Penh, Cambodia, 26 February. Available from: www.gevans.org/speeches/speech568.html. [06 December 2016].

Evans, G 2016, 'R2P: The Next Ten Years' in A Bellamy and T Dunne, (eds), *Oxford Handbook of the Responsibility to Protect*, pp. 913–931. Oxford University Press, Oxford.

Freedom House 2016, 'Anxious Dictators, Wavering Democracies: Global Freedom under Pressure'. Available from: https://freedomhouse.org/report/freedom-world/freedom-world-2016. [06 December 2016].

Fung, C 2016, 'China's Troop Contributions to U.N. Peacekeeping', United States Institute of Peace, 26 July. Available from: www.usip.org/publications/2016/07/26/china-s-troop-contributions-un-peacekeeping. [06 December 2016].

Gallagher, A 2012, 'A Clash of Responsibilities: Engaging with Realist Critiques of the R2P', *Global Responsibility to Protect*, vol. 4, no. 3, pp. 334–357.

Gallagher, A 2015, 'The Responsibility to Protect Ten Years on from the World Summit: A Call to Manage Expectations', *Global Responsibility to Protect*, vol. 7, no. 3, pp. 254–274.

Gjozo, E 2016, 'Let Russia Own Syria', *The National Interest*, 15 September.

Gray, C 2001, 'No Good Deed Shall Go Unpunished' in K. Booth, (ed.), *The Kosovo Tragedy*, pp. 302–306. Frank Cass, London.

Guéhenno, J-M 2015, 'The World's fragmenting Conflicts', International Crisis Group: The Future of Conflict, 26 October. Available from: https://medium.com/the-future-of-conflict/the-world-s-fragmenting-conflicts-7d9c2eac98d6. [06 December 2016].

Hehir, A 2013, 'The Permanence of Inconsistency: Libya, the Security Council and The Responsibility to Protect', *International Security*, vol. 38, no. 1, pp. 137–159.

Hehir, A 2015, 'The Dog That Didn't Bark?: A Response to Dunne and Gelber's Analysis of RtoP's Influence on the Intervention in Libya', *Global Responsibility to Protect*, vol. 7, no. 2, pp. 211–224.

Hehir, A 2016, 'Assessing the Influence of the Responsibility to Protect on the UN Security Council during the Arab Spring', *Cooperation and Conflict*, vol. 51, no. 2, pp. 166–183.

Hehir, A and Murray, RW 2012, 'Intervention in the Emerging Multipolar System: Why R2P will Miss the Unipolar Moment', *Journal of Intervention and Statebuilding*, vol. 6, no. 4, pp. 387–406.

Hobson, C 2016, 'Responding to failure: The Responsibility to Protect after Libya', *Millennium*, vol. 44, no. 3, pp. 433–454.

Human Rights Watch 2000, 'Introduction', *World Report 2000*. Available from: www.hrw.org/legacy/wr2k/. [06 December 2016].

Human Rights Watch 2015, *World Report 2015*. Available from: www.hrw.org/sites/default/files/world_report_download/wr2015_web.pdf. [06 December 2016].

International Committee of the Red Cross 2015, 'World at a Turning Point: Heads of UN and Red Cross issue joint warning', 30 October. Available from: www.icrc.org/en/document/conflict-disaster-crisis-UN-red-cross-issue-warning. [06 December 2016].

Jackson, R 2000, *The Global Covenant: Human Conduct in a World of States*, Oxford University Press, Oxford.

Jones, S 2015, 'One in every 122 people is displaced by war, violence and persecution, says UN', *The Guardian*, 18 June. Available from: www.theguardian.com/global-development/2015/jun/18/59m-people-displaced-war-violence-persecution-says-un. [06 December 2016].

Kaldor, M 2003, *Global Civil Society: An Answer to War*, Polity, London.

Kersten, M 2015, 'The Responsibility to Protect Doctrine is Faltering. Here's Why', *The Washington Post*, 8 December. Available from: www.washingtonpost.com/news/monkey-cage/wp/2015/12/08/the-responsibility-to-protect-doctrine-is-failing-heres-why/. [06 December 2016].

Ki-moon, B 2016, 'Mobilizing Collective Action: The Next Decade of the Responsibility to Protect', Report of the Secretary-General, A/70/999–S/2016/620.

Kissinger, H 2012, 'Syrian Intervention Risks Upsetting Global Order', *Washington Post*, 2 June. Available from: www.washingtonpost.com/opinions/syrian-intervention-risks-upsetting-global-order/2012/06/01/gJQA9fGr7U_story.html. [06 December 2016].

Leblow, RN 2003, *The Tragic Vision of Politics*, Cambridge University Press, Cambridge.

Lombardo, G 2015, 'The Responsibility to Protect and the Lack of Intervention in Syria: Between the Protection of Human Rights and Geopolitical Strategies', *International Journal of Human Rights*, vol. 19, no. 8, pp. 1190–1198.

Lowenkron, B and Reiss, M (2016) 'Pragmatic Primacy: How America Can Move Forward in a Changing World', *The National Interest*, 11 September.

Luck, E 2015, 'The Responsibility to Protect at Ten: The Challenges Ahead', Stanley Foundation, Policy Brief, May.

Luttwak, E 1999, 'Give War a Chance', *Foreign Affairs*, vol. 78, no. 4, pp. 36–44.

Mills, K 2015, 'Syria and the Mediterranean Refugee Crisis: A Failure of International Responsibilities', *Huffington Post*, 5 October. Available from: www.huffingtonpost.co.uk/kurt-mills/syria-refugee-crisis_b_8231874.html. [06 December 2016].

Molloy, S 2006, *The Hidden History of Realism*, Palgrave Macmillan, Basingstoke and New York.

Morris, J 2013, 'Libya and Syria: R2P and the Spectre of the Swinging Pendulum', *International Affairs*, vol. 89, no. 5, pp. 1265–1283.

Morris, J 2016, 'The Responsibility to Protect and the use of force: Remaking the Procrustean bed?', *Cooperation and Conflict*, vol. 51, no. 2, pp. 200–215.

Newman, E 2016, 'What Prospects for Common Humanity in a Divided World? The Scope for R2P in a Transitional World Order', *International Politics*, vol. 53, no. 1, pp. 32–48.

Osborne, S 2015, 'Refugee Crisis: Families could freeze to death after leaders warn EU could "fall apart" if it fails to reach deal', *The Independent*, 27 October. Available from:

www.independent.co.uk/news/world/europe/refugee-crisis-families-could-freeze-to-death-after-leaders-warn-eu-could-fall-apart-if-it-fails-to-a6708776.html. [06 December 2016].

Pape, R 2012, 'When Duty Calls: A Pragmatic Standard of Humanitarian Intervention', *International Security*, vol. 37, no. 1, pp. 41–80.

Posen, B 2015, *Restraint: A New Foundation for U.S. Grand Strategy*, Cornell University Press, Ithaca, NY.

Ralph, J 2015, 'R2P at 10: Looking Beyond Military Intervention', OpenCanada, 21 May. Available from: www.opencanada.org/features/r2p-at-10-looking-beyond-military-intervention/. [06 December 2016].

Robertson, G 2002, *Crimes Against Humanity*, Penguin, London.

Rotmann, P, Kurtz, G and Brockmeier, S 2014, 'Major Powers and the Contested Evolution of a Responsibility to Protect', *Conflict, Security and Development*, vol. 14, no. 4, pp. 355–377.

Slaughter, A-M 2011, 'A Day to Celebrate, but Hard Work Ahead', *Foreign Policy*, 18 March. Available from: www.foreignpolicy.com/articles/2011/03/18/does_the_world_belong_in_libyas_war?page=0,7. [06 December 2016].

United Nations High Commissioner for Refugees 2015, 'World at War: UNHCR Global Trends'. Available from: http://unhcr.org/556725e69.html. [06 December 2016].

Valentino, B 2011, 'The True Costs of Humanitarian Intervention', *Foreign Affairs*, vol. 90, no. 6, pp. 60–73.

Walzer, M 2011, 'The Case Against Our Attack on Libya', *The New Republic*, 20 March 2011. Available from: https://newrepublic.com/article/85509/the-case-against-our-attack-libya. [06 December 2016].

Weiss, T 2014, 'Military Humanitarianism: Syria hasn't killed it', *The Washington Quarterly*, vol. 37, no. 1, pp. 7–20.

Williams, M 2007, *Realism Reconsidered*, Oxford University Press, Oxford.

PART I
Rethinking fundamental principles

1

GLOBAL CONSTITUENT POWER

Protests and human rights[1]

Anthony F. Lang, Jr.

Introduction

The enthusiasm for human rights that emerged in the post-Cold War era has been undermined by a resurgence of sovereigntist claims from Russia and China along with cultural resistance to the liberal ideal of the individual in the Middle East and elsewhere. Can human rights still be protected and promoted? This chapter defends human rights not from a liberal cosmopolitan position but from a global constitutional one. Though some work in global constitutionalism has made a defence of rights from a broadly cosmopolitan position (Kumm 2009), this chapter instead argues that a truly global constitutional order with rights at its heart requires a robust constituent power as the basis by which such rights can be defended. More specifically, this means that protest movements and global activism will promote and protect rights more effectively than efforts to perfect legal texts or rely on judicial bodies (both global and national) to defend them. Of course, legal texts and judicial activism are central to rights, but when they become ossified standards of certainty or promote idealized normative orders, rights will be undermined. Moreover, a legalist defence of rights can easily be hijacked by powerful agents, whereas the constitutional idea I defend here is less susceptible to such moves.

The chapter proposes a theory of global constituent power and how human rights play an important role in the co-constitution of the global constitutional order in which rights are central. The theoretical basis for my argument is drawn from James Wilson, an American founder who argued that a constitution must be representative in all its aspects, not simply in the legislature. Moreover, he argued against the enumeration of a bill of rights because he believed that the structure of a government would lead the people toward a continued engagement with and demand for their rights through properly designed institutional forms. For Wilson, rights were not set in stone as a singular universal ideal but were constantly up for negotiation by the people whose sovereignty constitutes the political order. To make concrete my argument, I look to the World Social Forum (WSF) and its efforts to create alternative global political spaces that rely on but also fundamentally challenge liberal ideas of human rights.

Global constitutionalism

A constitution is the set of principles and rules that govern a society. A constitutional political and legal order enables and constrains political decision making. Four principles make manifest these limiting and enabling functions: the rule of law, a balance/separation of powers, constituent power, and rights.

The rule of law is the idea that a political order should be organized so that decisions result from a rule based system that has emerged from a legislative process. The historical emergence of constitutionalism came in response to governance by individuals who cared little or nothing for consistency and fairness (Bingham 2011). The rule of law is not simply the existence of a legal code, however. Law must arise from a legislative process, one that reflects a diversity of interests and allows a community not simply to create law but to engage in the practice of politics in order to prevent the rule by law rather than of law (Ginsburg and Simpser 2014).

The separation of powers is the next crucial element of a constitutional system. As with the rule of law, the separation of powers is a device for ensuring that no one political actor has too much power or can direct the political system to his/her own purposes. In ancient and medieval contexts, the separation of powers arose from the need for different social classes to be represented in the political order. This separation evolved in the early modern period into a separation of functions rather than classes or forms, becoming the balance of power in a constitutional order, as the functions of the legislature, executive and judiciary came to serve different roles that ensured that no one agent (particularly the executive) could dominate the political system. Montesquieu (1748 [1989]) has become the most famous theorist in the history of political thought to develop this idea, though his version was based on a somewhat idealized picture of the British constitutional system. The separation of powers provides a means not only to limit power but also to enable power by channelling it into productive and useful ends.

Constituent power, the third principle, is defined as the idea that a constitutional order is one that rests upon the people. This idea is sometimes referred to in French as *pouvoir constituant* due to the heritage of the French Revolution and its theorist, Emmanuel Joseph Sieyès, better known as Abbe Sieyès. In his pamphlet, 'What is the Third Estate', Sieyès gave voice to the people and argued for their centrality in the creation of a constitutional system (Sieyès 1789 [1970]). The idea of constituent power is not the same as representation, but is the source of authority for a constitution, often made manifest in the convention that drafts the constitution itself. This power, however, should not be confined to any historical moment, but relies on a continued engagement of the people with their rulers and with the structure of the system.

The final principle that plays a part in constitutional theory that is often the most prominent in 'popular' conceptions of constitutionalism is that of rights. Rights, either in a domestic or global context, have increasingly become part of constitutional theory and practice. The classic legal definition of rights comes from Wesley Hohfeld, an American theorist of the early twentieth century: rights are justified demands we make on others (Hohfeld 1946 [1918]).[2] This definition is not the only or final one, of course, though it does lay out some important features of rights. Rights are not a form of charity, but are demands we can legitimately make. Further, rights arise in a communal context and so require some exchange among individuals. Rights are, in other words, at that intersection of politics and law where I have located constitutionalism more generally. Many assume that constitutional theory can be reduced to the protections that rights afford especially through the exercise of judicial review. Ronald Dworkin famously argued that rights are trumps in political life, a basis against which all other practices must be measured (Dworkin 1977). However, as will become clear in my discussion of Wilson that follows, if we reduce rights to the written constitutional text, we fail to appreciate how rights arise from and depend on political engagement across a range of different political spaces.

How do these principles relate to global constitutionalism? Some argue that for any global order to be constitutional, it must be tied to a specific constitutional text. Bardo Fassbender has been a leading proponent of the view that the global constitutional order is found in the UN Charter (Fassbender 2009). Certain strands in international legal theory also focus on the way in which judiciaries and legal texts define international law, which has been described as the 'constitutionalization' of international law (Klabbers *et al.* 2009). There has also emerged a literature on legal pluralism that relates to global constitutionalism, one that derives from efforts to negotiate the relationship between legal orders in European states and the European Union (Maduro 2009).

Political theorists have also contributed to this literature. Some of these works take a cosmopolitan approach, drawing on Immanuel Kant, particularly his political writings, and propose a move toward a global constitution. Jürgen Habermas has made this argument in the context of European Union politics, drawing on Kant's *Perpetual Peace* essay to propose an evolution from state to state international law to cosmopolitan law (Habermas 2001, 2006). Garrett Wallace Brown draws on not only the *Perpetual Peace* essay but a wide range of Kant's work on political philosophy and public law to explore the potential for a global constitutional order (Brown 2009, 2012). Jean Cohen has recently argued that the idea of federalism might be a better way to negotiate the space between individuals and institutions than the cosmopolitan or legal pluralist arguments noted above that results in what she calls 'low intensity constitutionalization' (Cohen 2012).[3]

International Relations theorists have also proposed constitutional interpretations of the global order. Liberal theorists, such as G. John Ikenberry suggest that the international order is becoming more constitutional as the rule of law and human rights become more prominent, an argument that assumes the triumph of American and British liberal ideas (Ikenberry 2006). A republican literature focuses on how balances and law promote and protect individual agents. These works draw on sources such as Aristotle and Vattel (Onuf 1998) and the American founders (Deudney 2007). Antje Wiener has drawn upon constructivist theories of international relations alongside of wide ranging interviews with European policy elites to propose the existence of an 'invisible constitution' in certain regional and international contexts (Wiener 2008).

As is evident from this brief review, there is a wide array of approaches to the study of global constitutionalism. Much of the work arising from moral and legal theory has focused on the rule of law. Those working within international relations theory and, to a lesser extent political theory, have been drawn to the separation of power. Constituent power, however, remains the least commonly addressed. This is perhaps because of its heritage as a theory of the nation state, i.e., as an effort to identify a particular 'people' that can come together and create a new political order. The difficulties of turning constituent power into constitutional form, particularly at the global level where so many competing agents and interests seem resistant to such a move, has also hindered efforts to find any evidence for constituent power at the global level (Loughlin and Walker 2007). The next section sets out a defence of global constituent power and links it to human rights at the global level.

Global constituent power and human rights

A constitutional order is one that rests upon the people. This constituent power differs from democracy which means the ongoing governance of a community by the people. The difference is perhaps best captured in seeing democracy as a form of government and constituent power as the basis for sovereignty, or the logic that underlies a political order. Martin Loughlin locates the idea in relation to the Enlightenment, seeing it as a rational foundation for rule that moved away from logics relying on divine rights or natural law. Instead:

> The concept comes into its own only when the constitution is understood as a juridical instrument deriving its authority from a principle of self-determination: specifically, that the constitution is an expression of the constituent power of the people to make and remake the institutional arrangements through which they are governed.
> (Loughlin 2014, p. 219)

This formulation relies on a reality for the 'people' who can engage in some form of self-determination. This is, of course, a major obstacle for any kind of global constituent power; that is, there does not exist a unified people at the global level who can construct a community. If this is the case, then there seems to be no grounds for advocating any kind of a global constituent power. Yet, one might argue that there is no 'people' at the national level either. That is, while we assume constituent power exists in an empirical people, we should perhaps look for the ways in which a constitution and a people are co-constituted.[4] Therefore, to identify constituent power, we need to identify the constitutional order that constructs the people. In what follows, I turn to the existing institutional structure of human rights as the 'constitution' with which and, at times, against which a global constituent power comes into existence. That is, my argument in what follows is that global constituent power exists in practices undertaken by people in moments of protest and activism, but their ability to undertake those practices results from and relies upon an existing structure of human rights ideas and institutions.

A few versions of global constituent power have been proposed (Negri 2009; Niesen 2014; Oklopcic 2014; Nootens 2015). One that parallels the argument in this chapter comes from Chris Thornhill, who argues that if we envision constituent power not as an effort to find a singular people but as a sociological ordering device, it can be found at the global level (Thornhill 2012). Thornhill looks to the origins of constituent power in the American and French Revolutions not as moments when these communities 'discovered' the people they represent but as devices employed by founders and activists to structure their political orders. More specifically, and related to the concerns of this chapter, those efforts were located in relation to rights. The order that constituent power created was designed to distinguish the people from an external normative will, whether that be an external political power (as the British were for the Americans) or an external normative force (as institutions such as the nobility and church were for the French). Hence, the purpose of constituent power in these revolutions was not 'to bind the political system to an external normative will, but to increase the inner consistency of the political system and to reduce its reliance on external actors' (Thornhill 2012, p. 384). Based on his reading of these key Enlightenment revolutionary moments, Thornhill suggests that current efforts to advance human rights can be seen as a similarly orienting device at the global level; that is, judicial orders that draw on human rights are institutions that can 'internalize constituent power as a projective aspect of the political system' (Thornhill 2012, p. 394).

Thornhill's argument suggests that regional and global judicial institutions provide the location for a constituent power that can advance human rights. Other accounts of constituent power eschew human rights as their foundation, looking instead to Marxist and critical theory resources to defend socio-economic equality as the basis for a just world order. One prominent example can be found in the work of Michael Hardt and Antonio Negri, whose collaborative works have articulated a space for a global constituent power in response to global economic injustice. In *Commonwealth* (2009) they advance this argument through a creative effort to find a global commons created by financial and trade structures but that can be refashioned to redistribute wealth. Their argument, however, does not find in rights a useful foundation for this redistributive effort, seeing the current human rights regime as dependent on liberal capitalism. Their alternative largely ignores existing human rights documents and institutions and instead seeks to develop a radical alternative.

While human rights may have links to liberal capitalism at their point of origin, this does not mean that they need to be ignored or dismissed in responding to global injustice. In fact, constituent power claims might be best understood as being co-constitutive with existing institutional structures of human rights. That is, without the UN system and its surrounding judicial and legal institutions, efforts to advance global justice and freedom would flounder. Some of the literature on human rights points to how this co-constitutive move is possible.[5] Andrew Vincent focuses on activism and citizenship as the place where rights can best be found (Vincent 2010). Vincent critically assesses the idea of the state, arguing that it remains indebted to a nineteenth century Hegelianism that reified a kind of quasi-natural community. This idealization of the state resulted in extreme attempts to clean and purify the state, culminating in abuses of individual rights and even genocide. Opposed to this, Vincent argues that the idea of a vigorous state based citizenship needs to be recovered, one that will best protect the rights of individuals both within it and globally. Similarly, Mervyn Frost has argued that if states developed in such a way as to perfect their practices, they can be the foundations for a world in which human rights can be protected. Frost proposes how states play a role in 'constituting human rights' by constituting the state as an entity that can protect them, a democratic state (Frost 2002).

Charles Beitz also argues for a political conception of rights, but one that is grounded in the international order as opposed to the state (Beitz 2009). Beitz argues that human rights can only really be understood globally or internationally, as a set of practices that resulted from events in the twentieth century and the responses to those events undertaken by state leaders and activists. The triumph of human rights is really an international or global one and should be understood as such. Beitz emphasizes the evolution of the human rights system of the United Nations as giving evidence for how rights should be understood globally rather than domestically. Christopher Reus-Smit traces the ways in which the current international order presumes a human rights framework, looking to the spread of a nation-state system as evidence for such a formulation. He sees individual rights as the foundation for not only the modern state, but an intersection of that state form with the global and international structures that seek to protect it (Reus-Smit 2013).

These different efforts to formulate human rights that parallel the idea of constituent power suggest some ways in which we might defend human rights. Much of this work, however, looks to the enumerations of rights in legal texts and the efforts of judicial bodies to defend those rights and, crucially, remain tied to their specific instantiation. The existence of documents such as the UN Universal Declaration of Human Rights, the two covenants on human rights from 1966, and related documents form a central part of the global constitutional order. The efforts of judicial institutions such as the International Criminal Court, the International Court of Justice, the European Court of Human Rights, and the Inter-American Court of Human Rights draw upon these and other documents to advance rights. Yet, are they enough? Do these documents and the judicial bodies that interpret and seek to enforce them provide the only guarantee we have for a strong human rights regime? In the next section, I turn to one American founder who believed that enumerating rights may not be the best way to advance them. Rather, only by ensuring that the people have continued access to and engagement with their constitutional order can human rights be truly defended and advanced. At the same time, as someone intimately involved in the creation of formal institutions that allowed for a people to remain constantly engaged with their government, Wilson's example suggests how constituent power and rights can be co-constitutive.

James Wilson and constituent power

James Wilson was born in Scotland in 1742 and in 1765 moved to the American colonies. Wilson's first contribution to the cause of American independence came with the publication of his *Considerations on the Nature and Extent of the Legislative Authority of the British Parliament* in 1774. In that text, he argued that the conflict with Great Britain resulted from an abuse of power by Parliament in their efforts to tax the colonies. But, more importantly, his critique of Parliament was based on its failure to be truly representative: 'parliamentary authority is derived solely from representation – that those, who are bound by acts of parliament, are bound for this reason only, because they are represented in it' (Wilson 1774 [2007], p. 19). This concern with representation continued throughout his career and became the central issue upon which he based many of his contributions to debates around independence.

Because of this pamphlet and other writings, Wilson served in the Constitutional Convention of 1787 as a representative of Pennsylvania, where he participated actively in the drafting of the Constitution. He worked on the Committee of Detail that took the deliberations of the convention and turned them into the written draft of the constitution. Though it is disputed, some have argued that Wilson wrote in the iconic first words of the constitution, 'We the People', having crossed out the phrase, 'We the States of . . .' (Wood 1972). Throughout the convention, Wilson's contributions were consistently aimed at ensuring representation.

Throughout his political activities, judicial opinions and scholarly writings, Wilson emphasized the importance of representation. He often employed the metaphor of a pyramid in his arguments, claiming that just as a pyramid's base is widely distributed in order to provide a secure foundation, so a government must have a similarly widely spread foundation in the people as a whole. While advancing this position, he was also aware of the dangers of representative government; he argued strongly against a unicameral congress, a view that arose from his concerns with legislative despotism (Wilson 1787 [2007], p. 97). As such, Wilson also argued for a powerful executive and judiciary. In the debates of 1787, he not only advocated for a single executive (others proposed a triumvirate), but more importantly argued for direct election of the president as opposed to the complex structure of the Electoral College (Wilson 1787 [2007], pp. 83–86). He was most certainly in the minority here but his argument arose from his strong belief that all branches of government ought to be based on some form of representation. Again, as noted in his advocacy for a bicameral legislature in both his own Pennsylvania and in the newly formed United States, this did not mean that any single institution should be dominant in a political system. Nevertheless, he did strongly believe that all institutions of government should be representative, not just the legislature (Wilson 1804 [2007], p. 699).

The importance of representative government derives from the importance of the rights bearing individual as a citizen. In his role as a Supreme Court Justice, he articulated this in his opinion in the case of *Chisolm v. Georgia* (1793).[6] The case considered by the Court concerned an individual in South Carolina who wished to sue the State of Georgia. Under the Articles of Confederation, this was illegal, as an individual could not sue a state of which he was not a citizen. However, with the new constitution, all were citizens of one country and so could sue the subsidiary parts thereof. This case was perhaps the most important case decided on by the Court during Wilson's tenure, though it was soon overturned by the passage of the eleventh amendment in 1785. In his opinion, Wilson argued that there is no sovereignty in the state but only in the citizen. He notes that the corollary of a sovereign is a subject and that there is no mention of subjects in the Constitution (only one in fact, which is prefaced by the word 'foreign'). As a result, the only sovereignty resides in the individual person, the rights bearing citizen.

In his defence of the constitution before the Pennsylvania ratifying convention in 1788, Wilson addressed a concern expressed by many in the post-convention debates; why was there no bill of rights appended to the constitution? Wilson argued that to list rights in the case of an already written constitutional text would give too much power to the government:

> A bill of rights annexed to a constitution is an enumeration of the powers reserved. If we attempt an enumeration, everything that is not enumerated is presumed to be given. The consequence is that an imperfect enumeration would throw all implied power in the scale of the government, and the rights of the people would be rendered incomplete. On the other hand, an imperfect enumeration of the powers of government reserves all implied power to the people; and by that means the constitution becomes incomplete. But of the two, it is much safer to run the risk on the side of the constitution; for an omission in the enumeration of powers of government is neither dangerous nor important as an omission in the enumeration of the rights of the people.
>
> (Wilson 1788 [2007], p. 195)

Wilson's argument against a written bill of rights rests not on a libertarian fear of government; rather, as someone who spent a great deal of time constructing a government, his concern is rather with the balance between the rights of the people and the powers of the government. A written constitution is necessary, but one that lists our rights simply freezes in place particular rights and gives the government the authority to interpret whether or not new rights claims are possible.

How then are the people to defend their rights? This is where the constituent power of the people play a crucial role. Wilson believed that only by ensuring the people a constant role in every branch of the governmental system could they ensure that their rights remain defended. As James Zink argues, Wilson believed that the constitution creates a system by which individual citizens are constantly educated and provoked to defend their rights. Their political agency emerges because the system gives them the ability to be engaged at all times in their own governance. Such a stance would enable individuals of future generations to engage in and craft their rights as new situations emerged (Zink 2014).

For Wilson, institutional design arising from constituent power is the best defence of rights. As noted below, representation is not the same as constituent power. Wilson's ideas about representation are perhaps closer to the idea of constituent power, only because he sought to design a system so that individuals could not only govern themselves (representation) but also prod those in positions of power to ensure continued adherence to the rights they deserve. The fact that the US Constitution could theoretically be rewritten if enough states move to ratify it is a further example of how constituent power was built into the US political system. The energy of citizens should be devoted to the perfection of that design rather than to debates about or enumeration of rights. Certainly, a person connects to others though the institutions they create and through the 'civic education' they constantly receive by their participation in and check upon the government. What is required, according to Wilson, is an institutional structure that gives individuals an ability to continually advance their constituent power and defend their rights. There most certainly exist institutions at the global level with constitutional like qualities, as described in section two of this chapter. But, do there exist places and opportunities for individuals to advance constituent power and defend their rights in relation to those institutions? And, do such practices rely on a simple liberal conception of rights enumerated in the human rights documents and treaties at the global level? The next section of this chapter proposes one particular set of practices that both rely on a global constitutional order but also seek to push and prod it forward into new and unexpected directions. In so doing, those engaged in these practices provide a hope for a new version of human rights, one that is co-constitutive with the existing order.

Global constituent power

In his exploration of the early American republic, Jason Frank proposes the idea of constituent moments. He argues that there exists a latent constituent power in political orders and that this power emerges in unexpected moments. A constituent moment is when:

> the underauthorized – imposters, radicals, self-created entities – seize the mantle of authorization, changing the inherited rules of authorization in

> the process. . . . Constituent moments invent a new political space and make apparent a people that are productively never at one with themselves.
>
> (Frank 2010, p. 8)

He explores efforts by founders such as John Adams to understand the role of the crowd in the American revolutionary period, both seeking to draw on them for the revolution yet also wary of them as new political orders are created. In fact, one of the most famous such mob moments was an attack on the house of Wilson in 1779. This resulted in part from his position as one of the wealthy elites in Philadelphia politics, in which role he defended merchants who refused to allow price controls. In what became known as the attack on 'Fort Wilson', a crowd agitating for such controls killed one officer as part of growing economic unrest in the city. This reflected the tensions identified by Frank as colonial founders sought to draw on the constituent power of the crowd but were wary of such efforts when they became an attack on American patriots such as Wilson who were trying to carve out a new political order. Frank suggests that it is precisely the uncertainty of the crowd that makes them such a powerful reminder of exactly what Wilson was articulating; that constituent power remains vested in the people (Frank 2010, pp. 91–92).

In this last section, I want to point to one global constituent moment of the last few years, or a series of moments linked together under the theme of the World Social Forum (WSF). In identifying this ongoing protest and activist movement in this way, I want to suggest that what makes these practices particularly important and powerful is that they are articulated in relation to the existing global constitutional order and, in particular, the human rights elements of that order. This does not mean, however, that they rely on the specific legal texts. These documents and codes may well be invoked, but the moments that merit the term 'constituent' are those that construct a political space within which rights can be defended, promoted and advanced by participants from different areas in the international/transnational/ global realm. Therefore, rather than rely on already existing institutional spaces, such as those in the UN system or various regional and international courts, these efforts seek to create new spaces and institutional frames. Like Wilson, I see the existence of an institutional order as crucial but also as a space in which the people can continue to advocate and perhaps even transform that same global constitutional order.

In 1998, a range of protests took place in Seattle, where activists came together to respond to the rules being formulated by the newly created World Trade Organization (WTO). This set a precedent in that these protests were not organized by any single institution but brought together a range of activists and NGOs concerned about the impact the WTO would have on environmental and labour rights in its promotion of free trade. The emergence of these shifting coalitions was derided by some as ineffective, though one might argue it was part of an ongoing constituent power that was emerging through new forms of global communication and interaction (Lang 2005).

The World Social Forum (WSF) sprang in part from this protest moment, but also connected with efforts to respond to wider neoliberal globalization processes.

In 2001, the first WSF took place in Porto Allegro, Brazil. Described as a collective, movement, or process (or all three together), the WSF has met every year since. In fact, in some years it takes place in a single location, while in other years it has been dispersed across different locations all happening at the same time. There is a strong emphasis on inclusion and freedom to speak, and throughout the meetings, there is reference to different forms of rights. In 2013 and 2014, the WSF met in Tunis in order to connect with the events of the Arab Spring. In so doing, it sought to link up national, regional and global processes. The 2016 WSF took place in Montreal. This meeting was the first to be held in the global North, though its organizers have argued it will continue to embody the spirit of the WSF by ensuring access to as many as possible around the world.

What is most relevant for my purposes here is that WSF is largely about the creation of spaces within which political activities of various sorts can take place. After the WSF there is no effort to summarize the outcome, as the organizers each year claim that they are not formally representative of global civil society. Nor is there an effort to create a single organizational structure but rather the goal is to provide a forum within which different organizations and struggles can become public and work toward an alter-globalization agenda.

There does exist a charter, though, one that sets out a moral vision for the WSF. Drafted and signed in 2001 in Porto Allegro, the World Social Forum Charter of Principles begins by noting it is:

> an open meeting space for reflection, democratic debates of ideas, formulation of proposals, free exchange of experiences, and interlinking for effective action by groups and movements of civil society that are opposed to neoliberalism and to the domination of the world by capital and all forms of imperialism, and who are committed to building a planetary society based on the human being.
> (World Social Forum Charter of Principles 2016)

It goes on to highlight that it is a 'world forum', one that is explicitly global. In article 4, it explicitly evokes a form of constituent power:

> 4. The alternatives proposed at the World Social Forum stand in opposition to a capitalist globalization process commanded by the large multinational corporations and the governments and international institutions at the service of their interests. These alternatives are designed to ensure that globalization in solidarity will prevail as a new stage in world history. This will respect universal human rights, and those of all citizens of all nations and the environment. This step will be supported by the international democratic systems and institutions that are at the service of social justice, equality, and the sovereignty of peoples.
> (World Social Forum Charter of Principles 2016)

These principles appear in the Constitutive Charter of the WSF 2016 in Montreal, which lays out more specific details for the 2016 meeting. But rather than list specific rights, the bulk of the charter is devoted to structural details of the different types of meetings and forums within which deliberation can take place. There are five 'values' articulated at the outset of the document: inclusion and openness; transparency; horizontality; self-management; and independence. These values, however, are not defined in terms of specific rights or obligations, but are largely about the construction of a particular type of organizational space for the meetings themselves. The bulk of the 2016 charter details the ways in which forums operate and how they deliberate.

There is, of course, no discussion here of an executive, judiciary, or legislature. There is also an explicit effort to refuse any kind of representational status for this forum or any other previous one. Yet, this effort provides us some insight into how a global constituent power may be located. As with Wilson, it does not seek to create a list of human rights that can be judicially defended but an institutional space(s) that is (are) capable of advancing rights in new and unexpected ways. Indeed, the themes of the Montreal WSF focus on social and economic rights, environmental rights, and indigenous peoples' rights. These are certainly not the traditional rights to property and life that Wilson would have defended, nor are they necessarily the rights to be found in the UN Declaration or in the related covenants. But this is precisely the point; when an institutional framework is created rather than an enumeration of rights in a legalized document, it will respond to the needs of those who inhabit those institutional spaces rather than reflect the particular understandings of those who may have inhabited related spaces in the past.

Conclusion

The WSF has little power to protect the freedom of speech in China, to save individuals suffering under oppression in the Syrian conflict, or to ensure the end of torture by the United States or United Kingdom in waging war on terrorism. It may appear to be a small voice in the wilderness without any purchase on the most important human rights violations. In addition, it has not always been as inclusive as its advocates have argued, though as an ongoing project, it continues to work toward creating a space in which democratic rights can be defended and advanced (Caruso 2012). And, along with the crowds of the early American Republic, such protest movements can be dangerous and disruptive to existing patterns of economic activity and settled lifestyles.

But, along with the Occupy Movements, Arab Spring, release of the Panama Papers, and other attempts to engage in global protest movements and NGO activism, the benefit of these kinds of activities can be found not only in the creation of new rights or demands for the enforcement of existing rights. There are clearly problems with supposing protest movements can advance human rights as different agendas can come into conflict. As one example, in the protests in Egypt in 2010–2011, labour groups had been advocating against the increasing neoliberal agenda of the state by drawing on international human rights treaty obligations signed by Egypt. Despite this, the uprisings in Tahrir Square did not advance any economic rights, and, indeed, the result has not been promising for human rights more broadly defined (Beinin 2012). At the same time, some protest movements do advance human rights, and, in so doing, demonstrate how international human rights agendas can contribute to the protection of domestic rights claims. Even in the United States, where there is a robust set of rights protections, some protest movements have turned to the global constitutional order of human rights to articulate and justify their demands (Merry *et al.* 2010).

Protest movements will continue to emerge around the globe. This chapter has sought to articulate how such movements can contribute to and simultaneously draw upon the global constituent power of human rights. The creation of common spaces within which political action can continue and within which rights can be protected requires further analysis (Hardt and Negri 2009; Murray 2010; Wenman 2013). This chapter has demonstrated efforts to create a new space within which global citizens can advocate for new modalities of rights, a global constituent power that might provide the best hope we have for defending human rights in this age of uncertainty.

Notes

1 Versions of this paper were presented at the University of Hamburg, City University London, and the University of Sheffield. At each one of these venues, comments and questions from participants were extremely helpful. For comments, thanks to Peter Niesen, Garrett Wallace Brown, and Patrick Hayden, and the editors of this volume.
2 Hohfeld's formulation of rights is more complex than this, but for my purpose here, the idea of demands made on others is most important.
3 William Schuerman argues that Cohen's account is not cosmopolitan enough, to which she responded with a defence of her argument as more pragmatic and realistic; Scheuerman 2014 and Cohen 2014.
4 I am indebted to Garrett Wallace Brown for this formulation.
5 The literature on human rights is vast, so the few citations here should not be seen as exhaustive, but rather are those that run parallel to the focus on constituent power which is my focus here. For an overview of some of the literature on human rights, see Forsythe 2006; for a collection of key readings on human rights, see Hayden 2001; for a short discussion of human rights as a form of international political theory, see Lang 2014.
6 At this time, there was no 'majority opinion', so each justice delivered his opinion and they were read in order of seniority.

References

Beinin, J 2012, 'Egyptian Workers and January 25th: A Social Movement in Historical Context', *Social Research*, vol. 79, no. 2, pp. 323–348.
Beitz, C 2009, *The Idea of Human Rights*, Oxford University Press, Oxford.
Bingham, T 2011, *The Rule of Law*, Penguin Publishers, London.
Brown, GW 2009, *Grounding Cosmopolitanism: From Kant to the Idea of a Cosmopolitan Constitution*, Edinburgh University Press, Edinburgh.
Brown, GW 2012, 'The Constitutionalization of What?', *Global Constitutionalism*, vol. 1, no. 2, pp. 201–228.

Caruso, G 2012, 'Toward an Emancipatory Cosmopolitan Project: The World Social Forum and the Transformation of Conflicts', *Globalizations*, vol. 9, no. 2, pp. 211–224.
Cohen, J 2012, *Globalization and Sovereignty: Rethinking Legality, Legitimacy and Constitutionalism*, Cambridge University Press, Cambridge.
Cohen, J 2014, 'Reply to Scheuerman's review of Globalization and Sovereignty', *Global Constitutionalism*, vol. 3, no. 1, pp. 119–141.
Deudney, D 2007, *Bounding Power: Republican Security Theory from the Polis to the Global Village*, Princeton University Press, Princeton, NJ.
Dworkin, R 1977, *Taking Rights Seriously*, Bloomsbury, London.
Fassbender, B 2009, *The United Nations Charter as the Constitution of the International Community*, Martinus Nijhoff, Amsterdam.
Forsythe, D 2006, *Human Rights in International Relations*, 2nd edn, Cambridge University Press, Cambridge.
Frank, J 2010, *Constituent Moments: Enacting the People in Postrevolutionary America*, Duke University Press, Durham, NC.
Frost, M 2002, *Constituting Human Rights: Global Civil Society and the Society of Democratic States*, Routledge, London.
Ginsburg, T and Simpser, A 2014, *Constitutions in Authoritarian Regimes*, Cambridge University Press, Cambridge.
Habermas, J 2001, 'Why Europe Needs a Constitution', *New Left Review*, no. 11, pp. 5–26.
Habermas, J 2006, *The Divided West*, Polity Press, Cambridge.
Hardt, M and Negri, A 2009, *Commonwealth*, Harvard University Press, Cambridge, MA.
Hayden, Patrick, (ed.) 2001, *The Philosophy of Human Rights*, Paragon Press, St Paul, MN.
Hohfeld, W 1946 [1918], *Fundamental Legal Conceptions as Applied in Judicial Reasoning*, Yale University Press, New Haven, CT.
Ikenberry, GJ 2006, *Liberal Order and Imperial Ambition: Essays on American Power and World Politics*, Polity Press, Cambridge.
Klabbers, J, Peters, A and Ulfstein, G 2009, *The Constitutionalization of International Law*, Oxford University Press, Oxford.
Kumm, M 2009, 'The Cosmopolitan Turn in Constitutionalism: On the Relationship between Constitutionalism in and beyond the State' in JL Dunoff and J Trachtman, (eds), *Ruling the World? Constitutionalism, International Law, and Global Governance*, pp. 258–325. Cambridge University Press, Cambridge.
Lang, AF, Jr 2005, 'Governance and Political Protest: Hannah Arendt on Global Political Protest' in AF Lang, Jr and J Williams, (eds), *Hannah Arendt and International Relations: Reading Across the Lines*, pp. 179–198. Palgrave, New York.
Lang, AF, Jr 2014, *International Political Theory: An Introduction*, Palgrave, London.
Loughlin, M 2014, 'The Concept of Constituent Power', *European Journal of Political Theory*, vol. 13, no. 2, pp. 218–237.
Loughlin, M and Walker, N, (eds) 2007, *The Paradox of Constitutionalism: Constituent Power and Constitutional Form*, Oxford University Press, Oxford.
Maduro, MP 2009, 'Courts and Pluralism: Essay on a Theory of Judicail Adjudication in the Context of Legal and Constitutional Pluralism' in JL Dunoff and J Trachtman, (eds), *Ruling the World? Constitutionalism, International Law, and Global Governance*, pp. 356–380. Cambridge University Press, Cambridge.
Merry, SE, Levitt, P, Serban Rosen, M and Yoon, DH 2010, 'Law from Below: Women's Human Rights and Social Movements in New York City', *Law and Society Review*, vol. 44, no. 1, pp. 101–128.
Montesquieu, C, II 1748 [1989], *The Spirit of the Laws*, reprinted in and trans. AM Cohler, BC Miller, HS Stone, (eds), Cambridge University Press, Cambridge.

Murray, D 2010, 'Democratic Insurrection: Constructing the Common in Global Resistance', *Millennium*, vol. 39, no. 2, pp. 461–482.
Negri, A 2009, *Insurgencies: Constituent Power and the Modern State*, translated by M Boscagli, University of Minnesota Press, Minneapolis.
Niesen, P 2014, 'Constituent Power: A New Foundation for International Political Theory?', *presentation at School of International Relations*, University of St. Andrews.
Nootens, G 2015, 'Constituent Power and People-as-the-Governed: About the "Invisible" People of Political and Legal Theory', *Global Constitutionalism*, vol. 4, no. 2, pp. 137–156.
Oklopcic, Z 2014, 'Three Areas of Struggle: A Contextual Approach to the Constituent Power of the "People"', *Global Constitutionalism*, vol. 3, no. 2, pp. 200–235.
Onuf, N 1998, *The Republican Legacy in International Thought*, Cambridge University Press, Cambridge.
Reus-Smit, C 2013, *Individual Rights and the Making of the International System*, Cambridge University Press, Cambridge.
Scheuerman, W 2014, 'Globalization, Constitutionalism and Sovereignty', *Global Constitutionalism*, vol. 3, no. 1, pp. 102–118.
Sieyes, E 1789 [1970], *Qu'est-ce que le Tiers état?* Roberto Zapperi, (ed.), Droz, Geneva.
Thornhill, C 2012, 'Contemporary Constitutionalism and the Dialectic of Constituent Power', *Global Constitutionalism*, vol. 1, no. 3, pp. 369–404.
Vincent, A 2010, *The Politics of Human Rights*, Oxford University Press, Oxford.
Wenman, M 2013, *Agonistic Democracy: Constituent Power in the Era of Globalization*, Cambridge University Press, Cambridge.
Wiener, A 2008, *The Invisible Constitution of Politics: Contested Norms and International Encounters*, Cambridge University Press, Cambridge.
Wilson, J 1774 [2007], 'Considerations on the Nature and Extent of the Legislative Authority of the British Parliament' in K Hall and MD Hall, (eds), *Collected Works of James Wilson*, pp. 3–31. Liberty Fund, Indianapolis, IN.
Wilson, J 1787 [2007], 'Remarks of James Wilson during the Federal Convention' in K Hall and MD Hall, (eds), *Collected Works of James Wilson*, pp. 80–171. Liberty Fund, Indianapolis, IN.
Wilson, J 1788 [2007], 'Remarks of James Wilson in the Pennsylvania Ratifying Convention' in K Hall and MD Hall, (eds), *Collected Works of James Wilson*, pp. 178–284. Liberty Fund, Indianapolis, IN.
Wilson, J 1793 [2007], '*Chisolm v Georgia*' in K Hall and MD Hall, (eds), *Collected Works of James Wilson*, pp. 351–366. Liberty Fund, Indianapolis, IN.
Wilson, J 1804 [2007], 'Lectures on Law' in K Hall and MD Hall, (eds), *Collected Works of James Wilson*, pp. 430–1275. Liberty Fund, Indianapolis, IN.
Wood, GS 1972, *The Creation of the American Republic, 1776–1787*, WW Norton Publishers, New York.
World Social Forum 2016, *World Social Forum Charter of Principles*. Available from: https://fsm2016.org/en/sinformer/a-propos-du-forum-social-mondial/. [08 December 2016].
Zink, JR 2014, 'James Wilson versus the Bill of Rights: Progress, Popular Sovereignty and the Idea of the US Constitution', *Political Research Quarterly*, vol. 67, no. 2, pp. 253–265.

2
A CRITICAL EXAMINATION OF 'HUMANITY'

Samuel Jarvis

Introduction

In a speech to the United Nations General Assembly in September 1999, Secretary-General Kofi Annan addressed the gap that had developed between traditional interpretations of the UN Charter and evolving humanitarian practice, in which member states had gradually begun to recognise further limits to state sovereignty. In direct response to the inaction of the Security Council in Rwanda, and its division in the case of Kosovo, Kofi Annan (1999) argued that, 'In both cases, the UN should have been able to find common ground in upholding the principles of the charter, and acting in defence of our common humanity'. Implicit in Annan's assessment of the previous moral failings of the UN, is the assumption that the defence of 'humanity' itself can and should act as a central guiding principle for UN member states. In response, Annan (1999) argued the case for a 'new commitment to humanitarian action' that needed to be 'universal, irrespective of region or nation' and underpinned by a 'broader definition of national interest'. Central to this new approach was the need for Security Council action to now be 'answerable to a higher authority, that of morality', in order to reject the absolutism of traditional sovereignty (Hopgood 2014, p. 190). Consequently, it is this recognition of a distinct moral concern for the threat posed by mass atrocity crimes to a collective humanity that would prove central to the original framing of the Responsibility to Protect (R2P) within the International Commission on Intervention and State Sovereignty (ICISS) report. However, the extent to which recognition of the moral plight of our common humanity can be used to ground state consensus, and how this triggers when the international community *should* intervene on behalf of others, remains a question left critically underexplored.

The philosophical and moral foundations of humanity's relationship to the R2P have for a long time remained a largely overlooked element of the R2P literature. Despite the language of humanity and appeals to it being a consistent feature in a wide range of R2P scholarship, from Nicholas Wheeler (2005) questioning whether the R2P is 'A victory for common humanity?' to Peter Hilpold's (2012) framing of the R2P as 'Intervening in the name of humanity', it is most often the case that humanity's normative status and value is one left assumed and/or unexplored. This appears strikingly at odds with the significant normative weight both scholars and diplomats continue to place on the concept of humanity, and the metaphysical heavy lifting they assume the word can provide to any moral argument. This can be illustrated in a number of examples, including Ramesh Thakur's (2015, p. 23) conceptualisation of the R2P as being one underpinned by 'our common humanity', and hence demanding 'an acceptance of a duty of care by all of us who live in zones of safety towards all those who are trapped in zones of danger'; as well as Gareth Evans (2008), who suggests that 'the case for R2P rests simply on our common humanity'. Thus, as Maja Zehfuss (2012, p. 862) has argued, 'most often "humanity" is not considered a category in need of explanation', leading to the assumption that 'it self-evidently deserves protection'. In both these examples, the concept of humanity provides the central philosophical principle underpinning the moral weight of their arguments, yet the concept is presented without further comment, and simply taken as an uncontested truth.

While more recent scholarship has looked to fill this void, such as an *International Politics* special issue on 'The Responsibility to Protect 10 years on from the World Summit (2016)', focusing more specifically on the relationship between humanity and the R2P, there still remains a tendency to overlook the complexities of humanity's moral foundations and its subsequent impact on the framing and construction of the R2P. One can highlight this oversight within the special issue, whereby the concept of common humanity is most often utilised as a theoretical benchmark in which to measure the current progress of the R2P. In this sense, the focus often concerns 'whether the Responsibility to Protect promotes a common humanity' (Waldorf 2016, p. 50); or the extent to which the R2P can represent an 'expression of common humanity' (Newman 2016, p. 32). Thus, rather than analyse the R2P as simply an attempt to live up to or put into practice the universal value of humanity, one must further interrogate the points of contestation within this relationship, in particular, the extent to which states recognise the link made between humanity's role in identifying collective harm and its ability to then motivate action through the framework of the R2P.

In light of this lacuna, it is necessary to ask what this theoretical oversight means for on-going debates about the R2P as well as our ability to still talk of a 'common humanity'. First of all, the lack of critical engagement with the concept of humanity has to some extent clouded normative judgements concerning both the centrality of humanity to the R2P's motivational capacity as well as its relation to issues of moral progress. The relative speed in which the R2P concept has moved from a loose abstract framework to an idea recognised by all states in the 2005 World Summit Outcome Document (WSOD) has thus been central to reinforcing the beliefs of many advocates that 'the normative arguments about R2P are largely won' (Bellamy 2015). However, this conflation between the R2P's normative progression and the relative progress of our collective humanity is at times misplaced. In addressing this oversight the chapter will examine the extent to which the recognition of a moral demand for protection, founded in the idea of a collective harm to humanity, can in fact influence states to take action on behalf of others. Through this more critical engagement on the relationship between humanity and R2P, the chapter highlights the significant contestation that still exists, in terms of how the moral demands founded in the R2P compete with the everyday constraints of international politics.

In order to break down this complex relationship the chapter is structured around two key questions. First, how does the concept of humanity underpin the moral claims that are central to the identification of universal 'human wrongs' (Booth 1999, p. 56)? In response to this question, the next section will focus on how to distinguish various aspects of humanity in order to ground our understanding of the distinctly human harm created by mass atrocity crimes. Building upon this theoretical outline, the chapter will second examine how the concept of humanity is used to underpin the moral and ethical framework of the R2P. In addressing this question, the chapter will analyse the key moral obligations created by the concept of humanity, and assess how these obligations have helped to inform and construct the central motivational qualities of the R2P. Through tracing the R2P's chronological emergence, alongside its engagement with the concept of humanity, the section will demonstrate how states have continued to challenge the link made between humanity's role in locating collective harm, and the subsequent call for humanity to be protected. The chapter will then conclude by highlighting the need to more critically engage with the normative tensions at play in the R2P concept, thus opening up space for a significant reassessment of how we qualify the ability of new humanitarian concepts such as the R2P to reflect moral progress and change.

Grounding the concept of humanity

In order to clarify the distinct characteristics that make up our understanding of what constitutes the idea of harm to humanity, the chapter will first focus on two specific complementary characteristics often used by philosophers in their examinations of humanity, namely *humanness* and *humankind*. Through exploring these dual characteristics, it will be possible to reflect on how both are essential elements in how we frame and categorise the crimes that are considered of greatest harm to us collectively. As Matthew Weinert (2015, p. 25) argues, notions of humanity are not simply used as 'diplomatic or academic flourishes' but can in fact be seen to 'exert influence on polices and ways of thinking about contemporary international relations'. This section will therefore help to demonstrate why there remains a need to further develop greater conceptual clarity on the diverse, yet central, elements of humanity, so as to better understand its moral significance in relation to categorising 'conscious shocking crimes' (Heinze 2009, p. 33).

Humanity can first be interpreted as referring to the quality of being human, encapsulated as what philosophers often call *humanness*. Humanity is thus the essence of what makes us human, which must be seen as an abstract property, rather than the human race or a set of individuals (Luban 2004, p. 90). In other words, there are certain basic values that are considered inherent to all human beings, such as a form of shared human dignity and our collective diversity as a species (Bauman 2001, p. 136; Renzo 2012). The consequence of this reading of humanity implies that there is something fundamental to being human and how we define these elements of humanness has a profound impact on our overall understanding of the concept of humanity.

Consequently, when we talk about a crime committed against humanity, we are often insinuating that the very basic moral sensibilities that are instinctive to human beings are challenged, and thus the foundations of human worth are directly under attack (Gyekye 2004). In this sense, we can also conceptualise humanness in terms of its relation to dehumanisation (Haslam 2006), whereby our ability to locate practices of dehumanisation, such as defining others as cockroaches instead of humans, helps to reinforce the value of recognising a shared humanness. We must therefore understand humans as having 'capacities which non-humans do not and which humans consider being so significant, as to make them the basis of an appropriate moral practice' (Parekh 1999, p. 147). The collective status of humanness is thus defined through 'individuals possessing certain species-specific capabilities', reinforcing the need to treat humans in a certain manner, not as inanimate objects (Parekh 1999, p. 147). The notion of humanness therefore allows us to set moral limits as to the categorisation of universal human wrongs (Booth 1999, p. 56), which can be seen to represent a direct affront to the human qualities we are all deemed to share.

In contrast, humanity can also be referred to as simply *humankind*, meaning the aggregation of all human beings. This requires the ability to accept that as human beings we all belong to one collective group and that this allows us to have interconnections with human beings as a whole. It is through greater identification with distant people that we can then expand our recognition of harm and therefore draw 'serious violations of human rights to the attention of a worldwide public' (Linklater 2009, p. 490). Thus, we can view crimes against humanity as crimes that not only harm the direct victim and their humanness, but also all human beings in the process (Renzo 2012, p. 449). The collective element of this understanding of humanity is based on the fact that we are all members of a human species, living in the confines of the planet, by which we are both constrained and interconnected by this reality. While it is difficult to argue that we are all directly violated by acts that supposedly 'stain the conscience of humanity', by referring to humankind one can suggest that a significant group representing human beings as a species has been directly affected as a singular body (Geras 2011, p. 49). Furthermore, if we assume that groups can be assigned responsibility as well as be the victim of harm, one can view certain acts as violating key interests of that group, for example, attacks on the diversity of culture and people; whereby humanity arguably has an interest in the maintenance of its relative diversity and security (Macleod 2010).

While both categorisations prove useful in breaking down different elements of what we often refer to as our common humanity, it is important to note that the two interpretations do not exist independently of one another. It is often the case that when people refer to humanity they interpret its existence as containing elements of both humankind and humanness. One can see this in a statement by Geoffrey Robertson (1999, p. 220), who claims that crimes against humanity 'diminish every member of the human race'. Implicit in this claim is the suggestion that certain crimes not only concern the whole of the human race, in regard to a collective understanding of humanity, but that these actions directly challenge and diminish human essence, which is key to the idea of humanness. In this sense, when we appeal to humanity in a motivational capacity, we are most often implicitly making reference to a dual conception of humanity, one that combines ideas of human interconnectedness with the individual characteristics of human nature. It is the way in which mass atrocity crimes supposedly challenge both these separate concepts of humanity simultaneously, that consequently reinforces the moral aversion shared by so many across the globe to the inherent wrong of such crimes. In this regard, addressing the problem of being human requires us to consider 'the processes by which those who are "outside" the human family become fully human and to whom dignity is accorded' (Weinert 2015, p. 27). The strength of humanity as a concept relevant to the R2P therefore lies in its ability to locate individual crimes within a collective framework of harm, whereby the defence of humanity can then be framed as a key objective for the international community at large.

However, there also remain those who directly question the value of appeals to any form of common humanity. As Ilana Feldman and Miriam Ticktin (2010, p. 1) highlight, any claim to be speaking on behalf of humanity is often one that is attempting to go beyond the categories of political, religious and social divides, in order to assert a fundamentally powerful universal position. Despite the assumed neutrality that is implied by the concept, an understanding of what humanity specifically represents and how we can define it is still severely contested. Due to the almost limitless interpretations of what humanity consists of it can often appear as though we should simply dismiss the concept all together, as ultimately an empty signifier; where despite universal claims to its ability to encompass all human beings, it is in fact 'so historically, geographically situated, as to have no meaning beyond its particular instantiation' (Feldman and Ticktin 2010, p. 2). Accordingly, one is reminded of Carl Schmidt's (2007, p. 54) famous critique in which he argued that 'whoever invokes humanity wants to cheat' and as such appeals to humanity can only open up the space for further inhumanity carried out in its name. This line of thought has led many to suggest that appeals to humanity are mostly used in a way that 'obscures that lives are valued differently' (Butler 2009, p. 50) and thus the imperative that is triggered by appeals to humanity is used to mask 'the complexity of the political situations' in which the term is applied to (Zehfuss 2012, p. 873).

Conversely, what these critiques attack is not necessarily the universal idea of humanity as a reflective guide to moral harm, but its role as a rhetorical tool used to legitimate action by state leaders, whether morally defensible or not. One must therefore separate out the meaning we place on humanity as a moral force for collective harm recognition and the belief that an appeal to humanity assumes the imposition of universal actions of protection. In this regard, humanity's relation to the politics of intervention practices is one that will often be defined by a diversity of legitimate but potentially conflicting ethical considerations (Lu 2007, p. 945); but that does not equate to the idea that humanity should simply be thought of as devoid of value or merit. This is present in the very critiques of the use of humanity outlined above, since it is clear that by resisting dominant universal narratives about humanity, they themselves posit a different categorisation of humanity as embedded in a universal condition of pluralism, which when taken seriously, acts as a common element shared by human beings writ large from which normative value should be attached.

The need to therefore acknowledge a separation in humanity's meaning can be best encapsulated by the language connected to its moral application. In this sense, whether or not we have a shared ideal of unconditional common humanity or agree on the actions performed in its name, the fact that we bring up the question of 'should we act' in the face of mass atrocity crimes in the first place, assumes that we do have some moral ideals and principles, by which we recognise and condemn certain acts as inhuman (Luban 2002, p. 99). Without a form of shared moral concept, the question of should we act in the face of mass atrocity crimes simply would not arise. Consequently, one can highlight how the concept of humanity has been constructed through language to form an essential part of our ability to define universal human harms. In this sense, it is important to acknowledge how even those who commit acts, considered as against humanity, frame their actions and motivations through an understanding of who is or isn't included in humanity. This is most often highlighted by the dehumanising language used by perpetrators, through the use of phrases such as 'rats' (Holocaust), 'cockroaches' (Rwanda Genocide) and 'maggots' (Uganda Cultural Revolution) to refer to victims. This is demonstrative of how the language of humanity is deeply embedded in our understanding of specific mass atrocity crimes, which are made obvious not only to the potential intervener, but also to those committing such crimes in the first place. Subsequently, the concept of humanity is arguably central to the language of mass atrocity, whereby appeals to the concept are heavily embedded in our thought processes. When we see mass atrocity crimes and label them as such, we are already acting and believing in the concept of humanity. Thus, what remains central to our understanding of humanity is its role in reinforcing an assumed moral wrong found within the actions of the perpetrators, and thus generating a harm that can be seen to transcend traditional sovereign borders. Yet, the extent to which the concept can provide more than a reflective point of reference for locating universal harm remains fundamentally contested.

Consequently, while the concept of humanity plays a central role in grounding our ability to locate the limits of human action and categorise certain crimes accordingly, it also remains critical to our understanding of what moral responsibilities states owe to those beyond their borders. In investigating this link more closely the chapter will next address the theoretical bond made between the concept of humanity and the R2P, in order to outline the role humanity plays in supporting a moral obligation for the international community to protect those threatened by mass atrocity crimes. In this sense, humanity is used to ground the concept of a wider international community, one that is able to recognise the idea 'that community is equally relevant internationally as it is domestically' (Bulley 2010, p. 447). This is the normative ambition that is subsequently fused into the creation of the R2P, placing the concept of humanity front and centre in its role as the guiding motivational force for action. The next section will therefore outline how these motivational elements have been drawn together within the construction of the R2P, and highlight the specific points of tension between the R2P's normative commitment to humanity and the creation of its pragmatic framework in the 2005 WSOD.

Humanity and the construction of R2P's moral framework

The R2P must be understood first and foremost as a commitment born out of previous inaction by the international community, in responding to genocides and mass atrocities across the globe. The starting point for reflection on these serious moral failings can subsequently be brought back to the aftermath of the Holocaust, in which states were in agreement that lessons must be learned and the mistakes of the past never repeated, in order for the crime of genocide to be outlawed once and for all. Consequently, as Adrian Gallagher (2013, p. 94) argues, it was the 'moral abhorrence felt toward the Holocaust' that dramatically altered 'international society's moral, constitutional and legal expectations', resulting in the establishment of the 1948 Genocide Convention. For the first time genocide was understood as an international concern, whereby states now recognised a legal obligation to override the rights of sovereignty wherever genocide was committed (Gallagher 2013, p. 115). Yet despite the initial moral outrage created by the crimes of the Holocaust, the events of the following decades would provide little support to the possibility of realising 'never again'. The response of the international community to the genocides of Rwanda and Bosnia demonstrated a lack of support for the principles underlying the Genocide Convention, as well as a general indifference in regard to the moral obligations states owe to those outside of their borders. The consistent failure to make the most conscience shocking crimes of greatest concern to states therefore drew many to call for a change in the way international society went about its approach to mass atrocity crime prevention and response.

Accordingly, it is still the symbolic language of 'never again' that arguably gives R2P much of its moral authority in international affairs and thus underpins a key motivational element of the concept. The language of 'never again' must therefore be understood in relation to the concept of common humanity, whereby mass atrocity crimes are considered so shocking to our collective humanity that we must all pledge to never let such crimes occur again. It is in relation to this moral framework that the R2P can be viewed as 'essentially a narrative of guilt on the part of dissident former UN diplomats', utilised in order to help 'operationalize moral determinism more effectively' (Lucas 2014, p. 37). While this particular reading may be rejected by some R2P advocates (Bellamy 2013), the statement does highlight how significant political failures of the past are very much interspersed within the very moral fabric of the concept. Thus, as Stephen Hopgood (2014, p. 182) argues, 'The politics of the R2P are intimately interwoven with the politics of stopping genocide' in which 'it was the ghosts of Rwanda and Srebrenica that haunted advocates'. Nevertheless, the R2P does claim to provide a new focus to debates regarding humanitarian intervention, whereby states are now tied to a stronger moral obligation and must work harder to both prevent and react to mass atrocity crimes across the globe. Consequently, its many supporters (Evans 2009; Peters 2009) describe the R2P as representing a fundamental shift in state practice; whereby the failures of the past will no longer be played out again and again.

Nonetheless, one must also recognise that long before the creation of the R2P, states were forced to wrestle with a variety of obligations and responsibilities not only to humanity, but to the management of international peace and security, domestic actors, as well as the influence of material factors, when weighing up the case for action. Often the cacophony of voices pulling and pushing from each side resulted in deadlock or indifference from the international community. This failure to act was therefore seen as representative of a moral inadequacy of states, whereby state actors were fundamentally unable to recognise the responsibilities they supposedly had to those threatened by such 'conscience shocking crimes'. As Secretary-General Ban Ki-moon reinforced in his 2012 R2P report, the tragic events of the past were underlined by the profound failure of 'individual states to live up to their responsibilities and obligations under international law, as well as the collective inadequacies of international institutions'. Consequently, if we understand the R2P as a moral imperative derived from our 'common humanity' (Welsh 2014, p. 127), then to what extent can the normative ambition of humanity be utilised by the R2P, in an attempt to better reinforce moral responsibilities for states? As this section highlights, the complex relationship between the foundational moral principle of humanity and its influence on the R2P's ability to forge greater state responsibility, is still one defined by political contestation. In tracing the development of the R2P one can therefore highlight how appeals to a collective obligation of protection have often resulted in the theoretical stretching of humanity's motivational influence.

ICISS

What is perhaps most significant about the formulation of the ICISS report is the decision to specifically build the concept of R2P around direct appeals to a common humanity. As Jennifer Welsh (2012) acknowledges, while the construction of the R2P in the 2001 ICISS document is based upon the idea of securing individual rights that are denied by persecution and violence, the responsibility of states to intervene to protect these rights is built around the collective idea of a common humanity. In this sense, the document is grounded on a moral imperative, by which certain crimes are seen to 'affect us all collectively, through the international harm principle' (Welsh 2012, p. 105). As the ICISS (2001, p. 75) proposal states, 'all human beings are equally entitled to be protected from acts that shock the conscience of us all'. The reasoning behind this principle therefore stipulates that humanity itself can be damaged by mass atrocity crimes, generating a 'moral responsibility for members of the international community to act' (Welsh 2012, p. 105). Due to the severity of the crimes committed, the responsibility generated by the R2P is then shifted upwards to the international level. This conception of R2P's moral framework has continued to define the approach taken by advocates when explaining how the R2P can generate consensus for protection. In this sense the R2P is often understood as 'the normative instrument of choice for converting a shocked international conscience into decisive collective action' (Thakur 2015, p. 23).

Correspondingly, as Michael Doyle (2015, p. 7) highlights, the R2P therefore attempts to 'redefine and broaden' the standard for authorisation of force, Chapter VII's 'international peace and security' clause, reflecting a desire to draw more attention to the effects mass atrocity crimes can have beyond their domestic impact. The motivation for the expansion of this understanding must be understood in relation to the concept of humanity. This is articulated by the argument that mass atrocity crimes pose the most serious threat to the very ideals humanity is built upon:

> Nothing has done more harm to our shared ideal that we are all equal in worth and dignity, and that the earth is our common home than the inability of the community of states to prevent genocide, massacre and ethnic cleansing.
> (ICISS 2001, p. 75)

The ICISS report explicitly states a need to 'strengthen the prospects for obtaining action. . . . in response to conscience-shocking situations of great humanitarian need' (ICISS 2001, p. 74). This statement again reinforces the centrality of the moral principle of humanity to the motivational strength of the overall R2P concept. Preventing and reacting effectively to mass atrocity crimes must therefore be considered a universal goal for the international community, based upon the importance of human dignity to the management of international society. Humanity in this sense provides an ability to theoretically locate the harm caused by mass atrocity crimes as well as define a moral obligation for states to protect and prevent such crimes. However, the scope of the international community's moral responsibility to act in such situations has continued to be a key point of contestation, whereby states have often firmly rejected the link made between the identification of mass atrocity crimes as a threat to collective humanity, and the subsequent call for humanity to be protected.

World Summit Outcome Document

In the years following the ICISS report, the R2P concept experienced a number of key setbacks in its development, most notably the changing security environment post-9/11, resulting in the highly controversial US led Iraq intervention (Weiss 2006). Yet, despite these initial setbacks, the R2P was able to gain considerable momentum during the 2005 Secretary General's High Level Panel on Threats, Challenges and Change, and following these negotiations states agreed to endorse a more refined principle of R2P in the WSOD. For supporters of the R2P, the 2005 WSOD was a major watershed moment in which the tragedies of the past had finally forced an 'historic shift in international relations' reinforcing the idea of a 'moral obligation to prevent and halt the most horrific crimes known to humankind' (Schmidt and Wolf 2012). However, as C.S.R. Murthy and Gerrit Kurtz (2016, p. 42) acknowledge, the disparate normative perspectives of contrasting states resulted in considerable contestation over agreement to the new formalisation of the R2P. Consequently, what emerged from the eventual agreement has often been referred to as 'R2P lite' (Weiss 2007, p. 117), due to the fact the agreement did not fundamentally address the issue of political will, particularly in regard to how the Council could move beyond deadlock in mass atrocity crime situations.

The construction of the R2P within the 2005 WSOD therefore acknowledged a specific pragmatic understanding of when states should have the responsibility to act. This obligation was expressed as being on a strict 'case by case' basis. In this regard, the R2P was specifically set up to balance various imperatives and procedural considerations, and thus in many ways contradicts the form in which the R2P was originally presented in previous discussions (Paris 2014, p. 579). As Peter Hilpold (2006, p. 65) argues, very little remained in the 2005 WSOD from the bold designs developed by the ICISS, and the HLP report. The agreement therefore underwent a number of significant changes to its language in which to help build international consensus (Bellamy 2006, p. 143). Thus, as Carsten Stahn (2007, p. 109) has highlighted, the strict conditions placed on the ability of states to use force clearly distinguished the WSOD from the more responsibility-driven approach of the previous ICISS report on collective security, and reflects the views of those states against the imposition of 'any legal obligation for Security Council members to support enforcement action in the case of mass atrocities'. In response to such demands, Paragraph 139 of the WSOD firmly locates the responsibility to protect within the framework of the Security Council and its powers under Chapter VII, and thus 'does not provide any new legal obligations on the part of states to prevent or respond to atrocities' (Welsh 2009, p. 4).

This reframing of the R2P within the 2005 WSOD agreement has since been described as a move to narrow the possibilities of implementing collective responsibility, whereby it is 'no longer the challenging framework of common humanity which creates the moral responsibility, but rather the specific political commitment of states to act through the UN to address potential or real atrocities' (Welsh and Banda 2010, p. 225). The 2005 WSOD is argued by Lars Waldorf

(2016, p. 56) to have shifted the focus from 'moral judgments about what shocks the conscience of humanity (ICISS 2001) to legal determinations about what violates international criminal law' and is thus seen to a have replaced 'subjective moral judgments (and selective political decisions) with something more consensual and more consistent'. This reading of humanity's changing role in relation to the R2P is significant and in many ways reflects how consensus was built through watering down the language of moral obligations in order to craft a pragmatic framework for action, which rejects the need to locate a higher authority above the state system. While it may appear as simply a vital move away from the emotive language of the ICISS document, in order to put into place a more rigid and workable doctrine, it also represents a significant rejection of the idea that the R2P can reshape the current global political system (Hopgood 2014, p. 193). In this sense, it reinforces the idea that an obligation for the international community is one that sits at the sovereign level, whereby humanity as a moral obligation is internally reflected on by states and thus does not dictate to sovereign powers.

The 2005 agreement must therefore be understood as reinforcing existing but fragile state agreement as to the potential of mass atrocity crimes to threaten international peace and security, rather than an attempt to create a distinctly new responsibility founded in the respect of human dignity and common humanity. As a consequence, states do still face what Adrian Gallagher (2012, p. 343) has referred to as a 'clash of responsibilities' 'between the international responsibility of states to assist other states and the national responsibility of states to pursue survival within anarchy'. Based upon these terms, it makes sense to classify the R2P as representative of a distinctly pragmatic framework of protection, defined by a 'duty of conduct' which at a minimum generates a 'responsibility to consider' the appropriate action concerning all incidents of mass atrocity crimes (Welsh 2013). While this more pragmatic interpretation of the R2P is clearly an attempt to shrink down the influence of moral obligations, the framing of a theoretical 'responsibility to consider' must also be understood and interpreted through the language of common humanity, which informs our ability to recognise why we should consider the harm of mass atrocity crimes in the first place.

Nevertheless, this normative shift does also open up further space for states to contest and reinterpret the moral demands created by humanity, and ultimately to challenge the link made between the process of threat identification and the corresponding obligation to act. In this regard, the moral demand for protection on behalf of a common humanity is one that is continually internalised within the confines of the political, and as such, the scope of the moral obligations attached to the concept are continually reshaped by the system of sovereign states. Subsequently, rather than see humanity as a moral benchmark to which state action must aspire, it is much more the case that the normative power of humanity provides a tool for driving action and critique that is consistently manipulated by states in an attempt to define the limits of moral concern. As Michael Barnett (2002, p. 181) has argued, what this may suggest is that the very institutions and concepts that we develop in order to create higher humanitarian ends can still often 'generate ethical principles that are disconnected from those in whose name they act'. Thus, the creation of the 2005 R2P agreement provides a normative space in which states can now more easily consider and define the political scope of protection on behalf of humanity, but this process of increased reflection does not necessarily correspond with the ability of the R2P to supposedly shift emotional shock and outrage into collective action on behalf of others.

Taking stock – ten years of the R2P

In the ten years since its official adoption, the R2P has been applied to a number of prominent mass atrocity cases, most notably the 2011 Libyan intervention, as well as its role in supporting more limited intervention and prevention practices in Côte d'Ivoire, Guinea and Kenya. Yet at the same time the R2P has also been unable to generate sufficient political interest or consensus as to the need for protection in cases including Syria, Sri Lanka and Sudan. This mixed picture of the R2P in its first decade of existence requires one to begin questioning the influence of the moral framework underpinning the R2P, and its role in grounding the scope of state obligations. Taking stock of the current R2P 'balance sheet' (Evans 2011), one can certainly highlight evidence of a continual process of R2P language becoming further embedded and commonplace within Security Council resolutions. As Jess Gifkins (2016, p. 13) highlights, 'R2P has been regularly reaffirmed in a wide array of conflicts and thematic issues'. Yet in spite of this changing reality, there still remains a considerable lack of consensus surrounding the moral obligations for protection, and in particular, discussions concerning the hierarchy of when and where the protection of humanity must be reinforced. For Aidan Hehir (2016, p. 171), the lack of Pillar III engagement has been a consistent feature of R2P discussions, and has arguably increased since the invocation of R2P language in regard to the 2011 Libya intervention, following which members have continued to hold diverse views on how Pillar III can be applied and when certain criteria demand its application (Morris 2016). This contestation has certainly not gone unnoticed and has as such remained a significant point of concern following the continuation of the Syrian crisis, as well as relatively inadequate responses by the UN to situations in Central African Republic and Burundi (Cinq-Mars 2016; Rugiririza 2016). Subsequently, the impact of the motivational force of humanity and its relation to the R2P has become a key point of discussion once again, in particular, the need to question how it can influence state decision making in mass atrocity crime situations (Tacheva and Brown 2015).

In the 2015 UN Secretary General Report on the R2P, Ban Ki-moon (2015) engaged directly with the apparent tension between the pragmatic and moral frameworks embedded within the R2P concept and most significantly, the role of humanity as a central normative element of the R2P. The document states that despite the 2005 WSOD calling on the Security Council to address atrocity crimes on a case-by-case basis, 'the Council's inconsistent response to situations featuring genocide, war crimes, ethnic cleansing and crimes against humanity continues to affect the standing of the responsibility to protect' (p. 13). Subsequently it is argued that, 'the Security Council has too often failed to live up to its global responsibility and find a common purpose, allowing narrower strategic interests to impede consensus and preclude a robust collective response' (p. 13). This common purpose is expressed through the distinctive harms created by the crimes of R2P, which are understood as 'a deep affront to humanity, to the very dignity of human beings' (p. 6). The concept of humanity is thus underlined as critical to building consensus as to the scope of the crimes that define the R2P as well as providing the key motivational force to compel states to drastically shift their behaviour. As the report goes on to outline, a key priority for the future must be making sure the protection of populations is 'elevated above political and strategic interests' (p. 16). The key to achieving this lies in the ability of states to recognise the R2P as an 'enduring obligation', whereby the responsibilities it creates cannot be turned on and off by states (p. 18). All this adds up to an enhanced pressure on states to make atrocity crime prevention and response a priority.

While the R2P clearly remains a work in progress, Ban Ki-moon's harsh words against the current practices of the Security Council highlight a strained relationship between humanity's moral demand for protection and the ability of the R2P to compel states to shift their behaviour accordingly. The complex relationship between humanity and the R2P therefore remains far from resolved. Subsequently, if the UN had the moral capacity to act in the cases of Rwanda and Srebrenica but failed to, can we confidently point to a different response in such situations in the future? The ability to fully address this question therefore requires the continuation of a more systematic engagement with the moral foundations of the R2P, in order to assess how normative concepts such as humanity influence the framing of the obligations states are believed to hold. Thus if we accept that the R2P does not create any higher law, such as restraints on the actions of the Security Council, then to what extent can normative obligations created by the notion of humanity compete 'in the sphere of "politics", the world of everyday decision-making' (Hopgood 2014, p. 193)?

Conclusion

In a 2013 speech on the future of R2P, Gareth Evans stated his strong belief that 'the imperative of our common humanity will eventually prevail'. With the growing traction of the R2P concept across the globe, demonstrated by numerous UN resolutions and continued institutional support, advocates have since articulated similar sentiments (Dunne 2013; Bellamy 2014). Yet by focusing on humanity as a higher moral cause driving future progress, it is often easy to overlook the complexity of its current normative interaction with the R2P, and its role as a central motivational component for the doctrine. Subsequently, the chapter has sought to address this significant lacuna in the current R2P literature, in which appeals to the concept of humanity and its relationship to the R2P have remained considerably under theorised. A significant impact of this oversight has been to view the development of the R2P as one that follows a linear path of progression, dictated by the higher moral good of humanity. This framing of humanity's normative role has therefore often led advocates to overstate humanity's role in helping the R2P convert emotional shock and outrage into collective action.

The limitations of the R2P in helping to reinforce this conversion process can be reflected on through revisiting a critical statement from the 2001 ICISS report, in which it was argued that, 'for all the rhetoric about the universality of human rights some human lives end up mattering a great deal less to the international community than others' (ICISS, p. 1). In the 15 years since this report, states have continued to contest the scope of their zones of moral concern, in which the hierarchy of human life has remained a consistent challenge to the universal ambitions of the R2P. Subsequently, it is vital to reflect on the processes through which those who are currently dehumanised can become recognised as fully human (Weinert 2015, p. 2). The politics of forging such agreement is therefore the arena in which the normative and motivational capacity of humanity must compete. Yet while the R2P can never be a quick fix to the problems of collective morality in the current state system, we must be prepared to more critically engage with the wider normative tensions that remain apparent in the R2P's construction. Attempts to bypass or overlook the normative elements of such debates will only allow for further confusion, as a supposedly uncontested moral principle continues to provide contrasting results. Consequently, while the concept of humanity is so often left under-theorised in the literature, there continues to be a tendency to overstate its apparent influence on generating consensus for responding to humanitarian crisis. In order to further address this oversight, it is vital that both academics and practitioners continue to reflect on how the language and moral demands created by humanity are internalised by states, and ultimately begin to challenge assumptions as to the ease from which its function as a generator of moral concern can in fact fully translate to effective consensus and response during mass atrocity crime situations.

References

Annan, K 1999, *Two Concepts of Sovereignty*, The Economist, 18 September. Available from: www.economist.com/node/324795. [10 December 2015].
Barnett, M 2002, *Eyewitness to a Genocide: The United Nations and Rwanda*, Cornell University Press, Ithaca, NY.
Bauman, Z 2001, *Community: Seeking Safety in an Insecure World*, Polity Press, Cambridge.
Bellamy, A 2006, 'Whither the Responsibility to Protect? Humanitarian Intervention and the 2005 World Summit', *Ethics and International Affairs*, vol. 143, no. 20, pp. 143–169.
Bellamy, A 2013, 'The Responsibility to Protect: Added value or hot air?', *Cooperation and Conflict*, vol. 48, no. 3, pp. 333–357.
Bellamy, A 2014, *The Responsibility to Protect: A Defence*, Oxford University Press, Oxford.
Bellamy, A 2015, *Still Hearing the Cries from the Graves: Srebrenica, R2P and the Struggle for Human Protection*. Available from: www.internationalaffairs.org.au/australian_outlook/still-hearing-the-cries-from-the-graves-srebrenica-r2p-and-the-struggle-for-human-protection/. [12 February 2016].

Booth, K 1999, 'Three Tyrannies' in T Dunne and N Wheeler, (eds), *Human Rights in Global Politics*, pp. 31–70. Cambridge University Press, Cambridge.

Bulley, D 2010, 'The Politics of Ethical Foreign Policy: A Responsibility to Protect Whom?', *European Journal of International Relations*, vol. 16, no. 3, pp. 441– 461.

Butler J 2009, *Frames of War: When is Life Grievable?* Verso, London.

Cinq-Mars, E 2016, *How the World Failed the Central African Republic*. Available from: www.washingtonpost.com/news/in-theory/wp/2016/02/18/how-the-international-community-failed-the-central-african-republic/. [17 March 2016].

Doyle, M 2015, *The Question of Intervention: John Stuart Mill and the Responsibility to Protect*, Yale University Press, Newhaven, CT.

Dunne, T 2013, 'Distributing Duties and Counting Costs', *Global Responsibility to Protect*, vol. 5, no. 4, pp. 443–465.

Evans, G 2008, 'The Responsibility to Protect: An Idea Whose Time Has Come . . . and Gone?', Lecture to David Davies Memorial Institute, University of Aberystwyth, 23 April, Available from: www.crisisgroup.org/en/publication-type/speeches/2008/the-responsibility-to-protect-an-idea-whose-time-has-come-and-gone.aspx. [16 February 2016].

Evans, G 2009, *The Responsibility to Protect, Ending Mass Atrocity Crimes Once and For All*, Brookings Institution Press, Washington DC.

Evans, G 2011, 'Interview: The "RtoP" Balance Sheet After Libya', e-International Relations. Available from: www.globalr2p.org/media/files/gareth-_interview-the-rtop-balance-sheet-after-libya.pdf. [12 January 2016].

Evans, G 2013, 'The Responsibility to Protect: Theory and Practice', presentation at China Institute of International Studies (CIIS) Conference on Responsible Protection: Building a Safer World, Beijing, 17 October. Available from: www.gevans.org/speeches/speech535.html. [9 March 2016].

Feldman, I and Ticktin, M 2010, *In the Name of Humanity*, Duke University Press, Durham, NC.

Gallagher, A 2012, 'A Clash of Responsibilities: Engaging with Realist Critiques of the R2P', *Global Responsibility to Protect*, vol. 4, no. 3, pp. 334–357.

Gallagher, A 2013, *Genocide and Its Threat to Contemporary International Order*, Palgrave Macmillan, Hounslow.

Geras, N 2011, *Crimes Against Humanity*, Manchester University Press, Manchester.

Gifkins J 2016, 'R2P in the UN Security Council: Darfur, Libya and beyond', *Cooperation and Conflict*, vol. 51, no. 2, pp. 148–165.

Gyekye, K 2004, *Beyond Cultures: Perceiving a Common Humanity*, The Council for Research in Values and Philosophy, Washington, DC.

Haslam, N 2006, 'Dehumanization: An Integrative Review', *Personality and Social Psychology Review*, vol. 10, no. 3, pp. 252–264.

Hehir A 2016, 'Assessing the Influence of the Responsibility to Protect on the UN Security Council During the Arab Spring', *Cooperation and Conflict*, vol. 51, no. 2, pp. 166–183.

Heinze, E 2009, *Waging Humanitarian War: The Ethics, Law, and Politics of Humanitarian Intervention*, SUNY Press, Albany, NY.

Hilpold, P 2006, 'The Duty to Protect and the Reform of the United Nations – A New Step in the Development of International Law?', *Max Planck Yearbook of United Nations Law Online*, vol. 10, no. 1, pp. 35–69.

Hilpold P 2012, 'Intervening in the Name of Humanity: RtoP and the Power of Ideas', *Journal of Conflict Security and Law*, vol. 17, no. 1, pp. 49–79.

Hopgood, S 2014, 'The Last Rites for Humanitarian Intervention: Darfur, Sri Lanka and R2P', *Global Responsibility to Protect*, vol. 6, no. 2, pp. 181–205.

ICISS 2001, 'The Responsibility To Protect: Report of the International Commission on Intervention and State Sovereignty', International Development Research Centre, Ottawa.

Ki-moon, B 2012, 'Responsibility to Protect: Timely and Decisive Response: Report of the Secretary-General', A/66/874–S/2012/578. Available from: www.responsibilityto protect.org/UNSG%20Report_timely%20and%20decisive%20response%281%29.pdf. [20 March 2016].

Ki-moon, B 2015, 'A Vital and Enduring Commitment: Implementing The Responsibility to Protect: Report of the Secretary-General', A/69/981–S/2015/500. Available from: www.un.org/en/preventgenocide/adviser/pdf/N1521764%202015%20SG%20Report%20R2P%20English.pdf. [25 March 2016].

Linklater, A 2009, 'Human Interconnectedness', *International Relations*, vol. 23, no. 3, pp. 481–497.

Lu, C 2007, 'Humanitarian Intervention: Moral Ambition and Political Constraints', *International Journal*, vol. 62, no. 4, pp. 942–951.

Luban, D 2002, 'Intervention and Civilization: Some Unhappy Lessons of the Kosovo War' in P De Greiff and C Cronin, (eds), *Global Justice and Transnational Politics*, pp. 79–116. MIT Press, Cambridge, MA.

Luban, D 2004, 'A Theory of Crimes Against Humanity', *The Yale Journal of International Law* vol. 29, pp. 85–167.

Lucas, G 2014, 'Revisiting Armed Humanitarian Intervention: A 25-year Retrospective' in DE Scheid, (ed), *The Ethics of Armed Humanitarian Intervention*, pp. 26–45. Cambridge University Press, Cambridge.

Macleod, C 2010, 'Towards a Philosophical Account of Crimes Against Humanity', *The European Journal of International Law*, vol. 21, no. 2, pp. 281–302.

Morris, J 2016, 'The Responsibility to Protect and the use of force: Remaking the Procrustean bed?', *Cooperation and Conflict*, vol. 51, no. 2, pp. 200–215.

Murthy, CSR and Kurtz, G 2016, 'International Responsibility as Solidarity: The Impact of the World Summit Negotiations on the R2P Trajectory', *Global Society*, vol. 30, no. 1, pp. 38–53.

Newman, E 2016, 'What prospects for common humanity in a divided world? The scope for RtoP in a transitional international order', *International Politics*, vol. 53, no. 1, pp. 32–48.

Parekh, B 1999, 'Non-ethnocentric Universalism' in T Dunne and N. Wheeler, (eds), *Human Rights in Global Politics*, pp. 128–159. Cambridge University Press, Cambridge.

Paris, R 2014, 'The "Responsibility to Protect" and the Structural Problems of Preventive Humanitarian Intervention', *International Peacekeeping*, vol. 21, no. 5, pp. 569–603.

Peters, A 2009, 'Membership in the Global Constitutional Community' in J Klabbers, A Petersand and G Ulfstein, (eds), *The Constitutionalization of International Law*, pp. 153–262. Oxford University Press, New York.

Renzo, M 2012, 'Crimes Against Humanity and the Limits of International Criminal Law', *Law and Philosophy* vol. 31, no. 4, pp. 443–476.

Robertson, G 1999, *Crimes Against Humanity*, New Press, New York.

Rugiririza, E 2016, 'What Hope for Burundi After All the Failed Initiatives?' Available from: www.justiceinfo.net/en/component/k2/25479-what-hope-for-burundi-after-all-the-failed-initiatives.html. [18 March 2016].

Schmidt, C 2007, *The Concept of the Political: Expanded Edition*, University of Chicago Press, London.

Schmidt, M and Wolf, A 2012, 'The Responsibility to Protect: a new norm to make "Never again" a reality'. Available from: http://icrtopblog.org/2012/12/05/the-responsibility-to-protect-a-new-norm-to-make-never-again-a-reality/. [15 February 2015].

Stahn, C 2007, 'Responsibility to Protect: Political Rhetoric or Emerging Legal Norm?', *The American Journal of International Law*, vol. 101, no. 1, pp. 99–120.

Tacheva, B and Brown, GW 2015, 'Global Constitutionalism and the Responsibility to Protect', *Global Constitutionalism*, vol. 4, no. 3, pp. 428–467.

Thakur, R 2015, 'R2P's "Structural" Problems: A Response to Roland Paris', *International Peacekeeping*, vol. 22, no. 1, pp. 11–25.

Waldorf, L 2016, 'Inhumanity's Law: Crimes against humanity, RtoP and South Sudan', *International Politics*, vol. 53, no. 1, pp. 49–66.

Weinert, SM 2015, *Making Human: World Order and the Global Governance of Human Dignity*, University of Michigan Press, Ann Arbor, MI.

Weiss, TG 2006, 'R2P after 9/11 and the World Summit', *Wisconsin International Law Journal*, vol. 24, no. 3, pp. 741-750.

Weiss, TG 2007, *Humanitarian Intervention*, Polity, Cambridge.

Welsh, J 2009, 'Implementing the Responsibility to Protect: Policy Brief'. Available from: www.elac.ox.ac.uk/downloads/r2p_policybrief_180209.pdf. [04 March 2016].

Welsh, J 2012, 'Who Should Act? Collective Responsibility and the Responsibility to Protect' in W Knight and F Egerton, (eds), *The Routledge Handbook of the Responsibility to Protect*, 1st edn, pp. 103–114. Routledge, Milton Park, Abingdon, Oxon.

Welsh, J 2013, 'Norm Contestation and the Responsibility to Protect', *Global Responsibility to Protect*, vol. 5, no. 4, pp. 365–396.

Welsh, J 2014, 'Implementing the "Responsibility to Protect": Catalyzing Debate and Building Capacity' in A Betts and P Orchard, (eds), *Implementation and World Politics: How International Norms Change Practice*, pp. 124–143. Oxford University Press, Oxford.

Welsh, J and Banda, M 2010, 'International Law and the Responsibility to Protect: Clarifying or Expanding States' Responsibilities?', *Global Responsibility to Protect*, vol. 2, no. 3, pp. 213–231.

Wheeler, NJ 2005, 'A Victory for Common Humanity? The Responsibility To Protect After the 2005 World Summit', *paper presented to The UN at Sixty: Celebration or Wake? conference*, 6–7 October, University of Toronto.

Zehfuss, M 2012, 'Contemporary Western War and the Idea of Humanity', *Environment and Planning D: Society and Space*, vol. 30, no. 5, pp. 861–876.

3

FAILED INTERVENTIONS AND THE INHERENT CONTRADICTIONS OF LIBERAL INTERNATIONALISM

Eric A. Heinze

Introduction

This chapter is about the theory and practice of liberal intervention—including humanitarian intervention—and the extent to which the failures and paradoxical outcomes of such interventions in practice are related to the inherent contradictions in liberal internationalist theory. Liberal intervention is the use of military force that is intended to protect or promote values in the target state that are of a "liberal" nature, namely human rights and democracy. Unlike other kinds of intervention, which are often undertaken for self-defensive or other self-serving reasons, liberal intervention is at least supposed to be undertaken primarily for the benefit of those residing in the state that is the target of such intervention, who are being denied their basic human rights, or are even victims of genocide or other forms of mass violence. Liberal interventions arguably enjoyed their most recent revival during the immediate post-Cold War era of the 1990s, though achieving mixed results, at best. While the humanitarian interventions during this period were highly criticized and perhaps poorly executed, there was still a general perception that they were driven by a genuine sense of humanitarianism in the foreign policies of the various western, liberal and democratic states carrying them out (Woodward 1995, p. 321). Yet moving into the twenty-first century, in particular after the 9/11 attacks and the US and UK-led invasion of Iraq, there was a sense that the case for liberal interventions had been "wrecked" (Clark 2003). Especially in post 9/11 interventions, we see a definite articulation of liberal justifications alongside what appear to be more self-interested and self-aggrandizing—that is, "realist"— motives (Wheeler 2002). The notion that humanitarianism and liberal values had been used as pretexts for the Iraq invasion revealed the deep hypocrisy in the policies of liberal states such as the US and UK, who routinely violated the very principles they were supposedly seeking to uphold. And such hypocrisy, of course, is to say nothing of the profound indifference that many influential liberal states showed toward the atrocities in Darfur, Sudan around this same time, not unlike Rwanda a decade before (Heinze 2007).

Such is the story of much contemporary practice of liberal intervention: it is undertaken in a highly selective manner by actors—themselves liberal states—who evidently seek to put their own interests before those of the people who reside in the target state; it has rarely improved the human rights situation in the target state; it almost invariably eventually results in regime change, thus requiring indefinite post-conflict occupation; and the establishment of democratic institutions, if it occurs at all, is rarely followed by a consolidation of liberal-democratic practices. In short, "liberal intervention" is hardly "liberal," in practice or outcome. One could always argue that these states are simply not abiding by the precepts of liberal internationalism at all in carrying out their interventions. In other words, interveners were using liberalism as an ideological justification to mask self-interested power politics, they frequently violated international law, used illiberal means and methods, or left a "heavy footprint" that marginalized local populations—thus rendering such interventions "illiberal."

On the contrary, this chapter suggests that this is indeed what liberal intervention entails, and that the purported "illiberal" practice and outcomes of recent interventions are precisely due to the contradictions inherent in the liberal theories articulated as justificatory bases for these interventions—especially those regarding the universality of human rights and the democratic peace. Utilizing the work of Beate Jahn (2013) and her "immanent critique" of liberal internationalism, this chapter will explore the internal contradictions of liberal internationalism as they pertain to the theory and practice of contemporary liberal intervention, drawing primarily from three cases as examples: the 1999 Kosovo intervention, the 2003 Iraq invasion, and the 2011 Libya intervention. I argue that contemporary liberal theories as they pertain to the practice of liberal intervention would deem many elements of these interventions as highly illiberal, or at least paradoxical. However, understood through Jahn's "Lockean" conception of liberal internationalism, these interventions appear more consistent with the underlying logic of liberalism, which, in both theory and practice, entails a heavy dose of power politics and even oppression.

The chapter will proceed in two broad steps. I first provide a discussion of contemporary liberal internationalism that is specifically relevant to the practice of intervention and describe how these theories have abstracted away from liberalism's historical practices—originally advocated by Locke—thus leading to the paradoxical normative prescriptions, and ultimately practices and outcomes, of contemporary liberal intervention. I focus here on the ways in which contemporary liberal theories seek to justify military intervention on the basis of 1) protecting human rights norms globally and 2) spreading liberal democracy to non-democratic states, utilizing Jahn's analysis of Locke as a way to interrogate these arguments. The second part of the chapter then examines the three aforementioned cases of intervention to illustrate these tendencies and show that interventions premised on liberal internationalism are likely to continue to fail or produce paradoxical outcomes, and should either be abandoned as a policy of liberal actors, or profoundly reformed in light of these inherent contradictions.

Liberal intervention and the origins of liberalism's contradictions

Liberal internationalism is said to entail a commitment to human rights, individual liberty, anti-imperialism, a law-governed international order, and the pursuit of international peace (Doyle 1999, p. 213; Hall and Hobson 2010, pp. 201–211). Yet it is well-known that much of the so-called "liberal project" entails spreading liberal values to other parts of the world and defending them where they are in peril. It is therefore no surprise that the world's most influential liberal states have made human rights and the spread of democracy central parts of their foreign policies (Charvet and Kaczynska-Nay 2008, pp. 260–280). Such a dynamic has led these liberal states to engage in numerous military interventions for the explicit purpose of defending these values. Yet these interventions have been highly selective and often violate international law, suppress individual liberty, and even cause more conflict and suffering. According to Jahn, such paradoxical outcomes are a result of the "abstraction of liberal principles away from the particular context of their constitution and dynamics of their development" (2013, p. 152). That is to say, liberal principles, such as human rights and individual freedom—upon which prevailing theories about contemporary liberal internationalism and intervention are based—have their origins in the political theory of John Locke, who articulated them to apply to a specific time and place (late seventeenth-century England) to promote the interests of a specific category of individuals (propertied males). So while contemporary liberal theories have abstracted away from these "pre-liberal" principles articulated by Locke, adapted them to various changing circumstances and contexts, and reformed them to be in conformity with contemporary sensibilities, their underlying dynamic remains fundamentally the same.

For Jahn, liberalism as articulated by Locke was a political project that sought to institutionalize the protection of the individual freedom of male property owners, and extend this freedom through government by consent (2013, pp. 52–53). However, in practice, this was achieved through the expropriation of commonly held property and by extending political freedom to some people (male property owners) and not others (non-property owners, colonial subjects). In abstracting away from these historical practices, contemporary liberal theories invoke abstracted and "sterilized" versions of these principles as applicable to entirely different contexts: contemporary world politics. So when contemporary liberals argue that a state's sovereignty is contingent upon respect for human rights (see Barkin 1998; Annan 1999; Roberts 1999), seek to grant the right of nonintervention to some states and deny it to others (Beitz 1979, p. 79; Fukuyama 1992; Doyle 1996; Rawls 2001, pp. 81–90), or use authoritarian means to achieve emancipatory ends, they are, in essence, repeating the underlying dynamics of Lockean liberalism: the establishment of liberal principles through the reproduction of unequal power relations (Jahn 2013, pp. 43–60). This dynamic is particularly pronounced in liberal theories that seek to justify liberal intervention on the basis of promoting and protecting universal human rights.

Universal human rights

Jahn argues that Locke articulated his political theory in the *Second Treatise* with the aim of providing solutions to a political crisis in the aftermath of extreme violence and religious and civil war in late seventeenth-century England. These crises seriously jeopardized the economic interests and liberties of the population, especially people such as Locke and his longtime employer, the Earl of Shaftsbury, who were landowners and merchants who "had become rich through trade with the colonies [and] who sought solutions to these problems based on property" (2013, p. 62). Locke therefore articulated a theory wherein individuals are imbued with a natural right to property as a basis for self-preservation, whereby the very fact of property ownership was constitutive of his freedom and liberty and acted as a check against absolutist government. With liberty effectively constituted by property, Locke argues that the chief end of government—which should be based on the consent of these propertied individuals—is thus the preservation of private property (2013, p. 43).

In describing how such an arrangement would be implemented in practice, Locke initially only sought to extend full political rights to the property-owning class, and sought to deny them to those without property until such time as liberal property rights could become embodied by the state. Locke thus aimed to extend this franchise by eventually turning all segments of society into property owners, providing them a stake in the continuance of such a political order. Of course, common property (in terms of land) capable of being privatized even in seventeenth-century England had become scarce, so Locke essentially offered the colonial settlements of America as the basis for expanding property ownership, therefore justifying and defending colonialism as a means to achieving liberalism at home.

> In practice, therefore, the realization of liberal principles [at home] (according to Locke) required the expropriation of other peoples' land and this goal could only be realized by the systematic exploitation of power differentials. . . . Locke thus provided a theoretical justification for the denial of political rights of some communities [colonial subjects], and hence for the practice of power politics in the international sphere.
>
> (Jahn 2013, p. 57)

The practice of power politics, therefore, does not have its roots solely in the (anarchical) nature of the international system, as realism would suggest, but rather in the logic of (Lockean) liberal principles.

Jahn also argues (2013, p. 159) that liberal states' tendency to pursue their own interests at the expense of advancing liberal principles in carrying out these liberal interventions (as will be examined below), lies in the fact that these interventions are justified on the basis of protecting and promoting allegedly *universal* liberal human rights norms. That is, the conventional liberal view is that human rights are universally valid (Donnelly 2003; Charvet and Kaczynska-Nay 2008) and, concomitantly, that there is a universal moral obligation for people (usually in liberal states) to come to the rescue of those whose rights are being systematically and grossly violated (Wheeler 2000, pp. 33–51; Shue 2004). One need look no further than the voluminous discourse on the Responsibility to Protect (R2P) as evidence of a deeply liberal movement intended to convince states to internalize this obligation (see Bellamy 2009). However, to the extent that universal human rights is a concept that has its roots in Lockean conceptions of individual rights, this "universal" concept is really an abstracted version of a principle (individual property rights), whose original theoretical and historical development was based on promoting the *particular* interests of property-owning men—that is, protecting their property and liberty from encroachment by the state (Jahn 2013, p. 159).

Liberal international norms such as human rights are therefore abstracted, universalized, and sterilized conceptions of a particular group's political interests. In practice, then, the realization of liberal principles such as human rights *requires* the existence of particular interests and actors willing to protect these interests for themselves. States that embody these norms and principles based on particular interests (liberal states) would therefore be unlikely to attempt to promote these norms globally if doing so potentially undermines the interests underpinning the liberal rights of their own populations—that is, their economic benefits, political consent, and individual rights. We should thus *expect* the practice of liberal intervention, insofar as it is inspired by these theories, to be conducted in a way that is consistent with upholding these benefits of liberalism at home for the interveners. How (and whether) a liberal state responds to a mass atrocity abroad, and the extent to which it persists in democratic state-building, then, is not a struggle between political self-interest and moral obligation, it is a struggle between competing moral obligations between one's own citizens and foreigners (Jahn 2013, p. 160)—and both sets of obligations are central to liberal internationalism.

In addition, to the extent that the realization of liberal rights in the Lockean sense requires granting these rights to some and denying them to others in practice, even universalized abstractions of these principles will have to be linked to particular interests and practices to be fulfilled, thus accounting for the tendency of contemporary liberal theories to identify liberal states as the embodiment of liberal principles, and extend them "the rights and privileges necessary to extend these moral institutions . . . while denying similar rights to morally less advanced political systems" (Jahn 2013, p. 162). While sovereign equality is very much a part of contemporary positivist international law, Locke understood international law to be analogous to the state of nature among individuals, which was governed by "natural law," wherein any person who "lives according to the laws of nature" can enforce these laws. Analogously, then, any state that generally abides by international law is empowered to enforce this law against states who violate it

(Locke 1980, pp. 9–10). Doyle (1997, p. 220) has even attributed to Locke the view that a "just conqueror" has the right to punish transgressors of the "law of nations" in order to deter future attacks and seek compensation.

Far from conceiving international law as the horizontal legal system of today whose actors enjoy sovereign equality and must consent to be bound by its rules, a Lockean conception of international law grants special privileges to more advanced (liberal) states and seems to see enforcement primarily as a matter of capabilities. Hegemony, inequality, and hierarchy, therefore, appear to be as central to a (Lockean) liberal conception of world politics as much as they are to a realist one. It should therefore not be surprising that contemporary liberal theories about intervention, often bemoaning the gap between positivist international law and liberal moral norms (Strauss 2009, p. 46), have advocated the reform of international law to permit intervention in certain cases (Buchanan 2003) and to make the right of nonintervention contingent upon respect for human rights (Barkin 1998; Donnelly 1998). By extension, it should also not be surprising that many liberal interventions have been violations of international law, leading some to opine whether such state practice was rendering humanitarian intervention legal under customary international law (Cassesse 1999).

The enterprise of liberal intervention—and perhaps even liberal internationalism *writ large*—has, in effect, established an unequal, hierarchical international system that imbues liberal states with more rights than non-liberal states—hardly the "equality before the law" that is normally associated with liberalism. Left to the discretion of powerful liberal states, then, the practice of liberal intervention is therefore as inconsistent and paradoxical as its articulation in liberal theory. So when interventions do occur, they are always fiercely contested, frequently violate international law, and entail a commingling of humanitarian and self-interested justifications. Likewise, many of these interventions have used means that seem inconsistent with a goal of promoting human rights in the target states, and at least in the short term (and very frequently in the long term) such interventions have commonly resulted in an escalation of atrocities, not their cessation. So despite eloquent and convincing arguments about the existence of moral obligations to protect human rights globally, the contemporary practice of liberal intervention suggests that this moral obligation is quite weak, given liberal states' tendency to prioritize the benefits of liberalism at home over defending liberal principles abroad.

Democratic institutions

Another set of ideas relevant to intervention that flow from liberal internationalism relate to the peaceful nature of democracies, and therefore entail a prescription for democratic states to spread this form of government to the non-democratic and illiberal parts of the world. Originating with Kant, the "democratic peace hypothesis" is well-known, as is the paradox that it provides philosophical justification for policies such as forcible regime change (á la Iraq) to replace non-democratic regimes with democratic ones (e.g. Doyle 1996; Desch 2007/8). The various democracy promotion policies inspired by democratic peace theory, however, have largely found their applications in the post-conflict context, focusing on establishing the institutions deemed to be necessary for a functioning democracy: separation of powers, an independent judiciary, and critically, electoral institutions. Yet, as the examples discussed below will show, these sorts of policies frequently require increasingly heavy-handed approaches on the part of the interveners in order to create the stability thought necessary for democracy to take hold, and even then, have largely failed to engender sustainable democratic practices.

While the failure of liberal democratic institutions to consolidate in states that were the target of liberal interventions can also be partially explained by the lack of commitment on the part of intervening liberal states, owing to the struggle between competing moral obligations (citizens versus foreigners), Jahn also suggests that there is another force at work, again with its origins in the abstraction of liberal principles away from their historical development. That is, by and large, the theory and practice of contemporary democracy promotion have focused on the creation of political institutions—most notably, electoral institutions (see Carothers 2004, pp. 7–74). When elections alone did not produce liberal democracy, analysts concluded that successful democratic political institutions needed to be based upon a liberal political culture, and therefore advocated for the creation of a variety of social and political institutions intended to constitute such a culture—anything from a free press, to civil society organizations, to political parties. Yet in numerous cases, even if free and fair elections were held, liberal democratic practices failed to take root, and in some cases, these efforts produced results that were decidedly illiberal (Jahn 2013, pp. 90–91). Such a dynamic logically leads either to the intervening actors giving up and ceasing these activities, or continuing to undertake ever more intrusive efforts, and therefore undermining the very goal they are trying to achieve—democratic self-government.

According to Jahn, however, the problem lies in the tendency of the liberal theories that inspired these policies to treat political institutions as the source of liberal political culture, as opposed to realizing that even in mature democracies, political institutions tend to be "vehicles for the organization and expression of existing social and political interests" (Jahn 2013, p. 91). Applying the Lockean conception, however, reveals that it is not political institutions, but rather *private property*, that is constitutive of individual freedom and hence a liberal political culture. In other words, one should not expect a liberal political culture to develop in a society where private property is not already broadly distributed, or where individual liberty is based on other characteristics (e.g. ethnicity, religion, etc.). When "liberal" political institutions are introduced in societies that lack a liberal political culture, it makes perfect sense for them to use those institutions as a basis to promote the interests of their own group (religious, national, etc.), rather than the protection of private property and individual liberty (2013, p. 91).

Again, interveners are faced with the option of withdrawing in the face of increasing costs—and thus abandoning liberalism abroad in favor of liberalism at home—or intensifying their efforts at state-building by pursuing more intrusive and heavy-handed approaches that marginalize some parts of the population. Jahn argues this should again not be surprising, since, after all, liberalism was not originally democratic. Also faced with the task of establishing liberal practices in a nonliberal environment, Locke advocated a "liberal despotism" that extended political rights to some and denied them to others until the state came to embody principles of private property and individual liberty. Far from democratic institutions being a precursor to liberalism, historically, the realization of liberal principles was only possible through the suppression of democracy (2013, pp. 93–94). According to this logic, efforts to establish liberal practices in nonliberal contexts *should* entail the oppression of illiberal forces until such time as private property is sufficiently widely distributed throughout a society, such that a majority of the populace has a positive stake in a political system whose purpose is the protection of private property and individual liberty.

Recent practice of liberal intervention

This section surveys some recent practice of liberal interventions that had paradoxical outcomes in order to illustrate and interrogate some of the propositions articulated above drawn from Jahn. I do not approach this discussion as a traditional case study analysis, but rather use the cases of the interventions in Kosovo (1999), Iraq (2003), and Libya (2011) to explore how some of the liberal theories discussed above (fail to) account for the following paradoxical aspects of these interventions: 1) the legality of the interventions under international law, 2) the stated motives of the interveners compared to the means of the intervention, and the overall selectivity of interveners, and 3) the short- and long-term outcomes of these interventions.

Legality

As indicated above, liberal internationalism professes a commitment to a rule-governed international system, so we would expect policies based on liberal internationalism to be consistent with international law. For the most part, the humanitarian interventions of the 1990s were consistent with international law in terms of *jus ad bellum*, which is to say they were authorized by the UN Security Council. But, as is well known, neither the Kosovo intervention nor the Iraq invasion obtained prior UN Security Council authorization. While the Libya operation was authorized by the Council, the force authorization was to protect vulnerable populations, not assist rebel forces in their effort to depose Gadhafi, which many observers noted was taking place, indicating to many states that NATO had exceeded the legal mandate given them by the Security Council (Erlanger 2011). While we might otherwise expect a liberal foreign policy to be consistent with international law, a Lockean analysis would suggest that to the extent that the interveners are liberal states and it can be argued that the target states have violated international law, then the interveners' liberal character, as well as their capabilities, give them the legal right to unilaterally enforce international law against outlaw states, who have no political rights under international law, owing either to their underdeveloped or "outlaw" status. Powerful liberal actors thus decide for themselves what is legal and when the law requires enforcement. To a certain extent, this arrangement reflects the international legal order of today—broadly understood to be a "liberal" order—whereby the great powers (P-5 of the UN Security Council) basically decide on whether a particular (non-self-defensive) use of force should be considered legal. However, many of the actors deciding on these issues are not themselves liberal states (Russia and China, namely). So when the Security Council fails to authorize a military action that seeks to uphold universal human rights, a Lockean analysis would suggest that the importance of this illegality is overstated, since it was a decision arrived at with the input of illiberal states who should have no say in such matters.

This would certainly be the case regarding the Kosovo intervention, whose illegality in practice was very much downplayed by the democratic states of the world, who largely supported it and argued it was morally justified, if technically illegal (Kosovo Commission 2000, p. 4). So for a Lockean liberal, and many contemporary liberals, what is important is not whether an intervention is technically legal or not, but whether it was undertaken and otherwise supported by liberal actors in the enforcement of (the liberal parts of) international law (human rights). The opposition of illiberal actors to the Kosovo operation, as well as charges by illiberal states that the Libya intervention exceeded the UN mandate, therefore, should not matter to the proponents of liberal internationalism to the extent that the decision of what is considered lawful is tainted by actors who are themselves routine violators of the law. Even the Iraq invasion, which was opposed by many authoritarian as well as liberal democratic states, would be excused from its technical illegality, given again that illiberal actors helped to determine this illegality, and second, that Iraq had been found, on numerous counts, to have egregiously violated international law and the interveners were liberal states intent on enforcing it. The illegality of an intervention would therefore not automatically disqualify it as a "liberal" intervention according to this Lockean interpretation, as well as many contemporary liberal approaches that argue international law should be reformed or interpreted in light of liberal human rights norms (e.g. Tesón 1988, 2003; Buchanan 2003; Buchanan and Keohane 2004, p. 19).

Selectivity, motives, and means

The humanitarian interventions of the 1990s, were, for the most part, considered permissible under international law, and also seemed to be mostly motivated by a genuine desire to promote human welfare, as opposed to the pursuit of more self-interested goals. Yet very early on in the supposed heyday of liberal intervention of the 1990s, liberal states began hedging their commitment to promoting human rights abroad. In the aftermath of the disastrous Somalia intervention, for example,

US President Bill Clinton signed a directive that severely circumscribed the situations under which the US would support or participate in humanitarian operations, including that US participation in any such multilateral operation must "advance US interests," which according to some observers, had a direct impact on the US's policy of indifference in Rwanda (Heinze 2007, p. 363). Likewise, by the time the Kosovo intervention went forward, both the US and UK made it very clear that they would not intervene unless their pressing national security interests were at stake (Roberts 1999, pp. 119–120). As a result, powerful liberal states would intervene in situations where they believed their national interests were at stake— that is, if the intervention could enhance (or defend) the benefits of liberalism domestically while simultaneously defending and spreading them abroad. We thus see a determined intervention in Kosovo, triggered largely in response to a single massacre in the village of Racak in which 45 civilians were killed (Clark 2001, p. 158), because, not only was it a moral imperative, but as President Clinton emphasized in his address, the situation threatened regional political and economic stability as well as the credibility and relevance of NATO as an alliance (Clinton 1999).

Regarding the Iraq war, the reasons for why the US and UK chose to invade Iraq are still very much contested. At least in US circles, however, there is strong evidence that its architects sought to fundamentally alter the politics of the region, ultimately realigning the Middle East in favor of the West by establishing Iraq as a democratic outpost in the region from which Western states could exert influence in their favor (Packer 2006). Interestingly, these were not the public justifications for going to war in Iraq in 2003, as these tended to emphasize the threat posed by Iraq, including its links to al Qaeda and possession of Weapons of Mass Destruction—that is to say, self-defensive or "realist" justifications (Roth 2004). As the (counter-) insurgency and occupation unfolded, allied behavior in Iraq evinced a clear desire to put their own interests above those of the local population. Whether it was securing the Iraqi Oil Ministry after the regime fell (versus, for example, protecting the local population), or the clear preference given to American and Western firms in the awarding of reconstruction contracts (Beelman 2003), the self-serving nature of this effort was evident. But it soon became increasingly clear that the interveners were not "greeted as liberators" as US Vice President Dick Cheney had promised, while the effort continued to produce adverse consequences not only for Iraqis, but in the domestic societies of the interveners in the form of serious violations of liberal principles, including racial profiling, violations of privacy, and economic recession before the intervention/occupation effectively ended in 2011 (see generally Darmer *et al*. 2004; Oatley 2015, pp. 127–149).

During the Libya intervention, which was observed by some to be a "classic" humanitarian intervention (Pattison 2011, p. 251), we likewise see the mixing of various motives. While humanitarianism and the need to protect civilian populations were proffered as the public justification—with some UN members even going so far as to invoke R2P (Weiss 2011)—there is some evidence to suggest that NATO powers were also concerned about how Gadhafi's erratic behavior, and the situation overall, might affect their other interests in the region. Both France and Britain had significant business interests in Libya (Stratfor 2011), while European powers were very concerned about refugees. Information released by WikiLeaks also revealed a deep concern in the US about how the instability in Libya would impact US and allied access to global oil markets (DiMaggio 2015, pp. 222–223). Thus, as many have argued, the Libya intervention was at least as much geostrategic as it was humanitarian (Murray 2013; DiMaggio 2015, pp. 220–224). Yet there was also a strong sense in especially US foreign policy circles that the so-called "Arab Spring," of which the Libyan revolt was a part, signified that "democracy was on the march," and that if the West allowed Gadhafi to follow through on his threats of atrocities (which, incidentally, harkened to the Rwanda genocide in his use of the word "cockroaches" to describe his opponents), that "100,000 people could be massacred and everyone would blame us for it" (cited in DiMaggio 2015, p. 220). Yet going to war on the basis of a threat is always going to be anticipatory, and similar to the Kosovo intervention, the scale and severity of the atrocities that were the basis for the Libya intervention have been called into question, raising the very strong possibility that the intervention did more harm than good in terms of human lives (Cockburn 2011; Chivers and Schmitt 2011).

In each of these cases, then, self-interested motives clearly commingled with any humanitarian or liberal motives for intervening. The foregoing discussion suggests this should not be surprising. Since "universal" human rights are abstractions of particular interests, efforts to protect them abroad must be consistent with preserving the benefits of liberal rights to a state's own populations (Jahn 2013, p. 160). Far from these states embodying the idea that they have a moral obligation to halt atrocities, in each of these cases, interveners based the intervention significantly (if not entirely) on the propensity of the intervention to accrue domestic benefits, even at the expense of those on whose behalf the intervention was supposedly undertaken. Liberal interventions are therefore inherently selective on the basis of the likely benefits (or at least lack of risks) to the populations of the intervening actors. This dynamic also explains why we see these interventions carried out using means and methods that prioritize the interveners' own combatants over vulnerable populations. As is well known, both the Libya and Kosovo operations relied on high-altitude bombing campaigns in order to avoid the political backlash of sustaining combat casualties—effectively pitting the human rights of the intervening communities against those of the supposed beneficiaries of the intervention. As a result, what is touted as a "universal moral obligation" is in practice understood as an "imperfect duty" (Nardin 2002, p. 23), whereby obligations to one's own citizens (even combatants) take priority over obligations to foreigners.

Short- and long-term outcomes

These interventions have each also produced outcomes—both in the long and short term—that were ostensibly not consistent with liberal principles. In the short term, of course, it is well known that during the Kosovo operation, the onset of the allied air campaign actually resulted in an escalation of the atrocities (Hehir 2010, p. 209). Ruling out using ground troops from the beginning, NATO could not physically separate the perpetrators from the victims, but had to rely on using air power to persuade Serb ruler Slobodan Milosevic to order his forces to cease the atrocities. The result was a 78-day air campaign that caused between 500 and 1200 civilian deaths (Human Rights Watch 2000). Likewise, in Libya, the (exclusively) air campaign is itself thought to have resulted in at least 72 civilian deaths (Human Rights Watch 2012). But the far heavier toll was in the ensuing chaos that resulted from the effort to oust Gadhafi, which was facilitated—if not intended—by the NATO intervention, resulting in hundreds of thousands of displaced people, routinized torture and summary execution, and according to the International Criminal Court, 10,000 total deaths by October 2011 (*International Business Times*, 2011). Regarding the Iraq war, while casualty reports vary widely, the first days of the so-called "shock and awe" invasion and occupation are thought to have caused 15,000 total Iraqi casualties, with over 4,000 of those being civilian noncombatants (Goldenberg 2003), while a study published in 2013 argued that 500,000 people had been killed as a result of the conflict between 2003 and 2011 (Hagopian *et al.* 2013).

The long-term outcomes of these operations have likewise painted a conflicting picture. While Kosovo was eventually liberated, declared independence from Serbia in 2008, it exists today as a disputed territory and a partially recognized state that required an extensive UN administrative mission until 2008, and as of 2016, 4,600 NATO troops still patrol the territory and the UN administration still performs basic civil administrative functions (KFOR 2016). Likewise, while Kosovo held its first parliamentary elections in 2007, they were largely boycotted by the Serbs, and ultimately resulted in a coalition government led by former KLA commander, Hashim Thaci, thought by Western intelligence agencies to have links to Albanian organized crime groups and who accuse him of effectively running a mafia state that engages in human and organ trafficking, drug smuggling, and racketeering (Sudetic 2015). And despite being urged by the UN to do so, the government in Kosovo has thus far not permitted some 100,000 Serbs to return to Kosovo who lived there prior to the intervention (Ristic 2014).

Post-invasion Iraq has been characterized by even more chaos and instability. After the fall of Saddam Hussein's government, an insurgency almost immediately erupted to challenge the allied occupation. The allied occupying authority appointed a Governing Council, which was followed by the transfer of sovereignty in 2004 to the Iraqi Interim Government, a caretaker government appointed by the US and its allies until elections could be held and a constitution drafted in 2005. Yet resistance from disaffected Sunnis and an uprising by the previously marginalized Shias eventually put the occupiers in the middle of a civil war between Iraq's main rival religious groups. While elections were held to establish a permanent government and constitution, they were largely boycotted by the Sunnis, resulting in the further empowerment of the majority Shia. All the while, the US and UK found themselves in the middle of a counter-insurgency with no end in sight, requiring escalating uses of force to establish security in the restive

"Sunni triangle." Yet the nadir of the occupation for the interveners was undoubtedly the 2006 publication of pictures of mostly US troops torturing and humiliating Iraqi detainees in Abu Ghraib prison, resulting in a political firestorm that severely damaged the US's credibility and commitment to human rights. Despite an eight-year occupation, intensive state-building, and training and equipping of thousands of Iraqi security forces to counter extremist threats, Iraq's politics emerged in the early 2010s as a Shia-dominated version of its former self, whose democratically elected Shi'ite ruler, Nouri al-Maliki, turned out to be an authoritarian who was adept at using his political power to intimidate his rivals (Carlstrom 2010). And this is, of course, to say nothing of the fact that post-invasion Iraq became a hotbed for extremist activity, as Sunnis disaffected by the empowerment of Shi'ites were socialized and radicalized within allied detention facilities, contributing to the creation of Al Qaeda in Iraq and Mesopotamia, which is today known as the Islamic State, or ISIS (Woods 2016).

Post-intervention Libya, by contrast, did not experience a lengthy occupation, counter-insurgency, or intensive state-building by interveners like Iraq did. Yet like Iraq, it has experienced ongoing sectarian violence, extremist violence, lawlessness and general chaos since its government was deposed with help from NATO forces. Even before Gadhafi's death, a National Transition Council was announced in February of 2011, which ruled until elections were held in July 2012—assisted by the United Nations Support Mission in Libya (UNSMIL) and United Nations Development Programme (UNDP)—to form a General National Congress (GNC) that was to draft a constitution. Yet violence continued throughout these processes, including militants storming the US embassy in Benghazi, resulting in a crackdown by the GNC and prompting them to pass a law banning Gadhafi-era politicians from running for office (Europeforum 2016). While elections were again held in 2014 to elect a legislature (House of Deputies), they were marred by violence and protest, resulting in extremely low voter turnout and leading disaffected Islamist groups to orchestrate a coup, forcing the newly elected government to flee the capitol (Al Jazeera 2014). The result was a government contested between the Islamist "Libya Dawn" coalition and the government in exile, though they agreed to a power-sharing agreement brokered by the UN in 2015. Importantly, the US, UK, and France continue to advise the Libyan military in its efforts to counter ISIS and other extremist groups, while the US, for its part, spent about $170 million through 2012 to address the humanitarian and security challenges, as well as to support capacity building, civil society, and electoral assistance (ReliefWeb 2012; Al Jazeera 2016). UNSMIL also continues to assist the transitional government to promote the rule of law, monitor human rights, build government capacity, and "ensure the transition to democracy" (UNSMIL n.d.).

If such powerful and influential liberal states are bringing their tremendous resources to bear in support of human rights and democracy in places such as Kosovo, Iraq, and Libya, why do they have such disastrous consequences? In all three cases, political institutions were established, internationally monitored elections deemed to be free and fair were held, and constitutions enshrining liberal principles were drafted, yet in none of these cases do we see anything resembling a functional liberal democracy emerging. Jahn's analysis would again suggest that the problem is that these policies have been inspired by theories that focus on liberal *political institutions* as the genesis of liberal practices, though the institutions that were established were, in effect, used as a means to reinforce and justify particular social and political interests (Jahn 2013, p. 90). Thus, when the ethnic Albanians were liberated from Serb oppression in Kosovo, the Shi'ites liberated from Sunni oppression in Iraq, and the various ethnic groups in Libya liberated from Gadhafi's tyranny, it is no surprise these newly empowered and "liberated" groups used the various institutions imposed by the intervening powers to promote the interests of their own community at the expense of their rivals, and not to establish freedom and individual liberty for all people. As Jahn suggests, the reason for this is that, following Locke, liberal political cultures have only been established historically when individual freedom is based on private property. Political institutions—even democratic ones—will therefore not translate into liberal practices unless the society in question has widely distributed private property (2013: p. 91).

While a discussion of property rights prior to these interventions is beyond the present scope, the literature suggests that there is not a particularly strong historical basis of property rights in any of these territories. Kosovo not only has a legacy of uncertain property issues stemming from the Ottoman era and their violent emergence from communist rule as part of Yugoslavia, it today faces the challenges of restoring property to the Serbian minority population who fled during the war prior to Kosovo's independence, privatizing numerous socially owned properties, facilitating women's property ownership, and a range of other property disputes (Joireman 2015). Both Iraq and Libya, former Ottoman and colonial territories, had highly insecure property rights under the respective Hussein and Gadhafi dictatorships. Both were characterized by frequent government seizure of private property and land reform policies that effectively socialized property and encouraged communal ownership, while Libya even abolished private property ownership in 1986 (USAID 2005, 2013). While further research would be required to determine whether progress in establishing and enforcing private property rights in these territories is related to improved and more sustainable liberal-democratic practices, it appears that perhaps Kosovo has had the most success, if modest, in this regard, at least compared to the persistent chaos and violence of Iraq and Libya. Though this certainly also has much to do with the small size and population of Kosovo compared to Libya and Iraq, *inter alia*.

Yet it does appear to be the case that interveners and other liberal actors have demonstrated superior commitment to achieving these goals in Kosovo versus Iraq and Libya. After all, 17 years later Kosovo is still occupied by NATO and enjoys substantial assistance from the EU Rule of Law Commission in Kosovo (EULEX) in developing their police, judiciary, and customs capacities. In Iraq, after allied troops all but completely withdrew in 2011 after a peak occupation force of well over 200,000, and after spending billions on democracy promotion, the US now has about 4,000 troops, and Britain has about 1,000, advising and assisting Iraqi forces in combatting ISIS (*Mirror* 2016), while the democracy transition activities are mostly coordinated by the UN (Caryl 2013). In Libya, the interveners left virtually no residual occupying force, save for advisers and monitors assisting in combatting ISIS. And while Libya did receive significant western assistance for bolstering civil society, education, and a free press, continuing US, EU, and UN efforts to implement the UN-brokered agreement are perceived by many groups in Libya as foreign interlopers meddling in Libya's internal affairs (Blanchard 2016).

Yet despite the various degrees of "footprints" left by interveners at different points of these interventions and occupations, tension still exists between the desire to allow self-determining and democratic politics to play themselves out, which would seemingly be what liberal theory would prescribe, except for the fact that it has resulted in the validation of authoritarian leaders or exacerbated sectarian and ethnic tensions. On the other hand, to avoid this and create the necessary stability for democracy to flourish, if interveners adopt more sustained and comprehensive policies in the target society, they are considered foreign interlopers who are usurping the liberal rights and freedom of the people of that society. But as Jahn's Lockean analysis would suggest, a genuine "liberal" intervention would indeed entail the usurpation of the liberal rights of the target population. That is, in practice and consistent with Locke's theory, the realization of liberal principles in a non-liberal environment historically required a *suppression* of democracy. Political rights were extended first to a property-owning class (and denied to others) under a "liberal despotism" until the state came to embody private property as the basis for liberal rights, and private property was sufficiently widely distributed throughout society (Jahn 2013, p. 96). Thus, again, we should not be surprised that contemporary liberal interventions often entail such intrusive policies, as interveners erroneously focus on establishing political institutions rather than cultivating a liberal political culture through private property.

Conclusion

This chapter has suggested that liberal interventions that have produced paradoxical outcomes or failed outright either to protect human rights in the short term, or establish liberal practices in the target state more long term, is a function of the internal contradictions of the liberal theories that inspired these policies. That is, to the extent that contemporary liberal theories contain these tensions between the need to abide by international law and yet reform it in light of liberal values, between the moral obligation to preserve liberalism at home versus the obligation to establish it abroad, and between the authoritarian means and emancipatory ends of promoting democracy abroad, we can expect policies to result in similarly contradictory outcomes. In carrying out such interventions, even liberal interveners frequently violate international law, prioritize their own interests over the supposed beneficiaries, and use authoritarian means to establish emancipatory practices. Yet when considering the specific historical development of liberal principles and the situations in which they were intended by their advocates to be applied, these outcomes do not seem as puzzling. While this analysis is intended to be more suggestive than definitive regarding the sources of these "failed" interventions, if correct, this analysis does have some pretty significant implications.

First, it suggests that to the extent that military interventions are conducted consistent with a grand strategy that is of a fundamentally liberal internationalist character, they are likely to produce these sorts of mixed outcomes. This has led some to suggest that the doctrine of humanitarian intervention and the democracy-promotion paradigm should be abandoned (Carothers 2004, p. 180; Menon 2016), making the task of the present volume all the more urgent. On the other hand, while in the context of liberalism it may be impossible to overcome the problems associated with competing moral obligations to co-nationals versus foreigners, if liberal states are going to continue to take seriously the practice of promoting liberal-democratic processes in other countries, they would be doing well to focus on the economic organization of the society in question (i.e. the protection of property rights), rather than seeking to immediately establish the institutions of democracy or use institutions as a means to cultivate a liberal political culture. Yet this would also seemingly entail significant interference in the socio-economic systems of target societies that do not have a tradition of established private property rights, again leaving interveners in the position of having to pursue intrusive policies to re-engineer a society's system of property rights, assuming they would be able to make and keep such a commitment if it begins to produce adverse consequences domestically. In the end, some of these tensions may ultimately be irresolvable, but it is nevertheless important to acknowledge and account for them if we are to search for alternate normative theoretical bases, ideas, and practices that may offer a way forward in improving the global human condition.

References

Al Jazeera 2014, "Libyans Mourn Rights Activist Amid Turmoil. Al Jazeera," June 26. Available from: www.aljazeera.com/news/middleeast/2014/06/libyans-mourn-rights-activist-amid-turmoil-2014626161436740827.html. [September 17, 2016].

Al Jazeera 2016, "Fierce Fighting Rages in Libya," Al Jazeera, July 26. Available from: www.aljazeera.com/indepth/inpictures/2016/07/fierce-fighting-rages-libya-160725115159385.html. [September 17, 2016].

Annan, K 1999, "Two Concepts of Sovereignty," *The Economist*, September 16. Available from: www.economist.com/node/324795. [September 17, 2016].

Barkin, JS 1998, "The Evolution of the Constitution of Sovereignty and the Emergence of Human Rights Norms," *Millennium – Journal of International Studies*, vol. 27, no. 2, pp. 229–252.

Beelman, M 2003, "US Contractors Reap the Windfalls of Post-War Reconstruction," International Consortium of Investigative Journalists, October 30. Available from: www.icij.org/project/windfalls-war/us-contractors-reap-windfalls-post-war-reconstruction-0. [September 17, 2016].

Beitz, CR 1979, *Political Theory and International Relations*, Princeton University Press, Princeton, NJ.

Bellamy, A 2009, *Responsibility to Protect: The Global Effort to End Mass Atrocities*, Polity Press, Cambridge.

Blanchard, CM 2016, "Libya: Transition and US Policy," *Congressional Research Services*, 13 May. Available from: www.fas.org/sgp/crs/row/RL33142.pdf. [September 17, 2016].

Buchanan, A 2003, "Reforming the International Law of Humanitarian Intervention" in JL Holzgrefe and RO Keohane, (eds), *Humanitarian Intervention: Ethical, Legal and Political Dilemmas*, pp. 130–173. Cambridge University Press, Cambridge.

Buchanan, A and Keohane, RO 2004, "The Preventive Use of Force: A Cosmopolitan Institutional Proposal," *Ethics and International Affairs*, vol. 18, no. 1, pp. 1–22.

Carlstrom, G 2010, "Nouri al-Maliki's 'Detention Squad,'" *Al Jazeera*, October 24. Available from: www.aljazeera.com/secretiraqfiles/2010/10/201010237530782302.html. [September 17, 2016].

Carothers, T 2004, *Critical Mission: Essays on Democracy Promotion*, Carnegie Endowment for International Peace, Washington, DC.

Caryl, C 2013, "The Democracy Boondoggle in Iraq," *Foreign Policy*, March 6. Available from: http://foreignpolicy.com/2013/03/06/the-democracy-boondoggle-in-iraq/. [September 17, 2016].

Cassesse, A 1999, "*Ex iniuria ius oritur*: Are We Moving towards International Legitimation of Forcible Humanitarian Countermeasures in the World Community?" *European Journal of International Law*, vol. 10, no. 1, pp. 23–30.

Charvet, J and Kaczynska-Nay, E 2008, *The Liberal Project and Human Rights: The Theory and Practice of a New World Order*, Cambridge University Press, Cambridge.

Chivers, CJ and Schmitt, E 2011, "In Strikes on Libya by NATO, an Unspoken Civilian Toll," New York Times, December 17. Available from: www.nytimes.com/2011/12/18/world/africa/scores-of-unintended-casualties-in-nato-war-in-libya.html?mtrref=undefined&_r=0. [September 17, 2016].

Clinton, WJ 1999, "Statement on Kosovo. University of Virginia Miller Center," 24 March. Available from: http://millercenter.org/president/speeches/speech-3932. [September 17, 2016].

Clark, D 2003, "Iraq Has Wrecked our Case for Humanitarian Wars," *The Guardian*, 12 August. Available from: www.theguardian.com/politics/2003/aug/12/iraq.iraq1. [September 17, 2016].

Clark, W 2001, *Waging Modern War: Bosnia, Kosovo and the Future of Combat*, Public Affairs, New York.

Cockburn, P 2011, "Amnesty Questions Claim that Gaddafi Ordered Rape as a Weapon of War," *The Independent*, June 23. Available from: www.independent.co.uk/news/world/africa/amnesty-questions-claim-that-gaddafi-ordered-rape-as-weapon-of-war-2302037.html. [September 17, 2016].

Darmer, KB, Baird, RM and Rosembaum, SE, (eds), 2004, *Civil Liberties vs. National Security in a Post-9/11 World*, Prometheus, New York.

Desch, M 2007/8, "America's Liberal Illiberalism: The Ideological Origins of Overreaction in US Foreign Policy," *International Security*, vol. 32, no. 3, pp. 7–43.

DiMaggio, AR 2015, *Selling War, Selling Hope: Presidential Rhetoric, the News Media, and US Foreign Policy Since 9/11*, State University of New York Press, Albany, NY.

Donnelly, J 1998, "Human Rights: A New Standard of Civilization?," *International Affairs*, vol. 74, no. 1, pp. 1–23.

Donnelly, J 2003, *Universal Human Rights in Theory and Practice*, 2nd edn, Cornell University Press, Ithaca, NY.

Doyle, MW 1996, "Kant, Liberal Legacies, and Foreign Affairs" in ME Brown, SM Lynn-Jones and SE Miller, (eds), *Debating the Democratic Peace*, pp. 3–57. MIT Press, Cambridge, MA.

Doyle, MW 1997, *Ways of War and Peace*, W.W. Norton, London.

Doyle, MW 1999, "A Liberal View: Preserving and Expanding the Liberal Pacific Union" in TV Paul and JA Hall, (eds), *International Order and the Future of World Politics*, pp. 41–66. Cambridge University Press, Cambridge.

Erlanger, S 2011, "Sarkozy Puts France at Vanguard of West's War Effort," *The New York Times*, March 20. Available from: www.nytimes.com/2011/03/21/world/europe/21france.html. [September 17, 2016].

Europeforum 2016, "Libya: Country Profile. Europeforum," January 27. Available from: www.europeanforum.net/country/libya. [September 17, 2016].

Fukuyama, F 1992, *The End of History and the Last Man*, Penguin, London.

Goldenberg, S 2003, "Up to 15,000 People Killed in Invasion, Claims Thinktank," *The Guardian*, October 29. Available from: www.theguardian.com/world/2003/oct/29/iraq.suzannegoldenberg. [September 17, 2016].

Hagopian, A, Flaxman, AD, Takaro, SA, Al Shatari, SA, Rajaratnam, J, Becker, S, Levin-Rector, A, Galway, L, Al-Yasseri, BJ, Weiss, WM, Murray, CJ, and Burnham, G 2013, "Mortality in Iraq Associated with the 2003–2011 War and Occupation: Findings from a National Cluster Sample Survey by the University Collaborative Iraq Mortality Study," *PloS Medecine,* vol. 10, no. 10, pp. 1–15.

Hall, M and Hobson, JM 2010, "Liberal International Theory: Eurocentric But Not Always Imperialist?," *International Theory*, vol. 2, no. 2, pp. 201–245.

Hehir, A 2010, *Humanitarian Intervention: An Introduction*, Palgrave, New York.

Heinze, EA 2007, "The Rhetoric of Genocide in US Foreign Policy: Rwanda and Darfur Compared," *Political Science Quarterly*, vol. 122, no. 3, pp. 359–383.

Human Rights Watch 2000, "Civilian Deaths in the NATO Air Campaign. Human Rights Watch," vol. 12, no. 1. Available from: www.hrw.org/reports/2000/nato/Natbm200-01.htm#P153_32943. [September 17, 2016].

Human Rights Watch 2012, "NATO: Investigate Civilian deaths in Libya. Human Rights Watch," May 14. Available from: www.hrw.org/news/2012/05/14/nato-investigate-civilian-deaths-libya. [September 17, 2016].

Independent International Commission on Kosovo (Kosovo Commission) 2000, *The Kosovo Report: Conflict, International Response, Lessons learned*, Oxford University Press, Oxford.

Jahn, B 2013, *Liberal Internationalism: Theory, History, Practice*, Palgrave, London.

Joireman, SF 2015, "Resigning Their Rights? Impediments to Women's Property Ownership in Kosovo," University of Richmond Scholarship Repository, Political Science Faculty Publications, Paper 44. Available from: http://scholarship.richmond.edu/cgi/viewcontent.cgi?article=1056&context=polisci-faculty-publications. [September 17, 2016].

KFOR 2016, "NATO's Role in Kosovo. North Atlantic Treaty Organization," Kosovo Force. Available from: http://jfcnaples.nato.int/kfor/about-us/welcome-to-kfor/natos-role-in-kosovo. [September 17, 2016].

International Business Times, October 26, 2011. "Libya: Civil War Casualties Could Reach 100,000". Available from: www.ibtimes.co.uk/libya-conflicting-death-toll-raises-questions-about-what-truly-happened-237895. [September 17, 2016].

Locke, J 1980, *Second Treatise of Government*, Hackett, Indianapolis, IN.

Menon, R 2016, *The Conceit of Humanitarian Intervention*, Oxford University Press, Oxford.

Murray, RW 2013, "Humanitarianism, Responsibility or Rationality? Evaluating Intervention as State Strategy" in A Hehir and RW Murray, (eds), *Libya: The Responsibility to Protect and the Future of Humanitarian Intervention*, pp. 15–33. Palgrave, London.

Nardin, T 2002, "The Moral Basis for Humanitarian Intervention" in A Lang, (ed.), *Just Intervention*, pp. 11–24. Georgetown University Press, Washington, DC.

Oatley, T 2015, *A Political Economy of American Hegemony: Buildups, Booms, Busts*, Cambridge University Press, Cambridge.

Packer, G 2006, *The Assassin's Gate: America in Iraq*, Farrar, Straus & Giroux, New York.

Pattison, J 2011, "Introduction: Roundtable: Libya, RtoP, and Humanitarian Intervention," *Ethics and International Affairs*, vol. 25, no. 3, pp. 251–254.

Rawls, J 2001, *The Law of Peoples*, Harvard University Press, Cambridge, MA.

ReliefWeb 2012, "US Government Assistance to Libya – Fact Sheet. ReliefWeb," 20 July. Available from: http://reliefweb.int/report/libya/us-government-assistance-libya-fact-sheet-20-july-2012. [September 17, 2016].

Ristic, M 2014, "UN Urges Kosovo to Help Refugees Return," *Balkan Insight*, June 13. Available from: www.balkaninsight.com/en/article/un-calls-serbia-kosovo-to-resolve-idps-issues. [September 17, 2016].

Roberts, A 1999, "NATO's 'Humanitarian War' Over Kosovo," *Survival*, vol. 45, no. 2, pp. 102–23.

Roth, K 2004, "War in Iraq: Not a Humanitarian Intervention" in *Human Rights Watch World Report 2004: Human Rights and Armed Conflict*, pp. 13–33. Human Rights Watch 2004, New York.

Strauss, E 2009, "A Bird in the Hand is Worth Two in the Bush: On the Assumed Legal Nature of the Responsibility to Protect," *Global Responsibility to Protect*, vol. 1, no. 3, pp. 291–323.

Shue, H 2004, "Limiting Sovereignty" in JM Welsh, (ed.), *Humanitarian Intervention in International Relations*, pp. 11–28. Oxford University Press, Oxford.

Stratfor 2011, "France, UK Have Differing Motives for Intervening in Libya" Forbes, [online] March 29. Available at: www.forbes.com/sites/energysource/2011/03/29/france-u-k-have-differing-motives-for-intervening-in-libya/#4dda04892816. [September 17, 2016].

Sudetic, C 2015, "The Bullies Who Run Kosovo," *Politico – Europe Edition*, [online] July 21. Available at: www.politico.eu/article/kosovo-hashim-thaci-un-special-court-tribunal-organ-trafficking-kla-serbia-milosevic-serbia-ramush/. [September 17, 2016].

Tesón, FR 1988, *Humanitarian Intervention: An Enquiry into Law and Morality*, Transnational, Dobbs Ferry, NY.

Tesón, FR 2003, "The Liberal Case for Humanitarian Intervention" in JL Holzgrefe and RO Keohane, (eds), *Humanitarian Intervention: Ethical, Legal and Political Dilemmas*, pp. 93–129. Cambridge University Press, Cambridge.

Mirror, March 11, 2016. "UK Sends More Troops to Fight ISIS with More than 1,000 Now in Region". Available from: www.mirror.co.uk/news/world-news/uk-sends-more-troopsiraq-7542634. [September 17, 2016].

United Nations Support Mission in Lybia n.d., "UNSMIL Mandate." Available from: https://unsmil.unmissions.org/Default.aspx?tabid=3544&language=en-US. [September 17, 2016].

United States Agency for International Development 2005, "USAID Iraq Local Governance Program: Land Registration and Property Rights in Iraq" USAID, January. Available from: http://humanitarianlibrary.org/sites/default/files/2013/05/PNADE241.pdf. [September 17, 2016].

United States Agency for International Development 2013, "USIAD Country Profile: Property Rights and Resource Governance: Libya," USAID, June. Available from: www.usaidlandtenure.net/libya. [September 17, 2016].

Weiss, TG 2011, "RtoP Alive and Well After Libya," *Ethics and International Affairs*, vol. 25, no. 3, pp. 287–292.

Wheeler, NJ 2000, *Saving Strangers: Humanitarian Intervention in International Society*, Oxford University Press, Oxford.
Wheeler, NJ 2002, "Humanitarian Intervention after September 11, 2001" in A Lang, (ed.), *Just Intervention*, pp. 192–216. Georgetown University Press, Washington, DC.
Woods, AK 2016, "ISIS Was Born in an American Detention Facility (and it Wasn't Gitmo)," *Lawfare*, February 3. Available from: www.lawfareblog.com/isis-was-born-american-detention-facility-and-it-wasnt-gitmo. [September 17, 2016].
Woodward, SL 1995, *Balkan Tragedy: Chaos and Dissolution after the Cold War*, Brookings, Washington, DC.

4

HUMANITARIAN INTERVENTION IN POST-AMERICAN INTERNATIONAL SOCIETY

Robert W. Murray

Introduction

For nearly 30 years after the end of the Cold War, the norms of international society were heavily influenced by the unipolar moment of American hegemony, where the US remained the sole superpower and a perceived consensus formed around western, liberal values, reinforced by American hegemony. In many ways, the unipolar moment was also the liberal moment, and a series of normative advances were made in world affairs including environmentalism, a greater recognition of obligation to alleviate poverty and humanitarian crises in the developing world, and a more human-centric conceptualisation of how, according to many, the post-Cold War era shifted focus from the 'international' to the 'global'. Among the most important elements of this supposed normative shift was the affirmation of human rights and an emerging normative consensus around humanitarian protection. Nowhere is this more evident than in the proliferation of debates around humanitarian intervention and, more specifically, the emergence of the Responsibility to Protect (R2P) doctrine in 2001.

An important part of international political theorising has been the effort to explain and to verify the claims made about normative transitions throughout the unipolar moment and whether states do, in fact, believe in a sense of duty or obligation when it comes to not only articulating, but also enforcing, norms such as human rights and humanitarian protection.[1] Naturally, there has been a tendency for much of this debate to be dominated by liberal and constructivist theorists, but thus far, there have been few efforts to balance those explanations with realist views. Among the reasons for incorporating realist and systemic views in modern international politics is to better explain and understand the impact of the transition occurring from the unipolar moment and American hegemony to what is quite clearly a multipolar structure of the international system and the rise of non-western great powers. How will the rise of states such as China and Russia impact the supposed normative consensus of the unipolar moment? What will happen to efforts to protect human rights when non-western states that challenge the western normative consensus play a larger role in international affairs and expand their relative spheres of influence? More importantly, how are scholars of international politics going to be able to approach and explain the effects of such transitions on the normative consensus and new trends when recent scholarship is predicated on assumptions that are, in many ways, inadequate?

Since its reorganisation in the early 1990s, the English School of international relations theory has been at the forefront of debates involving human rights, humanitarian intervention, and the R2P doctrine. Those that use the international society or society of states approach promote it as a middle way of theorising international politics due to its ability to incorporate features from both systemic (or realist) and domestic (liberal and critical theory) perspectives. This typology is grounded in the English School's differentiation of levels of theorising, which distinguishes between the system, international society and world society, and is arguably more capable of providing novel insight into a greater array of explanatory variables than many other approaches to exploring international political events or trends. A noticeable tendency in the works that fall within the English School since the end of the Cold War has been its preoccupation with debates about humanitarian intervention.[2] Particular emphasis has been given to world society views of how states approach human rights and interventionism with a significant number of School adherents arguing that humanitarian intervention norms have become more widely accepted and enforced. It is in this light that the English School can be employed to evaluate whether norms of humanitarian intervention and R2P have, in fact, become accepted by states and what will happen to these norms as the international system continues its evolution from unipolar to multipolar.

This chapter will use an English School approach to argue that, while there is validity in the claim that interventionism as a norm of world affairs has grown in both prominence and significance since the end of the Cold War, though still never fully implemented, we are now seeing a transition from the post-Cold War, western international society to a post-American international society. This transition is marked by the changing trends in the international system and the rise of new great powers that fundamentally challenge the pro-intervention and western-liberal thesis. As a result of this ongoing evolution in international society, it is highly unlikely that interventionism and R2P will be realised as consistent doctrines of humanitarian protection. As such, it is far more likely that humanitarian intervention will be even more precarious in post-American international society than it is currently.

Post-Cold War American international society

At the conclusion of the Cold War, both the United States and the USSR were forced to contemplate the nature of the post-Cold War international order, and what part each side would play. It was evident to most onlookers that the US was about to embark upon a moment of unipolar hegemony, while the status and power capabilities of the former USSR were uncertain. With the Cold War coming to an end and a major shift in the polarity of the international system, the world saw the formation of a new international society that, many argue, was far more solidarist in character than pluralist given its liberal-western orientation. Adhering to Hedley Bull's framework for understanding how to identify the type of international society in a particular historical period, the best way to demonstrate how either solidarists or pluralists understand the classification of post-Cold War international society is best done by examining three elements: common interests, rules and institutions.

For solidarists, the common interests of the post-Cold War international society differ somewhat from those seen throughout the Cold War. The self-interested nature of states is not necessarily brought into question, but how states come to define their self-interest changed. Security maximisation remains the primary motivator for states, but security is no longer understood in the narrow definition of national security, which is taken from realist conceptions of self-help. Instead, many solidarist scholars, such as Nicholas Wheeler, Tim Dunne, Andrew Linklater and others, are pointing to the need to focus on how security affects the world society level of analysis in English School thought. According to Alex Bellamy and Matt McDonald: 'In this society, the boundaries of community extend beyond the state and the overall purpose of the society is the protection of individual security' (Bellamy and McDonald 2004, p. 313). By looking to the domestic sphere, solidarist accounts of security attempt to discuss the responsibility of states in securing individuals, not simply statist interests, and attempt to extend the understanding of security beyond the systemic concerns for hard power alone.

Individual or human security is contingent upon a notion that states are moral agents and are obligated to protect the natural rights of humanity, which is understood to be inherently connected. Solidarist scholars differ somewhat on their interpretations of the extent of human interdependence, but there is some common ground among them in terms of humanity being the ultimate referent for the policies of states (Linklater and Suganami 2006, pp. 242–246). In terms of supporting a view of the interconnected nature of humanity in world society, Linklater makes a strong case. Rather than attempting to prove the notion of a like-minded or normatively universal humanity, Linklater claims that individuals in world society are linked by basic physical vulnerability:

> The main point to make is that the bonds and attachments between strangers may rest entirely on the almost universal experience of being similar to, but not necessarily equal with (or identical to) others, and in being exposed as part of one's biological heritage to similar vulnerabilities to mental and physical suffering. It is striking that some of the earliest formulations of the defence of cosmopolitanism in Western moral and political theory grounded the perspective in such universal vulnerabilities of the body. This is hardly extraordinary given that mutual recognition of shared mental and physical

vulnerability provides the most readily available means of projecting forms of solidarity across the boundaries of established communities – and across the boundaries that are deemed to exist between human and non-human forms of life.

(Linklater 2007, p. 138)

An essential point here, however, is that while solidarists like Linklater may see humanity as the driving concern for theory, they maintain the primacy of the state as the vehicle through which security of the individual is to be attained. This argument is supported by Linklater as he argues:

In this perspective, international societies are the key level of analysis because they have been the main steering mechanisms which independent communities have devised for organising increasing levels of global interconnectedness. As organisers of humanity, they have been the vehicles through which certain universal ethical potentialities could be released and embedded in collective efforts to ensure that the relations between social groups do not cause unnecessary suffering to peoples everywhere.

(Linklater 2007, p. 148)

The common interest for states in international society, according to solidarist scholars, is to protect the natural rights intrinsic to all individuals in world society. This account of the society of states tends not to pay close attention to the anarchic constraints of the international system, but instead examines more closely the relationship between international society and world society.[3] To achieve this concern for individual security, the rules of modern international society are also divergent from those seen throughout the Cold War.

When discussing Cold War international society, the rule of non-intervention and strong state sovereignty was perceived as vital to maintaining the stability of the balance of power. Solidarists argue that the international society that emerged immediately after the Cold War overcame these constraints and that human security is only guaranteed by an alteration to the rule of non-intervention. Bellamy and McDonald focus on this argument as a means for suggesting an English School discourse on security as they contend:

[T]he focus on justice rather than order, and human rights rather than a conception of sovereignty as non-intervention, allows us to think of ways of redressing human rights abuses and to question the centrality of the state as the primary referent of security. Solidarism suggests, for example, that sovereignty and human rights may be two sides of the same coin: a state's sovereignty may indeed be legitimised and supported (and the sovereignty of the international society more broadly with it) if the state does indeed provide human security for its citizens.

(Bellamy and McDonald 2004, p. 326)

It is difficult to envision post-Cold War international society as rejecting the typical rule of non-intervention, but solidarists use strong empirical evidence to support their claims. Examples of changes within the UN and reform efforts hint at clear changes to the rules of international society itself. Wheeler points to the emerging practice of humanitarian intervention throughout the 1990s as a sign that the rules of post-Cold War international society were contingent upon interventionism becoming an accepted method for states to uphold or achieve the common interest of individual security (Wheeler 2000, pp. 285–310). What is often overlooked in these discussions is the important point that, despite the rise of normative recognition around humanitarian intervention, there remained a strong link to state national interest as the predominant motivation for states to decide whether or not to intervene. Thus, as the norm of non-intervention began to evolve, the challenge became how to better protect populations experiencing humanitarian emergencies but also confronting the limitations of state self-interest in determining whether or not states would choose to intervene on behalf of others. One of the most important outcomes in this debate surrounding the rule of non-intervention is found in the 2001 Responsibility to Protect (R2P) document.

Produced by the International Commission on Intervention and State Sovereignty (ICISS 2001), R2P suggests that states can no longer hide behind the excuse of sovereignty when it comes to averting humanitarian disaster. Sovereignty, according to this view, is not absolutely guaranteed under positive international law, but instead becomes a conditional right. To attain this right, states must ensure the protection of their populations. Section 2. 15 of the ICISS report states:

> Thinking of sovereignty as responsibility, in a way that is being increasingly recognized in state practice, has a threefold significance. First, it implies that the state authorities are responsible for the functions of protecting the safety and lives of citizens and promotion of their welfare. Secondly, it suggests that the national political authorities are responsible to the citizens intern ally and to the international community through the UN. And thirdly, it means that the agents of state are responsible for their actions; that is to say, they are accountable for their acts of commission and omission. The case for thinking of sovereignty in these terms is strengthened by the ever-increasing impact of international human rights norms, and the increasing impact in international discourse of the concept of human security.
> (ICISS 2001, p. 13)

Though it is arguable that alterations to state sovereignty and the *need* for interventionism have not taken place in practice, the normative development and popularity of R2P in forums such as the UN suggests there has been an ideational shift in state perceptions of sovereignty and non-intervention, but that shift remains limited given its inability to overcome how states pursue their national interests. Of course this change also comes as a result of the increase in the number of intrastate conflicts and civil wars since the end of World War II.[4] Cold War international society was occupied primarily with stemming the tide of nuclear war among the superpowers, but with the end of the Cold War, the solidarist agenda has been dedicated to seeing international society as the forum in which to discuss, debate and actually protect human rights.

In terms of institutions within the solidarist conception of post-Cold War international society, there are many of the same primary and secondary institutions that were in existence in Cold War international society, but there have also been some important changes and additions. In his discussion of contemporary institutions, Barry Buzan highlights those that are essential in maintaining the state-centrism of the English School, such as territoriality, diplomacy and great power management, but he is also sure to make some additional contributions to the various institutions that govern a solidarist idea of post-Cold War international society (Buzan 2004, p. 187). Added to the list of primary institutions are the equality of people, the market, nationalism and environmental stewardship. Buzan explains that the growth in many world society factors since the end of the Cold War has altered the institutional agenda in modern international society, allowing for factors such as humanitarian intervention, the liberal economic markets and the environment to become vital considerations for all states. To protect these primary institutions and adhere to the common interest of individual security and well-being, Buzan describes the importance of bodies such as the United Nations High Commission for Refugees, the World Trade Organization, the International Monetary Fund, the United Nations Department of Peacekeeping Operations, the United Nations Framework Convention on Climate Change and the Intergovernmental Panel on Climate Change (Buzan 2004, p. 187).

The primary responsibility of states, according to the solidarist agenda, is not to focus on mitigating anarchy and making advances in hard power technology alone, but is coupled, if not surpassed, by a desire to secure the rights and lives of humanity. Solidarists believe the rules of international society have changed from those that governed the Cold War, especially the understandings of sovereignty as absolute to a shift that defines sovereignty as a conditional right. Institutions continue to play a critical role in the governance of modern international society, but the types and range of institutions, both in the primary and secondary sense, are larger in number and are heavily influenced by the normative concerns of world society. It is easy to see that many states and international organisations have begun to discuss these norms and values underscored by solidarists, but the empirical evidence supporting their enforcement and implementation remains questionable. Dorothy Jones notes:

> Sincerity of intent has often been overbalanced by sincerity of national interest and even more often by sincerity of grievance. Basically, for whatever reason, the states have never succeeded in creating an environment in which they felt safe enough to live together without arms and the resort to arms.
>
> (Jones 1991, p. 135)

However, even with the recognition that norms such as humanitarian protection and interventionism have grown and flourished, at least rhetorically, since the end of the Cold War, the claims about state self-interest and security from the pluralist perspective certainly cannot be ignored.

It is difficult to deny that the foreign policy strategies of states have changed substantially since the end of the Cold War. International society became a forum in which states could more openly discuss and try to implement normative policies aimed at improving the conditions within world society, and international institutions made very public claims about their desires to reform in order to meet the needs of the global populous.[5] What must also be taken into account, however, is the continued relevance of the international system in describing the way states interact and behave in the post-Cold War era, and how systemic concerns impacted human rights. On one hand, solidarist values are playing a larger role in the ways states are attempting to achieve their self-interest, but apprehension about implementing these norms translates into a society of states where basic territorial security considerations have been retained for western states and other states; particularly those in the developing world have been pressured politically, diplomatically and, at times, militarily, to adhere to a more solidarist agenda.

In the pluralist view, states seek to cooperate at a minimalist level in international society so they do not disrupt the stability of the international system and end up potentially having to go to war with one another. In order to protect this common interest, the rules of post-Cold War international society are arguably much the same as they were throughout the Cold War – premised on non-intervention and minimalist cooperation. To claim, as solidarists do, that sovereignty has become more of a conditional right than an absolute one is difficult to prove, especially given states' reluctance to act consistently in protecting vulnerable populations. Robert Jackson discusses this point as he claims:

> Human rights in current international law are subject to the consent of sovereigns, however. The cosmopolitan society of humankind is legally – not to mention politically – inferior to the international society of sovereign states. Independent governments are free to decide whether or not to be signatories to human rights instruments. They may feel under a moral obligation to sign. They may come under political pressure to sign. They may believe it is in their interests to sign. They are under no legal obligation to do so, however. Although there is a growing moral imperative in international society to protect human rights which derives from domestic standards and international influence of Western democracies, sovereign rights still have priority over human rights in international law.
>
> (Jackson 1993, p. 46)

Jackson's observations soon after the end of the Cold War continue to have relevance. States never moved away from seeking to attain national security in favour of human security. Discussions of such ideas have sometimes resulted in complete inaction on the parts of states. There can be no better examples than the genocides in Rwanda and the Darfur region of Sudan, as well as the ongoing inaction to ISIS acts of genocide against Yazidis and Christians which have not been the focus of the wider western and Russian action in Syria and Iraq. These major human rights atrocities occurred after the Cold War ended and in an era when solidarists have been describing international affairs by looking to variables such as world society, natural rights, global citizenship and cosmopolitan ideals. Even with the perceived victory of the UN adopting the R2P doctrine in 2005, albeit in a weaker form than that seen in the original ICISS document, there has not been any consistent implementation or enforcement of the doctrine by the UN or any other agency. While noble in theory and rhetoric, there is little hope of seeing this document used in practice in either its 2001 or 2005 version. Kim Nossal explains why this is the case:

> [D]espite the nominal endorsement of the [R2P] agenda at the United Nations, in real terms this endorsement is entirely symbolic, since there are at least two members of the security council, the Russian Federation and the People's Republic of China, that do not really believe in R2P, and thus can be counted on to use their veto to block any security council approval of R2P initiatives that even marginally touch their interests.
> (Nossal 2005, p. 1029)

The debate over the use and relevance of R2P in post-Cold War international society serves to demonstrate the pluralist contention about the need to focus more on interstate conflict and the behaviour of states in the system, rather than reducing international relations to world society concerns alone. Pluralists in the modern era do not discount the possibility of changing the way that politics in the post-Cold War society of states is conducted, but the primary institutions, such as sovereignty and great power management are as relevant as human-centric variables at this time in the history of international politics. Consequently, any shifts to a purely solidarist notion of foreign relations strategy might prove destabilising at the systemic level because of the disruption to balance of power logic posed by individual-focused proposals for state action. Bellamy and McDonald discuss this point by showing how the pluralist political agenda is guided by the warnings of both Bull and E.H. Carr out of the belief that 'the forceful articulation of political values would destabilise international order and make it harder for states to provide security for their citizens' (Bellamy and McDonald 2004, p. 314). Moreover, Jackson finds a serious problem in trying to enforce the human security agenda emphasised by solidarists. This notion presents a possible threat to international order due to the fact that there is no consensus on what human rights are, and thus 'the consistent enforcement of human security around the world is impossible' (Jackson 2000, p. 214).

Jackson concedes that primary institutions have changed and become more world society-focused, but does not agree with Buzan's logic which places these institutions on the same level as those that affect national security. Without national security, Jackson argues, there can be no hope of realising progress in issues such as economics or the environment, but these are not interpreted as security issues. He argues that 'an economic depression might threaten my personal welfare as well as the national welfare, but it is no threat to my safety or my country's security' (Jackson 2000, p. 195). Therefore, the pluralist agenda, often associated with the traditional realist idea of international relations, is more concerned with maintaining stability among self-interested states in an anarchic system than it is with trying to impose values.[6] In the modern context, states are not consistently acting on solidarist rhetorical values. It is this dichotomy between solidarist aspirations and pluralist actions that makes the contemporary society of states so intriguing, yet disappointing.

While human rights and the enforcement of norms such as R2P have become far more prominent since the end of the Cold War, the issue of enforcement remains highly contentious. Some argue that the discussion and institutional recognition of norms not only speaks to the solidarist thesis of a human-centric method of conceiving state security and responsibility, but that this has increased human rights protection. As Bellamy argues:

> Taking the three tests together (practice, recognition of rights and duties, criticism of clear violations), there are strong grounds for concluding that over the past few years RtoP has emerged as an international norm. This is most obvious in the underlying changes to practice, whereby international responses to genocide and mass atrocities have become more common and more focused on protecting populations.
>
> (Bellamy 2015, p. 171)

While there is validity in claiming that norms around protection and R2P have grown, the lack of enforcement or a consistent framework through which to implement such norms begs the question of how successful such normative progress has been, and more, why implementation has yet to take place. As Aidan Hehir notes in this volume, there is a stark divide between the quantity and quality of R2P when it comes to invocation and efficacy. As a norm, there is no doubt that R2P has grown in both prominence and recognition. This growth has impacted state behaviour, especially in terms of both guilt and shaming of states around their lack of prevention of atrocity and rarely acting in the face of such humanitarian crisis (Evans 2015). Yet, even in the face of R2P being affirmed by the Security Council in 46 resolutions (Global Centre for R2P 2016), the world is left to ask, as the Chair of the UN High Level Panel on Peace Operations, José Ramos-Horta did: 'why is it that, in the face of such a sophisticated normative framework to protect civilians, we keep failing?' (Ramos-Horta 2015).

Despite raising awareness for atrocities and provoking important debates, R2P has not itself directly prevented or halted mass atrocity crimes since its endorsement by the UN in 2005, evidenced most obviously by situations in states such as Syria,

Darfur and Sri Lanka. But why? If the normative framework of R2P has expanded to the point of UN Security Council invocation, how is it that R2P has yet to become an enforcement framework as opposed to an important normative and rhetorical tool? In many ways, the interplay between English School solidarism and pluralism helps to explain this dichotomy.

The post-Cold War international society has been, in many ways, a solidarist experiment in that a clear normative agenda under US unipolarity emerged that replicates western, liberal norms. However, the systemic constraints of anarchy and pluralist views about security, balance of power, and war have not disappeared or been overcome. As such, while there may be a desire for international society to behave and speak according to solidarist norms, states cannot abandon their security concerns or the impact of an anarchic system that continues to be an element of constraint around consistent implementation of R2P.[7] Even more troubling is that, despite US hegemony that would seem to favour a pro-human rights and democracy agenda, there has been relatively little progress made towards an enforceable international framework for rights protection. Among the key reasons for this lack of progress has been the failure on the part of international society to effectively negotiate an international order that is able to balance pluralist concerns of security, balance of power, and sovereignty with solidarist values such as civilian protection. As English School scholars such as Bull, Jackson and others contended, order can incorporate provisions for change but must balance moral values and political practice, and it must be consensual among the states that make up international society. Bull warned: 'We should be aware of the danger of what might be called *mindless* universalism, the assumption that all our own values apply equally to other societies, even if they do not recognize it' (Bull 1979).

Further, English School scholars have warned against the presumption that western-liberal solidarist values would inevitably bring about a more moralistic universal order and not simply privilege the states in positions of power trying to extend their own value system.

Most problematically, *even when genuinely held*, the promotion of global values will work to entrench the power and special interests of particular states or groups of states. The paradox of universalism is that the successful promotion of 'universal' or 'global' values, even if they are to some degree genuinely shared, will often depend on the willingness of particularly powerful states to promote them and will work to reinforce the already marked inequality of power and status among states and regions (Alderson and Hurrell 2000, 63).

Following this logic, it becomes apparent that among the limitations of post-Cold War international society was the presumption by western states that there was a universal consensus regarding rights protection and humanitarian intervention. Instead, the rise in solidarist rhetoric and norms without the subsequent action to enforce the norms and ideas being promoted can be seen as a lack of acceptance on the part of non-western states in particular to the normative framework being proposed, as well as a lack of interest on the part of western states to sacrifice national interest to enforce the values they claimed to hold. If, under the conditions of a western-dominated international society, only limited progress was made, what can be expected from the evolution towards a multipolar system and a post-American international society?

Intervention in a post-American international society

As the international system continues its evolution from unipolar to multipolar, it is inevitable that international society will also undergo a significant transition.[8] With a greater number of great powers involved in the functioning of the international system, and the ongoing decline of US hegemony, the norms and institutions within international society will be forced to change and acclimatise to the constraints posed by the evolution at the systemic level. Such change will undoubtedly see a more pluralist type of international society, especially given the fact that the emerging great powers are non-western powers with vital interests and spheres of influence that they will want to pursue and enforce. The ongoing transition to post-American international society is going to largely impact a number of issues within the society of states, perhaps none so much as human rights and humanitarian intervention.

As with any other historical international society, the institutions of post-American international society will be, in large part, determined by how great powers interact at the systemic level, as well as how the preferences and norms of world society react to or influence international affairs. With powers such as Russia and China rising, the US continuing its relative decline, and other regional powers playing a significant role in world events, it is unlikely that international society will maintain its current normative structure and institutional framework. How exactly international society will evolve is yet to be known, but an argument can be made by determining how the basic institutions of international society can evolve with a multipolar system such as the one currently emerging. Moreover, the ongoing devolution from a centralised or truly international society to regional is quite likely to continue, which leaves key issues such as human rights protection and other western norms very much in doubt.

Despite the progress pointed to by many scholars in the post-Cold War period regarding social norms and a greater recognition and acceptance of human rights and the duty to protect them, the evidence from the post-Cold War international society was far more rhetorical and discursive than it was actionable. Scholars largely preferred a narrative of solidarism during the era of American hegemony, yet despite the supposed progress made in areas such as environmental protection, rights and inequality, and post-statism, international society struggled to implement and enforce the myriad of conventions and doctrines aimed to both articulate and create robust legal frameworks that could see solidarist norms realised. The triumph of *postmodern international society* was, to put it simply, greatly exaggerated.[9]

In the emerging post-American international society, traditional institutions such as diplomacy, war, the balance of power, the state, international law and sovereignty will all be forced to evolve with a shifting systemic framework. If the argument holds that the post-Cold War international society was largely rhetorically solidarist without completing the supposed transition from *international* to *world* society, the more pluralist society that will emerge will be even less likely to see progress on world society-linked institutions and variables. This point is, perhaps, most important in the context of human rights and humanitarian intervention. What substantial progress has been made on normative frameworks for humanitarian protection that includes the various types of interventionism is both uncertain and precarious in an evolving system and society of states.

Starting with the 1992 *An Agenda for Peace*, through to the advent of the R2P doctrine in 2001 which was later endorsed by the UN in 2005, the issue of rights protection and meaningful doctrines for humanitarian intervention has come a long way. No longer can individual states or multilateral organisations sit back and allow human populations to suffer without significant pressure to act. The sheer number of interest groups and advocacy organisations, combined with international bodies established to promote awareness and action for humanitarian emergency, has led to a level of global awareness on a scale previously inconceivable. Focusing specifically on R2P, which is part of the intervention debate but certainly is not equated with humanitarian intervention, Bellamy argues:

> Through [R2P], the international community has come to view emerging crises through the prisms of atrocity prevention and response – focusing on what the world can do to protect populations from genocide, war crimes, ethnic cleansing and crimes against humanity. Inevitably, as the principle has come into widespread diplomatic use it has aroused controversy. But international debate has shifted in the past half decade. Where once UN Member States debated the merits of RtoP itself, now they debate its implementation in difficult and complex situations.
>
> (Bellamy 2013, p. 5)

Yet, despite the obvious normative growth of awareness and debate surrounding both humanitarian intervention and more often R2P, why are these norms not being enforced consistently, and moreover, when evaluating the prospects for achieving a framework for humanitarian protection how can international society seek to overcome current hurdles to implementation as the future society of states looks to be even more complex?

Among the major problems facing debates about interventionism and R2P is the automatic relationship made between 'protecting' and two controversial concepts – boots-on-the-ground militarism and regime change. The decision to rely on the UN Security Council under its Chapter VII mandate as the primary body through which to determine humanitarian action at the international level is a key obstacle to ever seeing successful and consistent implementation, given the competing political interests of the Permanent Five members of the Security Council and other limitations of the UN system (Morris 2016; Gifkins 2016). In most cases, if a potential intervention, especially those that could lead to overt military action and regime change, could infringe upon or affect the interests of Russia and/or China, they have shown little hesitation in using their veto. This situation is likely to worsen in a multipolar international system where both China and Russia will see their relative spheres of influence increase and feel emboldened by the inability of the US or western coalitions to deter or impact their decisions in the same way that was seen throughout the era of American hegemony.

Conclusion

Much attention has been paid to focusing on the preventative mechanisms of intervention in R2P and R2P's diplomatic success as a means of identifying and halting atrocity and emergency before a situation declines into crisis, as well as in an effort to overcome the challenges posed by seeking Security Council approval for formal military involvement. What remains to be seen, however, is whether preventative and diplomatic measures alone can be as effective as necessary, given the expected difficulties the evolving systemic structure will pose for states in international society trying to make rapid decisions about helping those in need and the structural constraints posed by both the UN Security Council and the system at large. If international society is paralysed by the interests of emerging great powers and systemic considerations, what options remain for humanitarian intervention and/or R2P in the emerging post-American international society?

The primary challenge is understanding that intervention and by extension R2P can be consistent with a pluralist society of states, if framed differently. Robert Pape, for instance, argues that an approach called 'pragmatic humanitarian intervention' would help to overcome some of the systemic and societal constraints of interventionism by adhering to three criteria:

> (1) an ongoing campaign of mass homicide sponsored by the local government in which thousands have died and thousands more are likely to die; (2) a viable plan for intervention with reasonable estimates of casualties not significantly higher than in peacetime operations and near zero for the intervening forces during the main phase of the operation; and (3) a workable strategy for creating lasting local security, so that saving lives in the short term does not lead to open-ended chaos in which many more are killed in the long term.
>
> (Pape 2012, p. 43)

Many pro-intervention and R2P advocates see value in trying to approach the concept through a more pragmatic or realistic lens, precisely given the obstacles these doctrines have encountered to date. According to Tim Dunne, Pape's contention is:

> [an] attempt to ensure that R2P is aligned with a traditional pluralist conception of how key international institutions work – including the

privilege of great powers on the UN Security Council who have the power to block action if they believe it to be contrary to their interests or detrimental to international order as a whole.

(Dunne 2015, p. 65)

Despite the noble intentions of developing pragmatic approaches to interventionism and R2P, the prospects for the future look bleak, despite the normative successes seen to date. Further, this bleakness would be the case in the current institutional framework of international society, but this is likely to worsen still as the evolution towards a new society of states continues. Finding ways of developing agendas for intervention in a pluralist international society is not easy, particularly when powers such as Russia and China have thus far shown themselves to be less than supportive of concepts such as R2P. One body of thought is to continue working within the context of existing conventions and doctrines to refine and improve them with the hope of someday seeing their enforcement. In this vein, Bellamy notes: 'If the first ten years of [R2P] were primarily about establishing the norm, the next ten should be about its implementation' (2015, p. 182). Another body of thought is to look beyond current frameworks and to build something new that better reflects the legal, structural and normative elements of international politics. Murray and Hehir exemplify this way of thinking as they argue:

> The existing system has reached an untenable impasse; intra-state mass atrocities will continue to destabilise international order and the mass human suffering they spawn will obviously degrade perceptions of the system's legitimacy. The alternative, moral suasion as advanced by R2P, has clearly failed, and thus it is surely time to think seriously about fundamental and far-reaching alternatives; to do so need not necessitate utopianism. Rather, what is required is a debate about the relationship between states and international law, and the extent to which the former can permit the latter to ensure a more consistent response to intra-state crises.
>
> (Murray and Hehir 2015, para. 11)

Whatever the future may hold for interventionism and human rights protection, the English School of international relations is well suited to serve as an effective theoretical framework for its development and explanation. The dichotomy between English School pluralism and solidarism lends itself very well to debates about interventionism, given the typical pragmatism v. aspirationalism that often defines intervention discussions. One lesson that can be derived from the English School in this context is to see an inextricable relationship between the normative interests of citizens and movements, explained by the English School as world society, the structure of the international system, and how states work to reconcile these factors in their foreign and global affairs policies. As the system continues its progression towards multipolarity, how the new structure of the international system will be received by world society, and how states will behave as a result, will undoubtedly be increasingly constrained especially in the area of humanitarian intervention.

An English School approach to this issue helps understand that the norms and values embodied in world society can only ever be realised through an accepted order in international society. The major failure in the post-Cold War international society dominated by western states and a supposed consensus around liberal values was that international order was never successfully renegotiated after the Cold War to allow for a shift from a Westphalian view of sovereignty to one articulated through R2P. Can such a renegotiation take place in a multipolar systemic structure and the emerging post-American international society that would allow for divergent approaches on various issues, including humanitarian intervention, to be both identified and accepted by both western and non-western states that could not only lead to a stable international order but one that could also see civilian protection as a core value? If the past is any indication, states will continue to privilege their own interests and security before considering the aspirational. Such a reality does not bode well for humanitarian intervention and civilian protection.

Notes

1   See for instance Pattison, J 2010, *Humanitarian Intervention and the Responsibility to Protect: Who Should Intervene?* Oxford University Press, Oxford; Murray, RW and Hehir, A 2012, 'Intervention in the Emerging Multipolar System: Why R2P will Miss the Unipolar Moment', *Journal of Intervention and Statebuilding*, vol. 6, no. 4, pp. 387–406; Bellamy, A 2015, *The Responsibility to Protect: A Defense*, Oxford University Press, Oxford; and Weiss, T 2016, *Humanitarian Intervention: Ideas in Action*, 3rd edn, Polity, Cambridge.
2   See the works of Alex Bellamy, Tim Dunne, Jason Ralph, Adrian Gallagher, Robert Murray, Cristina Stefan, Justin Morris, and Nicholas Wheeler.
3   For an extensive discussion of world society and the solidarist relationship, see Buzan, B 2004, *From International to World Society? English School Theory and the Social Structure of Globalization*, Cambridge University Press, Cambridge.
4   For more on the changes to warfare since the end of World War II, see Holsti, K 1996, *The State, War, and the State of War*, Cambridge University Press, Cambridge.
5   See, for instance, Annan, K 2000, *We the Peoples: The Role of the United Nations in the 21st Century*, United Nations Department of Public Information, New York.
6   This builds on Bull's earlier warnings about the Grotian idea of international society, which is now more closely related to solidarism. See Bull, H 2000, 'The Grotian Conception of International Society' in *Hedley Bull on International Society*, pp. 95–118, Macmillan, Houndmills.
7   See Murray, RW 2012, 'The challenges facing R2P implementation' in WA Knight and F Egerton, (eds), *The Routledge Handbook of the Responsibility to Protect*, pp. 64–76. Routledge, London.
8   For more on the causal connection between the structure of the international system and prospects for R2P, see Murray, RW and Hehir, A 2012, 'Intervention in the Emerging Multipolar System: Why R2P will Miss the Unipolar Moment', *Journal of Intervention and Statebuilding*, vol. 6, no. 4, pp. 387–406.
9   For more on the idea of postmodern international society, see Buzan, B and Little, R 2000, *International Systems in World History: Remaking the Study of International Relations*, Oxford University Press, Oxford, as well as Buzan, B 2004, *From International to World Society? English School Theory and the Social Structure of Globalization*, Cambridge University Press, Cambridge.

References

Alderson, K and Hurrell, A 2000, 'The Continuing Relevance of International Society' in K Alderson and A Hurrell, (eds), *Hedley Bull on International Society*, pp. 54–73. Macmillan Press, Houndmills.

Annan, K 2000, *We the Peoples: The Role of the United Nations in the 21st Century*, United Nations Department of Public Information, New York.

Bellamy, A 2013, 'The Responsibility to Protect: Towards a "Living Reality"', United Nations Association, UK. Available from: www.una.org.uk/sites/default/files/UNA-UK%20Alex%20J%0Bellamy%20R2P%20Briefing%20Report%20no.%201.pdf. [5 May 2016].

Bellamy, A 2015, 'The Responsibility to Protect Turns Ten', *Ethics and International Affairs*, vol. 29, no. 2, pp. 161–185.

Bellamy, A and McDonald, M 2004, 'Securing International Society: Towards an English School Discourse of Security', *Australian Journal of Political Science*, vol. 39, no. 2, pp. 307–330.

Bull, H 1979, 'Western Values in a Hostile World'. Talk. Foreign Affairs Club, London.

Bull, H 2000, 'The Grotian Conception of International Society' in *Hedley Bull on International Society*, pp. 95–118, Macmillan, Houndmills.

Buzan, B & Little, R 2000, *International Systems in World History: Remaking the Study of International Relations*, Oxford University Press, Oxford.

Buzan, B 2004, *From International to World Society? English School Theory and the Social Structure of Globalization*, Cambridge University Press, Cambridge.

Dunne, T 2015, 'The English School and Humanitarian Intervention', in RW Murray, (ed.), *System, Society and the World: Exploring the English School of International Relations*, 2nd edn, pp. 60–67. E-International Relations, Bristol.

Evans, G 2015, 'R2P: Looking Back, Looking Forward', Keynote Address, Phnom Penh, Cambodia, 26 February. Available from: www.gevans.org/speeches/speech568.html. [18 July 2016].

Gallagher, A 2016, 'Conceptualising Humanity in the English School', *International Theory* vol. 8, no. 2, pp. 341–364.

Gifkins, J 2016, 'R2P in the UN Security Council: Darfur, Libya and beyond,' *Cooperation and Conflict* vol. 51, no. 2, pp. 148–165.

Global Centre for R2P 2016, 'UN Security Council Resolutions Referencing R2P'. Available from: www.globalr2p.org/resources/335. [18 July 2016].

Holsti, K 1996, *The State, War, and the State of War*, Cambridge University Press, Cambridge.

International Commission on Intervention and State Sovereignty (ICISS) 2001, *The Responsibility to Protect*, International Development Research Centre, Ottawa.

Jackson, R 1993, *Quasi-States: Sovereignty, International Relations and the Third World*, Cambridge University Press, Cambridge.

Jackson, R 2000, *The Global Covenant: Human Conduct in a World of States*, Oxford University Press, Oxford.

Jones, D 1991, *Code of Peace: Ethics and Security in the World of the Warlord States*, University of Chicago Press, Chicago, IL.

Linklater, A 2007, 'Towards a sociology of global morals with an "emancipatory intent"', *Review of International Studies*, vol. 33, pp. 135–150.

Linklater, A and Suganami, H 2006, *The English School of International Relations: A Contemporary Reassessment*, Cambridge University Press, Cambridge.

Morris, J 2016, 'The Responsibility to Protect and the use of force: Remaking the Procrustean bed?', *Cooperation and Conflict*, vol. 51, no. 2, pp. 200–215.

Murray, RW 2012, 'The challenges facing R2P implementation' in W Andy Knight and F Egerton, (eds), *The Routledge Handbook of the Responsibility to Protect*, pp. 64–76. Routledge, London.

Murray, RW & Hehir, A 2012, 'Intervention in the Emerging Multipolar System: Why R2P will Miss the Unipolar Moment', *Journal of Intervention and Statebuilding*, vol. 6, no. 4, pp. 387–406.

Murray, RW and Hehir, A 2015, 'The Need for Post-R2P Humanitarianism', *Open Canada*. Available from: www.opencanada.org/features/the-need-for-post-r2p-humanitarianism/. [5 May 2016].

Nossal, KR 2005, 'Ear Candy: Canadian policy toward humanitarian intervention and atrocity crimes in Darfur', *International Journal*, vol. 60, no. 4, pp. 1017–1032.

Pape, R 2012, 'When Duty Calls: A Pragmatic Standard of Humanitarian Intervention', *International Security*, vol. 37, no. 1, pp. 41–80.

Pattison, J 2010, *Humanitarian Intervention and the Responsibility to Protect: Who Should Intervene?* Oxford University Press, Oxford.

Ralph J & Gallagher A 2015, 'Legitimacy Faultlines in International Society. The Responsibility to Protect and Prosecute after Libya', *Review of International Studies*, vol. 41, no.3, pp. 553–573.

Ramos-Horta, J 2015, 'Preventing Conflicts, Mediating the End of Wars, Building Durable Peace', Fifth Annual Gareth Evans Lecture, 8 October. Available from: www.globalr2p.org/media/files/gelramos-horta.pdf. [16 July 2016].

Stefan, C 2011, *Humanitarian Intervention and the Responsibility to Protect: Security and Human Rights*, Routledge, London.

Wheeler, N 2000, *Saving Strangers: Humanitarian Intervention in International Society*, Oxford University Press, Oxford.

PART II
'Protection' and peacekeeping

5

THE UNCERTAINTIES OF INTERNATIONAL PROTECTION

Kelly Staples

Introduction

Key texts of global governance such as the Fourth Geneva Convention, Universal Declaration of Human Rights, and Convention on the Status of Refugees, all produced in the wake of the Second World War, can be read in part as acknowledgements of the vulnerability of being 'beyond the pale' of national protection (Larking 2014). New landmarks in international protection, notably the Responsibility to Protect (R2P) doctrine, which affirms an international responsibility to 'help to protect populations from genocide, war crimes, ethnic cleansing and crimes against humanity', have further conceptualised the notion of international protection. However, the weaknesses in practice of international protection are obvious. 2015 was characterised by persistent reports of aid workers and civilians being targets of military airstrikes, drowning refugees, and unchecked crimes against humanity. This chapter discusses the uncertainties of international protection. It has been argued that 'a proliferation of protection concepts' (Stevens 2013) has led to confusion. In addition, there has been substantial debate about the normative status of protection concepts (e.g. Thakur and Maley 2015), and consideration of whether to replace 'old, outdated and ineffectual norms' with 'robust new powerful ones' (Francis and Popovski 2012, p. 12). On this basis, recent debates about civilian protection (Holt *et al*. 2009; Bellamy and Williams 2010; Francis *et al*. 2012) have sought to identify relatively unambiguous protection concepts related to specific contexts and practices. This chapter argues that many of the problems of international protection arise not at the conceptual level, but in its interaction with other key aspects of international relations. The challenges of international protection, like those related to human rights more broadly, hinge on wider questions of authority, compliance and commitment in international relations. While this complicates rather than simplifies our understanding of protection, it provides for approaches that avoid fatalism, utopianism and abstraction.

This chapter considers the protection of civilians during armed conflict (POC), looking at the long-established principle of civilian immunity and its status in relation to parties to armed conflict and to peacekeeping operations. The role of the host state in protecting its civilians or wider populations, the failure of which is often the basis for external action for the purposes of protection, is addressed only indirectly. The chapter does not, therefore, consider in-depth the practices of state protection of which war crimes, 'persecution' under the 1951 Refugee Convention, or 'manifest failure to protect' (R2P) are the antithesis. However, it is worth noting that the background assumption of all forms of international protection is the principle of state responsibility. Furthermore, the first set of protective practices examined in this chapter (POC under international humanitarian law (IHL)), though external to states in terms of authority, is primarily targeted towards states in its prohibitions. It is also worth remembering that external actors will often have to work not only together, but also with states (Holt et al., p. 3), a fact that has often led to disagreement and ambiguity.

Various studies report substantial divergence and uncertainty in the meaning of protection. Alex J. Bellamy and Paul D. Williams point to 'a lack of consensus on what protection ought to entail, where the sources of protection . . . lie, and how those sources relate to one another' (2010, p. 128). Hugh Breakey refers to peacekeeping conceptions of protection that are 'plastic and amorphous' (2012a, p. 42). On refugee protection, a seminal article of 1989 noted that 'the word protection is often unclear' (Goodwin-Gill 1989, p. 6), with the intervening years leading to even greater 'definitional uncertainty' (Stevens 2013, p. 234). And it is routinely noted that R2P remains 'clouded in . . . controversy and ambiguity' (Sarkin 2009, p. 57) due to 'widely divergent' state understandings (Hehir 2013, p. 8).

The first section of the chapter outlines the approach to protection concepts to be taken, which draws on work by a range of authors concerned with the normative status of civilian protection. Considerable attention has been devoted in recent literature to the question of whether 'third parties have been granted authority to implement, interpret, and apply' relevant rules (Abbott et al. 2000, p. 401). This chapter goes beyond 'delegation' or legal authority to consider the epistemic and political status of the protection concepts under review, focusing heavily on the limiting or enabling scope of consent and consensus. Looking first at POC under IHL, and then at peacekeeping, the chapter assesses in each case the clarity (or ambiguity) of the concept, the degree of consensus on it, and whether there are sources of legal or political authority for marshalling the compliance, consent and commitment of relevant actors. In conclusion, the chapter argues that the legal status of international norms cannot be understood in isolation from their epistemic and political status, which can often render them more ambiguous than they initially appear. It argues, furthermore, that this ambiguity is not necessarily a weakness.

Sources of civilian protection

I have suggested already that the *authority* of any conception of protection – that is, the extent to which it is binding on, or what we might call 'constitutive of

(Frost 1996) a practice such as warfighting or peacekeeping – cannot be determined in isolation from its epistemic and political aspects. Nor can it be separated out from other international norms, including the fundamental norms of sovereignty and non-intervention. Protection, which manifests concern with the 'life, liberty and security of person' (United Nations 1948, Art3) of individual people inevitably interacts with sovereignty. Though some constraints on the latter will garner substantial agreement, the continuing importance of state compliance and consent, and the consequent difficulty of securing international commitment, make international protection an inherently controversial subject.

International protection takes various forms. On the one hand, there are well-established legal protections, such as those directed towards civilians in armed conflicts (for example the Fourth Geneva Convention or 'GCIV') or towards refugees (the 1951 Convention relation to the Status of Refugees and its 1967 protocol). Customary IHL also provides legal protections against a range of atrocity crimes, and since 2005, we can also refer to the policy and practice of pillars two and three of the R2P, adopted by the UN General Assembly in 2005 with the aim of clarifying and enhancing responsibilities for the protection of populations from genocide and mass atrocities.

Drawing on an approach outlined earlier by Bellamy (2009), Breakey distinguishes in a discussion of civilian protection concepts between norms (strong), principles (weaker) and concepts (weakest) as a heuristic device for assessing the status of different concepts. He also draws on Kenneth W. Abbott et al. 's (2000) account of legalisation, which assesses it on three dimensions: Obligation, Precision, and Delegation, where 'Capital letters indicate high levels on the dimension, lower-case letters indicate moderate levels, and subscript letters indicate low levels' (Breakey 2012b, p. 72). Delegation, which 'gauges whether states have been willing to *delegate* authority to external institutions' (Breakey 2012b, p. 72) proves to be particularly important for understanding whether or not a given concept is authoritative in the context of a sovereign state system. Here, I look not only at the 'whether' of delegation, but also the 'why' (or 'why not'). Taking seriously the claim that in the absence of 'enforcement measures, rules will deteriorate over time' (Lang Jr. 2007, p. 255), the chapter accounts for the continuing weakness in practice of ostensibly precise rules and (in the case of combatant POC) unconditional obligations.

To understand the scope of legal authority requires us to look beyond precision to the more social notion of consensus. In political theory, there is a close, though complex, relationship between consensus and legitimacy, although this relationship has until quite recently been 'widely ignored' in International Relations (IR) (Clark 2007, p. 2). Consensus is itself a much debated concept, though it can be argued that any persuasive notion of 'good conduct' requires considerable agreement within the relevant society or on the part of relevant actors (Frost 2012). Common sense dictates that this is especially the case in the absence of strong obligations or effective means of adjudication or sanction, or indeed where we might wish to work towards these. In a discussion of consensus and authority in relation to the UN Security Council, Bruce Cronin differentiates between consensus and consent. He argues that the historically indispensable requirement for individual state consent, exemplified in treaty-based international law can now be supplemented, or even over-ridden by more general consensus (Cronin 2008, p. 64). While the current chapter does not find much evidence of 'collective international consensus' *overriding* individual state consent, both play a role in relation to the epistemic authority of protection concepts.

Some have disputed the importance of consensus to international law, with Bellamy going so far as to call it 'a fiction', or at the very least, significantly 'mediated by power' (2007, p. 84). Certainly, the consent (in the strong sense) of weaker parties to international rules can be disputed. However, a more instrumental consensus, derived from reciprocal interactions and relating to the 'rules of the game or procedures' (Sartori cited by Pasquino 2016, p. 203) is frequently said to be a condition of international norms (Keohane 1986, p. 1). Arguably, the very 'basis of responsibility is reciprocity' (Groves 2006, p. 1). In Rene Provost's analysis, reciprocity is 'one of the bases on which legitimate norms can be established to link participants variously positioned in a regime like international humanitarian law' (2012, p. 17). A quite 'basic reciprocity' has arguably been 'essential for the functioning of international law' (Bellamy 2007, p. 84). Research into consensus in 'legal, political and social settings' (Boudreau *et al.* 2010, p. 868) tends to emphasise the challenges of achieving consensus on difficult problems (Boudreau *et al.* 2010), and the importance of active communication including dissent in trying to avoid deadlock (Pasquino 2016). Going forward I argue that the degree of commitment to participation in protection on the part of relevant actors is at least as important as (and can sometimes be in tension with) conceptual clarity. Real commitment will entail communication, dissent, and disagreement, all of which are vital to sustaining reciprocal practices and fostering authoritative protection practices.

Combatant protection of civilians

Bellamy and Williams identify six 'streams of thought and policy' on civilian protection, associated variously with: IHL; humanitarianism; the UN Security Council; peacekeeping mandates; regional arrangements; and R2P (2010, p. 131). This chapter is concerned only with IHL, or what Breakey terms 'combatant POC' (2012a), and peacekeeping POC. Given that this aspect of international protection has the longest history, emerging from Just War theory and first embodied in a treaty in the First Geneva Convention of 1864, I address 'combatant POC' here first. This conception has its source in the ostensibly binding Geneva Conventions (a consent based form of international law) (see Cronin 2008) and in what is commonly called customary IHL. IHL, then, is 'that body of norms that protects certain categories of persons and property and prohibits attacks against them during the course of armed conflicts' (Bassiouni 1998, p. 200). It is quite commonly argued that IHL is the strongest conception of protection, attaining the status of a settled norm. Breakey characterises it as having the status in policy and law of a norm insofar as there is 'a shared expectation of appropriate behaviour by actors with a given identity' (2012a, p. 42). The expectation in relation to appropriate combatant behaviour is said to be that 'We must not harm or unduly risk harm to non-combatants' (Breakey 2012a, p. 45). Using Abbott *et al.*'s device, Breakey concludes that combatant POC is [O, P, d], in other words, high on obligation, high on precision, and moderate on delegation: 'The Geneva Conventions and Additional Protocols unquestionably dictate legal obligations, they have a high degree of preciseness, and in many (though not all) instances, external courts and ad hoc tribunals are able to adjudicate upon them' (2012b, p. 73).

On this account, it is delegation that must be strengthened for a more legalised regime. In William Maley's view, 'the development of enforcement mechanisms' for upholding the laws of armed conflict has had a positive impact, though he accepts that the impact of the International Criminal Court in this respect 'remains to be seen' (Maley 2015, pp. 257–258).

This supports Breakey's assessment in which the necessary (though insufficient) conditions for stronger delegation are in place (see Abbott *et al.* 2000, p. 406). Cherif M. Bassiouni also affirms the strength of obligation, contrasting the relative clarity and strength of IHL, which deals with war crimes, by comparison to international law on genocide and crimes against humanity. He argues that this derives from the fact that the former are less politically sensitive to states as they 'frequently are committed by individual combatants acting on their own' (Bassiouni 1998, p. 202). Even when war crimes result from state action, they can often be treated as if this were the case by scapegoating 'bad apples' (Human Rights Watch 2004, p. 1). This contrasts with genocide and crimes against humanity, which are generally a matter of 'deliberate state action or policy'. In these areas, governments 'are not . . . for political reasons, desirous of removing the ambiguities' (Bassiouni 1998, p. 202). Even in the face of quite broad and deep consensus that 'widespread and systematic attack[s] directed against any civilian population' (Rome Statute of the International Criminal Court 1998, Art7.1) are wrong, states have proved reluctant, in his view, to clarify or consent to 'normative provisions applicable to crimes against humanity and genocide' (Bassiouni 1998, p. 203).

Combatant POC can be seen to combine legal and political strengths. On the one hand, we have precise obligations under international law, and a moderate degree of delegated authority criminalising violations. On the other, we arguably have substantial consensus, sustained by the reciprocal interest of parties to conflict. Maley identifies a degree of consensus 'across societies and cultures' (2015, p. 257) and the influence of reciprocity as a constitutive aspect of the relationship between parties to a conflict:

> A distinctive feature of the laws of armed conflict is how widely they have come to be accepted. One reason, beyond any doubt, is reciprocity. A military that does not meticulously observe its obligations under international humanitarian law is poorly placed to demand that . . . the status of its civilian population be respected.
>
> (Maley 2015, p. 257)

On the face of it then, the picture is far from a realist one; rather a pluralist one in which mutual interest, custom and practice have led to consensus around precise and authoritative rules of conduct, in spite of some continuing ambiguity around their application to non-state actors, multinational forces and non-international armed conflicts (see Geiß 2006; Provost 2012; Ferraro 2013).

However, the merest glance at the world today raises challenges in respect of the ostensible strength of combatant POC. Severe and ongoing breaches of the principle of civilian immunity cast serious doubt on the influence of the civilian immunity norm on the behaviour of 'weapon bearers and their political operatives' (ICRC 2010). 2013 saw a record high in attacks – killings, woundings and kidnappings – against aid workers (Aid Worker Security 2015). It is now widely acknowledged that civilians, for the first time in history, are often the intended target of attacks. Perhaps particularly shocking in recent months has been the increased violence against patients and medical personnel. In 2015, seventy-five hospitals managed or supported by the humanitarian organisation Médecins sans Frontières (MSF) were bombed (MSF 2016), leading the organisation to issue a strongly worded condemnation of 'four of the five permanent members' of the Security Council for their association 'with coalitions responsible for attacks on health structures' (Liu 2016).

How is this protection gap to be understood? Views differ on the 'significance of individual criminal responsibility as an enforcement tool for IHL', with Provost arguing in respect of both state and non-state actors that, 'given the limited appetite of states for universal jurisdiction and the limitations on the competence and capacities of international tribunals, the likelihood of either type of prosecution appears too remote to suggest a significant compliance pull' (2012, p. 26).

While the establishment of the ICC in 2002 offers *prima facie* evidence of delegation and hence of enhanced enforcement prospects, there are pertinent critiques in relation to the Court's impact on protection. The uneven reach of the ICC has arguably politicised enforcement. First, it is often held to have an Africa-bias (Moss 2012, p. 9). This is exacerbated by a second line of criticism, which regards the Court's relationship to the UN Security Council. The latter's powers of referral and deferral, and the fact that three of the five permanent members have not consented to the jurisdiction of the Court is of serious concern (see Moss 2012), and creates an asymmetry at odds with the reciprocity that was historically a strength of IHL. There is a further asymmetry in terms of the Court's power over peacekeepers. 'Deficiencies in the laws governing peacekeeping operations' make for the immunity, or even impunity, of UN peacekeeping troops (Freedman 2014; Du Plessis and Pete 2004). Sadly, peacekeepers have not always been above attacks on civilians, with distressing 'reports of UN peacekeepers committing severe crimes against the people they are meant to protect' with almost 'total impunity' (Du Plessis and Pete 2004, p. 5, 8). This is of serious concern. As Robin Geiß has argued: 'Patterns of compliance are far more unstable if the aforesaid factual asymmetries are coupled with legal asymmetries and a profound divergence of interests between the parties involved' (2006, p. 766).

Of course, actors, even states, sometimes comply with rules even in the absence of delegated legal authority. Andrew T. Guzman's compliance theory of international law considers the impact of political sanctions and reputational costs. Reputational costs, he argues, can be severe 'when the obligation is clear and the violation is unambiguous' (Guzman 2002, p. 1863). While according to Guzman, ad hoc measures (either punitive, such as sanctions, or more positive, such as communication) can be effective in achieving compliance, he finds that overall, both direct and reputational sanctions are 'weakest when the stakes at issue are large' (2002, p. 1883). Recent experience vindicates this claim. Guzman's theory in fact 'predicts that international law will have the smallest impact in those areas of great importance to countries' (2002, p. 1873). The Assad regime in Syria, for example, continues to have the support of Russia and Iran, and is by no means a fully pariah regime. Military sanctions are hardly predictable either, as the indifference of the UN Security Council members – in spite of Obama's famous 'red line' of 2012 – to Assad's use of chemical weapons in 2013 demonstrates. Neither have 'reputational costs' obviously affected the calculus of regimes battling for their survival in a multipolar world in which they can generally maintain a degree of patronage.

Is there still evidence that parties to conflict have a reciprocal interest in the observance of the rules of IHL? Determining the status of international customs is 'not only a challenging legal exercise, but one that is fraught with political considerations' (Bassiouni 1998, p. 220). Part of the explanation can be found in the increase in inter-state war, the blurring of the line between combatants and civilians, the increased power of non-state actors, and renewed conflict between the P5, all of which have been discussed at length in recent years. Consensus, or at least reciprocity, was identified earlier as being a key strength of combatant POC. As we have seen, authoritative norms are closely related to reciprocal interactions, or the consent of relevant actors to 'be bound by a norm on the basis that they thereby obtain a benefit' (Provost 2012, p. 18). In contemporary conflicts, the balance of reciprocity has clearly altered. Arguably, a more negative, tit-for-tat reciprocity (Geiß 2006, p. 777), in line with Tim Dunne's observation that 'human wrongs . . . can 'cascade' throughout global politics just as quickly as human rights' (Dunne 2007, p. 44) now prevails. Complexity and asymmetry in contemporary war have been key factors. The dizzying array of parties, including non-state actors, to current conflicts, and imbalances and asymmetries in power, weaponry, and civilian vulnerability distort the simple reciprocity underpinning Maley's explanation for the strength of the norm of civilian immunity. Armed non-state actors in particular often do not 'feel bound to abide by rules that they have neither put forward nor formally adhered to' (Geneva Call n.d.).

Without wishing to paint too pessimistic a picture, or to succumb to a simple realist explanation of military and state behaviour, it seems clear that armed actors will continue to find reasons, ideological or prudential (Bellamy and Williams 2010, p. 130), to violate the precise legal obligations relating to POC in conflict. Overall, the current constellation of civilian protection under IHL is one in which the precise legal obligations are undermined by political factors, notably the continuing requirement for parties to conflict to actively comply. David Rieff's characterisation of the twentieth century remains apt: 'no century had better norms and worse realities' (Rieff 2003, p. 70, cited by Bellamy and Williams 2010, p. 128).

Peacekeeping protection of civilians

In this section I address peacekeeping POC, the demand for which arises in part out of the weaknesses of IHL already outlined, in particular the continuing propensity of armed actors to target civilians. Civilian protection is now an important dimension of peacekeeping operations (PKOs), though the status of this concept needs to be understood in the context of other founding principles of peacekeeping. PKOs, like humanitarianism more broadly, traditionally require impartiality and 'minimal and proportionate use of force' in self-defence or defence of mission (Holt *et al.* 2009, p. 10). Peacekeeping also rests explicitly on host-state consent and Security Council consensus. Impartiality has historically been an under-defined and ambiguous principle (Vohra 1996, p. 63), though it has been clarified in recent years. By contrast, host-state consent and minimal use of force are precise norms. In effect, these specify negative requirements: *do not* deploy without host-state consent and *do not* use force except in self-defence or defence of mission. It could be argued that there is also obligation in the UN Charter and delegated authority on the part of the International Court of Justice in respect of 'the threat or use of force against the territorial integrity or political independence of any state' (United Nations 1945, Art2.4). However, the enduring strength of conceptions of host-state consent and minimal use of force derives more obviously from their basis in a procedural consensus derived from states' reciprocal interest in sovereignty and non-intervention. As we will see going forward, the strength of these normative aspects of peacekeeping has seriously complicated efforts to articulate an effective peacekeeping civilian protection concept.

In order to assess peacekeeping POC, I look again in this section for conceptual authority, taking what I am choosing to call epistemic authority (which addresses clarity and consensus) first. At first glance the core meaning of peacekeeping POC seems to be imprecise. Hitoshi Nasu identifies a continuing lack of definition 'despite the fact that numerous UN documents have been produced in relation to this topic' (2012, pp. 126–127).

In a 2009 report, jointly commissioned by the Department of Peacekeeping Operations and the Office for the Coordination of Humanitarian Affairs of the UN, it was noted that:

> The Secretariat and peacekeeping missions do not have a clear understanding of the Council's intent regarding 'protection of civilians' mandates. In this regard, one source of confusion has been the multiple meanings the Council has attached to the term 'protection of civilians' in peacekeeping mandates, and its relationship to various concepts of protection.
>
> (Holt *et al.* 2009, p. 6)

Confusion over the Security Council's intended meaning has led relevant actors to 'struggle over what it means for a peacekeeping operation to protect civilians, in definition and in practice' (Holt et al. 2009, p. 4).

In Breakey's account, 'peacekeeping POC' is not yet a settled norm, but is rather a 'principle'. Principles are not associated with expectations, or appropriate behaviour, but do imply a 'shared understanding that can function as a basis for action' (Breakey 2012a, p. 42). He classifies peacekeeping POC as $[_o, p, _d]$, or low on obligation, moderate on precision, and low on delegation:

The obligation of peacekeepers to provide decent protection, within their mandate and capacities, to civilians around them is not a legal obligation and there are no external courts empowered to adjudicate it. There is, however, sufficient preciseness to the duty that we may be confident in determining failures to perform it in at least some instances (Breakey 2012b, p. 73).

The failures he has in mind are notorious peacekeeping failures of the 1990s, such as Rwanda and Srebrenica. For him, peacekeeping POC is guided therefore by the notion that: 'Taking responsibility for peace enforcement in an area necessarily involves taking responsibility for the protection of civilians in that area' (Breakey 2012a, p. 41). He argues that the relevant objectives, capacities and roles are 'becoming settled' through 'developments in doctrine, training, methods and institutionalization', but fall short of the status of a norm (Breakey 2012a, p. 42).

Victoria Holt, Glyn Taylor and Max Kelly's UN-commissioned report identifies three conceptions. There is, on the one hand, the 'broad normative framework that prohibits violence against civilians', addressed in the first section of this chapter. Next there is a conception spanning 'the full range of humanitarian and peacebuilding activities in which the UN system engages', which is beyond the reach of this chapter. Finally, we have the 'narrower concept of "physical" protection supported by the peacekeeping mission' (Holt et al. 2009, p. 6). In trying to ascertain the core meaning of 'protection of civilians' as applied to PKO mandates, Holt, Taylor and Kelly's report focuses on this last, narrower conception. The narrow version of peacekeeping is relatively precise, holding that:

> When a protection crisis occurs, United Nations personnel cannot stand by as civilians are threatened or killed. They must use every tool available to them to protect civilians under imminent threat. Each and every peacekeeper, whether military, police or civilian, must pass that test when crisis presents itself.
>
> (Ramos-Horta 2015, p. 11)

'Protection of civilians', left undefined in Breakey's normative assessment, is increasingly articulated, then, to intend the use of force by peacekeepers to 'help prevent and halt acts of extreme violence' (Holt et al. 2009, p. 6). It is now quite widely accepted – in principle – that peacekeepers will sometimes be required to use force to 'protect civilians under imminent threat of physical violence' (Holt et al. 2009, p. 3).

While the long-standing commitment to consent, impartiality and minimal use of force had the benefit of being in conformity with states' sovereignty concerns, it left PKOs vulnerable to the charge of being bystanders to war crimes or even crimes against humanity (Power 2001). Recent years have seen a paradigm shift in peacekeeping. After undisputed failures in the 1990s, the UN sought to clarify the meaning of impartiality and its implications for the legitimate use of force. The Brahimi Report, published in 2000, affirms that: 'Impartiality is not the same as neutrality or equal treatment of all parties in all cases for all time, which can amount to a policy of appeasement.' Lakhdar Brahimi makes it clear that where there are 'obvious aggressors and victims . . . peacekeepers may not only be operationally justified in using force but morally compelled to do so' (2000, para. 50). This has led to policies of 'robust peacekeeping' and peace enforcement. The former involves 'the use of force at the tactical level with the authorization of the Security Council and consent of the host nation and/or main parties to the conflict' (DPKO/DFS 2008, p. 34). 'Peace enforcement' mandates, by contrast, are authorised under Chapter VII of the UN Charter and do 'not require the consent of the main parties and may involve the use of force at the strategic or international level' (DPKO/DFS 2008, p. 34).

PKOs now generally have a mandated role to play in POC: 'UNSC mandates have shifted from allowing POC to requiring it' (FCO 2015, p. 3). Today, mandates regularly authorise the use of 'all necessary means, within the limits of . . . capacity and deployment' to carry out PKO mandates. In recent years MONUSCO (Democratic Republic of Congo), MINUSCA (Central African Republic) and MINUSMA (Mali) have all been authorised with permissive Chapter VII mandates. However, it remains to be seen how effective these shifts have been. As late as 2010, Roberta Cohen argued that peacekeeping missions continue to prove 'a great disappointment to those in need of protection' (2010: 49). In 2014, the UN Office of Internal Oversight Services (OIOS) reported that of 507 incidents involving civilians between 2010 and 2013, only 20 per cent:

> provoked an immediate PKO response. A show of force to deter was also rare and, even with mission staff on site during an attack (or threatened attack) against civilians, force was almost never used. When it was, it was more often when troops were engaged in self-defence or defence of UN personnel and property. Only four missions reported ever firing a warning shot and only three had fired a shot with lethal intent.
>
> (FCO 2015, p. 7)

In spite of the regular inclusion of POC in PKO mandates today, 'force is almost never used to protect civilians actually under attack' (FCO 2015, p. 7). MONUSCO was accused in 2012 of failing 'spectacularly in its most fundamental mission: protecting civilians' (Hatcher and Perry 2012). Neither is it clear that the authorisation in 2013 of the UN's 'first ever offensive combat force' (FCO 2015, p. 3), a Force Intervention Brigade deployed in the Democratic Republic of Congo has much improved civilian protection. After early successes against the Rwanda-backed M23 militia group, the brigade has been criticised for inaction and accused of politicisation (Fabricius 2014).[1] In 2015, Ramesh Thakur noted that while 'the numbers and activities of civilian protection actors have grown, there does not seem to have been a commensurate increase in actual protection' (Thakur 2015, p. 23).

A 'Comprehensive review of the whole question of peacekeeping operations in all their aspects', led by Jose Ramos-Horta, was undertaken in late 2014 and early 2015. The final 'HIPPO' report (High-level Independent Panel on Peace Operations), published in June 2015, sets out a range of changes needed for the UN to be more effective 'in preventing and ending conflicts' and 'making and sustaining peace' (Ramos-Horta 2015, p. 3). A Council of Foreign Relations response lauds the emphasis on prevention as 'refreshing and overdue', but notes the underlying and unaddressed contradiction between what is needed and member states' 'persistent shortsightedness in failing to dedicate the time and resources necessary to prevent armed conflicts and to adequately respond to them when they do break out' (Call 2015).

How is this commitment gap to be explained? As noted, Breakey sees peacekeeping POC as entailing low levels of obligation and delegation in spite of progressive clarifications on its requirements. For a host of reasons, peacekeeping POC is not amenable to the kind of precise obligations found in IHL, which already (in principle, though not at the level of enforcement) address peacekeepers. Firstly, peacekeeping POC, in contrast to combatant POC, is the basis for action rather than restraint. In their research on the DPKO, Francis and Popovski reported the view that 'historically international humanitarian law has been about what *not* to do, whereas POC is about what *to* do' (Francis and Popovski 2012, p. 84). Law in general, and international law in particular, is generally concerned with the articulation of clear negative rules of the form 'do not . . .'. The importance of context to peacekeeping also necessarily entails a degree of flexibility and responsiveness (DPKO/DFS 2010, p. 3). Furthermore, in moving from combatant POC to peacekeeping POC, we are moving from obligations on actors already implicated in a conflict to the assignment of roles and responsibilities to external actors. Whereas IHL is universal in its prohibitions on intentional attacks on civilians, peacekeeping POC is more targeted, particular, and limited; 'PKOs are not resourced or designed to protect all civilians in a conflict' (FCO 2015, p. 1). In addition, the reliance of PKOs on the consent-based participation of troop contributing countries is at odds with binding obligations (as seen in their reluctance to consent to being under the jurisdiction of the ICC). In their explanation of the 'impediments to transforming ambitions to protect civilians into realities on the ground', Holt *et al.* also point to the lack of political support on the part of the Security Council (2009, p. 2).

Operational problems also abound. PKOs are by their very nature deployed in tense and potentially violent situations where 'the security situation can change very quickly', 'with limited or insufficient resources, and with partners who . . .

lack the will or capacity to do their part' (United Nations Peacekeeping n.d.). Operations often lack a unified chain of command (FCO 2015, p. 8) and accountability structures are weak (Du Plessis and Pete 2004; Lutz et al. 2009, p. 15). Significant challenges remain in relation to peacekeeper training, conduct and discipline in spite of focused attention in this area (Lutz et al. 2009). There is evidence on the ground that PKOs comprised even of troops from troop contributing countries (TCCs) broadly supportive of robust peacekeeping tend towards a conservative approach to the use of force (FCO 2015, p. 8). This may again relate in part to an absence of reciprocity in the relationship between TCCs and the largest financial contributors to the peacekeeping budget (Coleman 2014, p. 32). Finally, and fundamentally, the enhanced scope for force risks clashing with sovereignty, undermining host-state consent and thus endangering specific PKOs as well as the legitimacy of peacekeeping more generally. UN PKOs clearly cannot act in ways that are in tension with the UN Charter that gives them their authority. They are therefore bound to observe the underlying principle of host-state consent with the effect that they remain unlikely to engage in any activity that threatens this.

Compliance and commitment issues

The demands of combatant civilian protection are relatively narrow and precise, with a weight of moral consensus behind them. However, the continuing and rising trend of attacks on civilians by powerful states and non-state actors alike demonstrates serious issues at the level of compliance and commitment. Moral consensus is not mirrored in practice; parties to conflict today do not fear prosecution or sanction and do not see expectations on civilian protection as shared rules of the game. On this point, at this moment, a degree of fatalism is probably right; the dynamics of conflict seriously weaken the prospects in practice for the norm of civilian immunity. What we might usefully call the global constitutional order (Lang Jr. and Wiener 2015) does not yet effectively enforce the negative obligations of IHL, nor does this prospect look imminent, especially in light of increasing tension between Russia and NATO.

The prospects for greater civilian protection, then, currently rest on the scope for greater commitment on the part of the international community. Here the right response is neither fatalism nor utopianism; positive developments can be identified, although 'unreconstructed Wilsonian aspirations' (Soffer 1997, p. 69) are not helpful. We can say confidently that host-state consent will continue to be a condition of PKOs for the foreseeable future for the reason that the status of POC can only be understood in relation to other principles, including the settled sovereignty norms articulated in the UN Charter. It is this background context that makes general consensus and the explicit consent of states so vital to sustaining a commitment to protection. Pluralism, sovereignty and multipolarity in world politics all mean that consensus is simultaneously necessary and difficult to achieve. Research indicates (and world politics demonstrates) that 'when problems are difficult, and communication is most needed, [consensus] will be least likely to occur' (Boudreau *et al.* 2010, p. 869).

The importance of consensus and consent are vividly illustrated by the rise and fall of the liberal internationalist vision of humanitarian intervention that began in the 1990s. Of course, there can be no teleology of consensus, and its pursuit necessarily entails dissent. Coordinating civilian protection will never be straightforward. There may, however, be concrete ways to strengthen commitment by enhancing reciprocity. A political approach to civilian protection need not be a fatalistic submission to *realpolitik*. Arguably, more political approaches will be better placed to acknowledge diversity and dissent, and work towards more ambiguous, pluralistic, committed versions that do not seek state compliance with pre-political rules, but foster participation in protection-practices. Bellamy and Williams make this point about paradox, diversity and consensus:

One of the principal strengths of the civilian protection norm – the breadth and depth of the normative consensus underpinning it – is also a source of weakness because there is little agreement . . . about what protection means, what it entails and which agents are best placed to provide it (2010, pp. 137–138).

However, it might just be that diversity and consensus are mutually supportive rather than paradoxical. Similarly, it may not be that precision comes later in the 'norm cycle' at the stage of socialization and crystallization (Francis *et al.* 2012, p. xiii), but rather that concepts guiding political action in a pluralistic context are necessarily ambiguous. Breadth of consensus will often entail considerable ambiguity, but this need not necessarily be a weakness (see also Widmaier and Glanville 2015). What protection entails will often be difficult to determine in the abstract. A wide range of activities can be directed towards protecting civilians, which leads Thakur to make the point that 'protection of civilians is an outcome, not an activity' (2015, p. 23).

This is not to say that protection concepts are totally open-ended; in the case of peacekeeping POC, there must be a good faith commitment from all parties to mitigating deliberate harm to non-combatants. Even on this, serious differences of opinion are bound to arise. While some have seen the MONUSCO Intervention Brigade as welcome evidence of peace enforcement, humanitarian groups including MSF have been fierce critics, holding the more expansive use of force in peacekeeping indirectly responsible for increased attacks on civilian objects including medical targets (Doyle 2013). I end the chapter by sketching a few mechanisms that might avoid infringing on sovereignty norms, promote more inclusive and participatory practice, and thereby strengthen the reciprocal basis of protection.

Provost has argued in respect of IHL that enhancing the reciprocity of interaction between parties to conflict will be one of the best ways of strengthening the norm of civilian protection. This, he argues, will require the creation of mechanisms that lower the costs of communication and cooperation (Provost 2012; see also Boudreau *et al.* 2010). When it comes to armed non-state actors, he identifies the positive work of Geneva Call in this regard. Of particular interest is the NGO's work in creating Deeds of Commitment as a means of creating more reciprocal interactions through communication and consensus-building.

On peacekeeping, Jonathan Soffer has argued that, for the 'patchwork enforcement necessary in an increasingly fractured world, the kind of ad hoc combinations of forces we see today may be the most rational response' (1997, p. 69). Several discussions about more inclusive models of peacekeeping are also to be found in the literature. It is arguable that greater commitment on the part of Europe and the Security Council, and greater attention to the views of the major TCCs would help strengthen the social dimension, including actors' responsibility to one another, and hence the authority of peacekeeping POC. As noted earlier, communication is vital to enhancing reciprocity, consensus, and hence a sense of shared responsibility. There is some evidence of useful practical measures in the peacekeeping literature that deadlock between different interests can 'be remedied by temporarily moving debate into a smaller and more insulated venue' (Coleman 2014, p. 32). Katharina P. Coleman identifies the importance of ensuring also 'that the concerns of smaller and less affluent TCCs and PCCs [Police Contributing Countries] continue to receive adequate consideration' (2014, p. 33). More reciprocal interactions might also result from greater EU involvement in peacekeeping. It has been suggested that: 'The increased European engagement [in MINUSMA] can provide useful common ground for the policy and finance debates . . . as well as create a broader coalition to improve the Security Council's consultations with TCCs on mandates' (Karlsrud and Smith 2015, p. 2).

The greater participation of the P5 is controversial, however. Since the Suez Crisis, there has been an 'unwritten rule . . . that the great powers would not directly be involved for fear that power politics would compromise the neutrality of peacekeeping missions' (Libben 2013, p. 2). This 'anything but the P5' rule has led, however, to a problematic situation where the P5 'are not prepared to provide the backbone of peacekeeping in terms of military capacities' (Guéhenno 2015). In any case, inclusive efforts must go way beyond the Security Council. Jean-Marie Guéhenno, the former Under Secretary-General of Peacekeeping Operations, recently argued that 'we need to find intelligent ways to involve troop contributing countries more. And the P5 must open up to the troop contributing countries' (2015). At the same time, reviving or reinvigorating UN bodies such as the Military Staff Committee (cf. Grove 1993; Soffer 1997) or the Secretariat (see Guéhenno 2015) could mitigate the threat to reciprocity posed by worsening Russia–NATO relations. Guéhenno takes the view that the goal must be the construction of a 'sense of shared responsibility' for PKOs (2015). Painstaking attempts to build a more cooperative, reciprocal basis for peacekeeping will be vital to this endeavour.

Conclusion

The chapter has attempted to demonstrate that even rules that seem, in the abstract, to be precise and obligatory, can fail to constrain behaviour in the absence of state consent. Clarity and apparent consensus can be easily overridden (and undermined) by the failure of relevant actors to follow the rules. Consent, and hence compliance and commitment are further weakened by political asymmetry and a lack of reciprocity. The challenges for international protection of fundamental human rights could hardly be greater, especially given the inherently anti-social character of contemporary war. However, specific mechanisms of consensus building can potentially foster more reciprocal bases for the operation of specific concepts. They may also, in turn, help leverage sanctions and reputational costs where norms are violated.

The chapter has also sketched out the argument that precision can be at odds with epistemic authority in the context of a pluralistic community. In the case of peacekeeping POC, precise 'rule-like' prescriptions are currently unfeasible, and arguably undesirable, for reasons outlined in the body of the chapter. The ambiguity of the concept relative to combatant POC, and the low level of obligations, might, however, provide space for the development of more participatory, consensual practices. High-level delegated authority is probably out of reach at this moment in history, and should not, therefore, be the goal. More moderate forms of delegation can, by contrast, coexist with a degree of imprecision or ambiguity. Though this form of delegation is not highly legalised (Abbott *et al.* 2000, p. 407), and is better suited to 'standard-like' than 'rule-like' prescriptions (Abbott *et al.* 2000, p. 413), it may be better able to reflect and support consensus. In the case of combatant POC, it would be difficult, not to mention undesirable, to re-open the prohibitions of IHL. The focus, instead, must be on attempting to secure a pluralistic, reciprocal basis in consensus between the relevant parties (including peacekeepers). Neither of these suggestions promises utopia, but they provide a provisional sketch of a framework for thinking about normative authority and enhanced civilian protection.

Notes

1 The FIB had been widely criticised for failing to tackle the threat to civilians posed by the FDLR armed group; however, in the wake of aid-worker kidnappings by this group, military action against it was resumed in May 2016.

References

Abbott, KW, Keohane, RO, Moravcsik, A, Slaughter, A-M and Snidal, D 2000, 'The Concept of Legalization', *International Organization*, vol. 54, no. 3, pp. 401–419.

Aid Worker Security 2015, 'Aid Worker Security Report 2015: Figures at a Glance'. Available from: https://aidworkersecurity.org/sites/default/files/HO_AidWorkerSecPreview_1015_G.pdf. [7 June 2016].

Bassiouni, MC 1998, 'The Normative Framework of International Humanitarian Law: Overlaps, Gaps and Ambiguities', *Transnational Law and Contemporary Problems*, vol. 8, no. 199, pp. 199–275.

Bellamy, AJ 2007, 'The English School' in M Griffiths, (ed.), *International Relations Theory for the Twenty-First Century: An Introduction*, pp. 75–87. Routledge, Abingdon and New York.

Bellamy, A 2009, *Responsibility to Protect: The Global Effort to End Mass Atrocities*. Cambridge: Polity.

Bellamy, AJ and Williams, PD 2010, 'Protecting Civilians in Uncivil Wars' in SE Davies and L Glanville, (eds), *Protecting the Displaced: Deepening the Responsibility to Protect*, pp. 127–161. Brill, Leiden.

Boudreau, C, McCubbins, MD, Rodriguez, DB, and Weller, N 2010, 'Making Talk Cheap (and Problems Easy): How Legal and Political Institutions Can Facilitate Consensus', *Journal of Empirical Legal Studies*, vol. 7, no. 4, pp. 868–885.

Brahimi, L 2000, *Report of the Panel on UN Peace Operations*, United Nations, New York.

Breakey, H 2012a, 'The Protection of Civilians in Armed Conflict: Four Concepts' in A Francis, V Popovski and C Sampford, (eds), *Norms of Protection: Responsibility to Protect, Protection of Civilians and Their Interaction*, pp. 40–61. United Nations University Press, Tokyo.

Breakey, H 2012b, 'The Responsibility to Protect and the Protection of Civilians in Armed Conflict: Overlap and Contrast' in A Francis, V Popovski and C Sampford, (eds), *Norms of Protection: Responsibility to Protect, Protection of Civilians and Their Interaction*, pp. 62–81. United Nations University Press, Tokyo.

Call, C 2015, 'What the UN Can Do to Fix Its Peacekeeping Mission', *Defense One*. Available from: www.defenseone.com/politics/2015/07/what-un-can-do-fix-its-peacekeeping-mission/118660/. [7 June 2016].

Clark, I 2007, *Legitimacy in International Society*, Oxford University Press, Oxford.

Cohen, R 2010, 'Reconciling R2P with IDP Protection' in SE Davies and L Glanville, (eds), *Protecting the Displaced: Deepening the Responsibility to Protect*. Brill, Leiden.

Coleman, KP 2014, 'The Political Economy of UN Peacekeeping: Incentivizing Effective Participation', *Providing for Peacekeeping*, vol. 7, no. 7, pp. 1–44.

Cronin, B 2008, 'International Consensus and the Changing Legal Authority of the UN Security Council' in B Cronin and I Hurd, (eds), *The UN Security Council and the Politics of International Authority*. Routledge, Abingdon; New York.

Doyle, M 2013, 'DR Congo Unrest: Fears over UN intervention', *BBC News*. Available from: www.bbc.co.uk/news/world-africa-23452735. [7 June 2016].

DPKO/DFS 2008, *United Nations Peacekeeping Operations: Principles and Guidelines (Capstone Doctrine)*, United Nations, New York.

DPKO/DFS 2010, *Draft DPKO/DFS Operational Concept on the Protection of Civilians in United Nations Peacekeeping Operations*, United Nations, New York.

Dunne, T 2007, ' "The Rules of the Game are Changing": Fundamental Human Rights in Crisis After 9/111', *International Politics*, vol. 44, no. 2/3, pp. 269–286.

Fabricius, P 2014, 'Is the Force Intervention Brigade Neutral?', *ISS Today*. Available from: www.issafrica.org/iss-today/is-the-force-intervention-brigade-neutral. [7 June 2016].

FCO 2015, 'Protection of Civilians (POC): Developments since 2009', *Research Analyst's Papers*, November.

Ferraro, T 2013, 'The Applicability and Application of International Humanitarian Law to Multinational Forces', *International Review of the Red Cross*, vol. 95, no. 891–892, pp. 561–612.

Francis, A and Popovski, V 2012, 'The Responsibility to Protect and the Protection of Civilians: A View from the United Nations' in A Francis, V Popovski and C Sampford, (eds), *Norms of Protection: Responsibility to Protect, Protection of Civilians and Their Interaction*, pp. 82–97. United Nations University Press, Tokyo.

Francis, A, Popovski, V and Sampford, C, (eds), 2012, *Norms of Protection: Responsibility to Protect, Protection of Civilians and Their Interaction*, United Nations University Press, Tokyo.

Freedman, R. 2014, 'When UN peacekeepers commit atrocities, someone has to act'. *The Conversation*, 17 November. Available from: http://theconversation.com/when-un-peacekeepers-commit-atrocities-someone-has-to-act-34317. [7 June 2016].

Frost, M 1996, '*Ethics in International Relations: A Constitutive Theory*', Cambridge University Press, Cambridge.

Frost, M 2012, *Ethics, Foul Play and War in International Relations*, Research Seminar, University of Hull. Available from: www2.hull.ac.uk/FASS/docs/Frost-ETHICS, FOUL PLAY AND WAR IN INTERNATIONAL RELATIONS.doc. [18 July 2016].

Geiß, R 2006, 'Asymmetric Conflict Structures', *International Review of the Red Cross*, vol. 88, no. 864, pp. 757–777.

Geneva Call n.d., 'How We Work: Deed of Commitment.' Available from: www.genevacall.org/how-we-work/deed-of-commitment/. [7 June 2016].

Goodwin-Gill, G 1989, 'The Language of Protection', *International Journal of Refugee Law*, vol. 1, no. 1, pp. 6–19.

Grove, E 1993, 'UN Armed Forces and the Military Staff Committee: A Look Back', *International Security*, vol. 17, no. 4, pp. 172–182.

Groves, C 2006, 'Philosophy and Non-Reciprocal Responsibility for Futures', *In Pursuit of the Future Working Papers*, pp. 1–18. Available from: www.cf.ac.uk/socsi/futures/wp_cg_responsibility200106.pdf. [8 December 2016].

Guéhenno, JM 2015, 'Fog of Peace: UN Peacekeeping Needs to Focus More on Political Strategy and Less on Troops', *Global Peace Operations Review*, (October). Available from: http://peaceoperationsreview.org/interviews/fog-of-peace-un-peacekeeping-needs-to-focus-more-on-political-strategy-and-less-on-troops/. [8 December 2016].

Guzman, AT 2002, 'A Compliance-Based Theory of International Law', *California Law Review*, vol. 90, no. 6, pp. 1823–1886.

Hatcher, J and Perry, A 2012, 'Defining Peacekeeping Downward: The U.N. Debacle in Eastern Congo', *Time*. Available from: http://world.time.com/2012/11/26/defining-peacekeeping-downward-the-u-n-debacle-in-eastern-congo/. [8 December 2016].

Hehir, A 2013, 'Introduction: Libya and the Responsibility to Protect' in A Hehir and R Murray, (eds), *Libya: The Responsibility to Protect and the Future of Humanitarian Intervention*, pp. 1–14. Palgrave, Basingstoke.

Holt, V, Taylor, G and Kelly, M 2009, 'Protecting Civilians in the Context of UN Peacekeeping Operations: Successes, Setbacks and Remaining Challenges', United Nations, New York.

Human Rights Watch 2004, 'The Road to Abu Ghraib', Washington DC: Human Rights Watch. Available from: www.hrw.org/reports/2004/usa0604/usa0604.pdf. [8 December 2016].

ICRC 2010, 'What We Do: Protection of the Civilian Population'. Available from: www.icrc.org/eng/what-we-do/protecting-civilians/overview-protection-civilian-population.htm. [7 June 2016].

Karlsrud, J and Smith, AC 2015, 'Europe's Return to UN Peacekeeping in Africa? Lessons from Mali', *Providing for Peacekeeping*, no. 11.

Keohane, RO 1986, 'Reciprocity in International Relations', *International Organization*, vol. 40, no. 1, pp. 1–27.

Lang Jr., AF 2007, 'Crime and Punishment: Holding States Accountable', *Ethics and International Affairs*, vol. 21, no. 2, pp. 239–257.

Lang Jr., AF and Wiener, A, (eds), 2015, *Handbook on Global Constitutionalism*, Edward Elgar Press, Cheltenham.

Larking, E 2014, *Refugees and the Myth of Human Rights: Life Outside the Pale of the Law*, Ashgate, Farnham.

Libben, J 2013, 'Development in P5 Participation in Peacekeeping Troop Contributions: Recent Chinese Engagement' in IPSA 23rd World Congress. Montreal. Available from: http://paperroom.ipsa.org/papers/paper_35696.pdf. [8 December 2016].

Liu, J 2016, 'MSF President to UN Security Council: "Stop these attacks"', *MSF*. Available from: www.msf.org/en/article/msf-president-un-security-council-stop-these-attacks. [7 June 2016].

Lutz, C, Gutmann, M and Brown, K 2009, 'Conduct and Discipline in UN Peacekeeping Operations: Culture, Political Economy and Gender', *Report submitted to the Conduct and Discipline Unit, Department of Peacekeeping Operations*.

Maley, W 2015, 'Humanitarian Law, Refugee Protection and the Responsibility to Protect' in R Thakur and W Maley, (eds), *Theorising the Responsibility to Protect*, pp. 249–265. Cambridge University Press, Cambridge.

Moss, L 2012, *The UN Security Council and the International Criminal Court: Towards a More Principled Relationship*, Friedrich-Ebert-Stiftung, Berlin.

MSF 2016, 'MSF to pull out of World Humanitarian Summit'. Available from: www.msf.org/en/article/msf-pull-out-world-humanitarian-summit. [7 June 2016].

Nasu, H 2012, 'Peacekeeping, civilian protection mandates and the responsibility to protect' in A Francis, V Popovski, and C Sampford, (eds), *Norms of Protection: Responsibility to Protect, Protection of Civilians and Their Interaction*, pp. 117–133. United Nations University Press, Tokyo.

Pasquino, G 2016, 'Consensus' in G Mazzoleni, KG Barnhurst, K Ikeda, RCM Maia and H Wessler, (eds), *The International Encyclopedia of Political Communication*, pp. 1–5. John Wiley & Sons, Chichester.

Du Plessis, M and Pete, S 2004, 'Who Guards the Guards? The ICC and Serious Crimes Committed by United Nations Peacekeepers in Africa', *African Security Review*, vol. 13, no. 4, pp. 5–17.

Power, S 2001, 'Bystanders to genocide', *Atlantic Monthly*, vol. 288, no. 2, pp. 84–108.

Provost, R 2012, 'Asymmetrical Reciprocity and Compliance with the Laws of War' in B Perrin, (ed.), *Modern Warfare: Armed Groups, Private Militaries, Humanitarian Organizations, and the Law*, pp. 17–41. UBC Press, Vancouver.

Ramos-Horta, J 2015, *Comprehensive Review of the Whole Question of Peacekeeping Operations in All Their Aspects*, United Nations, New York.

Rieff, D 2003, *A Bed for the Night: Humanitarianism in Crisis*, Simon & Schuster, London.

Rome Statute of the International Criminal Court 1998, 2187 UNTS 3.

Sarkin, J 2009, 'Why the Responsibility to Protect (R2P) as a Doctrine or (Emerging) Norm to Prevent Genocide and Other Massive Human Rights Violations is on the Decline: The Role of Principles, Pragmatism and the Shifting Patterns of International Relations', *Politorbis*, vol. 47, no. 2, pp. 51–64.

Soffer, J 1997, 'All for One or All for All: The UN Military Staff Committee and the Contradictions within American Internationalism', *Diplomatic History*, vol. 21, no. 1, pp. 45–69.

Stevens, D 2013, 'What Do We Mean by Protection?', *International Journal on Minority and Group Rights*, vol. 20, no. 1, pp. 233–262.

Thakur, R 2015, 'R2P's "Structural" Problems: A Response to Roland Paris', *International Peacekeeping*, vol. 22, no. 1, pp. 11–25.

Thakur, R and Maley, W, (eds), 2015, *Theorising the Responsibility to Protect*, Cambridge University Press, Cambridge.

United Nations 1945, *Charter of the United Nations and Statute of the International Court of Justice*, San Francisco, CA.

United Nations 1948, *Universal Declaration of Human Rights*, New York.

United Nations Peacekeeping n.d., 'Protection of Civilians'. Available from: www.un.org/en/peacekeeping/issues/civilian.shtml. [7 June 2016].

Vohra, S 1996, 'Impartiality in United Nations Peace-Keeping', *Leiden Journal of International Law*, vol. 9, no. 1, pp. 63–85.

Widmaier, WW and Glanville, L 2015, 'The Benefits of Norm Ambiguity: Constructing the Responsibility to Protect across Rwanda, Iraq and Libya', *Contemporary Politics*, vol. 21, no. 4, pp. 367–383. Available from: http://dx.doi.org/10.1080/13569775.2015.1014178. [8 December 2016].

6

UN PEACEKEEPING AND THE PROTECTION OF CIVILIANS' NORM

Tom Keating

Introduction

Contemporary conflicts have taken an extraordinary toll on civilian populations. It has become exceedingly difficult for civilians to stand aside from the violent clashes that mark these civil conflicts. The civilian casualties alongside the rapidly escalating number of internally displaced persons attests to the catastrophic effects for civilians caught in the crossfire. Even more troubling has been the deliberate targeting of civilians in many of these conflicts. Much of this violence is gender-based as women and girls are particularly vulnerable, systematically abused by all sides and, at times, by interveners as well. Threats and acts of violence have been extended with ever-increasing frequency to humanitarian workers and their facilities such as hospitals and displacement camps. In addition to being subjected to violent acts, civilian populations displaced by conflict also become vulnerable to other risks that endanger their health and livelihoods. These secondary and tertiary effects of conflict and displacement increase the casualty count by a significant margin.

This is not as it was supposed to be. International humanitarian law was established primarily to prevent civilian populations from falling victim to the violent conflicts that might invade their communities. These laws were designed to restrict the activities of combatants and require them to limit their activities so as not to endanger the lives and livelihood of those who were not directly engaged in the conflict. In recent years, however, such laws are ignored with impunity as civilian casualties outnumber those of combatants. This disregard has been displayed not only by disorderly non-state or non-traditional forces, but also by those of national governments and even foreign interveners whose aerial bombing campaigns, at times, have been less discriminate than claimed and whose interventions seem more concerned with protecting their own forces than civilians at risk. In the midst of such practices and in response to its own past failures to protect civilian populations from violent harm, the United Nations (UN) has embraced the principle of protection of civilians (POC) and made it a cornerstone of its peacekeeping operations since 1999.

The prevalence of POC mandates as part of contemporary UN peacekeeping operations (UNPKOs) has enhanced the significance of these operations not only as primary security supports for populations at risk in conflict situations, but also as a means to institutionalise a norm that would strengthen the international human rights and humanitarian law regimes. The POC norm has become a central tenet of the UN's security mandate and assumed a singular significance for both the norm and the organisation. The UN Secretary General Ban Ki-Moon has described POC as 'the defining principle' of the organisation (UN Department of Public Information 2012). This chapter explores the potential contribution that UNPKOs can make both in advancing POC in armed conflicts and reinforcing the civilian protection norms enshrined in international humanitarian law. This chapter begins with a brief review of the evolution of the POC in armed conflict norm within the UN, with particular attention to its inclusion in the mandate of UNPKOs. It considers the political factors that gave rise to and have sustained this mandate's inclusion in UNPKOs over nearly two decades. The chapter also reviews various assessments of the effectiveness of these mandates as an instrument for the protection of civilians in principle and practice. Since UNPKOs reflect a degree of consensus among members of the UN Security Council (UNSC), does the addition of POC mandates to these operations represent agreement among member governments on the principle of civilian protection? Do UNPKOs provide a means for advancing both the norm and practice of the POC principle? Alternatively, what are the implications of this expanded mandate of civilian protection and the additional burdens it places on UNPKOs for both the efficacy and legitimacy of these operations and the principles they are intended to support?

The UN and POC

The norm of civilian protection in times of combat has a long and chequered trajectory emerging from the battlefields of Europe in the nineteenth century. Civilian protection found articulation in international humanitarian law in the mid-twentieth century, specifically the Fourth Geneva Conventions adopted in 1949, and was reinforced with adoption of Additional Protocols in 1977. The adoption of these conventions reflected the greater risks that civilians face in modern conflict and extended protection to individuals and agencies such as the International Committee of the Red Cross (ICRC) that provide assistance to populations at risk. As Melissa Labonte has noted, international humanitarian law 'articulates specific provisions that must be followed to ensure the protected status for civilians in times of war' (Labonte 2012, p. 997). The ICRC and other humanitarian organisations have consistently defended the law, called for its universal application, and sought accountability for those who have violated it. It is, however, quite evident that the law has been violated repeatedly and widely. These violations in recent years result, in part, from the blurred lines between state controlled armed forces and non-state combatants engaged in contemporary intra-state conflicts. Many of these non-state combatants lack both the legal standing and the legal training that states are generally considered responsible for providing for their military personnel. The laws of war and with them international humanitarian law are often ignored. It is perhaps in response to this blatant disregard and the reigning impunity that surrounds violations that the UN has taken up the cause.

> Across the board, the United Nations is more engaged with human protection than ever before: combating sexual and gender-based violence, keeping children out of armed conflict, limiting small arms, light weapons and anti-personnel mines, establishing regional tribunals and supporting the International Criminal Court, operationalising genocide prevention and the responsibility to protect.
>
> (Nambiar 2011, p. 925)

The most prominent example of this has been in the organisation's extensive effort to develop the concept and practice of POC.

On 17 September 1999, the UNSC unanimously approved Resolution 1265 that addressed the threats to civilian populations and to those providing assistance to such populations, as well as called on the UN through peacekeeping mandates and other measures to give priority to the protection of these civilians at risk. The resolution: 'Notes the importance of including in the mandates of peacemaking, peacekeeping and peace-building operations special protection and assistance provisions for groups requiring particular attention, including women and children.' The resolution also encourages the Secretary-General 'to continue consultations on this subject and to take concrete actions aimed at enhancing the capacity of the United Nations to improve the protection of civilians in armed conflict' (UN Security Council 1999/1265). Later that same year the UNSC established a peacekeeping operation for the tenuous peace that had been arranged in Sierra Leone (UNAMSIL). In establishing UNAMSIL the Council included as part of the mandate that peacekeepers should take necessary action to protect civilians under threat of violent harm (UN Security Council 1999/1270). In adopting these resolutions the member states of the Council were responding to the persistent threats to civilian populations that had emerged in the civil conflicts that marked the post-Cold War period. They were also acknowledging the organisation's own failure in protecting the victims of the Rwandan genocide of 1994 and the Srebrenica massacre of 1995. On those occasions, the UNSC was unwilling to revise its mandate to the peacekeeping forces already deployed in Rwanda and actually drew down the number of contingents deployed as the killing spree intensified. Srebrenica had been identified as a safe area in the Bosnian conflict watched over by UN peacekeepers, but UN forces stood aside as thousands of Bosnians were collected and summarily murdered by Serbian forces. These incidents while horrific on any level, were especially disturbing for the UN, as the organisation had peacekeeping forces in place who failed to respond. In line with traditional UNPKO mandates, the UN forces were not mandated to protect civilians, let alone to use force in doing so. Subsequently, in adopting POC mandates, the UNSC has been reframing the nature of peacekeeping operations to give priority to human rights and human security concerns. As Ole Jacob Sending and Benjamin de Carvalho have written:

> [T]he dominant anchor for discussions of security in the contemporary era starts and ends with the rights-endowed individual, whose sanctity must be protected and upheld. The accent in international security discourse turns not so much on 'peace' or 'territory', but on the protection of rights-endowed individuals.
> (Sending and de Carvalho 2012, p. 198)

While such a position has not been wholly adopted by all UN member governments, it has served as an important influence and has been added to a mix of more traditional UN concerns over sovereignty, territorial integrity, and non-intervention.

The persistent threats to civilian populations and the humanitarian networks deployed to support them since 1999 have kept the UN seized of the issue of civilian protection. A number of additional resolutions have been adopted by the Council reaffirming the POC principle and specifying its application to particular groups, specifically humanitarian workers (UN Security Council 2003/1502; 2014/2175), health care workers (UN Security Council 2016/2286), and journalists and media personnel (UN Security Council 2006/1738; 2015/2222). A further indication of the UN's persisting interest in POC can be found in the 12 reports that the Secretary General has issued on the theme and the numerous UNSC meetings devoted to the issue. The Secretary General in regular updates to the organisation has reported on the state of POC in different conflict zones, the challenges facing peacekeeping operations in these areas, and has offered recommendations for strengthening efforts for protecting civilians and improving the work of peacekeeping operations in this area (see, for example, UN Secretary General 2015).

> For a decade, the UN Security Council has . . . expressed its resolve to support more effective missions, and to put a greater spotlight on the protection of civilians, as seen by its series of statements and resolutions, and the request that the Secretary-General issue regular reports on the protection of civilians in armed conflict.
> (Holt et al. 2009, p. 2)

In addition to this considerable body of internal examination and deliberation has been the actual peacekeeping operations. Most importantly has been the Council's tendency to include a POC mandate in peacekeeping operations. By 2016 over 90 per cent of UN peacekeepers were operating under a POC mandate. The POC norm has received a significant degree of support from the UN and from all parts of the organisation – the Secretariat, the UNSC, and the General Assembly. This institutional support has helped to legitimise and institutionalise the norm and thereby reinforce its standing in international humanitarian law. It also demonstrates a considerable level of consensus among member governments on the core principles involved. As with many other principles of international law, however, its effective application has proven to be problematic. Adopting POC mandates has not meant that member governments have been willing to expend the material resources or the political will required to ensure their effective implementation. It does, however, demonstrate a shared concern with the problem, an acceptance of the norm of civilian protection, a willingness to use the UN as an instrument for addressing the problem, and the recognition that some level of material support will be necessary to do so. An examination of efforts to apply POC through UNPKOs reveals the limits of such support and some important qualifications of the norm itself.

POC and UN peacekeeping operations

In 1999, the UNPKO for Sierra Leone (UNAMSIL) was given a mandate 'within its capabilities and areas of deployment, to afford protection to civilians under imminent threat of physical violence, taking into account the responsibilities of the Government of Sierra Leone' (UN Security Council 1999/1270). This was the first of what would be a series of similar resolutions that expanded peacekeeping operations into the area of civilian protection. Among additional peacekeeping operations that have been mandated to protect civilians are the UN Stabilization Mission in the Democratic Republic of Congo (MONUSCO), the UN Operation in Cote d'Ivoire (UNOCI), the UN Interim Force in Lebanon (UNIFIL), the UN Mission in Liberia (UNMIL), the UN Stabilisation Mission in Haiti (MINUSTAH), the UN Interim Security Force for Abyei (UNISFA), the UN Mission in the Republic of South Sudan (UNMISS), the UN Multidimensional Integrated Stabilization Mission in the Central African Republic (MINUSCA), and the UN Multidimensional Integrated Stabilization Mission in Mali (MINUSMA). The wording and specific mandates have varied somewhat from one mission to the next, but each one has tended to acknowledge similar principles such as the primary responsibility of national authorities and the need for special attention in response to the extraordinary risks confronting women and children among vulnerable populations. For example, the UNMIL mandate explicitly acknowledges the responsibility of the local government in asking UN peacekeepers in what has been a common directive, 'To protect, without prejudice to the primary responsibility of the Liberian authorities, the civilian population from threat of physical violence, within its capabilities and areas of deployment' (UN Security Council 2003/1509). Others, such as the mandate for MINUSTAH in Haiti specifies the nature of the threat in affirming peacekeepers 'to protect civilians under imminent threat of physical violence' (UN Security Council 2004/1542). The POC mandate for peacekeeping forces in Côte d'Ivoire raises one of the core conundrums that have plagued these POC mandates: that protection should be done 'without prejudice to the primary responsibility of the Ivorian authorities, within its capabilities and areas of deployment and welcomes steps taken by UNOCI to move to a more preventive and pre-emptive posture in pursuit of its priorities and in active defence of its mandate, while underlining the need to continue such an effort, without prejudice to the agreed basic principles of peacekeeping' (UN Security Council 2004/1528). The basic principles of peacekeeping, of course, refer to the cooperation of host governments and the limited use of deadly force by UN troops. Over time and depending on local conditions, mandates have provided some greater latitude for peacekeeping troops. For instance, UNMISS forces are mandated: 'To protect civilians under threat of physical violence, irrespective of the source of such violence, within its capacity and areas of deployment, with specific protection for women and children' (UN Security Council, 2014/2155). The mandate also emphasises that POC must be given priority in decisions about how peacekeeping forces are to be deployed, the implication being that even government forces might be engaged in practices that might threaten civilian populations and that peacekeepers needed to be more assertive in carrying out their mandate. How to do this while recognising the primary responsibility of the host government poses a profound dilemma.

Collectively these resolutions represent a significant shift in focus for the organisation, yet the actual wording of these mandates reflects some important compromises that have allowed the UNSC to move forward, despite some profound differences that continue to exist among member governments over the primacy of human rights and the appropriateness of intervention. One compromise has been the repeated recognition of the host government's primary responsibility for civilian protection. Such wording occurs even in circumstances where host governments have been complicit in violating international humanitarian law by threatening or harming civilians. Its inclusion, however, reflects a concern that UN forces might undermine or usurp the sovereign authority of host governments. It represents the strong support for 'traditional' peacekeeping within the organisation. While China and Russia are the permanent members of the UNSC who take this position, they are not alone among UN member governments in doing so, as the view is shared more widely by states from Latin America, the Middle East, Africa and South Asia. On a more practical level, however, the addition of such a provision also acknowledges that host government support is critical in any sustainable programme of civilian protection. UNPKOs have never been adequately supported politically or materially to offer an effective challenge to governments in power and if they are to have any lasting effect must work with, or at times where this is not possible, around them. On balance, however, by recognising the authority and primary responsibility of local governments, these UNPKOs not only keep within the boundaries of traditional UN peacekeeping that has relied on host government acquiescence in allowing UN peacekeepers into their country, but also serve to reinforce the ultimate responsibility of local governments and thus enable these governments to be held to account when abuses persist. In the end, it must be these local governments that secure the protection of civilians.

Another area of considerable importance in these mandates has been the matter of the use of force and how both the Council through its mandates and the troops on the ground have dealt with this matter. As can be seen in the above resolutions there is seldom any explicit reference to the use of force in establishing peacekeeping operations. On occasion, a resolution will call on the forces to use all necessary means to protect civilians, but more common has been the absence of any such reference. The mandates thus provide no clear direction if and when deadly force may be used. The ambiguity in some of the particulars of these mandates would seem indicative of profound differences on the issue of how civilian protection is to be operationalised and the role that force should play in this task. The result has been to leave the question open and leave field commanders in the position of having to make the call on the ground.

What then is one to make of UN efforts in this area? Do POC mandates matter? There is good evidence to indicate that the actual performance of many of these UNPKOs have been less than successful in protecting civilians. That is not to say that they have had no success nor to exaggerate the extent of the failure. Yet the operations that have mandated POC provisions have yet to offer the sustained secured environment that civilian protection requires. Fulfilling expanded mandates has been an ongoing concern for the UN since peacekeeping operations have taken on additional responsibilities beginning in the early 1990s. The Brahimi Report on UN peacekeeping released in 1999 first raised concerns about UNPKOs taking on the added responsibility of protecting civilians. As the report noted:

> The potentially large mismatch between desired objective and resources available to meet it raises the prospect of continuing disappointment with United Nations follow-through in this area. If an operation is given a mandate to protect civilians, therefore, it also must be given the specific resources needed to carry out that mandate.
>
> (United Nations 2000, pp. 62–63)

It is evident that after more than a decade of seemingly empowering resolutions by the UNSC to protect citizens, and numerous operations with sizable number of UN forces deployed into conflict settings, the organisation's ability to carry out these mandates has met with, at the very best, modest results.

While acknowledging the effectiveness of some UN operations and their ability to provide temporary and geographically limited zones of protection, the paucity of resources leaves the many UNPKOs mandated to protect civilians with no real chance of doing so to a significant and sustainable degree. The sheer complexity of the task is itself, overwhelming, but, as Alan Doss, the Secretary General's Special Representative for the Congo mission notes, even more so when resources have been so severely limited.

> How do you protect people, but at the same time, disarm and dismantle foreign and local armed groups? How do you do it in a place such as the

Kivus, help end a crisis, but at the same time, do it in a way that protects people? You know, ending the crisis is essentially a political task, protecting civilians in some ways a humanitarian task. . . . So these are complex issues, and sometimes, as I say, there are contradictory elements in our mandate, which puts a huge pressure on a mission, and frankly is leading us sometimes into rather uncharted waters.

(Sending and de Carvalho 2012, p. 201)

The list of failed opportunities to protect civilians has been outlined in some detail by many observers (Holt *et al.* 2009; Deschamps *et al.* 2015; Johnson 2015). The Secretary General has also repeatedly outlined the difficulties that specific operations have confronted in his regular reports on civilian protection, citing 17 such cases in his 2015 report. Outside observers have reached similar conclusions. 'The inclusion of POC in the mandates of peacekeeping operations has generated a range of challenges: confusion about the operational implications, coordination problems, the lack of proper training, and the mismatch between mandates and resources' (Sending and de Carvalho 2012, p. 197).

In spite of, or perhaps because of, the poor performance to date, the organisation's interest in enhancing its ability to protect civilians has been repeatedly demonstrated by the amount of interest and effort displayed in examining its own practices and refining its processes, with the intent of improving its practice and making POC implementation more effective. It may be that 'How effectively the UN responds, or is perceived to have responded, to protect civilians at risk has become a central criterion of UN legitimacy' (Shesterinina and Job 2016). It would also, however, reflect the extreme vulnerability affecting so many people and a recognition on the part of governments that some effort to protect them is essential, even though there is still a profound reluctance to sacrifice other interest in doing so. In response to this and general concerns about the organisation's performance in this area, the Secretary General also established a panel of experts to examine the UN's own experiences in implementing POC mandates (UN Security Council 2015). The High Level Independent Panel on Peacekeeping Operations (HIPPO) released its report in 2015 and concluded, among other findings that:

Significant progress has been made in promoting norms and frameworks for the protection of civilians. And yet, on the ground, the results are mixed and the gap between what is asked for and what peace operations can deliver has widened in more difficult environments.

(UN Secretary General 2015, p. 11)

Additionally, the Department of Peacekeeping Operations (DPKO) undertook its own review of policy and issued new policy guidelines for these operations. The policy recognizes the core principles of peacekeeping operations:

The continuing applicability of the principles of peacekeeping: Peacekeeping operations operate with the consent of the host state, impartiality and the use of force primarily in self-defence and as otherwise authorized by the Security Council, including for the protection of civilians.

It also accepts the need for a comprehensive approach to the problem; 'Ensuring the protection of civilians requires concerted and coordinated action between uniformed and civilian components of a mission under the mission's Protection of Civilians strategy' (UN Department of Peacekeeping Operations 2015, p. 7). It also recognises the need to work with and as part of local resilience efforts:

> Actions to protect civilians should be planned in consultation with women, men, girls and boys of the local community and with a view to empowering them and supporting the mechanisms and community-based organisations they have established to ensure their own protection.
> (UN Department of Peacekeeping Operations 2015, p. 7)

Furthermore, it noted the need to be attentive to the gendered dimensions of the threat to civilians: 'Such perspective will enable to ensure all actions are tailored to the specific needs of women, girls, boys and men, but also designed to address the disproportionate impact of conflict and post-conflict situations on girls and women' (UN Department of Peacekeeping Operations 2015, p. 8).

The guidelines identify three levels of response that POC operations can be engaged in depending on local conditions and available resources. The first level focuses on preventive measures such as dialogue and engagement with the conflicting parties, mediation and working with potential perpetrators of violence. A second level of response will most likely entail the use of more overt protection measures, including military force in aid of protection in order to prevent direct harm when civilian populations encounter more direct threats of violent harm. A third level would address the need to create or help to support the creation of a more sustainable environment to reinforce and maintain a secure environment for civilians, including such measures as security sector reforms or disarmament, demobilization and reintegration practices (Johnson 2015, p. 4).

The adoption of these policy guidelines reflects an attempt by the organisation to refine its peacekeeping practices in such a manner that enables troops in the field a better opportunity to protect civilians more effectively. It represents the delicate balance that has been used to push the practice of peacekeeping ever further into areas that protect individuals and human rights, in a manner that will be compatible with other members' concerns for retaining the core principles of traditional UN peacekeeping practices. It suggests an attempt to design a programme that will satisfy all the disparate interests that come together in the organisation.

As has been widely documented, these operations have shown only limited degrees of success in meeting the responsibilities with which they have been charged. The failure of operations during the 1990s was tied, in part, to the failure to have in place explicit mandates from which field commanders could empower their troops to threaten and ultimately use deadly force when civilians were threatened by combatants. It is evident that more explicit mandates in the area of civilian protection have raised expectations of the capacity of UN forces leading many vulnerable peoples to seek out UN troops when threatened. It is also apparent that the raised expectations have required a reconsideration of the circumstances under which UNPKO forces are allowed and required to use force, yet a degree of ambiguity continues to surround the mandates pertaining to the use of force for UN operations.

A review of UNPKOs mandated to protect civilians found that force had almost never been used by peacekeeping forces to protect civilians (UN General Assembly 2014). The issue becomes whether this is a problem with the mandates or with the troops that have been deployed. This seemingly permissive wording has been treated quite differently, and much more conservatively on the ground by UN peacekeeping forces. Although one might want to hold the troops on the ground responsible for not exercising their mandates, including the use of force to the fullest extent possible, it is important to consider the context in which these forces are required to operate.

> Whether peacekeepers use force depends largely on how their commanders interpret their mandate. There are a number of practical questions force commanders face; which civilians should be protected? What is the area of protection? What means can peacekeepers use to protect? Should they use force or other means? If they do use force, how much can they use? Protecting 'civilians under imminent threat of physical violence' is not, therefore, as clear, on an operational or tactical level, as it might initially appear in the Security Council protection mandate.
> (Nadin *et al.* 2014, p. 108)

In response to this concern the UNDPKO undertook a review of past practices and issued an updated policy for UNPKOs, including a revised set of guidelines for field operations that specifically addresses these and other issues. In their 2015 review of field operations, the DPKO provided a more definitive interpretation of how the POC mandate was to be implemented:

> [T]he protection of civilians mandate for civilian, military and police components in United Nations peacekeeping is defined as follows: *all necessary means, up to and including the use of deadly force, aimed at preventing or responding to threats of physical violence against civilians, within capabilities and areas of operations, and without prejudice to the responsibility of the host government.*
> (UN Department of Peacekeeping Operations 2015, para. 13; emphasis in original)

This is intended to provide a clearer set of guidelines, yet field conditions might continue to lean heavily against the use of force unless and until other conditions change. Foremost among these would seem to be the capabilities of the forces in place.

Recent experience demonstrates that mandates alone are not sufficient. A change in UNPKOs' mandates does not, in and of itself, empower peacekeeping operations for effectively mitigating the worst effects of violent conflict on civilian populations. Clarification of these mandates is of obvious importance, but as indicated a field commander's decision to use force will continue to be influenced by other considerations. There are any number of rather obvious reasons for this. Capabilities are clearly central in enabling any peacekeeping operation to protect civilians, as are local conditions and relations with other forces in the field, including those of the host government. As Hilde Johnson notes:

> The impact that this revised definition will have on the performance of the contingents will largely depend on capabilities and the contingents' own willingness to take risks. This is about resources: the numbers of troops compared to the challenge and capabilities, mobility in difficult terrain, and the flexibility and agility of the troops and their willingness to act more robustly.
>
> (Johnson 2012)

Without exception all UNPKOs are under-resourced for meeting their mandates. In discussing her experiences in Sudan, Johnson maintains that:

> Both prior to the crisis and during the civil war, the mismatch between UNMISS' mandate and its resources were glaring, making it close to impossible for the mission to deliver on that mandate and provide physical protection to civilians under threat.
>
> (Johnson 2012)

Numbers alone are not the only solution, but there is evidence that UNPKOs can be successful, if properly mandated and resourced (Hegre *et al.* 2015). Research indicates that the size of UN peacekeeping deployments does matter. Lisa Hultman and her colleagues have argued that the size of UN deployments does have an effect on civilian casualties and that an increased police presence of even modest proportions can also have a noticeable effect in reducing casualties (Hultman *et al.* 2013). 'Moreover, a recent OIOS report noted that some missions, namely UNAMID and UNMISS, felt "weak, outnumbered and stretched across vast areas, making the use of force only a paper option"' (Nadin *et al.* 2014, p. 113). Robust mandates are of little use for operations with a vast scope of responsibilities and little capacity to effectively control even a small part of this area. That being said, the mere presence of troops and police personnel can and does act as a deterrent mitigating violent acts against civilian populations. More of each in any conflict setting will have some benefit as it will allow these peacekeepers to cover a wider range of territory and maintain vigilance over a larger group of people or to demonstrate a larger force presence within more confined areas. Therefore the peacekeeping operation must be sufficiently resourced to be capable of acting in a more robust fashion. Capabilities are of utmost importance for any of these operations to be effective in carrying out their mandates.

The repeated concerns raised about the lack of resources for such tasks makes it clear that there is as yet no significant amount of political will on the UNSC or among member governments to provide the resources necessary for these POC mandates. This despite the fact that there are sound economic motivations for pursuing more robust UN operations. 'Considering the extreme human cost and the negative externalities caused by civilian atrocities, UN military troops and police units can be regarded as fairly economical options for the UN to enhance human security' (Hultman *et al*. 2013, p. 14). The gap between the resources that member governments are willing to provide for their own interests compared to those they are willing to provide for UN peace operations is made startling clear in comparing the US government's military commitments to Iraq in 2008 with those it provides to the UN.

Consider the spending on UN peacekeeping troops worldwide in 2008 compared to the spending on US troops in Iraq in 2008. The UN allocated $6.7 billion to peacekeeping for fiscal year 2007–2008 and deployed 91,172 personnel worldwide. The United States was responsible for 26 per cent of the UN peacekeeping budget in 2008, accounting for $1. 74 billion, or about $19,000 per blue helmet. Comparatively, the United States deployed approximately 145,100 troops to Iraq in fiscal year 2007–2008, and the Congressional Research Service estimates that the United States spent $127.2 billion on military operations in the country for a total of approximately $877,000 per troop (Hultman *et al*. 2013, p. 14).

Yet if one were to consider the economic and security benefits that could potentially be achieved through larger UN operations, member governments might come to realise the value of UN operations for their own interests. It is perhaps this very recognition that encouraged the Obama administration to bring together peacekeeping supporters in September 2015 and launch an appeal to bolster the UN's resources for peacekeeping operations. It is not difficult to identify limited resources as a problem for the UN. The more difficult task will be convincing member governments to change their policies and to increase their contributions of money and personnel so that larger deployments become possible.

Paul Williams, among others, has called attention to the gap between the efforts to protect civilians from immediate harm/violence and neglect of the structural conditions that place them at risk (Williams 2013). One recurring problem in working on capacity building and longer-term sustainability has been the problem of time-limited mandates and shifting attentions and resources as new problems arise. The political pressure to respond, however inadequately, has taken precedence over a more-focused, better-resourced, longer-term approach to the structural problems in conflicting societies that have placed civilians at risk in the first instance and will continue to render them vulnerable unless and until these structural conditions are addressed.

The paucity of resources has been matched by 'a paucity of thinking about coercive tools' (Welsh 2011, p. 161). It is abundantly clear that UN peacekeepers have been reluctant to use deadly force as a means for dealing with threats to civilians, even when such threats have been imminent. One reason may be uncertain mandates. Another reason may be asymmetrical balance of forces in any particular situation. Yet another may be an individual force commander's unwillingness to engage. Yet even if these were to be overcome, a problem with more coercive tools is that it becomes difficult to protect civilians from their adverse effects, even when these might be indirect. This problem is not limited to the situation on the ground. The many civilian casualties resulting from aerial bombing campaigns, themselves launched to protect civilians, attests to one of the problems involved in using force for the purpose of civilian protection. There is a need for instruments that are less risky for vulnerable populations, more likely to be used, and more effective in offering protection. Disarmament measures and security sector reforms are often discussed in this respect. Johnson has argued that security sector reform remains a critical yet undeveloped piece of the POC mandate as government forces in many of these post-conflict settings are untrained in international humanitarian law and have no experience with proper POC activities. Police training is helpful here because it is important to reform security forces as they can quickly become spoilers in efforts to implement POC mandates and very much complicate the peacekeepers' efforts to work effectively with the local government in carrying out their mandates. Given the continued importance of host government acceptance of UNPKOs for many Council members, more attention needs to be devoted to bringing host governments security forces into the process or, at the very least, keep them from becoming spoilers and part of the problem.

Giving attention to security sector reform may indeed be an arena in which the various interests on the UNSC may coalesce. It would appeal to those who want to see a more effective UN role in the protection of civilians. It would at the same time acknowledge the critical role of the host state in assuming responsibility for this task over the long term. Those concerned about UNPKOs usurping their mandate and undermining a host government's sovereignty should be able to align in support of a more concerted effort in the area of security sector reform. As Johnson argues:

> [G]iven the scale of the challenge, and the fact that there are limits to what UN peace operations can do, investment in security sector reform and training in POC operations in relation to uniformed forces of host governments can help make protection a reality rather than rhetoric for civilians in many countries.
>
> (Johnson 2015, p. 11)

The most viable long-term solution is one that provides for a more robust and sustainable secured environment in which these civilians might live. There have been any number of suggestions as to how peacekeepers might contribute to such an environment, but their most immediate and still most significant contribution can be in stabilising a conflict situation through their presence.

Conclusion

The inclusion of POC mandates in UNPKOs represents a significant development in the evolution of multinational peacekeeping. It also reinforces a shift in emphasis towards greater attention to issues of human rights and human security. It provides an operational focus and means for advancing an important norm and suggests a degree of commitment to respect and seemingly to enforce international humanitarian law. The most important development in this area has been the persistence of the UNSC's support for the POC as both a principle and as a practical mandated objective for UNPKOs. This suggests a significant level of consensus among members of the Council that could be cultivated. The Council is an inherently political institution in which national interests will inevitably and always hold sway. Given this reality, the extent of support for the POC norm is noteworthy and while major gaps remain between the idea and the practice, the advancement of the idea among such a disparate group of states as exists on the UNSC should not be dismissed. The failure to adequately realise POC in conflict situations, of course, remains deeply troubling. On the other hand, it might be that those member governments of the UN who wish to advance the norm and the practice need to take greater advantage of the opportunities that remain available. This means, for a start, that member governments must provide substantially more assistance to these efforts. Research has demonstrated that the presence of larger forces, either military or policing, can have an impact on mitigating violence against populations at risk, even without resorting to the use of deadly force. Greater attention to secured environments also enables humanitarian organisations better access to such populations, reducing the secondary and tertiary risks to which displaced populations fall vulnerable. More resources would also allow the UN to work more constructively with host governments, a process that should make such efforts more amenable to those members of the Security Council who are reticent to support regime change.

It would seem both important and possible to bring the different national interests on the UNSC to a shared commitment to mitigate violence against civilians provided that it can be accomplished without abandoning the triumvirate of peacekeeping principles – state consent, neutrality and limited use of force. It is evident that the UNPKOs have, at times, been able to operate with greater degrees of vigilance, force and effectiveness even while adhering to these seemingly burdensome constraints. Navigating through and around these core peacekeeping principles is the stuff of specific mandates in specific circumstances. Given the advances that have been made it would seem untimely and counter-productive to abandon the effort completely at this stage because it has not met all concerns or because it has failed in any particular conflict. The norm of civilian protection has attained a higher priority even among those member governments most inclined to resist interventions. In view of this, it would seem that paying attention to the mandates that have been established and working to ensure that they are properly resourced and effectively and ethically managed will demonstrate their value and serve as a model for their wider application in the years ahead.

References

Deschamps, M, Jallow, HB and Sooka, Y 2015, *Taking Action on Sexual Exploitation and Abuse by Peacekeepers: Report of an Independent Review on Sexual Exploitation and Abuse by International Peacekeeping Forces in the Central African Republic*. Available from: www.un.org/News/dh/infocus/centafricrepub/Independent-Review-Report.pdf. [7 December 2016].

Hegre, H, Hultman, L and Nygard, HM 2015, 'Peacekeeping Works: An Assessment of the Effectiveness of UN Peacekeeping Operations', *Conflict Trends*, I. Available from: www.prio.org/Publications/Publication/?x=7613. [7 December 2016].

Holt, VK, Taylor, G and Kelly, M 2009, *Protecting Civilians in the Context of UN Peacekeeping Operations: Successes, Set- backs and Remaining Challenges*, Independent study jointly commissioned by the UN Department of Peacekeeping Operations and the Office for the Coordination of Humanitarian Affairs, New York.

Hultman, L, Kathman, J and Shannon, M 2013, 'United Nations Peacekeeping and Civilian Protection in Civil War', *American Political Science Review*, vol. 57, no. 4, pp. 875–891.

Johnson, HF 2015, 'Capacity to Protect Civilians: Rhetoric or Reality?', Challenges Forum Policy Brief 2015:4. Available from: www.challengesforum.org/PageFiles/8235/Policy%20Brief%202015_4_WEBB.pdf. [7 December 2016].

Labonte, MT 2012, 'Whose responsibility to protect? The implications of double manifest failure for civilian protection', *The International Journal of Human Rights*, vol. 16, no. 7, pp. 982–1002.

Nadin, P, Cammaert, P and Popovski, V 2014, 'Prioritising the Protection of Civilians', *Adelphi Series*, vol. 54, no. 449, pp. 103–126.

Nambiar, V 2011, 'The Protection of Civilians and the United Nations', *Strategic Analysis*, vol. 35, no. 6, pp. 921–926.

Sending, OJ and de Carvalho, B 2012, 'Conclusion' in OJ Sending and B de Carvalho, (eds), *The Protection of Civilians in UN Peacekeeping*, pp. 197–202. Nomos, Baden-Baden.

Shesterinina, A and Job, BL 2016, 'Particularized Protection: UNSC Mandates and the Protection of Civilians in Armed Conflict', *International Peacekeeping*, vol. 23, no. 2, 240–273.

United Nations 2000, Report of the Panel on UN Peace Operations, A/55/305 – S/2000/809, New York: UN, 2000.

United Nations Department of Peacekeeping Operations/Department for Field Support 2015, *The Protection of Civilians in United Nations Peacekeeping*, DPKO/DFS Policy, 1 April.

United Nations Department of Public Information 2012, ' "Responsibility to Protect" Comes of Age, Secretary General Tells Conference, Stressing Need to Prevent Conflict Before It Breaks Out', SGSM/14068, 18 January.

UN General Assembly (2014) 'Evaluation of the Implementation and Results of Protection of Civilian Mandates in UN Peacekeeping Operations', A/68/787, 7 March.

United Nations Secretary General 2015, *Uniting our Strengths for Peace, Politics, Partnerships and People*, Report of the High-Level Independent Panel on UN Peace Operations, 16 June.

United NationsSecurity Council 2015, 'Report of the Secretary General on the protection of civilians in armed conflict', S/2015/453, 18 June.

United Nations Security Council Resolution 1999/1265, on the Protection of civilians in armed conflict, 17 September 1999. Available from: https://documents-dds-ny.un.org/doc/UNDOC/GEN/N99/267/94/PDF/N9926794.pdf?OpenElement

United Nations Security Council Resolution 1999/1270, *Sierra Leone*, 22 October 1999. Available from: www.un.org/en/ga/search/view_doc.asp?symbol=S/RES/1270(1999) [7 December 2016].

United Nations Security Council Resolution 2003/1502, on the Protection of United Nations personnel, associated personnel and humanitarian personnel in conflict zones, 26 August, 1999. Available from: http://www.un.org/en/sc/documents/resolutions/

United Nations Security Council Resolution 2003/1509, *Liberia*. Available from: www.un.org/en/ga/search/view_doc.asp?symbol=S/RES/1509(2003). [7 December 2016].

United Nations Security Council Resolution 2004/1542, *Haiti*, 1 June 2004. Available from: www.un.org/en/ga/search/view_doc.asp?symbol=S/RES/1542(2004). [7 December 2016].

United Nations Security Council Resolution 2004/1528, *Côte D'Ivoire*, 27 February 2004. Available from: www.un.org/en/ga/search/view_doc.asp?symbol=S/RES/1528(2004). [7 December 2016].

United Nations Security Council Resolution 2006/1738, on the Protection of civilians in armed conflict, 23 December. Available from: http://www.un.org/en/sc/documents/resolutions/.

United Nations Security Council Resolution, 2014/2155, Reports of the Secretary-General on the Sudan and South Sudan, 27 May 2014. Available from: www.un.org/en/ga/search/view_doc.asp?symbol=S/RES/2155(2014). [7 December 2016].

United Nations Security Council Resolution 2014/2175, on the Protection of civilians in armed conflict, 29 August, 2014. Available from: http://www.un.org/en/sc/documents/resolutions/.

United Nations Security Council Resolution 2015/2222, on the Protection of civilians in armed conflict, 27 May 2015. Available from: http://www.un.org/en/sc/documents/resolutions/.

United Nations Security Council Resolution 2016/2286 on the Protection of civilians in armed conflict, 3 May 2016. Available from: http://www.un.org/en/sc/documents/resolutions/.

Welsh, J 2011, 'Civilian Protection in Libya: Putting Coercion and Controversy Back into R2P', *Ethics and International Affairs*, vol. 25, no. 3, pp. 255–262.

Williams, PD, 2013, 'Protection, Resilience and Empowerment: United Nations Peacekeeping and Violence against Civilians in Contemporary War Zones', *Politics*, vol. 33, no. 4, pp. 287–298.

7

FROM SHOWPIECE INTERVENTIONS TO DAY-TO-DAY CIVILIAN PROTECTION

Western humanitarian intervention and UN peacekeeping

Jonathan Gilmore and David Curran

Introduction

This chapter explores two contrasting approaches to the use of military assets in protection of civilians (POC) operations. Since the 1990s, there has been a growing, though by no means evenly accepted, sense that external actors have responsibilities to protect civilians in conflict-affected societies from large-scale human rights violations. Following the difficult experiences in Somalia, Bosnia, Rwanda and Kosovo during the 1990s, the use of military intervention for POC roles has become an important feature in both UN peacekeeping and Western foreign policies. Although there are certain commonalities in the infusion of such responsibilities into the policy discourse of both prominent Western states and the UN, there are significant differences in the modes of action used to effect protection.

The chapter argues that this divergence is reflected in the emergence of 'showpiece' and 'subtle' approaches. On the one hand, Western states have opted for ostentatious and conspicuous 'showpiece' interventions that have aimed to achieve rapid civilian protection effects through the use of overwhelming force, often in the form of air power. While emphasising their humanitarian credentials, these approaches have also been characterised by risk aversion and the use of technological solutions to insulate Western citizens from harm. On the other hand, the evolution of civilian protection within UN peacekeeping has reflected a relatively steady and subtle approach, characterised by the development of increasingly sophisticated civilian protection guidance and the embedding of these responsibilities into ground-level peace operations. This is partly driven by normative concerns over the role and responsibilities of UN operations, as well as pragmatic assessments of the means available to it.

The chapter argues that this means that there is a disparity between the two civilian protection actors that are surveyed. Those Western states that undertake 'showpiece' interventions arguably do so with a very limited depth of commitment, prioritising the speed in which the intervention can take place and maintaining physical distance from the conflict environment. States may offer a great deal of rhetorical space to concepts such as the Responsibility to Protect (R2P), but there is little evidence that this is mainstreamed into actual policy. It is also seen in action, whereby states demonstrate a reliance on 'risk-transfer' warfare, using air power, and supporting local armed factions, to avoid deploying personnel in theatre. Alternatively, the United Nations, an actor that suffers from an inherent lack of rapidity in its deployment, has spent a great deal of time in creating a suite of policy responses to facilitate greater depth in its activities, through longer-term forms of deployment in closer proximity to the conflict-affected society. It has developed policy and guidance that mainstreams civilian protection and, with a large number of soldiers deployed, the UN has the potential to operationalize this. However, as shall be seen, the UN is hamstrung in its capacities to implement such policies through issues of overstretch, lack of rapidly deployable forces, and the principles that govern peacekeeping.

By exploring the contrast between short-term, conspicuous and high-intensity humanitarian interventions conducted by Western states, and subtler, less visible and potentially more legitimate approaches taken by UN peacekeepers, the chapter invites reflection on the question of 'who protects'. The first section of this chapter examines the recent approaches of Western states to armed civilian protection, those of NATO states and the US and UK in particular. The second section examines the infusion of civilian protection responsibilities into the practice of UN peacekeeping and the scope and limitations of subtler approaches.

Between doing something and nothing: Western 'showpiece' interventionism

The foreign policy of prominent Western states has become closely intertwined with the promotion of human rights and the protection of civilians during violent conflicts. The sense that military force might have a role to play in this, and that state sovereignty should not be an insurmountable obstacle to protecting human rights, was evident in elements of international responses to crises in Northern Iraq in 1991, in Somalia in 1993 and in Bosnia between 1992 and 1995. However, it was the failure of the international community to provide an adequate response to the 1994 Rwandan Genocide that catalysed much of the subsequent policy development on POC. Western states were major drivers in the emergence of the concept of humanitarian intervention during the 1990s and their advocacy has been particularly influential in supporting the growth of the R2P concept. The United States has provided considerable support for the R2P under both the Bush and Obama Administrations. The Obama Administration has been particularly supportive of POC responsibilities, with human rights a central component in what might be tentatively referred to as the Obama Doctrine (Murray 2013, p. 150). Support for the role armed intervention might play in POC operations was evident from the start of Obama's presidency, featured in his 2009 Nobel Peace Prize acceptance speech, where he argued that 'all responsible nations must embrace the role that militaries with a clear mandate can play to keep the peace' (Obama 2009). In more practical terms, the Obama Administration augmented these commitments in the Presidential Study Directive on Mass Atrocities (PSD-10) in August 2011, which explicitly affirmed the prevention of genocide and mass atrocities as 'a core national security interest and a core moral responsibility of the United States' (White House 2011).

Commitments to the practice of humanitarian intervention have also become a significant feature of British foreign policy. Such commitments to humanitarian intervention were a prominent feature of Tony Blair's (1999) 'Doctrine of the International Community' speech, which outlined the reasoning for the then recent intervention in Kosovo. More recently, that the use of military force to protect civilians, with or without Security Council authorisation, was a legitimate feature of UK foreign policy, was reasserted in the government's legal opinion on the proposed intervention in Syria in August 2013 (HM Government 2013). At the UN, Britain has also been overtly supportive of further embedding the R2P concept into the practice of international society, with former UN ambassador Mark Malloch-Brown advocating the development of an 'R2P culture', unifying approaches to the prevention of mass atrocity crimes (UN General Assembly 2009, p. 7). Explicit references to the R2P can be found in the *UK Government Strategy on the Protection of Civilians in Armed Conflict* (FCO 2010), and POC roles are emphasized in recent UK peacekeeping doctrine (MOD 2011, 4–1).

At the same time, limitations have been evident in both the US and the UK translation of POC/R2P responsibilities into practice. Ralph (2014) notes that while commitments to the R2P are a common feature of UK foreign policy discourse, they have yet to be 'mainstreamed' into the UK's conflict prevention architecture, with the risk that national interest priorities may come to obstruct timely response to mass atrocity situations. Similarly, Junk (2014) identifies a very cautious use of R2P language by US policymakers, particularly in a domestic setting, expressing support for civilian protection objectives without creating any sense of any legal obligation. Frequent rhetorical references to the R2P by US and UK policymakers are thus carefully crafted to limit the practical commitments that might flow from emergent civilian protection norms.

Given the proliferation of civilian protection language within the foreign policy of these prominent Western states, it is easy to exaggerate the extent to which these states have volunteered their armed forces for POC operations. Armed humanitarian intervention by Western states has been the exception, rather than the rule, when considering incidences of violence that might fall within the understanding of contemporary civilian protection concepts such as the R2P. However, in the cases where the desire to 'do something' in response to mass atrocity crimes has actually manifested itself in military action, the preference has been for conspicuous, 'showpiece' interventions, enacted using remote techniques that aim to insulate Westerners from the risks associated with violent conflict. Although over a decade apart from one another, the military interventions in Kosovo and Libya demonstrated such characteristics. More recently, in attempting to shape the direction of the Syrian Civil War, Western states have again married overt expressions of concern for the plight of Syrian civilians under attack by regime forces or insurgent groups (notably Islamic State), with similarly remote forms of intervention.

Remoteness in civilian protection operations has been typically associated with the use of airpower. The use of airpower enables rapid forms of response to emerging crises, with minimal exposure of Western service personnel to the ground level risks of the conflict environment. The 1999 intervention in Kosovo, though followed by a subsequent ground-level stabilisation operation (KFOR), was principally conducted using NATO air power in the short 'Operation Allied Force' campaign from 24 March to 10 June. For Roberts (1999, p. 110), the avoidance of risk to Western military personnel was central to the path of action chosen by NATO for the Kosovo intervention. The harm caused by inaccurate targeting and unexploded ordnance from the extensive use of cluster munitions during the campaign raised important questions about the utility of airpower as a means of protecting civilians. The dependence on airpower has been a similar feature of intervention in Libya and to a lesser extent in Syria. In Libya, NATO's 'Operation Unified Protector' sought to effect the protection of Libyan civilians solely through the use of airpower, with no ground-level intervention. This mode of protection was largely determined by the Security Council mandate, which explicitly forbade the deployment of ground forces, most likely in response to Russian and Chinese concerns. However, it also arguably concurred with the preferences of prominent Western states, anxious to avoid ground-level deployments in the wake of the Iraq and Afghanistan campaigns. As with 'Operation Allied Force' in Kosovo a decade earlier, NATO's air campaign relied heavily on the use of airpower and was relatively short in duration, lasting from 23 March to 24 October 2011.

Although the scope for multilateral action in Syria has been precluded by Russian and Chinese use of the veto in the Security Council, Western-led intervention, with at least a partial civilian protection focus, has been intimated at key points. At these points, the focus on airpower as the primary mode of Western response has remained evident, whether proposed interventions were realised or not. The August 2013 chemical weapon attacks on the Damascus suburb of Ghouta provided the impetus for a more assertive international response to crimes committed by Syrian government forces. However, what became apparent when US and UK policymakers began to articulate their vision of such a response was that it would involve no ground-level commitment. President Obama made repeated use of the phrase 'no boots on the ground' when discussing possible responses to the Ghouta attacks (see for example Obama 2013a; 2013b). Similarly, although the precise character of the proposed UK response was not fully clarified during the House of Commons debate on Syria on 29 August 2013, the extensive deployment of ground troops appeared not to be envisaged and the use of airpower the more likely option.[1] Given the defeat of the UK government's Parliamentary motion on Syria in August 2013, and the subsequent reluctance of the US to take action unilaterally, the Ghouta chemical attacks elicited no military intervention. However, the use of airpower to protect civilians again came into focus, following the rapid advance of Islamic State (IS) in Iraq and Syria in the summer of 2014. Although military operations against IS have commonly been framed as counter-terrorist actions, serving national security imperatives, official justifications have also emphasised the profoundly detrimental impact of IS on human rights in territories under their control.[2] Once again, with the exception of small numbers of special forces and military trainers, Western airpower deployed over Iraq and Syria has been accompanied by no significant ground-level military presence.

In the absence of ground troop deployment, Western interventions in Libya and Syria have made direct use of local forces as potential agents of civilian protection. During 'Operation Unified Protector', the Libyan National Transitional Council (NTC), an umbrella group of anti-Gaddafi factions, effectively became local allies in a POC operation. British foreign secretary William Hague (2011) referred to the NTC as the 'legitimate political interlocutors', when announcing the UK's decision 'to support and advise the NTC on how to better protect civilians'. The NTC's careful control of the rebel narrative, with their commitments to a free and democratic Libya where human rights would be respected, was also particularly effective in positioning them as a local agent of a Western liberal agenda (see NTC 2011). The complex ground-level dynamics of the Syrian Civil War have made the identification of a similar 'moderate' local proxy more difficult. However, in the absence of more substantial ground-level civilian protection operations, the Free Syrian Army have become identified as appropriate recipients of Western patronage. Although they are party to the conflict, as with the NTC in Libya, an implicit understanding of Western policymakers is that they might act as local agents of civilian protection. As David Cameron (2015, emphasis added) argued in his justification for the extension of British airstrikes to Syria:

> ISIL presents a serious military threat to the tens of thousands of moderate Syrian fighters who are opposed to both the Assad regime and to ISIL, and who are under attack from both. These groups were at the heart of the peaceful protests that sprung up in 2011, when thousands of Syrians took to the streets to demand their freedom and dignity ... Coalition military action against ISIL will help to relieve some of the pressure on these groups, *enabling them to better protect Syrian civilians* and to focus on their true objective – political transition in Syria.

As in Libya, the broader war aims of 'moderate' Syrian insurgents were framed as synonymous with the objective of protecting civilians under attack from the Assad regime and Islamic State. Western patronage of local proxies thus appears based on the assumption that certain combatant factions have the capability to be used in POC operations, in lieu of Western ground forces.

The preference for remote approaches to civilian protection seems paradoxically at odds with the recent development of more sophisticated Western military concepts for POC operations (see Giffen 2010; Sewall *et al.* 2010; PKSOI 2013). These approaches emphasise the physical protection of local populations, but also the longer-term development of a protective environment, through good governance reforms, the rule of law, and the development of a sustainable economy (PKSOI 2013, p. xi). Moreover, the emphasis in contemporary stabilisation and civilian protection concepts is on proximity to local populations, in order to better ascertain their needs and concerns, and the challenges facing the society in question (Ministry of Defence 2009, p. 79; PKSOI 2013, p. 95). Increasing the physical distance between Western military personnel and the civilians they are charged to protect largely precludes the close engagement demanded by these operational concepts.

The recent approaches of Western states to armed civilian protection therefore reflect a form of 'remote cosmopolitanism', whereby the language and focus of operations emphasises moral solidarity with distant populations, but where the military techniques adopted seek to maintain physical distance from the intended beneficiaries of the operation (Gilmore 2015, pp. 187–195). It is in this way that the 'depth' of Western commitment is deliberately limited, in favour of speed, efficiency and risk management. 'Depth' of commitment relates, in this context, both to the level of physical proximity to the POC operation that a state is willing to expose its personnel and to the longevity of its state's commitment. For Western states, the relative shallowness of their commitment to POC operations is revealed in a distinctive preference for modes of involvement where easy extrication from the conflict is assured, with a marked aversion to long-term and immersive ground-level commitments.

The adoption of remote approaches is in keeping with broader trends in Western warfare. Indeed, Western humanitarian interventions have demonstrated the characteristics of what Shaw (2005) referred to as 'risk transfer war'. This mode of warfare is characterised by the use of technological solutions to ensure that the wars can be fought at minimal risk to political elites. This involves ensuring that such wars are strictly time limited and minimise the physical risk to Western service personnel by using airpower and local proxy actors (Shaw 2005, pp. 71–97). The distancing facilitated by this approach leads to a transfer of the risks inherent in war, away from Western soldiers and onto local civilian populations. In the period since Shaw's initial formulation of 'risk transfer war', advances in technology such as unmanned aerial vehicles (drones) and the more extensive use of special forces and private military companies, has significantly enhanced the capability of Western states to wage wars by 'remote control' (see Rogers 2013). Tellingly, this trajectory has been further reflected in suggestions that unmanned technologies could be usefully employed in future POC operations (Kennedy and Rogers 2015; Whetham 2015).

The use of remote methods results in a fundamental tension between the mainstreaming of humanitarian language and expressions of cross-border moral solidarity, and military practices that accentuate distance and asymmetry in the value of human life. While Western interventions have been 'showpieces', in their conspicuous declarations of humanitarian intent, the modes of military response with which they have been associated have sought to limit Western exposure to dangerous conflict environments. The result is a form of humanitarian theatre, where the rhetorical performance of civilian protection, through the profusion of public claims and deliberation, comes to overshadow the practices through which it might be achieved. Reflecting on the UK debate over military action in Syria, Tara McCormack (2016) notes the way in which the expansion of Parliamentary oversight of the use of military force and the consequent improvements in democratic accountability, have paradoxically emerged in tandem with the more frequent resort to remote forms of war, which allow for military action with 'less skin in the game'.

The modes of military action adopted by Western states undertaking POC operations are influenced by several significant constraints. While they do not necessarily pose insurmountable obstacles to the use of national militaries for POC roles, they must be taken into account as important limitations on their potential efficacy. The concerns of Western political elites about the stability of domestic public opinion provide perhaps the most significant basis for risk-averse and remote approaches to civilian protection. For the US in the post-Vietnam period, the so-called Weinberger–Powell doctrine created an emphasis on short-duration military actions, enacted using overwhelming force to achieve a decisive outcome (see Weinberger 1984; Powell 1992). The underlying objective here was to avoid drawn out overseas military entanglements and the subsequent erosion of domestic support for the deployment. Although long-term operations in both Afghanistan and Iraq undermined the Weinberger–Powell doctrine significantly, the difficulties experienced there appear to have driven a partial return to the doctrine's premises. The drawdown of US forces in Iraq and Afghanistan, alongside greater circumspection in the use of military force, was a central feature of the Obama Administration's foreign policy (see Quinn 2011; Obama 2014). However, in line with the principles of risk-transfer war, the use of 'human and technological surrogates' – in the form of drones, special forces and local proxies – has allowed the Administration to continue overseas military operations in the face of diminished public support for large-footprint deployments (Krieg 2016, p. 99). War weariness and the erosion of support for overseas deployments are similarly evident in the UK. Analyses of public opinion have revealed significant opposition to overseas interventions in the wake of Iraq and Afghanistan, with negative perceptions of these mission's levels of success and considerable cynicism regarding their true objectives (Clements 2013; Gribble et al. 2014). The constraints of public opinion have not gone unnoticed, with UK Parliamentarians calling on the government to focus more on 'strategic communication', explaining the objectives of intervention to an often sceptical general public (H of C Defence Committee 2014, p. 45).

For both the US and the UK, this declining public enthusiasm for overseas military interventionism has been exacerbated by the 2008 economic crash and subsequent programmes of austerity economics. In material terms, this has reduced the funding available to respective national militaries and potentially weakened their capacity to respond quickly to emerging crises (see Ministry of Defence 2010; British Army 2013; US Department of Defense 2013). However, in more ideational terms, the implementation of austerity politics across Europe increases the likelihood of greater public resistance to expensive overseas operations aimed at protecting non-citizens from large-scale human rights abuse. Legitimate questions might be raised as to why costly overseas military operations should be funded, at a time when public spending is severely constricted closer to home.

When considering the role of Western states as agents of armed civilian protection, the legacy of operations in Iraq and Afghanistan are ultimately transient influences. While these might have been influential on the character of Western action in Libya and Syria, their influence is likely to decay over time as political contexts change. Indeed, the sense that the public are intrinsically casualty adverse has been challenged, with the suggestion that public perceptions of success in overseas operations are more important than casualty figures in determining the strength of popular support (Eichenberg 2005; Aldrich *et al.* 2006). In this respect the framing of POC operations and the way in which they are narrated to domestic audiences may have a very significant impact in developing a consistent support base. However, this in itself presents a significant challenge in a period of internet-enabled mass communication, where images of conflict zones are more easily accessible through citizen-journalism and where a multitude of dissenting voices can contest the power of states to define the narrative of the intervention. The implications of this are that Western states may continue to experience difficulty in mobilising support for ground-level POC operations, long after the shadow of the War on Terror has passed.

Proximity and subtlety, yet little speed? POC in UN peacekeeping

Much like the evolution of Western approaches, the development of POC activities in UN peacekeeping came primarily as a result of the organisation's catastrophic failures in Rwanda and Bosnia Herzegovina during the 1990s. As the UN found out in these theatres, the legitimacy and credibility of peacekeeping will be rendered meaningless if systematic violence against civilians occurs in the midst of a peacekeeping deployment. The UN's response to failures during this period was led by Secretary General Kofi Annan, who pushed the UN to institutionalise POC activities. The 1999 Report of the Special Committee on Peacekeeping Operations (otherwise known as the 'Brahimi Report') suggested that peacekeepers 'who witness violence against civilians should be presumed to be authorized to stop it, within their means' (United Nations 2000, p. 11). Significant developments in this area have been reflected in Security Council Resolutions, UN guidance and policy, and peacekeeper deployments.

Security Council Resolutions are the clearest way of identifying the UN's policy on POC. The Security Council has both passed a number of resolutions specifically on POC, as well as incorporating these resolutions into UN peacekeeping mandates. Since 1999, the Security Council has continually created resolutions specifically addressing civilian protection themes.[3] For instance, UN Security Council Resolution 1296 (2000), made clear the gravity placed on POC, stating that targeting of civilian populations and the 'committing of systematic, flagrant and widespread violations of international humanitarian and human rights law in situations of armed conflict' may constitute a threat to international peace and security.[4] POC was – and is – one of three 'cross-cutting resolutions'. These resolutions (the other two issue areas being Women, Peace and Security, and Children in Armed Conflict), would in the words of Victoria Holt and Tobias Berkman (2006, pp. 3–4) be an *implied* goal of a peace operation and not a driving force for intervention. Nevertheless, POC has gained significant traction in peacekeeping mandates, being invoked regularly to justify giving strong Chapter VII coercive mandates to individual operations. In 1999, only one operation specifically mentioned civilian protection;[5] now, 95 percent of deployed personnel[6] operate under mandates that contain POC responsibilities (Ladsous 2014). Institutionalising POC in such mandates can arguably give UN operations a better chance of responding to sudden and significant surges in violence against civilians. Amanda Murdie and David Davies (2010, p. 58) identify that if a peacekeeping operation includes a 'formal humanitarian purpose' that focuses 'specifically to the conditions of citizens in the conflict-prone state', the chances are that it will improve the human rights situation in the state.

Policy guidance from the Department of Peacekeeping Operations has followed the development in mandates. In 2010, the *Draft DPKO/DFS Operational Concept on the Protection of Civilians in United Nations Peacekeeping Operations* (United Nations 2010) was released. The concept outlined a systematic, three tiered approach to POC in peacekeeping operations, largely following the UN's prevention-peacekeeping-peacebuilding approach.[7] Tier 1 refers to *Protection through political process* (missions are based on political processes that should be centred around protecting civilians). Tier 2 – *Providing protection from physical violence* – 'involves protecting civilians from physical violence, which includes any of the mission's efforts to prevent, deter, and if necessary, respond to situations in which civilians are under the threat of physical violence'. This is where UN missions are authorised to use military force, if necessary, and within their means. Tier 3 focuses on the development of peacebuilding processes and 'supporting the establishment of an environment that enhances the safety and supports the rights of civilians'.

In 2015, the DPKO/DFS published *Implementing Guidelines for Military Components of United Nations Peacekeeping Missions*, a series of guidelines aimed at focussing on 'physical protection of civilians against violence in any form or manifestation by the perpetrator, including but not limited to armed groups, non-state actors and state actors (where applicable) individually or collectively at operational and tactical levels' (United Nations 2015, p. 2). The guidelines outline the DPKO's strong stance on the role of military personnel reacting to potential threats to the civilian population, with recommendations that rules of engagement (RoE) be aligned to POC objectives. Additionally, the guidelines outline 'operational accountability', where a failure to act in circumstances warranting the use of all necessary means to protect civilians (where the RoE and mandate allow for such action) 'may amount to insubordination', as 'failure to use force in accordance with a PKO's mandate may create the perception that the PKO is lacking the requisite will to perform its mandate' (United Nations 2015, p. 10). At a tactical level, the guidance outlines advice on the conduct of POC tasks, including presence and posture, reporting, adherence to RoE, early warning, and engaging communities, with the last of these outlining the wider non-enforcement mechanisms that military personnel can use (such as community liaison and communication skills). This has a resultant impact on peacekeeper training, with the inclusion of a focus on 'local cultural sensitivities, early warning indicators, gender dynamics, and referral arrangements in the specific mission area' as well as mission specific scenario-based simulation (United Nations 2011, United Nations 2015, p. 11).

Policy development is only part of the equation. Equally (if not more) importantly is that personnel are deployed in large enough numbers to operationalise such policy. Here, UN peacekeeping – with over 100,000 uniformed personnel in the field – has a notable difference to remote methods outlined above. Lisa Hultman, Jacob Kathman and Megan Shannon (2013, pp. 879–880) suggest that if adequately composed of military troops and police, peacekeeping operations 'are effective at stifling anti-civilian violence and saving innocent lives, and that the more police/troops deployed on peacekeeping operations, the higher the likelihood that violence against civilians decreases'. In practice, there have been cases where increasing the number of peacekeepers has assisted in civilian protection during peacekeeping operations. The United Nations Mission in South Sudan (UNMISS), offers an example of this. UNMISS was originally created to assist in the consolidation of peace in the country, and the strengthening of the Government of South Sudan capacity building of the country. However, increasing insecurity, driven by the break-up of the government into two opposing camps, led to outbreaks of violence in the country. Importantly, the government itself has become one of the belligerent groups (International Crisis Group 2014, pp. 6–7). This had notable impacts on the mission. The most prominent of these impacts is that over 70,000 civilians sought refuge in UN bases (UN News 2011). In turn, militia groups targeted the UN bases. This led, in December 2013, to the death of two Indian peacekeepers, who were killed while carrying out direct protection activities at a UN base in Jonglei State. The reaction by the Security Council was to reinforce the UNMISS operation with 5500 troops and 440 police (UN Deptartment of Public Information 2013). The mandate for the operation was also realigned to one that offered direct civilian protection – guarding bases where civilians are sheltering (UN Deptartment of Public Information 2014). Although there have been debates over the longer-term ability of UNMISS to continue to provide direct forms of civilian protection (particularly in the absence of a peace agreement), the UN's strengthening of the operation undoubtedly contributed to the protection of vulnerable civilians.

When compared to the approach taken by Western states to armed civilian protection operations, one of the significant benefits of UN peacekeepers is the *close proximity* in which peacekeeping troops are deployed to populations at risk of violence. While mobility difficulties are often cited as a major limitation of UN peacekeepers, particularly in large theatres of operation such as the DRC, the ground-level presence provides a means of engaging with the conflict-affected society not available through the use of airpower alone. This yields obvious benefits in understanding the local conflict dynamics and in providing a rapid response to immediate threats to civilian well-being, both of which are more in keeping with recent Western conceptual developments on POC than the remote approaches that have transpired in practice. It also provides a more coherent and transparent international presence than the external sponsorship of local armed actors, who are already parties to the conflict.

In addition to the proximity to the intended beneficiaries of intervention, it is also arguable that UN peacekeeping operations, the product of Security Council mandates and intrinsically linked to the principle of host nation consent, enjoy greater legitimacy than Western states acting as agents of civilian protection. Rather than conspicuous, showpiece interventions, peacekeepers with a POC mandate have the capacity to effect protection with greater *subtlety*, while carrying out their other mandated tasks. Civilian protection by militaries need not always involve the direct application of force. Local negotiation, a visible ground-level deterrent and the role played by ancillary peacekeeping tasks – disarmament, security sector reform and confidence building between divided communities – could provide a much less invasive mode of civilian protection than interventions led from the air. Peacekeeping provides a platform for more locally legitimate, contextually appropriate and subtle forms of protection. It is in this area where conflict resolution scholarship has sought to link the theories and practices of conflict resolution to the activity of peacekeeping operations (Woodhouse and Ramsbotham 2005).

The themes of consent and legitimacy draw out the first of several potential limitations of UN peacekeepers as agents of civilian protection. In peacekeeping, state consent has largely been an absolute requirement (United Nations 2008, pp. 31–32). This leads to two problems in operationalising POC in UN missions. First, a state that hosts a peacekeeping operation may itself be perpetrating abuse on civilians. Returning to UNMISS, the mission was originally created to assist in the consolidation of peace in the country, and the strengthening of the Government of South Sudan. However, the government itself became one of the belligerent parties to the conflict, highlighting significant limitations regarding the concept of consent and increasing the risk that the UN may become an overt participant in the conflict. Second, UN peacekeeping may be seen as a potential intervening force into a country where a state is perpetrating abuse. This was arguably the case regarding the drive to deploy the UNAMID operation in Darfur, where in De Waal's (2007, p. 1043) view the mission was burdened with the weight of 'wildly inflated' expectations of civilian protection, particularly as the host state (Sudan) was (and continues to be) reluctant to offer consent to a mission primarily designed to protect vulnerable civilians from violence. As a result of this issue of host state consent, major troop-contributing countries placed pressure for a clear distinction to be made between consent-based peacekeeping operations and interventions under the R2P, which may not require the consent of the host government (Curran 2015, p. 150). Importantly, the Secretary General argued that '[w]hile the work of peacekeepers may contribute to the achievement of RtoP goals, the two concepts of the responsibility to protect and the protection of civilians have separate and distinct prerequisites and objectives' (United Nations 2012, p. 5).

Unlike those examples of Western led intervention (outlined above), UN peacekeeping suffers from institutional limitations that hinder quick and effective deployment. This is felt in the departments of peacekeeping operations (DPKO) and field support (DFS), where the ratio of headquarters staff to field personnel is nearly 1:100. When placed in comparison to NATO, which has a ratio of 1:18, the level to which the DPKO is 'overstretched' is clear (Center on International Cooperation 2009, p. 2). Additionally, the ability of the UN to physically get 'boots on the ground' in a quick and effective manner is a significant challenge. This has been a perennial challenge to the UN throughout its history, and one that successive high level reports on peacekeeping reform have sought to amend. Yet it still persists. In his address to the UN Special Committee on Peacekeeping Operations (the C34), Head of the DPKO Herve Ladsous (2015) stated that the UN's six-month force generation process needs to be shortened dramatically, with 'specialized capabilities that are critical in the start-up phase of an operation' being prioritised. More recent studies have outlined the range of internal and external pressures influencing the UN's capacities to deploy quickly and effectively, ranging from political will, budgetary limitation, burdens to individual troop contributors, and higher risks of deployment (Langille 2014, p. 3).

Further challenges have emerged in operationalising POC mandates in theatre. This is most notable in a 2014 report of the UN's Office for Internal Oversight Services (OIOS), which sought to examine how UN peacekeepers operating under POC mandates interpreted the mandates, and importantly for this discussion, the extent to which force was used as a mechanism to protect civilians when under attack (UN General Assembly 2014). Importantly, the OIOS report highlighted a significant shortfall in peacekeepers' actions. Through examining Secretary Generals' Reports from 2010 to 2013,[8] the report found that out of the 507 incidents involving civilians reported, 'only 101, or 20 per cent, were reported to have attracted an immediate mission response'. This meant that in the other 406 cases (80 per cent), missions did not report a response to incidents where civilians were attacked (UN General Assembly 2014, pp. 7–8). It went on to state that where missions were deployed 'on site' at the time of an attack or threatened attack, force was 'almost never used'. This was partly a result of UN mandates, described in the report as sometimes being 'skimpy on the detail'. In the case of unclear mandates, contingent leaders were left to interpret mandates differently, with some contingents 'more willing to use force than others' (UN General Assembly 2014, p. 13).

Although the DPKO argued cogently that UN's POC strategies are not purely based on using force (Department of Peacekeeping Operations, 2014), high expectations are placed on missions with POC mandates, particularly if the Security Council continues to authorise missions to use force to protect civilians. As the

OIOS states, 'successes in prevention do not, in the opinion of civilians, offset failures to intervene when they are under attack' (UN General Assembly 2014, p. 7). Just as the gap between civilian protection rhetoric and action remains pertinent for Western states, a significant burden of expectation rests on UN peacekeepers to honour their mandated responsibilities, whether political, conceptual and material support is forthcoming or not.

Conclusion

When considering the implications of the approach taken by Western states to armed civilian protection operations, two important shortcomings emerge. First, they reveal a significant lack of depth of commitment to such operations. There is a distinct preference for conspicuous and high-profile forms of humanitarian intervention, but also ones that involve rapid and transient forms of action. The speed of intervention effectively becomes prioritised over the depth of intervention. The lack of depth is reflected in a preference for operations involving low proximity of Western military personnel to the conflict environment and for short-term commitment. In an era of austerity economics and in the shadow of drawn-out campaigns in Iraq and Afghanistan, the appetite of Western states for 'deeper' and more complicated, long-term ground level operations is likely to remain very limited. The problem here is that in the search for low-risk and remote forms of action, little opportunity is available to ascertain and reshape the ground level dynamics of the conflict-affected society. The use of air power has the obvious potential for causing collateral civilian harm. Similarly, the overt sponsorship of local armed factions as 'surrogates' for an international ground presence has the risk of escalating violence or supporting war aims that may not actually be compatible with the aim of civilian protection.

The increasing prominence of POC operations within UN peacekeeping presents opportunities to carry out civilian protection operations as one component of an established multidimensional operation. Embedding POC responsibilities in this way allows for subtler forms of ground-level protection that may have greater legitimacy in the eyes of both local populations and the international community than more conspicuous forms of Western intervention. Such protection mechanisms afford flexibility in response to micro-level changes in the conflict environment and present less of an affront to the tradition of state sovereignty. However, UN peacekeeping continues to suffer from extensive problems of limited rapid deployment capability, and the expectations generated by the inclusion of POC responsibilities have the potential to highlight weaknesses in the UN's capabilities or, more problematically, draw the UN further into conflicts as an active participant.

This presents challenges in operationalising international responses to situations where civilian populations are facing the threat of violence. On the one hand there are highly advanced military capacities under the control of Western member states, but they may not possess the required levels of legitimacy or the inclination to fully commit to expansive ground-level operations. On the other hand, the body with greater legitimacy – the UN – may not have the capacity to act sufficiently and rapidly when a civilian population is experiencing violence. One possible response to this would be to channel the desire of Western states to 'do something' about mass atrocity crimes into higher levels of involvement in UN peacekeeping. The increased role for Western military forces could expand the capabilities of UN peacekeepers as agents of civilian protection considerably, particularly as national militaries from Europe and North America are some of the world's most technologically advanced forces. There are some indicators that such a re-engagement with UN peacekeeping might be emerging from UK and US forces (see Prime Minister's Office 2015; Obama 2015). However, the emphasis in these renewed commitments is on backline support, training and the contribution of niche technological capabilities, rather than the more politically sensitive provision of ground-level personnel. Once again, the desire for low-risk and limited-depth commitments becomes evident. Greater Western involvement in UN peacekeeping would also not square the circle in situations where a state not hosting a UN operation targets its own civilian population. As UN peacekeeping remains a fundamentally consent-based activity, it would not matter how well equipped a peacekeeping force is: if host state consent is not forthcoming, it would be exceptionally difficult to initiate a peacekeeping mission. As UN peacekeeping missions are also reliant on a Security Council mandate, the same would apply in situations such as Syria, where fundamental disagreements exist between permanent members.

The practical implementation of POC/third pillar R2P missions remains curiously under-examined. Beyond the broader debate around whether humanitarian intervention or the R2P have become norms in international society, there is an important issue of how existing state-based military tools might actually be adapted to serve post-state civilian protection ends. Both the 'showpiece' and 'subtle' approaches discussed in this chapter reflect attempts to make existing military modes of operation fit new responsibilities. In both cases, significant limitations are apparent and the question of 'who protects' thus remains one of fundamental importance and worthy of further exploration.

Notes

1 See Hansard HC Deb 29 Aug 2013, vol. 566, cols 1425–1436.
2 Systematic sexual violence, the murder of gay people and the persecution of the Yazidi ethnic group are frequently cited here. See for example, Cameron (2015, pp. 1–10).
3 See UN Security Council Resolutions 1265 (1999), 1296 (2000), 1674 (2006), 1738 (2006),1894 (2009) on Protection of Civilians.
4 United Nations Security Council Resolution 1296 (19 April 2000).
5 The United Nations Assistance Mission in Sierra Leone (UNAMSIL). See UNSC Resolution 1270 (1999).
6 As of April 2016, the UN had 104,279 uniformed personnel deployed in the field. See www.un.org/en/peacekeeping/resources/statistics/contributors.shtml [5 July 2016].
7 Seen for instance in the UN's *Peacekeeping Principles and Guidelines* (United Nations 2008).
8 Note that the reporting period here was 2010–2013, and thus did not take into account attacks on UN bases in South Sudan.

References

Aldrich, J, Gelpi, C, Feaver, P, Riefler, J and Thompson Sharp, K 2006, 'Foreign Policy and the Electoral Connection', *Annual Review of Political Science*, vol. 9, pp. 477–502.

Blair, T 1999 'The Doctrine of the International Community', speech given at the Economic Club, Chicago, 24 April.

British Army 2013, *Transforming the British Army: An Update*, Ministry of Defence, London.

Cameron, D 2015, 'Prime Minister's Response to the Foreign Affairs Select Committee's Second Report of Session 2015–16: The Extension of Offensive British Military Operations to Syria', Memorandum to the Foreign Affairs Select Committee, House of Commons, London.

Center on International Cooperation 2009, *Peacekeeping Overstretch: Symptoms, Causes, and Consequences: Background Paper for the Thematic Series 'Building More Effective UN Peace Operations'*, CIC, New York.

Clements, B 2013, 'Public Opinion and Military Intervention: Afghanistan, Iraq and Libya', *The Political Quarterly*, vol. 84, no. 1, pp. 119–131.

Curran, D 2015, 'The European Union and Pillar Three' in D Fiott and J Koops, (eds), *The Responsibility to Protect and the Third Pillar: Legitimacy and Operationalization*, pp. 146–170. Palgrave Macmillan, Basingstoke.

Department of Peacekeeping Operations 2014, 'Annex I, Comments on the draft report received from the Department of Peacekeeping Operations and the Department of Field Support' in UN General Assembly, *Evaluation of the Implementation and Results of Protection of Civilians Mandates in United Nations Peacekeeping Operations: Report of the Office of Internal Oversight Services* (A/68/787), United Nations, New York.

De Waal, A 2007, 'Darfur and the Failure of the Responsibility to Protect', *International Affairs*, vol. 83, no. 6, pp. 1039–1054.

Eichenberg, R 2005, 'Victory Has Many Friends: US Public Opinion and the Use of Military Force, 1981–2005', *International Security*, vol. 30, no. 1, pp. 140–177.

Foreign and Commonwealth Office 2010, *UK Government Strategy on the Protection of Civilians in Armed Conflict*, FCO, London.

Giffen, A 2010, *Addressing the Doctrinal Deficit: Developing Guidance to Prevent and Respond to Widespread or Systematic Attacks Against Civilians*, The Stimson Centre, Washington DC.

Gilmore, J 2015, *The Cosmopolitan Military*, Palgrave Macmillan, Basingstoke.

Gribble, R, Wessely, S, Klein, S, Alexander, D, Dandeker, C and Fear, N 2014, 'British Public Opinion after a Decade of War: Attitudes to Iraq and Afghanistan', *Politics*, vol. 35, no. 2, pp. 128–150.

Hague, W 2011, 'Foreign Secretary Announces Assistance to the National Transitional Council in Libya, and the Expansion of the UK Diplomatic Team in Benghazi', 20 April. Available from: www.gov.uk/government/news/foreign-secretary-announces-assistance-to-the-national-transitional-council-in-libya. [16 December 2016].

Hansard (2013) HC Deb, vol. 566, cols. 1425-1436, 29 August.

HM Government 2013, 'Chemical Weapon Use by Syrian Regime: UK Government Legal Position', 29 August. Available from: www.gov.uk/government/publications/chemical-weapon-use-by-syrian-regime-uk-government-legal-position/chemical-weapon-use-by-syrian-regime-uk-government-legal-position-html-version. [16 December 2016].

Holt, V and Berkman, T 2006, *The Impossible Mandate? Military Preparedness, the Responsibility to Protect and Modern Peace Operations*, The Henry L. Stimson Center, Washington.

House of Commons Defence Committee 2014, *Intervention: Why, When and How?* TSO, London.

Hultman, L, Kathman, J and Shannon, M 2013, 'United Nations Peacekeeping and Civilian Protection in Civil War', *American Journal of Political Science*, vol. 57, no. 4, pp. 1–17.

International Crisis Group 2014, *South Sudan: A Civil War by Any Other Name, Africa Report No. 21710*, International Crisis Group, Brussels.

Junk, J 2014, 'The two-level politics of support – US foreign policy and the responsibility to protect', *Conflict, Security and Development*, vol. 14, no. 4, pp. 535–564.

Kennedy, C and Rogers, J 2015, 'Virtuous Drones?', *The International Journal of Human Rights*, vol. 19, no. 2, pp. 211–227.

Krieg, A 2016, 'Externalizing the Burden of War: The Obama Doctrine and US Foreign Policy in the Middle East', *International Affairs*, vol. 92, no. 1, pp. 97–113.

Ladsous, H 2014, 'Statement by Under-Secretary-General to the Special Committee on Peacekeeping Operations', New York, 24 February.

Ladsous, H 2015, 'Statement of Under-Secretary-General for Peacekeeping Operations, Debate of the Fourth Committee on Peacekeeping', New York, 28 October.

Langille, P 2014, *Improving United Nations Capacity for Rapid Deployment*, International Peace Institute, New York.

McCormack, T 2016, 'The Emerging Parliamentary Convention on British Military Action and Warfare by Remote Control', *RUSI Journal*, vol. 161, no. 2, pp. 22–29.

Ministry of Defence 2009, *Joint Doctrine Publication 3–40: Security and Stabilisation – The Military Contribution*, Development, Concepts and Doctrine Centre, Shrivenham.

Ministry of Defence 2010, *The Strategic Defence and Security Review*, Ministry of Defence, London.

Ministry of Defence 2011, *Joint Doctrine Note 5/11: Peacekeeping – An Evolving Role for Military Forces*, Development, Concepts and Development Centre, Shrivenham.

Murdie, A and Davis, DR 2010, 'Problematic Potential: The Human Rights Consequences of Peacekeeping Interventions in Civil Wars', *Human Rights Quarterly*, vol. 32, no. 1.

Murray, D 2013, 'Military Action but not as We Know It: Libya, Syria and the Making of an Obama Doctrine', *Contemporary Politics*, vol. 19, no. 2, pp. 146–166.

National Transitional Council 2011, 'A Vision of a Democratic Libya', 29 March. Available from: www.ntclibya.org/english/libya/. [9 May 2012].

Obama, B 2009, 'Remarks by the President at the Acceptance of the Nobel Peace Prize', Oslo City Hall, Norway, 10 December.

Obama, B 2013a, 'Statement by the President on Syria', The White House, Washington, 31 August.

Obama, B 2013b, 'Remarks by the President in Address to the Nation on Syria', The White House, Washington, 10 September.

Obama, B 2014, 'Remarks by President Obama at the United States Military Academy Commencement Ceremony', West Point, New York, 28 May.

Obama, B 2015, 'Memorandum for the Heads of Executive Departments and Agencies: United States Support to United Nations Peace Operations', The White House, Washington DC, 28 September.

Peacekeeping and Stability Operations Institute 2013, *Protection of Civilians: Military Reference Guide*, US Army War College, Carlisle, PA.

Powell, C 1992, 'US Forces: Challenges Ahead', *Foreign Affairs*, vol. 71, no. 5.

Prime Minister's Office 2015, 'Press Release: PM pledges UK troops to support stability in Somalia and South Sudan', London, 28 September.

Quinn, A 2011, 'The Art of Declining Politely: Obama's Prudent Presidency and the Waning of American Power', *International Affairs*, vol. 87, no. 4, pp. 803–824.

Ralph, J 2014, *Mainstreaming the Responsibility to Protect in UK Strategy*, UNA-UK Briefing Report No. 2, United Nations Association – UK, London.

Roberts, A 1999, 'NATO's "Humanitarian War" over Kosovo', *Survival*, vol. 41, no. 3, pp. 102–123.
Rogers, P 2013, 'Security by "Remote Control": Can it Work?', *RUSI Journal*, vol. 158, no. 3, pp. 14–20.
Sewall, S, Raymond, D and Chin, S 2010, *The MARO Handbook*, Carr Centre/US Army Peacekeeping and Stability Operations Institute.
Shaw, M 2005, *The New Western Way of War*, Polity Press, Cambridge.
United Nations 2000, *The Report of the Panel on United Nations Peace Operations*, United Nations, New York.
United Nations 2008, *United Nations Peacekeeping Operations Principles and Guidelines*, United Nations, New York.
United Nations 2010, *Draft DPKO/DFS Operational Concept on the Protection of Civilians in United Nations Peacekeeping Operations*, United Nations DPKO, New York.
United Nations 2011, *Specialized Training Materials on Protection of Civilians and Prevention and Response to Conflict-Related Sexual Violence*, United Nations, New York.
United Nations 2012, *Responsibility to Protect: Timely and Decisive Response: Report of the Secretary General*, A/66/874, United Nations, New York.
United Nations 2015, *Implementing Guidelines for Military Components of United Nations Peacekeeping Missions*, United Nations, New York.
United Nations Department of Public Information 2013, 'Unanimously Adopting Resolution 2132, Security Council Increases United Nations Mission's Military Presence In South Sudan', 24 December. Available from: www.un.org/News/Press/docs/2013/sc11230.doc.htm. [5 August 2014].
United Nations Department of Public Information 2014, 'United Nations Mission in South Sudan to suspend current activities, re-focus priorities, peacekeeping chief tells Security Council', 18 March.
United Nations General Assembly 2009, *97th Plenary Meeting of the United Nations General Assembly*, A/63/PV. 97, New York, 23 July.
United Nations General Assembly 2014, *Evaluation of the implementation and results of protection of civilians mandates in United Nations peacekeeping operations: Report of the Office of Internal Oversight Services* (A/68/787), United Nations, New York.
United Nations News Centre 2011, *Ban, Security Council welcome South Sudan ceasefire agreement*, 23 January. Available from: www.un.org/apps/news/story.asp?NewsID=46992&Cr=south+sudan&Cr1=#. U9-nRlZ59UO. [5 August 2014].
United Nations Security Council Resolution 1999/1265, New York, United Nations.
United Nations Security Council Resolution 1999/1270, New York, United Nations.
United Nations Security Council Resolution 2000/1296, New York, United Nations.
United Nations Security Council Resolution 2006/1674, New York, United Nations.
United Nations Security Council Resolution 2006/1738, New York, United Nations.
United Nations Security Council Resolution 2009/1894, New York, United Nations.
US Department of Defense 2013, *Defense Budget Priorities and Choices: Fiscal Year 2014*, Department of Defense, Washington DC.
Weinberger, C 1984, *The Uses of Military Power*, speech given to the National Press Club, Washington DC, 28 November.
Whetham, D 2015, 'Drones to Protect', *The International Journal of Human Rights*, vol. 19, no. 2, pp. 199–210.
White House 2011, 'Presidential Study Directive on Mass Atrocities/PSD 10', 4 August.
Woodhouse, T and Ramsbotham, O 2005, 'Cosmopolitan Peacekeeping and the Globalization of Security', *International Peacekeeping*, vol. 12, no. 2, pp. 139–156.

8

THE RESPONSIBILITY TO PROTECT OR THE PROTECTION OF CIVILIANS

Which policy brand is more 'successful'?

Catherine Jones

Introduction

In the current international discourse, and particularly after the authorisation of international action regarding Libya (2011) and Côte D'Ivoire (2011), the dual concepts of the Responsibility to Protect (R2P) and the Protection of Civilians (POC) have been increasingly used in tandem. While these two concepts are clearly related they are not, as seems to be commonly misunderstood, synonyms.

When both concepts become internationally prominent at the end of the 1990s it was the POC that was the clearer and more accepted international norm. Indeed the first use of R2P was in Resolution 1674 on the Protection of Civilians in Armed Conflict (UN Security Council 2006/1674). Suggesting that the POC agenda already had more traction than R2P, a point that is verified by the fact that in between the draft (November 2005) and the final version of the resolution in April 2006, the language on the inclusion of R2P was watered down – indeed it significantly shifted from a specific call for member states and the international community to act (Draft UN Security Council Res 2005, p. 4), to a recalling of the commitment made in 2005 (UN Security Council 2006/1674, paras. 4, 8).

Hence, the different origins and normative evolution of these concepts should suggest that of these two concepts POC should continue to be more internationally resonant and accepted. However, since 2005 it is R2P that has become central to discussions of humanitarian intervention, peacekeeping and protection. In a yet more mystifying dimension of the relationship between these concepts, in looking at the discussion and claimed successes of the use of R2P within the UN and the related NGOs (full discussion below), the successes of the use of POC has been consistently appropriated by advocates of R2P. In exploring this puzzle this chapter seeks to respond to two questions: why has the discourse on R2P and POC become merged in spite of their different historical and practical origins? And does it matter? In concluding, the chapter indicates the longer term implications for both R2P and POC.

At this moment then the relationship between the R2P and POC can be seen as two separate but related conceptual products. Branding as a commercial practice emerged as a tool to differentiate between competing products. This chapter makes the claim that by viewing POC and R2P as competing conceptual products, and by identifying branding as a process that is relevant in international politics, this approach may contribute to understanding and explaining this puzzle. R2P has developed or spawned three distinct advocacy non-governmental organisations (NGOs), an academic journal, traction in the international academic and western policy literature, whereas POC has been subject to fewer promotion activities. Hence, in responding to the research questions this chapter explores the significance of policy branding in relation to R2P and POC. It explores the implications that the 'brand' of R2P is stronger, and clearer, and ironically more toxic, than POC within (and outside) the UN square mile, yet, the comparatively less developed policy brand of POC is more successful – in terms of being included in resolutions and informing UN mandates. This observation creates a number of interrelated puzzles but the chief one addressed here is: why does the 'brand' of R2P continue to exist despite its negative associations?

The argument presented here is that POC and R2P occupy a competitive policy space within the UN and because of the overlap between their agendas their relationship and distinct identities have become blurred. Indeed, as a result of the brand development of R2P this blurring has been actively created. Yet, the brand of R2P – despite being a global public policy – is only widely accepted and recognised within the New York UN bubble; wherein this policy has been advocated and developed by a particular international policy elite and the politics of its global acceptance has followed. In trying to create global acceptance, branding has become a crucial element of R2P in New York. In contrast, POC brand development is in some respects much weaker, for example in terms of international recognition, but at the broader global level (within national governments) it has greater recognition. In part this seems to relate to its different route to creation, which has been the identification of a problem, political advocacy for a solution, and then the development of a policy.

The origins and evolution of the responsibility to protect and the protection of civilians

The origins of R2P are well known in the academic and policy literatures. Therefore, for the purposes of this chapter a cursory overview will suffice.[1] The concept originated with Francis Deng (1996) and was then given a practical form in the report of the International Commission on Intervention and State Sovereignty (ICISS 2001); thereafter it was transformed into an internationally acceptable formulation in the World Summit Outcome document (hereafter WSOD) (UN General Assembly 2005). It has clear historical antecedents to humanitarian intervention (HI) although it was designed to attempt to overcome the problems commonly associated with HI. Yet, despite this goal these challenges may prove to be inescapable following the practice of R2P. The key factor in this narrative is that the origins of the concept were outside the institution of the UN and did not originate with a state-based entity, but rather rested on some key individuals including Edward Luck, Ramesh Thakur and Deng.

At the moment when R2P became endorsed by states in the WSOD (UN General Assembly 2005, paras. 138–140) its scope was significantly narrowed and only sought to commit states in instances where there is evidence that four crimes (genocide, war crimes, ethnic cleansing, and crimes against humanity) will be, have been, or are being committed. It has been associated with a large smorgasbord of tools (including sanctions, peace keeping, political negotiations) and provides the United Nations Security Council (UNSC) with a significant latitude in crafting international responses (Curran *et al.* 2015). Since its acceptance in 2005, the concept has been subject to refinements, the creation of a Special Office within the UN, the creation of Special representatives of the Secretary General, and is the subject of an annual General Assembly debate as well as a UNSG report. In addition to these intra-UN developments R2P has also attracted the attention and creation of specific NGO champions dedicated to spreading the ideas of R2P and encouraging practical and academic developments of the concept.

Hence, key features of the development of R2P are that it was developed through political negotiations and processes initially outside the state-based international structures. It was an attempt to shape when, where, and with what justifications understandings of sovereignty could be mutated to allow for international actors to take responsibility and action against crimes against humanity. It also had a clear audience, which the concept needed in order to be accepted by state missions to the UN in New York. Hence, R2P had clear political champions and a clear advocacy network: it was and continues to be a policy brand.

In contrast, POC in Armed Conflict protocols have their heritage in International Law. Indeed, the importance and international obligation to protect civilians in armed conflict dates back to the Hague conventions of 1899 and 1907 as well as the 1949 Geneva conventions (Solf 1986). However, international activity around these issues was reinvigorated in 1999 when the UN Secretary General requested a report from the Office for the Coordination of Humanitarian Assistance (OCHA) and the UNSC subsequently adopted UNSC Res 1265 (1999). Within these international legal obligations the focus is on the behaviour of combatants. Their application is focused on actions within the – strictly bounded – context of armed conflict. Hence, rather than setting out the criteria for action to protect populations against the four crimes (as in R2P), POC has a more narrowly defined set of obligations – that all parties to conflict must respect and protect non-combatants, and these obligations apply to contexts including natural disasters and civil conflicts.[2]

As a result of the engagement of the international community and particularly OCHA (and more recently the International Criminal Court) the achievement of these goals has also been limited to encouraging parties to comply, providing humanitarian assistance, and seeking recourse to punish violations. The scope and agenda of POC is less overtly political than R2P. Indeed, the main focus of POC is apolitical, it is a legal instrument with clear practical applications. This is not to imply, the most political body in the world – the UNSC – is not a participant in ensuring the protection of civilians, but rather because this agenda does not seek to infringe on sovereignty or re-interpret it, there is less political controversy surrounding and hampering its application. Indeed, because of the international legal status of POC it, in part, relies on sovereign states to ensure its application.[3]

Given these two separate evolutions, why have these two agenda come to be used as synonyms? In short, the answer is clear, because of the wide ranging activities of R2P, the activities of POC can be seen as a sub-set of the same agenda. In order to demonstrate and achieve the aims of R2P it is also necessary to provide the protection of civilians within an armed conflict. So, is it important that the lines between these concepts have become blurred? The argument that this chapter presents makes it clear that the distinction between these concepts should be maintained, and in part that is because of the dangers of the political policy brand of R2P.

International politics and policy branding

The need to have an idea about a product arises because of a need to differentiate between similar products; hence, brands and branding are also inherently linked to competition – whether that is a competitive market place or a competitive policy arena. The development and deployment of a 'brand' with a good and clear reputation, identity and culture (Anholt 2013, p. 2) can assist a product or policy to gain greater traction than competitors (Wong and Merrilees 2007, p. 385). An implication of this observation is that brands may be developed in any competitive environment including within international politics.

In the past, brands have been seen as a hallmark of excellence: good brands have emerged as a result of a relationship to a quality product (Anholt 2013, p. 7). The product itself was fundamental and if the quality or currency of the product diminished so too did the brand, this can be seen to be true in the commercial as well as the policy worlds (Marsh and Fawcett 2011, p. 517). However, in some more recent literature, an argument has emerged that the best branding can overcome poor products (Aronczyk and Powers 2010, p. 6), or a lack of content within the product.

Hence, there is a growing potential for the emergence of a disconnection between the product and the brand. So, rather than seeing a brand as a hallmark of a product's quality it is perhaps more useful to adopt Peter van Ham's phrase that 'A brand is best described as a customer's idea about a product' (van Ham 2001, p. 2). Ideally, this idea will relate to images of the quality of a product, but, a successful brand is distinct from a successful product in this sense. As a result, 'Branding acquires its power because the right brand can surpass the actual product' (van Ham 2001, p. 3). This then enables the criteria of success for a brand to be distilled from the success of a product.

In addition, brands also seek to create an emotional response in the consumer (van Ham 2001, p. 2; Aronczyk 2009, p. 292; Aronczyk and Powers 2010, p. 7). The development of this emotional response is then reflected in the customers' ideas about the brand and is related to the development of 'trust' but also in an idea of the 'good' (van Ham 2001, p. 3).

Within the realm of international politics the advent of brands and processes of branding have the potential to demonstrate 'changes in the nature of the international environment' (Browning 2015, p. 196); chiefly that an aspect of neoliberal governance, that of commercialisation of politics and policies, is becoming endemic. Rather than the primacy of so-called hard power, soft power and branding are now core tools of power politics. But, unlike soft power, branding may be seen as the power of being able to 'sell' a policy, not only the development of an attractive policy. Indeed, as the context in which international politics changes so too has the nature of power (Lukes 2005). A component of this neoliberal governance is the ability to 'sell' a policy to the world, and a part of this is being able to develop a successful brand. A feature of this process is the creation of international brands (whether policy or nation) that also have the potential to (re)enforce images of what 'good citizenship' looks like (Aronczyk and Powers 2010, p. 7; Browning 2014, p. 196).

Hence, in the past two decades a number of political brands have begun to emerge; whether those brands are connected to nations, organisations, or particular policies. Despite the potential link between brands and politics the concept of international brands and branding is relatively new to the field of international politics. Indeed, to date the preponderance of the academic literature has focused on nation branding (for example, Browning 2014; Browning 2015; van Ham 2008), although there has been some useful discussion on policy branding (Fawcett and Marsh 2012), but the arena of international policy development and branding has been overlooked. More importantly for this chapter, but under acknowledged in the literature, is that a policy brand is developed around a specific policy content whereas a political brand may contain a number of separate policies. This chapter is concerned with the individual policy brands of POC and R2P.

Even more significantly for this discussion is that within evolution of this discourse the 'international' dimension refers to the audience of the brand rather than the development of the 'brand'. As a development to this literature, this chapter instead explores the idea that, because of the importance of international institutions and the creation of global policy elites, it is also important to explore the 'international' with respect to both the development and audience of a brand. This section then sets out some key elements of the branding literature and how it may be applied to the case of international policies. Crucially, it sets out criteria for understanding whether a brand can be regarded as 'successful'.

How are brands created?

Within the literature on marketing, brand development is linked to product development. Products are created and acquire a reputation and distinct identity – things that separate them from similar products – through a process of interaction between the consumer and the seller as the quality and capabilities of the product improve and the brand credibility increases. Marketing of a 'brand' is therefore the agent driven component of a process that seeks to enhance and reinforce positive acceptance. But, the creation of the brand itself is an iterative interaction between the audience and the sender.

In this process the agents of brand creation are important and they need to have a clear rationale behind their actions. Although these agents are often companies in the commercial world, in nation branding they can be governments or a subset of a government bureaucracy. In the case of the policy transfer literature (see for example, Marsh and Fawcett 2011; Fawcett and Marsh 2012) the agent was a government agency. In achieving policy transfer to other systems not only do they gain control of an international agenda they also tend to achieve domestic control of the agenda – as rival policies or competitors are marginalised and removed from the debate.

In the international policy arena the net of potential 'branders' is much wider. It can include governments seeking to demonstrate their policies' international applications, they can be consortia of like-minded states, or they can be internationally adept political or policy elites. In this sense there are overlaps with the literature on norm entrepreneurship (for example Finnemore and Sikkink 1998), wherein individuals or states can champion new norms or practices seeking to gain greater adoption to achieve a tipping point whereby the norm becomes the internationally accepted practice. In some sense this allows for a relatively small group of individuals to dominate international discourse. Branding can be used as a part of this process. In the same way as commercial branding, norm entrepreneurs seek to marginalise and remove competitors and by so doing ensure that a brand (or a norm) reaches the pinnacle of the international hierarchy.

In these interactions and the development of policies that can become brands there is also a further important dynamic identified in the literature, that is whether a political process and narrative initiates a policy (politics → policy) or whether a policy is created and is then subject to politics (policy → politics) (Marsh and Fawcett 2011, p. 524). As noted by Marsh and Fawcett the policy → politics process is becoming increasingly evident (2011, p. 525); however, it does also have implications for the legitimacy of policies and raises questions about the accountability of individuals and networks who champion them.

Who or what is the audience of an international policy brand?

A significant component of a brand is that the audience must be identified in order for the brand to be targeted. In consumer marketing the development of a brand

and associated marketing practices is usually proceeded by consumer surveys, research, and competitor analysis. Indeed the success of a brand can then be measured in relation to the market share the product has within a particular target grouping (in nation branding this has also led to a metric that enables measurement of success (Fetscherin 2010)).

Within the world of nation branding, there is also a clear sense of who is the target for the product, for example, 'Incredible India', 'Wonderful Indonesia' or 'Malaysia, truly Asia' campaigns had a clear objective of encouraging tourism particularly from Western Europe and North America. But, as van Ham suggests, it is more than just making a state an attractive holiday destination, it is concerned with a more holistic view of an experience that someone can have in a particular place (van Ham 2008, p. 127). As such, place branding is about a relationship between the brand and the consumer – it is as much about the identity or the preferred identity of the consumer and how that self-referential identity can become externally recognised by an association with a place also recognised as imbuing the same set of identities.[4] As noted by Christopher Browning, the process of branding of Scandinavian states (and Finland more specifically) as good international citizens involves both an internal (domestic) audience and an external (international) audience. As a result, the internal audience is simultaneously the target and the product of the brand, as it seeks to associate certain properties with both the place and people of those states (2014, p. 207).

The audience for nation brands is therefore a complicated mesh of domestic and international identities that are represented in different media. It seeks to set out an attainable reality for the people of the place and the people who may interact with the place.

However, within policy branding the problem of the audience may be further complicated as it is not only associated with a cacophony of different audiences (across different cultural and linguistic divides) but is also associated with, and complicated by, the aspirational aspect of the audience and the brand: the type of place 'we' want the world to be. Hence, the policy has a constitutive effect in that it needs to create its own audience – the audience may not in this sense be predetermining and demarcated but rather is created by blending a number of different attributes of elites, diplomats and states. The 'we' in this sentence is therefore the audience of the brand but it is even less defined than in the case of nation branding. This approach to international audience identification is therefore congruent with the concept of a brand as a relational platform between a consumer and seller (Aronczyk and Powers 2010, p. 7). Importantly there is also a role or relationship between the brand and the consumers wherein the consumers participate in the continued relevance of the brand (Aronczyk and Powers 2010, p. 7) by buying into the brand as related to a consumer's (self) identity; they also buy into the need for the brand to continue to be associated with the particular properties they derive from it – for example a status.

A further complicating factor is related to the ability for policy brands to transcend cultural, philosophical, linguistic and ethical divides. As commercial brands have been internationalised it has been noted that there is a potential challenge in how brands are translated or transliterated into a local language or to be appropriate to a local audience (Zhang and Schmitt 2001); a particular issue here is whether the translation is done on an approximation of the sounds of the words or the content of the product.[5] In terms of international policies the issue of translation can also be considered a broader issue because, although concepts can be accurately linguistically translated, the transference of the intellectual content is more difficult. As shall be demonstrated in the discussion below this has been a challenge for R2P and it may help to explain why the resonance of the concept has remained relatively limited to the New York square mile and the audience remains centred on English-speaking diplomats.

Nonetheless, within the literature on nation branding the audience as a co-creator of a brand is seen as being a foundation for success and this may help with issues of cultural distance. As Melissa Aronczyk identifies, the development of a diverse group of grassroots supporters helps to create a successful nation brand (2009, p. 293).

What demonstrates a brand's success?

If a brand is successful it needs to be easily recognisable and identified, without the need for continued reinforcement. Three features that are attested as important in the commercial world are directly related to the reduction of risk for the consumer. Key indicators of a successful brand are therefore, the perception of quality and credibility (seen as a display of trustworthiness and knowledge) (Erdem *et al.* 2006, p. 35). At the international level these attributes are needed to be perceived by the target audience and this often means that they need to straddle cultural and linguistic divides. In addition there needs to be some identification and recognition of a brand as being appropriate.

Adding to these three indicators for an international brand, and borrowing from the literature on international norms acceptance, there is also a need for a successful brand to be ever-present, even in the absence of continual and specific marketing practices. For example, the success of a brand needs to be disaggregated from the success of the branding processes – the logic here is simple, if a brand is recognisable because it is continuously advertised then it would indicate that the brand has little continual resonance. Therefore, in addition to the three indicators set out above we also have a measure of strength of a brand – or the embedment of a concept – that is the degree to which it is dependent on continual marketing.

From this limited discussion then emerge three core indicators of a 'brand's' success:

1 diversification of the architects of the brand;
2 circulation – the policy or the brand is used with increasing frequency – this may be through the use of consumers or branders. Related to this is the issue of space or market share – the brand or product needs to hold a dominant and/or increasing share of the 'market' within a particular designated audience;

3   familiarity – there is a need for the policy to be used consistently – implying the same approach to a concept by all the parties that use it.

The next section takes these three indicators of the success of policy brands to discuss which concept of POC or R2P is more successful.

Brand 'R2P' versus brand 'POC'

According to the data from the Global Centre for the Responsibility to Protect, R2P has 'informed' 46 resolutions since January 2006 (Global Centre 2016). To contextualise this data, during the time between the first recorded use and the most recent use of R2P, there have been 633 resolutions passed by the UNSC (as of June 2016), that equates to 7.2 per cent of all resolutions having a reference to R2P. Moreover, the creation of the special office for prevention of genocide and R2P, the annual debate in the General Assembly, all indicate the relevance of the concept and policy in this sphere. Ostensibly, then, it may be shown that R2P has become a key concept and tool within the UNSC and this may then suggest that it has been successful.

However, in looking in more detail at these resolutions, this simple 'counting' approach to the use of R2P readily becomes insufficient. Within these resolutions the language of R2P is often used in conjunction with POC and in some it is almost indistinguishable which is the guiding concept; that is, rather than using excerpts of resolutions (as in the Global Centre's useful data sheet) it is essential to read and understand the document holistically. For example, in Resolution 1975 on the Côte D'Ivoire, one of the most celebrated uses of R2P as it followed on the heels of Resolution 1973 on Libya, the terms in the resolution are closely in line with the agenda of POC rather than R2P:

> [R]eaffirming the primary responsibility of each State to protect civilians and reiterating that parties to armed conflicts bear the primary responsibility to take all feasible steps to ensure the protection of civilians and facilitate the rapid and unimpeded passage of humanitarian assistance and the safety of humanitarian personnel, recalling its resolutions 1325 (2000), 1820 (2008), 1888 (2009) and 1889 (2009) on women, peace and security, its resolution 1612 (2005) and 1882 (2009) on children and armed conflict and its resolution 1674 (2006) and 1894 (2009) on the protection of civilians in armed conflicts.
> (UN Security Council 2011/1975, p. 2, emphasis added)

As noted above, the recourse to the humanitarian aspects of protection, the context of the conflict underway and the list of resolutions that refer to the POC agenda rather than R2P, this suggests that at this time POC was the primary concept and R2P was only in the background. Indeed, of the other listed references to R2P in UNSC documents, in resolution 1674 (2006) and 1894 (2009) both explicitly refer back to the concept of R2P but this is done in the overall context of a resolution on POC.

This issue of concept confusion or conceptual overlap also emerges among the states seeking to encourage and propel R2P and its developments. For example, in the 2015 informal debate in the General Assembly, the Republic of Korea – one of the hosts of an R2P focal point in 2016 – discussed the successes of R2P and POC as if they were a part of the same concept (Ji-Ah 2015).

An issue here is clearly the overlap between the concepts and policies of R2P and POC – it is difficult to identify which of these competitive policies is more accepted in the international arena, hence the reasoning behind this chapter's approach to exploring the issues of the brands of each R2P and POC.

Are R2P and POC 'brands'?

How should we conceptually understand R2P? Is it a concept or an element of a concept? A norm? Or a collection of norms? Or possibly regime? These questions have swirled around R2P since its inception.[6] In this chapter, a different approach is considered: whether R2P and POC may more accurately be understood as international policy brands. If this is the case then it would mean that perhaps R2P and/or POC have different 'success criteria'.[7] Instead of the success of the concept being defined as only the concept being fully implemented or civilians being adequately protected from crimes and in armed conflict, interstitial success criteria might emerge and shift evaluations of success towards being whether the brand has resonance within the policy community, or whether it is subject to invocation in international fora. In this sense, failing to recognise the difference between the success of a brand rather than the success of the concept may have significant disastrous outcomes, especially if the interstitial success criteria of the brand begin to compete or overshadow the overall objective. In this chapter the focus is therefore on whether it is appropriate to consider R2P and POC as brands, and which is the more successful brand; it is hoped that this can then contribute to a more fully developed understanding of these two international entities.

Before pursuing the discussion of which brand is more successful it is necessary to consider whether it is possible to consider both concepts to be 'brands'. As noted above, brands are intended to give a product (or in this case concept) greater market traction; they operate in competitive spaces; and they seek to create an emotional connection with their target audience.

1) Diversifying the architects of the brands

In the case of R2P and POC the target audience could be assumed to be international elites, particularly those within international organisations, but it could also be presumed to be diplomats, statesmen and citizens. In essence the policies offer a destination or a teleological or normative good to be aimed for, which the endorsement and activation of a policy should seek to ensure. The audience of the brand becomes those states and elites that 'buy-in' to that final destination. They are not predetermined nor seemingly pre-targeted. As will be noted later in the case of R2P, the call to create 'R2P focal points' is a part of this brand–audience creation process.

As noted above who and how a brand is created are central to its success. In the case of POC the drive and development of the concept arose from within the politics of the UN and the bureaucracies related to international law. There was a clear 'need' identified and it was subject to international politics – within the Security Council, Department of Peacekeeping Operations (DPKO), International Criminal Court, OCHA, and other bodies to work through the politics in order to create a policy. Having done so, the policy has then been applied to a number of different settings; because of its route to development there is a notable level of comfort with which departments are responsible for each element of the policy, because the policy implementation was developed in tandem with the concept. As discussed in other chapters in this volume, the DPKO has made efforts to incorporate the mandate of the POC into each operation, it has embedded training on POC into its training programmes, and troop contributing countries have also incorporated some POC training into their own training centres operations. Hence, the idea of POC and the implementation of the policy have been clearly linked.

Adding to the problems of the architects of the brand and the policy → politics approach of the branders is the issue of the credibility of the architects and the process of the development of the relationship between the audience and sender. For example, in the 2015 General Assembly debate on R2P (September 2015) Singapore claimed:

> Cynicism over the relevance of the R2P concept is not unjustified when, time and again, national interests outweigh moral imperatives in the calculations of major powers whether to take 'timely and decisive' action. It is difficult for the normative agenda of R2P to advance when the concept is undermined through its subjective application, sometimes through the actions of its strongest proponents.
> (Tan 2015; also, participant observation Sept. 2015)

These inconsistencies in application are – to an extent – understandable because of the nature and purpose of the Security Council. However, as the branders and their credibility are undermined there is significant damage to the brand itself.

R2P started life as a policy and was championed by elites but the inclusion of discussions in developing the ICISS documents was an attempt to foster engagement from grassroots (ICISS 2001). In order to become a UN policy it was amended by the politics (in the move and the distance between the ICISS recommendations and the WSOD). In terms of the development of the product this approach has, as a result, been problematic. For example, it was only in 2009, five years after the acceptance of the concept, in a UN Secretary General's report that the issue of implementation was raised. Although, in line with the nation branding literature, there has been a significant development of civil society groups and focal points, which suggests that there have been and continue to be a number of attempts to generate a self-referential audience and advocacy network for the brand. Despite these attempts, the policy also has had difficulty in becoming embedded as a practice within the UN operations, the creation of a separate office – lauded by some as a being a hallmark of success – may indicate that R2P is lacking a natural 'home'. This is problematic for the development and refinement of the product as a policy with clear tools within the UN system but it is also problematic because of the turf wars and the silo-based operating patterns that exist within the organisation. Hence, although there have been attempts to follow the pattern of nation branding and develop the brand as an iterative interaction between audience and senders, there is a disconnection between the audience in terms of grassroots advocates (civil society groupings) and the audience in terms of the end-users (the ability to use the concept within the UN).

This brief discussion leads to an interesting mini-conclusion, that the policy of POC is more recognisable, implementable and therefore successful than R2P within the broader audience that includes states (capitals and missions), bureaucracies, and policy elites, at least in part because the brand development has been following the policy development. Whereas, the policy first approach of R2P has met with some significant problems, not least related to the credibility of the branders and the iterative interaction between the sender and the audience. More significantly, where R2P has experienced greatest resistance to acceptance, there is clearly an emerging counter narrative that POC is a separate concept with a separate – non-political – implementation strategy.

In relation to the model for assessing success this suggests that, despite the visibility of the brand of R2P, the continual contest over its implementation and therefore application undermines its claims to be a successful brand.

2) Circulation of the brand

As noted above, and at the very heart of the research puzzle in this chapter, R2P seemingly has the greater circulation. This suggests that as a 'brand' it is stronger and therefore more successful than POC. But, it is important to situate this circulation narrative within the audience of the brand.

The General Assembly (UNGA) holds an annual interactive dialogue on R2P, and this is seen as being a major achievement that underscores the acceptance and relevance of the norm. However, although the UNGA is a good place for a debate it is not the body that authorises or 'buys' the concept, rather that is the UNSC. The question then arises whether it is more appropriate for R2P to be debated in the UNGA or whether the thematic debates on the POC are more indicative of the comparative successes of the brand? As the key body for implementing both concepts or norms or brands is the UNSC then it is reasonable to suggest that it is in respect to this audience that evaluations of the circulation of the brand should be made.[8]

In looking back at the text of the UNSC Res 1674 (2006), the placement of R2P within a discussion on POC gives an indication that POC as a brand or concept is towards the pinnacle of a hierarchy. Furthermore, as has been noted in other places, the text of the language on R2P used in UNSC Res 1674 (2006) was identical to the words of the WSOD (UN General Assembly 2005). The discussion of R2P has swirled around the UNGA, been discussed in Secretary General Reports, and occasionally been included in UNSC documents; there is still a focus on discussing the concept or on discussing how to implement the concept. Hence, although there has been increased circulation of the words 'R2P' in the UN to date there remains little substantive policy development.

In looking at the direct competition between the two concepts in respect to the conflict in Syria, it is noteworthy that on issues of the protection of civilians and provision of humanitarian assistance there has been a consistently approved approach by the UNSC and the correlating UN agencies (see for example, UNSC, S/PV. 7660 2016). In contrast, attempts to achieve a resolution and action on Syria under the auspices of the R2P have been consistently rebuked (see, UNSC, S/PV. 6711 2012; also UNSC, SC10356 2012).

In looking in more detail at the usage of the terms of POC and R2P in the work of the UNSC – identified as being the key end-user audience for both brands – it becomes apparent that while POC is being increasingly used in documents and mandates to inform peacekeeping practices on the ground, R2P's usage, although it is increasing, is more superficial and inconsistent. As POC developed from within the UN bodies there have been a number of substantive developments to attempt to consistently implement and refine the UN responses on this issue. For example, in 2013 a draft operational concept was produced by the departments of Peacekeeping and Field Operations (DPKO/DFS 2013).

However, POC and R2P are not only relevant to the UNSC as an audience; both concepts need to be embedded within the lexicon and practice of the UN member states (both at mission level and in their global contributions through states' own militaries, police, and civilian experts). At present, there have been moves to embed and operationalise the concept of POC within the DPKO, NATO, the EU and the African Union (Gordon 2013). POC has also been included in the training programmes of peacekeeping training centres (see for example, Kofi Annan International Peacekeeping Training Centre 2016). Nonetheless, it should be acknowledged that within the operationalisation documents, including in the UK Ministry of Defence document (FCO 2016) POC and R2P have been linked – but this is (as noted below) a problem within the operationalisation of POC in the UN and in other states' approaches (including Australia and Canada) (Gordon 2013).

In contrast, and looking at the broader audience engagement with these two concepts the circulation narrative is partially reversed. Considering for example, the academic literature, Routledge publishers alone have 23 books with titles that contain the phrase 'The Responsibility to Protect' whereas there is only one on 'The Protection of Civilians' (for data see Routledge 2016). Oxford University press also reflects this trend in having five books with R2P in the title and only one with POC in the title (OUP 2016). This taken together with the presence of three civil society groups on R2P and a dedicated journal suggests within the civil society and academic worlds R2P is the more circulated and common concept.

3) Familiarity with the brands of R2P and POC

As previously noted, a brand may be deemed to be successful if it is able to draw 'custom' and the highest market share with their specified audience. Therefore, a crucial component of the R2P and POC story here is whether they are competing in identical, overlapping or different market spaces.

It is apparent from the 2015 informal dialogue that not only is there still considerable diversity in the levels of understanding of the concept of R2P but there is a significant disparity between the ability and process of implementation across both concepts. Moreover, in 2015 there was a significant move towards some states (notably Syria) viewing R2P as the 'politicization of the protection of civilians' (Syria 2015; also participant observation Sept 2015).

The development of the Responsibility While Protecting (RWP) (see UNGA, 2011, paras. 11(h), 11(g); Evans 2012) and Responsible Protection (RP) (Zongze 2012a; Zongze 2012b) suggest that there are also challenges to the understanding and application of the concept outside the UN in New York. The creation and championing of these concepts – although they have not stood the test of time for their application and development – suggests that the brand of R2P was in an increasingly (rather than diminishingly) contested policy space. The ability of R2P to overcome these competitors shows that it was a stronger and more viable international policy than these alternatives.

In the case of the audience of R2P, in relation to the branding literature, there is a key element in the narrative of the localisation of the brand. As noted above, there have been competitors to R2P in the form of RWP and RP; however, there has also been a lack of translation and multiple transliterations of the phrase and assessments of concept – demonstrating limited localisation of the brand outside the English-speaking world. As discussed in Jones (2015), China's approach to the concept was limited until the intervention in Libya, and before then there was very little academic discourse on the topic. The comments made by China in the supplementary materials for the ICISS did not become incorporated into the major recommendations and conclusions for the document. Indeed, as noted by Liu (2014), even after 2011 the academic and policy engagement with R2P was on a case-by-case basis rather than at a conceptual level.

These two examples, Brazil (with the Responsibility While Protecting proposal) and China (with the Responsible Protection proposal), taken together indicate that the process of localisation for the brand of R2P is at best incomplete. It exists as a clear concept in New York and in several state capitals (notably among the friends of R2P), but even among UNSC permanent members it has not developed into an accepted local brand within their states.

A further problem that arises here is the recurring issue of the relationship between these two concepts. Even within the various branches of the UN there are different approaches, for example as noted by Stuart Gordon, the DPKO use the two in tandem whereas OCHA is keen to separate the two and maintain their distinctive identities (2013). Between the different advocacy networks for R2P there are also distinctions, for example as noted above the Global Centre tends towards fusing the two concepts, whereas the Asia Pacific Centre maintains the distinctions – particularly with respect to the contexts in which they apply (Gordon 2013).

Despite this confusion between the concepts, in contrast to R2P, POC has not experienced any counter narratives, although it has been subject to contest among troop-contributing countries and differences of opinion within the UNSC in terms of how POC can be achieved within the context of Peace Operations. For example, the central issue regards the use of force to protect civilians (see, What's In Blue 2016; UNSC, SC12396 2016).

Conclusion: success of the brands?

R2P has a clear identity, and among a narrow audience it has a market but the space it operates in within the UN and in the global context is seemingly facing increased competition rather than reduced competition. At the same time, rather than reducing the risk to consumers of applying the brands, the invocation of the concept of R2P – especially since 2011 – appears to have carried a greater risk. Indeed, the discussion of the term as 'toxic' in some policy arenas is emblematic of the problems that R2P faces. This chapter sought to set out an argument as to whether we should consider R2P and POC as brands rather than concepts or norms. In doing so, it sought to acknowledge that positioning, visibility and circulation are elements in being able to see POC and R2P as brands and also measure their success as such. Within this approach the chapter has claimed that R2P is the weaker brand with respect to the audience 'buying' it – that is within the state missions of the UN. But, it is a stronger brand in terms of advocacy networks.

Why then does the brand persist? As noted earlier, a key purpose of a brand is to reduce the perceived risk of the product to the consumer. But, R2P – if this narrative of branding is compelling – actually seems to increase the risk for the consumer. So although this branding story is crucial to understanding a part of the initial puzzle it clearly is not a holistic and all-encompassing answer. One argument that could help explain this is that in different contexts R2P – however contested – opens up a policy space; and within these contested spaces it acts as a lightning rod for the issues with humanitarian intervention. By creating a forum for discussion, research and marketing around humanitarian intervention – R2P has created space for policies to be contested and engage with new narratives. By opening up this space, R2P may create audiences more willing to engage with POC because of their aversion to R2P as a discourse (in some sense POC is the more acceptable of two challenging policies). But, crucially, branding is a part of this narrative too.

Notes

1. For a fuller and more detailed exposition of the origins of R2P see for example, Evans and Sahnoun 2002; Bellamy 2009.
2. IASC definition of protection is available from OCHA (2016).
3. As noted by Paul Schroeder, state sovereignty is an essential precondition for international relations and the creation and respect for international law (Schroeder 1994, p. 6). In addition, as noted by Waldemar Solf (1986, pp. 124–125) the developments to the POC conventions were all predicated on the respect for the inviolability of states as the signatories to international treaties.
4. This approach to identities is also evident in the broader literature on identity verification whereby a self-perception is verified by other actors. See for example Stets and Harrod 2004.
5. This relates to a broader literature in applied linguistics regarding different approaches to translation. See for example Bassnett 2002, pp. 23–24. There is also an issue with translations and their applications in social science research. See for example Temple 1997.
6. Considerations of R2P as a norm, or an emerging norm have been discussed at length since 2005 (see for example Bellamy 2011, pp. 8–26; Stahn 2007) however we should consider R2P has recently been subject to new inquiry including in Orchard 2016; Job and Shesterinina 2016.
7. As noted in an International Development Simulation based on the Haitian Disaster, if different actors involved have different success criteria – even if the broad objective is the same – the pathways to being successful can lead different contributors into competing behaviours. See for example, Inside Disaster (2016), available from: http://insidedisaster.com/haiti/experience [25 August 2016].
8. There is a caveat here that it is not that other audiences are not important and their circulation of the norm are not important or are unproblematic, but rather for the brevity of this chapter the focus must be on the link between success criteria for the brand.

References

Anholt, S 2013, 'Beyond the Nation Brand: The Role of Image and Identity in International Relations', *Exchange: The Journal of Public Diplomacy*, vol. 2, no. 1, pp. 6–12.

Aronczyk, M 2009, 'Research in Brief How to Do Things with Brands: Uses of National Identity', *Canadian Journal of Communication*, vol. 34, pp. 291–296.

Aronczyk, M and Powers, D 2010, 'Blowing up the Brand' in M Aronczyk and D Powers, (eds), *Blowing up the Brand: Critical Perspectives on Promotional Culture*, 1st edn, p. 1-28. Peter Lang, New York.

Bassnett, S 2002, *Translation Studies*, 3rd edn, Routledge, New York.

Bellamy, AJ 2009, *The Responsibility to Protect: The Global Effort to End Mass Atrocities*, Polity, Cambridge.

Bellamy, AJ 2011, *Global Politics and the Responsibility to Protect: From Words to Deeds*, Routledge, Abingdon, Oxford.

Browning, C 2014, 'Nation Branding and Development: Poverty Panacea or Business as Usual', *Journal of International Relations and Development*, vol. 19, no. 1, pp. 1–26.

Browning, C 2015, 'Nation Branding, National Self-Esteem, and the Constitution of Subjectivity in Late Modernity', *Foreign Policy Analysis*, vol. 11, no. 2, pp. 195–214.

Curran, D, Fraser, T, Roeder, L, Zuber, R 2015, *Perspectives on Peacekeeping and Atrocity Crime Prevention*, Springer, New York.

Deng, FM 1996, *Sovereignty as Responsibility: Conflict Management in Africa*, R.R. Donnelley & Sons, Harrisonburg, VA.

DPKO/DFS 2013, Draft DPKO/DFS Operational Concept on the Protection of Civilians in United Nations Peacekeeping Operations. Available from: www.peacekeeping.org.uk/wp-content/uploads/2013/02/100129-DPKO-DFS-POC-Operational-Concept.pdf. [13 June 2016].

Draft UNSC Resolution 2005, 21 November. Available from: www.responsibilitytoprotect.org/index.php/about-rtop/related-themes/2966-poc-and-rtop. [7 June 2016].

Erdem, T, Swait, J and Valenzuela, A 2006, 'Brands as Signals: A Cross-Country Validation Study', *Journal of Marketing*, vol. 70, pp. 34–49.

Evans, G 2012, 'Responsibility While Protecting', *Project Syndicate*, 27 January. Available from: www.project-syndicate.org/commentary/responsibility-while-protecting#MKc0ZIeBPQ6YeY2z. 99. [15 June 2016].

Evans, G and Sahnoun, M 2002, 'The Responsibility to Protect', *Foreign Affairs*, vol. 81, no. 6, pp. 99–110.

Fawcett, P and Marsh D 2012, 'Policy Transfer and Policy Success: The case of the Gateway Review Process (2001–2010)', *Government and Opposition*, vol. 47, no. 2, pp. 162–185.

FCO 2016, UK Government Strategy on the Protection of Civilians in Armed Conflict. Available from: www.gov.uk/government/uploads/system/uploads/attachment_data/file/32950/ukstrategy-protect-cvilians-arms-conflict.pdf. [15 June 2016].

Fetscherin, M 2010, 'The Determinants and Measurement of a Country Brand: The Country Brand Strength Index', *International Marketing Review*, vol. 27, no. 4), pp. 466–479.

Finnemore, M and Sikkink, K 1998, 'International Norm Dynamics and Political Change', *International Organization*, vol. 52, no. 4, pp. 887–917.

Global Centre 2016, UN Security Council Resolutions referencing R2P. Available from: www.globalr2p.org/resources/335. [10 June 2016].

Gordon, S 2013, 'Protection of Civilians: An Evolving Paradigm?', *Stability: An International Journal of Security and Development*, vol. 2, no. 2. Available from: www.stabilityjournal.org/articles/10.5334/sta.cb/. [15 June 2016].

ICISS 2001, *The Responsibility to Protect*, International Development Research Centre, Ottawa.

Inside Disaster 2016, *Simulation: Haiti Earthquake*. Available from: http://insidedisaster.com/haiti/experience. [25 August 2016].

Ji-Ah, P 2015, 'Statement by Ambassador Paik Ji-Ah Deputy Permanent Representative of the Republic of Korea to the United Nations', 8 September. Available from: www.globalr2p.org/media/files/republic-of-korea-1.pdf. [10 June 2016].

Job, B and Shesterinina A 2016, 'The Responsibility to Protect: A Necessary Normative Reorientation', *paper presented at OCIS*, University of Queensland, 5 July.

Jones, C 2015, 'The Evolution of China's Role in Peacekeeping and Atrocity Crime Prevention' in D Curran, T Fraser, L Roeder, R Zuber, (eds), *Perspectives on Peacekeeping and Atrocity Crime Prevention*, pp. 109–128. Springer, New York.

Kofi Annan International Peacekeeping Training Centre 2016, 'Protection of Civilians in Africa Course', *KAIPTC*. Available from: www.kaiptc.org/Training/Documents/2014/02-PSO/FACTSHEET-KAIPTC-Protection-of-Civilians-in-Africa.aspx. [15 June 2016].

Liu, T 2014, 'Is China like other Permanent Members? Governmental and Academic Debates on R2P' in M Serano and T Weiss, (eds), *Rallying to the R2P cause: International Politics of Human Rights*, pp. 148–170. Routledge, London.

Lukes, S 2005, *Power: A Radical View*, Palgrave Macmillan, London.

Marsh, D and Fawcett, P 2011, 'Branding, Politics and Democracy', *Policy Studies*, vol. 32, no. 5, pp. 515–530.

OCHA 2016, 'Thematic Areas: Protection'. Available from: www.unocha.org/what-we-do/policy/thematic-areas/protection. [13 June 2016].

Orchard, P 2016, 'The Responsibility to Protect Regime: Contestation and Consolidation', *paper presented at OCIS*, University of Queensland, 5 July.

OUP 2016. Available from: https://global.oup.com/academic/?cc=gb&lang=en& [15 June 2016].

Routledge 2016. Available from: www.routledge.com/ [15 June 2016].

Schroeder, PW 1994, 'The New World Order: A Historical Perspective', *ACDIS Occasional Paper*, pp. 1–28.

Solf, WA 1986, 'Protection of Civilians against the effects of hostilities under customary international law and under protocol I', *American University International Law Review*, vol. 1, no. 1, pp. 117–135.

Stahn, C 2007, 'Responsibility to Protect: Political Rhetoric or Emerging Legal Norm?', *The American Journal of International Law*, vol. 101, no. 1, pp. 99–120.

Stets, JE and Harrod, MM 2004, 'Verification across Multiple Identities: The Role of Status', *Social Psychology Quarterly*, vol. 67, no. 2, pp. 155–171.

Syria 2015, 'Statement of the Syrian Arab Republic at the Informal Dialogue on the Responsibility to Protect', 8 September. Available from: www.globalr2p.org/media/files/syria-5.pdf. [10 June 2016].

Tan, K 2015, 'Statement by Singapore Permanent Representative Ambassador Karen Tan at the Informal Meeting of the General Assembly on the Responsibility to Protect', 8 September. Available from: www.globalr2p.org/media/files/singapore.pdf. [10 June 2016].

Temple, B 1997, 'Watch Your Tongue: Issues in Translation and Cross-Cultural Research', *Sociology*, vol. 31, no. 3, pp. 607–618.

United Nations General Assembly 2005, *World Summit Outcome Document*, GA/60/L. 1 held on 15 September 2005.

United Nations General Assembly 2011 document, A/66/551-S/2011/701, 11 November.

United Nations Security Council Resolution 1265 1999, 17 September. Available from: https://documents-dds-ny.un.org/doc/UNDOC/GEN/N99/267/94/PDF/N9926794.pdf?OpenElement. [13 June 2016].

United Nations Security Council Resolution 1674 2006, 28 April. Available from: www.responsibilitytoprotect.org/files/final%20poc%20resolution.pdf. [7 June 2016].

United Nations Security Council Resolution 1975 2011, 30 April. Available from: www.un.org/en/ga/search/view_doc.asp?symbol=S/RES/1975%282011%29. [10 June 2016].

United Nations Security Council Document, S/PV. 6711 2012, 4 February. Available from: www.un.org/en/ga/search/view_doc.asp?symbol=S/PV. 6711. [15 June 2016].

United Nations Security Council Document, S/PV. 7660 2016, 30 March. Available from: www.un.org/en/ga/search/view_doc.asp?symbol=S/PV. 7660. [15 June 2016].

United Nations Security Council Press release, SC10356 2012, 4 February. Available from: www.un.org/press/en/2012/sc10536.doc.htm. [15 June 2016].

United Nations Security Council Press release, SC12396 2016, 10 June. Available from: www.un.org/press/en/2016/sc12396.doc.htm. [15 June 2016].

van Ham, P 2001, 'The Rise of the Brand State: The Postmodern Politics of Image Reputation', *Foreign Affairs*, vol. 80, no. 5, pp. 2–6.

van Ham, P 2008, 'Place Branding: The State of the Art', *The ANNALS of the AAPSS*, vol. 616, no. 1, pp. 126–149.

What's In Blue 2016, 'Ministerial-level Meeting on the Protection of Civilians in the Context of Peace Operations', *What's In Blue*, 9 June. Available from: www.whatsinblue.org/2016/06/ministerial-level-debate-on-the-protection-of-civilians-in-the-context-of-peacekeeping-operations.php. [15 June 2016].

Wong, HY and Merrilees, B 2007, 'Multiple Roles for Branding in International Marketing', *International Marketing Review*, vol. 24, no. 4, pp. 384–408.

Zhang, S and Schmitt, BH 2001, 'Creating Local Brands in Multilingual International Markets', *Journal of Marketing Research*, vol. 38, no. 3, pp. 313–325.

Zongze, R 2012a, 'Responsible Protection', *China Daily*, 15 March. Available from: www.chinadaily.com.cn/cndy/2012-03/15/content_14837835.htm. [15 June 2016].

Zongze, R 2012b, 'Responsible Protection: Building a Safer World', *CIIS*, 15 June. Available from: www.ciis.org.cn/english/2012-06/15/content_5090912.htm. [15 June 2016].

PART III
The responsibility to protect and beyond

9
NORM COMPLEXITY AND CONTESTATION
Unpacking the R2P

Alan Bloomfield

Introduction

Given that debating the Responsibility to Protect (R2P) norm has become a veritable academic cottage industry, a flurry of articles, journal special editions and books appeared in 2015 and 2016 to mark the tenth anniversary of R2P being endorsed at the 2005 World Summit. A range of views were offered concerning whether R2P had become a 'mature', 'established', or *entrenched* norm: Alex Bellamy argued that it had (2015, p. 161) while Edward Newman was more sceptical (2016, p. 34). It is not easy to decide which side to favour in this debate. The dilemma is neatly captured in a recent article by Gerrit Kurtz and Philipp Rotmann; they argued on the one hand that efforts to promote R2P had contributed to creating the situation whereby:

> Compared to the 1990s . . . there is a much greater and more widespread readiness today to politically support actions that are deemed necessary to protect populations from mass atrocities, and even to make active contributions in that direction if compatible with other strategic interests.
> (Kurtz and Rotmann 2016, p. 6)

But on the other hand, they asserted that 'R2P did not become an effective means of mobilising political will or effective action' (2016, p. 6). This chapter builds on this theme by exploring exactly what R2P is intended to achieve in a 'motivational' sense. It does so by unpacking R2P to examine its components and the relationships between them, but the analysis goes further than the traditional three-pillar formulation to identify *five intended constitutive effects*.

The purpose is to demonstrate how R2P's components are intended to constitute actors and thereby bolster and reinforce one another; in other words,

R2P's framers wanted to ensure that the norm became incorporated into all, or at least most, states' identities on the basis that if such occurred it would affect how they formulated their interests and therefore also affect their behaviour. The five effects are called 'intended' because the position advanced here is that they have not yet achieved their purpose, being to reliably and consistently affect international actors' – mainly states' – behaviour.

Thus while I accept that promoting R2P has contributed to the steady advance of the broader anti-atrocity agenda, I argue the R2P norm itself will only have a limited effect on states' behaviour until the notion of conditional sovereignty is more firmly entrenched, because until this occurs the cost of non-compliance will be insufficient to induce the sort of widespread compliance that R2P's advocates seek and that may be necessary to sustain R2P itself against the powerful 'abuse' critique. And this is unlikely to happen unless more states become self-motivated to punish behaviour that deviates from the undertakings made at the 2005 World Summit. Until then R2P will likely remain a well-meaning but only weakly and indirectly effective statement of intent.

The overarching theme of this volume, as discussed in the Introduction, is that contemporary events – global economic crisis, the rise of powerful authoritarian regimes, instability in the Middle East, etc. – have 'dampened, if not quenched, the optimism that characterised post-Cold War liberal internationalism'. This chapter mainly focuses on the problems the R2P agenda is currently facing in the wake of stiffening resistance to the norm prompted by the conduct and outcome of the Libyan intervention in 2011, which has become most starkly illustrated in the ongoing crisis in Syria.[1] But as a consequence of recent events some have offered advice on how to reinvigorate R2P. For example, Justin Morris recently called for removal of the most coercive Pillar III elements to 'inoculate' the other components of R2P from 'normative contamination' (2016, p. 209; see also Graubart 2015; Hobson 2016). The chapter therefore concludes with a brief discussion of what might be done to breathe new life into the R2P agenda on the assumption that doing so constitutes just one element, but an important one, of the wider effort to construct a more entrenched and effective liberal world order.

Judging R2P's progress: what norms (are supposed to) do

Before R2P can be unpacked we need to consider how one might go about assessing whether a norm is entrenched or not and also explain contemporary understandings of how norms affect actors.

Scholars seem to be coalescing around two positions regarding how to assess whether R2P is entrenched. What might usefully be thought of as the 'forgiving standard' claims that a norm is entrenched when it affects debates about behavioural responses. For example, after claiming R2P had become 'established' Bellamy said 'as Jennifer Welsh argues, [R2P] is primarily a responsibility to *consider* taking actions to protect . . . a "responsibility to try", as Edward Luck puts it' (emphasis in original, 2015, p. 171; see also Dunne and Gelber 2014). Critical scholars have enunciated this position more clearly: Sassan Gholiagha claims R2P 'opens discursive spaces in which a politics of protection becomes possible, even though not always enacted' (2015, p. 1087); while Papamichail and Partis-Jennings say R2P provides 'a domain for deliberation and discursive action' (2016, p. 85).

No doubt R2P sometimes operates in this way. But this does not necessarily mean it is entrenched. Newman, for example, prefers a more 'demanding standard':

> The declaratory proscription of [mass atrocity crimes] ... and agreement that the UN Security Council may respond to such ... has effectively universal support.... [T]herefore, this may be seen as a norm, even if the operationalisation of the principle is uneven and contested. A different, and more demanding, definition of a norm places more emphasis on the practice of states in upholding and implementing principles and commitments.... For [R2P] to be [judged] ... meaningful ... it would need to reflect a shared understanding among states about appropriate behaviour *and* a demonstrable commitment to act collectively to prevent or address proscribed activities.
>
> (2016, p. 34, emphasis in original)

This chapter applies the more demanding standard and so takes the position that we should not consider a norm entrenched until the behaviour required by it has become essentially 'normal' (Hurrell 2002, p. 143). This is not to suggest that there cannot be any deviation from the norm's proscriptions and/or prescriptions; Friedwich Kratochwil and John Gerard Ruggie argued decades ago that 'no single [violation] refutes a norm. Not even many such occurrences necessarily do' (1986, p. 767). Diana Panke and Ulrich Petersohn have argued more recently that an entrenched norm only 'dies' (or is replaced) after a 'violation cascade' occurs; in other words, violation becomes common and is not ordinarily punished (2011, pp. 721–726). Inverting this logic suggests new norms can be considered entrenched when they are generally complied with and when violations ordinarily attract punishments of some sort.

Newman (2016), Kurtz and Rotmann (2016) and Stephen Hopgood (2014) have all observed that compliance with the Pillar III obligation for the international community to assume responsibility for protection when individual states fail to do so is not yet normal. This chapter is not the place to exhaustively tally up all the 'successful applications of the Pillar III responsibility to assume protection' against the 'non-applications of Pillar III in ostensibly relevant circumstances', but it seems reasonable to observe that there have been more of the latter than of the former, suggesting compliance with Pillar III is not yet normal. Instead, this chapter focuses more on *punishments* because unless deviance can be punished the prospects of R2P becoming 'fully' entrenched arguably remain poor. So, what sort of punishments should we regard as sufficient? Bellamy claimed R2P is entrenched because most actors accept that non-compliance 'should attract criticism' (2015, p. 163). And Hopgood, who is unconvinced Pillar III-type measures are normally applied, readily concedes that it is 'harder than it was to publicly murder your own citizens with impunity . . . [doing so] generate[s] increasing amounts of adverse publicity and political pressure' (2014, p. 183). It is therefore uncontroversial to accept that 'naming and shaming' violators *might* be effective. Thomas Risse and Kathryn Sikkink's 'spiral model' of human rights norm diffusion, for example, theorised how international criticism might cause oppressive regimes to shift from normative resistance (i.e. claiming 'the right' to 'restore order' by abusing human rights) to factual denials of oppression, which might cause them to 'become "entrapped" in their own rhetoric', which might lead to 'norm compliance becom[ing] habitual' (1999, pp. 23–33). Yet they also admitted such pressure *might not work* (i.e. they cited the Tiananmen Square incident, p. 25).

Thus more stringent punishments than social disapproval alone would seem necessary to convince the more recalcitrant actors to comply. Martha Finnemore and Kathryn Sikkink's classic norm dynamics model recognised this; they argued that while norm entrepreneurs try to diffuse new norms by striving to ensure elites in particular become constituted by it, those entrepreneurs also typically strive to ensure the norm 'becomes institutionalized in . . . international rules and organisations . . . clarifying what, exactly, the norm is and what constitutes violations . . . and spelling out specific procedures . . . [for] disapproval and sanctions for norm breaking' (1998, p. 900). Jutta Brunnée and Stephen J. Toope have also argued – with explicit reference to R2P – that while 'enforcement is not the *sine qua non*' of a norm's effectiveness, 'when posited rules are consistently evaded or undermined without legal consequence, the rules themselves are compromised because the community of practice recognizes that the declared rule is hypocritical, or that power is being abused without response' (2010a, p. 193).[2]

These observations suggest that punishments would have to be reasonably 'costly', like sanctions of various kinds and even the application of military force. But before we explore how R2P's components might work together to exert these sorts of pressures we need to consider how norms are assumed to affect actors' behaviour.

Following Anthony Giddens (1984), 1990s-era constructivists accepted that norms 'emerge from the actions and beliefs of actors . . . and in turn norms shaped those actions and beliefs by constituting actors' identities and interests', and these scholars showed that norms have testable effects on states' behaviour (Hoffman 2010, pp. 1–3). The general argument is that by constituting actors an entrenched norm creates 'felt effects'; actors 'feel' it is legitimate, and therefore 'right' to comply with it (Finnemore and Toope 2001, p. 749). Norms therefore produce *proscriptive* and *prescriptive* effects. Proscriptive effects are simple – certain actions are prohibited – but prescriptive effects vary somewhat; some are *permissive*, they 'enable' or 'make possible' actions but do not demand them – some discretion remains – while *directive* norms 'require' particular actions. Thus norms' effects can be usefully plotted along a simple spectrum, with proscriptive and directive effects as book-ends and permissive norms in between (Glanville 2006, p. 155;[3] Sandholtz 2016, p. 11). Further, a norm may actually contain several (intended) effects. R2P is exemplary;

its components are intended to have various different, but connected effects. The discussion below also distinguishes between the *targets* of these effects according to a simple dichotomy, namely, some effects target individual actors while others target collections of actors.

Finally, this analysis proceeds on the basis that R2P does not, as a whole, create *legal* obligations. Not everyone agrees: Anne Orford has argued that R2P is part of customary international law even though it 'is not a form of law that imposes duties'; instead, it 'confers powers . . . [and] allocates jurisdiction' (2011, p. 25). But Brunnée and Toope found R2P 'falls short on several of the legality criteria' (2010a, p. 192). Luke Glanville's work on this matter is instructive. He found that states' Pillar 1 undertaking – to protect populations within their borders – was firmly embedded in international law independently of the 2005 World Summit Outcome Document (WSOD), meaning it can be considered a duty or legal obligation (2012, p. 3). But Glanville also found that the WSOD and the other 'sources' of R2P – such as the 2001 International Commission on Intervention and State Sovereignty (ICISS) report, the 2009 UN Secretary-General's report, etc. – are not ordinary or 'classic' sources of international law (2012, p. 14). Accordingly, the Pillar II undertaking to assist should not be considered a duty (Glanville 2012, p. 25). And regarding Pillar III's undertaking that the international community should assume the responsibility to protect when a state breaches this duty, only a single International Court of Justice ruling suggested states (i.e. effectively the international community's agents: see below) *must* act to prevent genocide (Glanville 2012, pp. 15–18), while the basis of the proposition that states must prevent the other three mass atrocity crimes was even weaker (Glanville 2012, p. 26). Further, failure to comply with the undertakings made in 2005 to act cannot be punished (Glanville 2012, p. 28), which leaves R2P somewhat lopsided; the Pillar I prohibition is legally binding, but states are not required to punish breaches (or offer Pillar II assistance to states that struggle to comply with Pillar I). Of course, this not just a problem in the R2P context; the enforcement problem applies to international law more generally.

Accordingly, Aidan Hehir is right to say that 'R2P does not constitute international law but is, rather, a political norm' (2011, p. 1338). This does not rule out the *possibility* of enforcement; indeed, R2P is *intended* to ensure that states that breach Pillar I (and an under-appreciated part of Pillar II) can be punished. But it does mean that for R2P to work as intended the actors who mete out these punishments will have to be motivated by political (and moral) concerns, not a sense of legal obligation (i.e. which would imply they were, at least in part, concerned about being punished for failing to act).

R2P's components and the connections between them

Since the UN Secretary General's 2009 report it has become conventional to talk of R2P's 'Three Pillars' (UN Secretariat), but I want to unpack it further, into five intended constitutive effects (ICEs). These are:

- ICE 1: states must not commit mass atrocities against populations within their borders.
- ICE 2: ICE 1-compliant states should *offer* assistance to other states who are struggling to fulfil ICE 1.
- ICE 3: states who are struggling to fulfil ICE 1 should *accept* assistance from ICE 1-compliant states.
- ICE 4: the international community should *incentivise* states to comply with ICEs 1, 2 and 3.
- ICE 5: ICE 1-compliant states should *support* the international communities' efforts under ICE 4.

To explain further, and to put this discussion in terms of the well-recognised three-pillars formulation, ICE 1 is essentially commensurate with Pillar I; it is intended to prohibit mass atrocities by motivating states to not commit such. Pillar II, however, has two ICEs; first, it is intended to induce the international community to *offer* assistance (ICE 2) to non-ICE1/Pillar I-compliant states and, importantly, it has been largely overlooked that Pillar II is also intended to induce target states to *accept* assistance (ICE 3).

I treat the first of the two ICEs in Pillar III – ICE 4 – as the 'glue' that is supposed to hold R2P together. It is intended to motivate the international community to incentivise compliance with ICEs 1, 2 and 3; specifically, the international community should *pressure* states to comply with ICEs 1 and 3 – which if successful should create both immediate remedial and future deterrent effects – and to also *reassure* actors that offers of assistance motivated by ICE 2 will not be squandered or refused. Finally, and because ICEs 2 and 4 are bedevilled by assignment and free-rider problems, Pillar III is also intended to motivate discrete actors to support the international community's collective assistance (ICE 2) and 'incentivising' (ICE 4) efforts. I treat this last intended effect – ICE 5 – as the single-most-important component of R2P. But I must deal with each in turn and consider the connections between them to illustrate why.

ICE 1: Prohibiting mass atrocities

ICE 1 – effectively Pillar I – is primarily intended to create a *self-proscriptive effect* operating on individual states. This effect is stated very definitively in paragraph 138 of the 2005 WSOD: 'Each individual State has the responsibility to protect its populations from genocide, war crimes, ethnic cleansing and crimes against humanity.' Ideally, every state would become constituted by this normative demand: it would become part of their identity and they would formulate their interests accordingly, meaning all states would 'see themselves' as 'human rights respecters' and consider committing mass atrocities 'unthinkable'.

While the main intended effect is obviously proscriptive – to prohibit actions – there is a logical flip-side in that ICE 1 implies states should take certain actions by, for example, establishing security services to maintain order and oversight bodies to ensure these services respect human rights. We can assume states have some means of keeping order because being a state implies some measure of 'positive' sovereignty (Jackson 1993, pp. 50–53). But without adequate oversight security services might threaten the population; thus states must create oversight bodies, possibly with international assistance. Nevertheless, the key intended effect of ICE 1 is to create a *universal* proscriptive felt effect. And if every state 'felt this way' the other pillars would be unnecessary. But R2P's framers recognised the expectation this would occur naturally was naïve, so they included the other pillars.

ICE 2: Offering assistance

We therefore come to the first of the two ICEs created by Pillar II. ICE 2 is already a well-recognised aspect of R2P. It arises from these words in paragraph 139 of the WSOD: 'We also intend to commit ourselves, as necessary and appropriate, to helping States build capacity to protect their populations . . . and to assisting those which are under stress before crises and conflicts break out.'

'Assistance' is now understood to range from transfers of financial resources and governance expertise to military assistance, including engaging in combat. But the target state must *consent*. Regarding the precise intended effect of ICE 2, two things should be noted. First, earlier in paragraph 139 the phrase 'international community' was used to describe what are now treated as Pillar III commitments, so the word 'also' suggests that the international community also assumes the responsibility to provide assistance; thus it seems ICE 2 creates a *collective-directive effect*. But, and second, the precise wording indicates that states only 'intend to commit' themselves, suggesting ICE 2 is not as directive as ICE 1 is prohibitive – some element of discretion remains – meaning ICE 2 actually creates a collective-*permissive* effect.

Together, therefore, these observations leave us with an assignation problem because it is unclear exactly what the 'international community' is. Toni Erskine has called the international community 'mythical' (2014, p. 139) and claimed that it is not a collective actor of the sort that can assume responsibilities (2014, p. 116). This implies strongly that the responsibility to offer assistance must be assigned to other more discrete actors, and because ICE 2 is permissive, a free-rider problem can also arise; some actors may fail to follow through on the undertaking they made in 2005, expecting others will provide the collective good (i.e. assistance that facilitates atrocity-prevention). But because the same problem arises vis-à-vis the burden of applying non-consensual pressure (i.e. ICE 4) this matter is explored more comprehensively later.

ICE 3: Accepting assistance

Somewhat strangely, nowhere in the voluminous R2P literature is it explicitly acknowledged that assistance must not only be offered, it must also be *accepted*. There are no words in the WSOD that indicate that states *must* accept assistance, but doing so would seem to be a logical corollary of ICE 1/Pillar I. It therefore seems perverse to conclude that ICE 3 creates a *self-permissive* effect; instead, it must create a *self-directive effect* on states, namely, to accept assistance to discharge the responsibility to protect populations within their borders.

Assistance is usually provided *conditionally*, on the expectation that sensitive coercive institutions such as security services and judiciaries (etc.) will be reformed.[4] Indeed, often states fail to protect because these very institutions threaten populations within their borders; they are the means by which those states enforce their rule, implying they are organised according to and staffed by persons who are constituted by normative understandings that prioritise *protection of the regime* above protecting the population. We cannot therefore assume that all states will accept assistance. Indeed, those states that threaten their own people most gravely and so are in most need of reform are presumably the most likely to reject assistance. North Korea is an extreme case, but it illustrates that sometimes very substantial changes in a state's identity would be required before it accepted assistance to radically reform the very mechanisms that sustain its ruling regime. It is for this reason that R2P advocates included a means of 'incentivising' compliance with ICE 3 (and ICEs 1 and 2 for that matter). Accordingly the following sub-section examines the first ICE created by Pillar III.

ICE 4: Incentivising compliance

At first glance ICE 4 may seem to be the most important ICE because it essentially holds R2P together. Yet ICE 4 requires the 'international community' to act, and it cannot do so unless discrete actors are motivated to act on its behalf by the constitutive effect of ICE 5, which makes the latter the most important component of R2P. But for the moment we must consider ICE 4 and the connections between it and ICEs 1, 2 and 3.

ICE 4 is essentially an enforcement mechanism. Thus on the face of it ICE 4 seems to be intended to create a *collective-directive effect*: in paragraph 139 of the WSOD the international community undertook, when a state failed to protect its population, to 'use appropriate diplomatic, humanitarian and other peaceful means, in accordance with Chapters VI and VIII' (i.e. mediation, arbitration, diplomatic pressure, etc.) and if these fail, to 'take collective action, in a timely and decisive manner, through the Security Council in accordance with the [UN] Charter, including Chapter VII'. But then the words 'on a case-by-case basis' follow, which seems to suggest the responsibility to assume responsibility for protection is actually collective-*permissive*. The discussion returns to this matter later because it suggests the potential for inconsistency is built into R2P, but for the moment we should recognise that most attention has focused on – and most resistance has been directed against – the Chapter VII coercive measures, which include sanctions (Article 41) and military force (Article 42). Thus at its most basic level ICE 4 is intended to alter the traditional interpretation of sovereignty and establish that it can, in some limited circumstances, be treated as *conditional*.

The UN Security Council is tasked with determining whether and how these sorts of measures should be deployed. It is a collective actor that can exercise responsibilities because, applying Erskine's criteria, it has a settled, 'corporate' identity, decision-making procedures, and means of transforming decisions into actions (2014, p. 119), but (again) discussion will return later to the Council because how a member state votes is determined by its interests and motivations, making this a matter for ICE 5. Accordingly, we must now explore the four specific intended sub-effects of ICE 4 that arise from its connections with ICEs 1, 2 and 3 (and note that while three sub-effects involve pressuring states, one concerns reassuring actors, which is why the overall effect of ICE 4 has been characterised as one that 'incentivises' compliance).

First, and most simply, ICE 4 is intended to create a *remedial* sub-effect: if a state breaches the ICE 1/Pillar I prohibition and is actively committing mass atrocities ICE 4 provides a mechanism for the international community to 'remedy the situation' (i.e. stop the atrocities). Second, and tied to the first sub-effect, ICE 4 is intended to provide a *deterrent* sub-effect. Assuming one or more states have previously been subjected to pressure that caused them to stop committing atrocities, these precedents should create a 'demonstration effect', deterring other states from committing atrocities in future.

These first two intended sub-effects are obvious (although it is not obvious they will always *work*). But ICE 4 is intended to create two other under-appreciated sub-effects through its connections to ICE 2 and ICE 3 (i.e. to Pillar II). The third effect is to *reassure* actors – states, but also non-state actors with the capability to offer assistance – that offers of assistance will be accepted. Why would actors need to be reassured in this way if they were strongly constituted by ICE 2? Consider that members of the international community may offer assistance, but a target state may recalcitrantly reject or, even more annoyingly, it might disingenuously accept aid but then not carry out promised reforms. If this happened often enough offers of assistance may dry up unless additional pressure could be exerted on recalcitrant or disingenuous states. Thus, by enabling the international community to, in effect, 'up the ante', ICE 4 is intended to bolster the confidence of those actors who offer assistance that it will actually be accepted and put to good use. The fourth sub-effect is the corollary of the third, namely, the threat that 'the ante might be upped' should pressure recalcitrant and disingenuous states to accept assistance and actually implement reforms. This fourth intended effect of ICE 4 is therefore a mixture of deterrents – to not refuse offers of assistance – and incentives to act, namely, to undertake reforms.

ICE 5: Supporting the international community

As noted earlier, arguably ICE 5 is the single-most-important component of R2P. It is intended to create a *self-permissive effect*, namely, to motivate discrete actors to support the international community's ICE 4 undertakings. Specifically, ICE 5 should motivate discrete actors to follow through on their ICE 2 undertaking to provide assistance, and also motivate them to support and facilitate efforts by the international community to pressure states that fail to comply with ICE 1/Pillar I to actually do so, and/or their ICE 3 obligation to accept assistance to do so. It should be noted that non-state actors might be motivated to – and capable of – discharging some of the undertakings made at the 2005 World Summit, such as offering assistance. But states remain the primary international actors because they dominate most international institutions, including the Security Council, which is crucial in the R2P context, and they are the most capable international actors because they can raise taxes and armies.[5] Thus ICE 5 is primarily directed towards motivating states.

But, as was also noted earlier, this means assignment and related free-rider problems arise. Assignment problems arise because the 2005 WSOD undertakings create 'imperfect' (Tan 2015, p. 133) or 'general' duties (Pattison 2008, p. 268), meaning the responsibility to support the international community's undertaking to provide aid or assume protection responsibilities is not assigned to specific actors. There are potential ways of resolving this problem. For example, the sample of states that are expected to provide assistance pursuant to ICE 2 could be reduced by removing all states that do not comply with ICE 1/Pillar I; it would be absurd to accept that an inveterate human rights abuser, such as North Korea, were qualified to do so. Then perhaps only states with good or excellent human rights records could be considered competent. According to Freedom House, 86 states are currently rated 'free' (2015). To reduce it further maybe only the most capable (i.e. the richest) states should be considered, although doing so inevitably raises fairness issues.

The same sort of process can be carried out to determine who should impose sanctions and/or military solutions. Other scholars have grappled more with these issues, especially military contributions, because these are likely to be more costly – especially politically – than offering assistance. James Pattison, for example, has argued that the 'most effective agent' should intervene (2008, pp. 265–267), although Kok-Chor Tan has observed that this is to some degree unfair (2015, p. 137). Tan also explored assigning responsibility to those states most at fault for causing the problem – perhaps a great power supported a brutal dictator, for example – although he notes it may be hard to establish proximity, quite apart from the practical and moral difficulties that arise when 'guilty parties' are expected to provide solutions (2015, pp. 139–140). Pattison has also considered whether 'special duties' might be assigned to states that are, for example, ethnically similar to a troubled state (2008, pp. 268, 272).

The key point is not that these various arguments about how to assign responsibility have the effect of forcing or coercing states – or even convincing them that they are legally obliged – to act on behalf of the international community. Instead, they must *motivate* states to act. They are political and/or moral 'factors to consider', offered by individual decision-makers (or their advisors) in internal debates about how to respond to humanitarian disasters, or states may direct them against other states. But these motivating arguments will usually have to contend with other considerations weighing upon decision makers. For example, competing normative considerations may suggest a state should not take military action because its soldiers sign up to defend their fellow citizens, not strangers (Huntington 1992). Practical resource allocation priorities also apply to both providing assistance and punishing deviance. There may of course be other cost-considerations that weigh on the side of providing assistance or meting out punishments; for example, doing either might arrest the instability in a neighbouring state which might otherwise spill over the border (Tan 2015, p. 124). But other non-neighbouring states may decide that the unstable state's neighbours will 'have to act' to contain the problem, meaning they don't need to 'waste' their own scarce resources. In other words, the motivating effect of ICE 5 likely faces contrary motivations in the form of a free-rider problem (Pattison 2008, p. 278; 2015, p. 196).

It is well recognised, of course, that assignment and free-rider problems can be overcome by creating institutions to both allocate responsibility and to burden-share. Tan has concluded that 'it does not appear that there is any satisfactory alternative to institutionalising the duty to intervene' (2015, p. 138). Pattison also treats institutionalisation as 'ideal' (2008, pp. 272–273), although he argues that the most effective actors should intervene, as a sort of stop-gap measure, because current institutions are flawed (pp. 273–274). They both reached these conclusions in the context of military intervention only, but essentially similar considerations apply vis-à-vis imposing sanctions. Similar reasoning also applies to providing assistance – that the ideal solution is to institutionalise – although because providing assistance is typically much less costly than military intervention – in terms of resources, and especially political capital – the parallel is not a perfect one. Nevertheless, we should consider whether institutional actors might be motivated – and capable – of supporting the international community's collective efforts to assist and punish deviance pursuant to ICE 4.

Regarding providing assistance first, the most obvious candidate is the UN, specifically, the part that most resembles an actor, the Secretariat. The UN did not, strictly speaking, provide R2P undertakings at the 2005 World Summit because it is not a state. Yet there is little doubt that recent Secretariats have been motivated to advance R2P. The last two UN Secretaries-General have been strong R2P advocates; Kofi Annan provided the initial momentum and was instrumental in ensuring paragraphs 138 and 139 made it into the WSOD. His successor, Ban Ki-Moon, also worked tirelessly by releasing annual R2P reports since 2009 and facilitating annual informal debates about R2P. In particular, Moon's 2009 report announced that R2P would be 'mainstreamed', as he put it, meaning all UN 'agencies, funds and programmes' would be expected to coordinate their activities to advance R2P (UN Secretariat, pp. 28–29). While Bellamy has been generally upbeat about the R2P-mainstreaming effort he was also honest about the obstacles it faced (2013, p. 177).

But the problem is not motivation but *capability*. The Secretariat's budget for 2016 and 2017 was only US$5.4 billion. It is difficult to know exactly how much it would cost to provide assistance sufficient to help a struggling state successfully discharge its Pillar I obligation – this is obviously a highly context-dependent matter – but I strongly doubt whether an annual budget of US$2.7 billion – which must, after all, cover the entire UN's 'staffing, travel, peacekeeping and administrative costs' (UN General Assembly 2015) – is sufficient. This chapter is also not the appropriate place to exhaustively survey how many resources other non-state actors such as regional organisations and NGOs can devote to such efforts. But it seems reasonable to assume that the majority, and probably a very large majority, of such assistance will have to be provided by states. Having said this, such assistance would likely be 'funnelled through' the UN, or at least states would coordinate with UN bodies; in other words, an institution already exists to facilitate states' efforts to provide assistance.

Regarding economic sanctions and military options, the Secretariat is strictly *incapable* because the UN Charter reserves these powers to the Security Council. But, as Hehir has argued, the five permanent members':

> response to any particular alleged or clear breach of [R2P] is entirely a function of the members' respective interests; there are no binding rules they must adhere to. . . . [Thus] R2P is predicated on an assumption that normative pressure will compel the P5 to alter the foreign policy calculus.
> (Hehir 2013, p. 152)

In other words, and because they all have the veto power, at minimum the five permanent members must *all* be motivated to define their interests in ways which lead them to authorise efforts to pressure deviant states on behalf of the international community. But the conduct and outcome of the Libyan intervention has led to deadlock in the Council when it comes to intervening in the appalling humanitarian crisis in Syria; two draft resolutions (UN Security Council 2011; UN Security Council 2012b) were vetoed by China and Russia after the text of each merely threatened the application of sanctions by *future* resolutions in the case of non-compliance, while another that did not even do that was also vetoed (UN Security Council 2012a). Then, in May 2014, both China and Russia vetoed a resolution that sought to refer the situation in Syria to the International Criminal Court's Prosecutor (UN Security Council 2014).

Thus the crux of R2P's problem is this. ICE 4 creates a collective-permissive effect: the international community undertook to assume R2P when a state fails to do so, although only on a case-by-case basis. But this 'entity' must act through the Security Council. ICE 5 must therefore motivate enough Council members to vote to apply pressure on a deviant state; nine members in total must be sufficiently constituted by ICE 5 to vote for a draft resolution that pressures deviant states and, crucially, ICE 5 must constitute the five permanent members sufficiently to ensure that they, at minimum, do not cast a veto. But at present Russia and China are not sufficiently constituted by ICE 5, they do not construe their interests in ways that facilitate the Security Council acting in ways that consistently apply pressure on actors who deviate from R2P's intended effects. Accordingly, because the Council is prone to deadlock the institution tasked with pressuring states that fail their ICE 1/Pillar I responsibility often cannot do so. In summary, there are two intended permissive effects in Pillar III – one for the international community to act (or not) and one for states to support it (or not) – and the fact they are permissive and not directive undermines efforts to ensure the 2005 undertakings are discharged *consistently*.

Could other institutions act on behalf of the international community? Certainly NATO has the capability and, according to Erskine it is a collective actor of the sort that can assume responsibilities (p. 120). And the African Union's Constitutive Act contains Article 4(h), which authorises 'the Union to intervene in a Member State . . . in respect of grave circumstances, namely: war crimes, genocide and crimes against humanity'. Yet the Charter's Article 53(1) says 'no enforcement action shall be taken under regional arrangements . . . without the authorization of the Security Council', relegating regional organisations to an informal 'gatekeeper' role only – such as pressuring Council members politically, as the Arab League did vis-à-vis Libya in 2011 (Bellamy and Williams 2011, p. 826) – or, presumably, deploying only 'other peaceful means' (such as diplomatic pressure). The R2P undertakings states made in 2005 did nothing to alter this; quite the contrary in fact, given paragraph 139 specifically tasks the Council alone with imposing Chapter VII measures.

Given that the Council regularly deadlocks and there is no legal way to bypass it to mete out punishments, some have claimed that there is a *responsibility to reform* (Welsh 2013, p. 140; Pattison 2015, pp. 204–205). Many reform proposals designed to enhance the international community's ability to protect threatened populations have been offered. The more radical ones call for entirely new institutions to replace the Security Council in R2P-relevant contexts (Ayoob 2010, p. 136), or to create a UN army to enforce R2P (Roff 2013), but the more modest proposals offered before the 2005 World Summit focused on reforming the Council. The 2001 ICISS report called for criteria ('precautionary principles') to guide the Council's deliberations about whether a 'threat to international security' existed (pp. 29–37). It also floated the idea of permanent members following a 'code of conduct' whereby they would not cast a veto unless their 'vital national interests were . . . involved' (2001, p. 51), and it considered whether the General Assembly and/or regional organisations could act if the Council was deadlocked (pp. 53–54). Later, the High-Level Panel convened by Annan in 2004 – ostensibly to 'discuss' and 'disseminate' the nascent R2P norm prior to the World Summit, but in reality to promote it – was cognizant of stiff resistance to the ICISS's recommendations, so it proposed that the permanent members 'declare their positions' before they voted (High-Level Panel 2004, p. 82); this would not have formally restricted the veto but it might have generated social pressure to not misuse it. But these initiatives all failed; indeed, all recent efforts to reform the UN Security Council, including those not substantially connected to the debate about R2P, have failed.

Conclusion

The broader implications of the preceding discussion are twofold. First, because there are fewer obstacles in the way of states supporting the international community's responsibility to offer assistance, there are good reasons to believe that it may become 'normal'; in other words, Pillar II might well become ever-more firmly entrenched which, hopefully, will steadily improve compliance with Pillar I. Granted, if pressure cannot be applied to recalcitrant and disingenuous states then the incentives to offer (ICE 2) and to accept (ICE 3) assistance might be reduced somewhat. Nevertheless, as long as states are sufficiently constituted by ICE 5 to bear the costs of providing assistance, institutional mechanisms exist that they can do so through, which should reduce the assignation and free-rider problems to some degree.

But it will be more difficult to normalise the international community's ICE 4 assumption of the responsibility to protect threatened populations. Even if many states are sufficiently motivated to overcome the assignation and free-rider problems to mete out costly and risky punishments, they face serious institutional hurdles in the Security Council and the fact that the UN Charter rules out alternative means of acting. Thus the institutional environment arguably magnifies, not alleviates, the assignation and free-rider problems. This in turn weakens the remedial and deterrent effects that ICE 4 is intended to create because it is difficult to *consistently* impose punishments of the sort that compel compliance with emerging norms.

On this last point, it is worth recalling Brunnée and Toope's warning that inconsistent application of a rule tends to provoke allegations of hypocrisy and abuse (2010b. Adrian Gallagher, for one, claims we should 'manage expectations' (2015, pp. 263–273) by essentially accepting what Hehir has called the 'permanency of inconsistency' (2013). But it is important to keep in mind what Ajish Joy has said about accepting this sort of logic too readily; Joy warned that 'while there is some merit in the argument it is better to intervene at least selectively rather than not intervening anywhere', he also observed 'selective application of R2P eventually corrodes it' (2011). Thus consistent application would likely achieve two intimately connected purposes: first, if the international community 'normally' assumed the R2P by punishing deviant behaviour the deterrent effect of ICE 4 would strengthen; and second, R2P would be more insulated from the powerful critique that it is prone to being abused (Brown 2013, pp. 265–268; Paris 2014, pp. 4–6, 10–11). Both would seem necessary before we can conclude R2P is an entrenched norm.

How might this situation be overcome? At least three broad means of entrenching the R2P norm come to mind. The first, institutional reform – especially of the Security Council – to facilitate efforts to pressure deviant states has already been canvassed. But we can largely discount this possibility, at least in the short- to medium-term, given how difficult it has been to achieve any sort of substantial reforms of this nature despite concerted attempts in the past decade or so. The other two means are related and are, arguably, more realistic options.

So, second, norm entrepreneurs could continue to promote an unchanged R2P to slowly but steadily socialise states, hoping that more – especially the institutionally critical, Security Council veto-holding states China and Russia – became constituted more strongly by ICE 5, meaning that they would begin to formulate their interests in ways which eased deadlock in the Council. And recall that Kurtz and Rotmann (2016) found that while R2P itself had not necessarily become 'an effective means of mobilising political will', it was part of what might be called a wider 'protection regime' that includes other human rights and humanitarian norms (Mills 2013) that *was* advancing. In other words, R2P might not have to 'do all the work' of socialising currently obstructive states in ways that fundamentally alter the manner in which they formulate their interests.

But Chris Brown has argued that the entire R2P project is predicated on finding middle ground between those who believe that sovereignty should be redefined and treated as conditional, at least in some circumstances, and those who consider this position 'an unacceptable assault on sovereignty' (2013, pp. 427–428). And Manjari Chatterjee-Miller has shown that states that experienced colonialism – about two-thirds of General Assembly members – remain 'very sensitive to any suggestions of external interference or coercion' (2013, pp. 50–54). Further, Xiaoyu Pu has bluntly asserted 'emerging powers' – virtually all of whom harbour anti-imperialist resentments of some kind or another – 'will change the distribution of power and also challenge Western domination of ideas and norms in international society' (2012, p. 365). It has therefore become common for contributors to the R2P debate to express the view – or the concern – that as geopolitical power shifts steadily from 'the West' to 'the Rest' the conditions for advancing R2P will likely become less forgiving (Welsh 2010, p. 428; Thakur 2013; Newman 2016). In short, it might also be somewhat unrealistic, or at least overly optimistic, to expect the Rising Rest will simply accept R2P in its current form.

Which brings us to the third option; it might be necessary to change the scope and content of R2P itself. Morris was cited at the outset in this regard. He believes we should excise the Pillar III military options while retaining the power to impose economic sanctions. Indeed, he claims ruling out military options will likely 'enhance the possibility that the Council will actually utilise [its Article 41 sanctions] powers' (2016, p. 209). Space restrictions prevent me from considering this matter at length, but I am concerned that his proposal would remove an important potential means of imposing pressure, even if such is only implied. Instead, reform proposals such as Brazil's 'Responsibility while Protecting' (2011) would seem to have more promise. This sought to circumscribe military options by, for example, ensuring that a military intervention did not result in a regime change, in part by establishing mechanisms for the Council to closely monitor R2P-inspired interventions.

Various other potential ways to reform the R2P norm itself have been offered. For example, the responsibility to rebuild was a prominent feature of the 2001 ICISS report, but is not an overt feature of the WSOD-version of R2P (although it is implicit in, or at least not ruled out by, Pillar II). Albrecht Schnabel has argued that reinserting this overtly would constitute 'a most useful "speech act" . . . [and]

reintroduce a new tool to rally quick, effective and sustainable global responses' (2012, p. 58). And building on Ramesh Thakur's call (2013), Jason Ralph and Gallagher have recently argued that greater consultation with rising non-Western powers regarding when to apply R2P in specific crises would likely help strengthen the norm by improving its legitimacy (2015, pp. 570–573). But I suspect these sorts of actors may also have to be included in efforts to renegotiate the very scope and content of R2P itself before the prospects of it becoming entrenched improve significantly.

Notes

1 Bellamy (2014) believes the connection is tenuous, but the weight of opinion is against him; see Brown (2013, p. 435), Thakur (2013), Ralph and Gallagher (2015), Morris (2016) and the most recent UN Secretary-General's report into R2P (UN Secretariat 2015).
2 For a more general discussion see Brunnée and Toope (2010b, pp. 350–355).
3 Glanville labels as 'prescriptive' what I (following Sandholtz) call 'directive'.
4 Although assistance might include the provision of military forces to help a state defeat rebels without expectations that the recipient-state undertakes substantial reforms.
5 Some multinational corporations are 'larger' than many states; Apple's revenue of $53 billion in 2015 was larger than 122 states' GDP. But the biggest states are much larger: for example, the United States' 2015 GDP – $17.8 trillion – exceeded Apple's revenue by a factor of 335. And corporations cannot raise armies.

References

Ayoob, M 2010, 'Making Sense of Global Tensions: Dominant and Subaltern Conceptions of Order and Justice in the International System', *International Studies*, vol. 47, no. 2–4, pp. 129–141.
Bellamy, AJ 2013, 'Mainstreaming the Responsibility to Protect in the United Nations System: Dilemmas, Challenges and Opportunities', *Global Responsibility to Protect*, vol. 5, no. 2, pp. 154–191.
Bellamy, AJ 2014, 'From Tripoli to Damascus? Lesson Learning and the Implementation of the Responsibility to Protect', *International Politics*, vol. 51, no. 1, pp. 23–44.
Bellamy, AJ 2015, 'The Responsibility to Protect Turns Ten', *Ethics and International Affairs*, vol. 29, no. 2, pp. 161–185.
Bellamy, AJ and Williams, P 2011, 'The New Politics of Protection? Côte d'Ivoire, Libya, and the Responsibility to Protect', *International Affairs*, vol. 82, no. 7, pp. 825–850.
Brazil 2011, 'Responsibility while Protecting: Elements for the Development and Promotion of a Concept', A/66/551–S2011/701, 21 September.
Brown, C 2013, 'The Antipolitical Theory of Responsibility to Protect', *Global Responsibility to Protect*, vol. 5, no. 4, pp. 423–442.
Brunnée, J and Toope, S 2010a, 'The Responsibility to Protect and the Use of Force: Binding Legality?', *Global Responsibility to Protect*, vol. 2, no. 3, pp. 191–212.
Brunnée, J and Toope, S 2010b, *Legitimacy and Legality in International Law: An Interactional Account*, Cambridge University Press, Cambridge.
Chatterjee-Miller, M 2013, *Wronged By Empire: Post-Imperial Ideology in India and China*, Stanford University Press, Stanford, CA.
Dunne, T and Gelber, K 2014, 'Arguing Matters: The Responsibility to Protect and the Case of Libya', *Global Responsibility to Protect*, vol. 6, no. 3, pp. 326–349.

Erskine, T 2014, 'Coalitions of the Willing and Responsibilities to Protect: Informal Associations, Enhanced Capacities, and Shared Moral Burdens' *Ethics and International Affairs*, vol. 28, no. 1, pp. 115–145.

Finnemore, M and Sikkink, K 1998, 'International Norm Dynamics and Political Change', *International Organization*, vol. 52, no. 4, pp. 887–917.

Finnemore, M and Toope, SJ 2001, 'Alternatives to "Legalization": Richer Views of Law and Politics', *International Organization*, vol. 55, no. 3, pp. 743–758.

Freedom House 2015, *Freedom in the World: Discarding Democracy, Return to the Iron Fist*. Available from: https://freedomhouse. org/report/freedom-world/freedom-world-2015#. V0-slLh96Uk. [10 August 2016].

Gallagher, A 2015, 'The Responsibility to Protect Ten Years on from the World Summit: A Call to Manage Expectations', *Global Responsibility to Protect*, vol. 7, no. 3–4, pp. 254–274.

Gholiagha, S 2015, ' "To Prevent Future Kosovos and Future Rwandas": A Critical Constructivist View of the Responsibility to Protect', *International Journal of Human Rights*, vol. 19, no. 8, pp. 1074–1097.

Giddens, A 1984, *The Constitution of Society: Outline of the Theory of Structuration*, Polity Press, Cambridge.

Glanville, L 2006, 'Norms, Interests and Humanitarian Intervention', *Global Change, Peace and Security*, vol. 18, no. 3, pp. 153–171.

Glanville, L 2012, 'The Responsibility to Protect Beyond Borders', *Human Rights Law Review*, vol. 12, no. 1, pp. 1–32.

Graubart, J 2015, 'War is not the Answer: the Responsibility to Protect and Military Intervention' in R Thakur and W Maley, (eds), *Theorising the Responsibility to Protect*, pp. 200–219. Cambridge University Press, Cambridge.

Hehir, A 2011, 'The Responsibility to Protect in International Political Discourse: Encouraging Sentiment of Intent or Illusory Platitude?', *International Journal of Human Rights*, vol. 15, no. 8, pp. 1331–1348.

Hehir, A 2013, 'The Permanence of Inconsistency: Libya, the Security Council, and the Responsibility to Protect', *International Security*, vol. 38, no. 1, pp. 137–159.

High Level Panel 2004, *A More Secure World: Our Shared Responsibility*, United Nations, New York.

Hobson, C 2016, 'Responding to Failure: the Responsibility to Protect After Libya', *Millennium – Journal of International Studies*, vol. 44, no. 3, pp. 433–454.

Hoffmann, MJ 2010, 'Norms and Social Constructivism in International Relations' in RA Denemark, (ed.), *The International Studies Encyclopedia*. Blackwell Reference Online. Available from: www.isacompendium.com. [10 August 2016].

Hopgood, S 2014, 'Last Rites for Humanitarian Intervention', *Global Responsibility to Protect*, vol. 6, no. 2, pp. 181–205.

Huntington, SL 1992, 'New Contingencies, Old Roles', *Joint Forces Quarterly*, Autumn, no. 2, pp. 38–43.

Hurrell, A 2002, 'Norms and Ethics in International Relations' in WE Carlsnaes, T Risse and BA Simmons, (eds), *Handbook of International Relations*, pp. 137–154. Sage, New York.

International Commission on Intervention and State Sovereignty (ICISS) 2001, *The Responsibility to Protect*, International Development Research Centre, Ottawa.

Jackson, R 1993, *Quasi-States: Sovereignty, International Relations and the Third World*, Cambridge University Press, Cambridge.

Joy, AP 2011, 'Almost Covert, Wholly Illegal', *Observer Research Foundation – Analysis*, 5 September. Available from: www.orfonline.org/research/almost-covert-wholly-illegal/. [10 August 2016].

Kratochwil, F and Ruggie, JG 1986, 'A State of the Art on an Art of the State', *International Organization*, vol. 40, no. 4, pp. 753–775.

Kurtz, G and Rotmann, P 2016, 'The Evolution of Norms of Protection: Major Powers Debate the Responsibility to Protect', *Global Society*, vol. 30, no. 1, pp. 3–20.

Mills, K 2013, 'R2P³: Protecting, Prosecuting, or Palliating in Mass Atrocity Situations?', *Journal of Human Rights*, vol. 12, no. 3, pp. 333–356.

Morris, J 2016, 'The Responsibility to Protect and the Use of Force: Remaking the Procrustean Bed?', *Cooperation and Conflict*, vol. 51, no. 2, pp. 200–215.

Newman, E 2016, 'What Prospects for Common Humanity in a Divided World? The Scope for R2P in a Transitional World Order', *International Politics*, vol. 53, no. 1, pp. 32–48.

Orford, A 2011, *International Authority and the Responsibility to Protect*, Cambridge University Press, Cambridge.

Panke, D and Petersohn, U 2011, 'Why International Norms Disappear Sometimes', *European Journal of International Relations*, vol. 18, no. 4, pp. 719–742.

Papamichail, A and Partis-Jennings, H 2016, 'Why Common Humanity? Framing the Responsibility to Protect as a Common Human Response', *International Politics*, vol. 53, no. 1, pp. 83–100.

Paris, R 2014, 'The "Responsibility to Protect" and the Structural Problems of Preventative Humanitarian Intervention', *International Peacekeeping*, vol. 21, no. 5, pp. 1–35.

Pattison, J 2008, 'Whose Responsibility to Protect? The Duties of Humanitarian Intervention', *Journal of Military Ethics*, vol. 7, no. 4, pp. 262–283.

Pattison, J 2015, 'Mapping the Responsibilities to Protect: a Typology of International Duties', *Global Responsibility to Protect*, vol. 7, no. 2, pp. 190–210.

Pu, X 2012, 'Socialisation as a Two-way Process: Emerging Powers and the Diffusion of International Norms', *Chinese Journal of International Politics*, vol. 5, no. 4, pp. 341–367.

Ralph, J and Gallagher, A 2015, 'Legitimacy Faultlines in International Society: the Responsibility to Protect and Prosecute after Libya', *Review of International Studies*, vol. 41, no. 3, pp. 553–573.

Risse, T and Sikkink, K 1999, 'The Socialization of International Human Rights Norms into Domestic Practices: Introduction' in T Risse, SC Ropp and K Sikkink, (eds), *The Power of Human Rights: International Norms and Domestic Change*, pp. 1–38. Cambridge University Press, Cambridge.

Roff, H 2013, *Global Justice, Kant, and the Responsibility to Protect: A Provisional Duty*, Routledge, Oxon.

Sandholtz, W 2016, 'Multiple Paths to Norm Replacement', *paper presented to Unsteady Lives: the Dynamics of Norm Robustness workshop*, ISA 2016, Atlanta, 15 March.

Schnabel, A 2012, 'The Responsibility to Rebuild' in WA Knight and F Egerton, (eds), *The Routledge Handbook of the Responsibility to Protect*, pp. 50–63. Routledge, Oxon.

Tan, K 2015, 'Humanitarian Intervention as a Duty', *Global Responsibility to Protect*, vol. 7, no. 2, pp. 121–141.

Thakur, R 2013, 'R2P after Libya and Syria: Engaging Emerging Powers', *Washington Quarterly*, vol. 36, no. 2, pp. 61–76.

United Nations General Assembly 2015, 'General Assembly Adopts United Nations Budget for 2016–17', 23 December. Available from: www.un.org/pga/70/2015/12/23/general-assembly-adopts-un-budget-for-2016–17/. [10 August 2016].

United Nations Secretariat 2009, *Implementing the Responsibility to Protect*, A/63/677, 12 January.

United Nations Secretariat 2015, 'A Vital and Enduring Commitment: Implementing the Responsibility to Protect'. A/69/981–S/2015/500, 13 July.

United Nations Security Council 2011. S/PV. 6627, 4 October.

United Nations Security Council 2012a. S/PV. 6711, 4 February.
United Nations Security Council 2012b. S/PV. 6810, 19 July.
United Nations Security Council 2014. S/PV. 7180, 22 May.
Welsh, JM 2010, 'Implementing the Responsibility to Protect: Where Expectations Meet Reality', *Ethics and International Affairs*, vol. 24, no. 4, pp. 415–430.
Welsh, JM 2013, 'Norm Contestation and the Responsibility to Protect', *Global Responsibility to Protect*, vol. 5, no. 1, pp. 365–396.

10

'WHY IS IT THAT WE KEEP FAILING?'

The responsibility to protect as a hollow norm

Aidan Hehir

Introduction

Those who believe that the Responsibility to Protect (R2P) is a dynamic force for change that has had, and will increasingly have, a positive influence on international relations, are correct to note that it has garnered widespread international support. States routinely affirm R2P and it has become embedded in international political discourse; most notably, it has increasingly been iterated in Security Council Resolutions. In this chapter, however, I challenge this conflation of invocation with efficacy; I argue that R2P's widespread affirmation and invocation cannot in itself be heralded as evidence of genuine, meaningful support for the concept, nor of its necessarily positive efficacy.

In his framework for determining the effectiveness and influence of norms, Jeffrey Legro notes that the existence of a norm does not in itself mean the norm is influential (1997, p. 34). A particular term/phrase/idea may command a degree of consensus and be widely used but still have minimal influence. I argue here that R2P's efficacy has often been based on an understanding of norms that overlooks the nuances Legro identifies. Rather than disputing that R2P is a norm, or declaring that norms are always insignificant, I argue that R2P has become a 'hollow norm'; a weak regulative – as opposed to constitutive – norm that has been endorsed and applied instrumentally. Focusing on R2P's popularity among states obscures the norm typology spectrum, variations in norm efficacy, the complex process by which norms are diffused and implemented, and the influence of power asymmetries on the evolution of norms.

Specifically, I argue that R2P has been framed and co-opted by states to the point that it is now largely devoid of prescriptive merit and, more ominously, often employed to serve mendacious interests that run counter to its ethos. R2P does not significantly raise the costs of non-compliance domestically with existing international human rights law, or significantly redress the problem of 'in-humanitarian non-intervention', namely inaction on the part of the international community in the face of egregious violations of international human rights law (Chesterman 2003, p. 54). R2P has, therefore, facilitated the perpetuation of a system that enables both the commission of intra-state mass atrocities, and inaction on the part of the 'international community'.

'Why is it that we keep failing?'

Whatever one might say about the efficacy of R2P, the passion of its advocates cannot be denied. While a number of prominent supporters of the concept have consistently advanced measured appraisals of its record and likely future influence (Weiss 2011; Welsh 2013), others have engaged in a form of celebratory rhetoric that had led them to be accused of peddling dangerously unrealistic expectations (Gallagher 2015b) and 'hubris' (Kersten 2015). Indeed, many statements reflecting on R2P's transformative influence do stray close to the hysterical; indicatively R2P has been described as 'the most significant adjustment to sovereignty in 360 years' (Gilbert in Axworthy and Rock 2009, p. 69), 'an enormous normative step forward, akin to an international Magna Carta' (Slaughter 2011), 'a brand new international norm of really quite fundamental importance and novelty . . . that is unquestionably a major breakthrough' (Evans 2009, p. 16), and an idea that 'has begun to change the world' (Bellamy 2015, p. 111). While these sentiments may justifiably be deemed hyperbole, perhaps even the triumph of reason over analysis as Justin Morris argues in his chapter in this book, there is undeniably some empirical basis for such claims.

If R2P had never advanced beyond the report of the International Commission on Intervention and State Sovereignty (ICISS) – and thus remained merely one of many recommendations made by the myriad panels and commissions established in the past 30 years – then the claims made about its efficacy could easily be dismissed as wilful naivety. But this is not the case. Unlike, for example, the detailed report *Humanitarian Intervention: Legal and Political Aspects* by the Danish Institute of International Affairs published around the same time as *The Responsibility to Protect*, the ICISS report was *not* ignored by the international community of states; there is no doubt, essentially, that R2P is today 'part of the worlds diplomatic language' (Welsh 2013, p. 378).

The UN Secretary-General published his eighth annual report on R2P in August 2016, and in September 2015 the General Assembly held its seventh 'Informal Interactive Dialogue' on R2P. Fifty-three states have now appointed an 'R2P Focal Point' (Global Centre for R2P 2016a) and 53 states (and the European Union) have joined the 'Group of Friends of the Responsibility to Protect' (Van Oosterom 2015). R2P has been invoked by the Security Council in 43 Resolutions (Global Centre for R2P 2017) and, despite the post-intervention crisis in Libya and the conflict in Syria, the Security Council's use of R2P increased after 2011 (Bellamy 2014, p. 26; Weiss 2014, p. 10; Adams 2015b; Global Centre for R2P 2016b).

The proliferation of R2P in official discourse and the growth in membership of groups such as the R2P Focal Points and the Group of Friends of R2P are regularly cited – not unreasonably – as evidence to back up the claims that R2P – though not a panacea – is positively influencing international relations. These arguments tend to be based on two central – and I suggest largely irrefutable – assertions; first, R2P commands global consensus, second, R2P is routinely invoked. In terms of the first assertion, it is claimed that R2P has been accepted by the global community of states; states rarely, if indeed ever, reject R2P and in fact routinely gather to express their support for the concept, thereby ostensibly giving R2P 'worldwide normative traction' (Evans 2016, p. 2). This is central to the narrative that R2P has real-world influence; indicatively, Alex Bellamy, Director of the Asia-Pacific Centre for the Responsibility to Protect, observed, 'R2P's greatest asset is the global consensus it commands' (2015, p. 83). Arguments made in support of the second claim note the precipitous rise in the use of the term 'responsibility to protect' at the highest levels of international discourse. Indicatively, the Global Centre for R2P publishes updates on references to R2P in Security Council Resolutions heralding this as evidence that the concept is exercising definite influence (Global Centre for R2P 2017). This is, indeed, a view held by a number of academic analysts who – again not unreasonably – note that irrelevant terms/ideas don't make their way (repeatedly) into Security Council Resolutions, General Assembly statements and Secretary-General Reports (Weiss 2014; Bellamy 2015; Gifkins 2016; Glanville 2016).

Yet, reflecting on the rise of R2P and the nature of contemporary international affairs it is hard not to feel a sense of cognitive dissonance; as noted in this book's introduction, in tandem with the irrefutable ascendancy of R2P we can see a marked degeneration in the very practices and ethos R2P seeks to cultivate. Global respect for human rights is in precipitous decline, state oppression is increasing, and the willingness of states to engage in expensive and time-consuming interventions has decreased. The celebratory rhetoric of R2P's proponents – and indeed the firm empirical evidence upon which they base these claims – clearly does not sit comfortably with the perilous state of human security in today's world.

How, then, can it be that R2P is so widely affirmed, so embedded in international political discourse, and the subject of myriad effusive statements extolling its radical influence, yet be unable to check this degenerative slide? As Nobel Peace prize winner, and Chair of the UN High Level Panel on Peace Operations, José Ramos-Horta asked, 'why is it that, in the face of such a sophisticated normative framework to protect civilians, we keep failing?' (Ramos-Horta 2015).

The answer to Ramos-Horta's question can be found by examining the nature of R2P's putative status as a norm. It has been widely claimed that R2P is a norm, and R2P's very efficacy is premised on a particular understanding of the influence of norms; indeed, norms are, according to Bellamy, 'the stuff of R2P' (2015, p. 59). To summarise this argument, R2P is deemed to constitute a norm by virtue of the widespread support it commands, its routine invocation and its non-legal character (Deng 2010; Welsh 2013; Evans 2016). As a norm, R2P shapes the framework within which state behaviour is determined and, through a process of rhetorical entrapment, compels states to act in certain ways (Dunne and Gelber 2014; Bellamy 2015: Glanville 2016). Conscious of the fact that R2P has manifestly *not* prevented certain mass atrocity crimes since 2005 – most notably in Darfur, Sri Lanka and Syria – proponents argue that, as is the case with all norms, R2P cannot be expected to work in every instance; norm violations do not necessarily constitute the death of the norm (Deitelhoff and Zimmermann 2013; Welsh 2013, p. 383; Hofmann 2015, p. 29; Glanville 2016). Thus, while states have engaged in intra-state mass atrocities and the international community has at times neglected to respond adequately, R2P has at least enabled the broader international community to condemn and shame those responsible. Despite occasional lapses in implementation, R2P has continued to win state support and this is, therefore, evidence that it is both robust and of growing influence.

The fundamentals of this argument are, to an extent, sound, and reflected in the broader literature on norms. Consensus *is* a prerequisite for any norm; repeated invocation *is* a necessary attribute of any putative norm; norms *do* exert influence through social shaming rather than legal censure; and norm violations *do not* necessarily signal the end of a norm (Chayes and Chayes 1993, p. 188; Sandholtz and Stiles 2009; Wiener 2008, p. 202; Panke and Petershon 2011, p. 721; Welsh 2014, p. 125). And yet, while there is, therefore, both theoretical and empirical evidence that can be marshalled to support the defence of R2P's efficacy, this rendering of R2P and the role of norms ultimately overlooks salient features of the consensus on R2P and the manner in which the term is so regularly employed; these are discussed in turn in the following section.

Interrogating the R2P norm

Following the end of the Cold War, research into the role of norms increased exponentially in line with the 'constructivist turn' in international relations (Checkel 1998, p. 324; see also, March and Olsen 1989; Ruggie 1993; Kowert and Legro 1996; Risse 1999; Wendt 1999; Acharya 2004). Interest in norms did, of course, precede the constructivist turn, having long been a central concern for English School scholars (Bull 1995; Dunne 1998).

Norms are conceived of as rules that do not necessarily have a legal basis or definite means of enforcement; they are based on conceptions of states as actors within a society that has generally agreed upon views on what is acceptable behaviour (Habermas 1992, p. 138; Finnemore and Sikkink 1998, p. 891; Wiener 2009, p. 183). As Legro notes, norms are the 'collective understandings of the proper behaviour of actors' (1997, p. 33). States thus abide by norms not because they are necessarily forced to, but rather because the community in which they operate shuns norm violators (Franck 1990, p. 24; Kowert and Legro 1996; Sandholtz 2008, p. 107).

The literature on norms (broadly) identifies three categories of norms: purported or 'challenger' norms that do not (as yet) meet the criteria for recognition as a norm; established norms that command consensus and are regularly invoked; and norms that have 'died' (Acharya 2004; Wiener 2004; Sandholtz 2008; Krook and True 2010, p. 104; Panke and Petersohn 2011; Labonte 2013, p. 50). While R2P's proponents are right to claim that R2P fits within the second category, such norms evidence divergent efficacy and a spectrum of characteristics; a particularly important distinction exists between 'regulative' and 'constitutive' norms, with the latter deemed to create new interests rather than just outline appropriate behaviour (Klotz 1995; Katzenstein 1996; Finnemore and Sikkink 1998, p. 891; Wendt 1999, p. 92).

With the emergence of post-positivist constructivism, earlier conceptions of a 'norm life cycle' leading to internalisation (Finnemore and Sikkink 1998, p. 896; Gholiagha 2015) have been superseded by a more nuanced understanding of the process of norm diffusion and efficacy, as exemplified by the non-linear diffusion model (Wiener 2009). The notion, therefore, that a norm emerges, reaches a tipping point and then cascades – often said to apply to R2P (Badescu 2010, p. 115) – is increasingly seen as overly simplistic and too deterministic. The influence exerted by R2P – like any norm – has to be appreciated, therefore, as subject to an array of factors – such as context, agency and contestation (Van Kersbergen and Verbeek 2007; Kelley 2008; Krook and True 2010, p. 106; Acharya 2013, pp. 469–470; Bloomfield 2016) – that highlight the complex means by which the influence and implementation of norms – particularly regulative norms – can be resisted and undermined (Kowert and Legro 1996, p. 483; Krook and True 2010, p. 104; Betts and Orchard 2014, p. 5; Bloomfield and Scott 2016). In the specific case of R2P, there are three features of its rise that undermine its efficacy.

The circumscribed consensus on R2P

As the consensus on R2P – evidenced by repeated state affirmation and the reluctance of states to reject R2P publicly – is held to be 'its greatest asset', it is clearly necessary to examine the nature of this consensus. Consensus on R2P overwhelmingly orientates around two particular aspects of the concept; the host state's responsibility to protect its own population, Pillar I in R2P parlance, and the international community's role in helping states develop the capacity to prevent and/or halt mass atrocities, known as Pillar II (Quinton-Brown 2013; Welsh 2014, p. 125; Glanville 2016). Notably absent from the consensus on R2P is agreement on Pillar III, which deals with the responsibility of the international community to take action when the host state is unable or unwilling to do so; this aspect of R2P – outlined in Paragraph 139 of the World Summit Outcome Document – calls for a 'timely and decisive response' that may require subverting the sovereign authority of the host state when it 'manifestly fails' to protect its people from one or more of the four crimes.

This circumscribed consensus is reflected in the statements by states at the General Assembly debates on R2P that invariably focus only on Pillars I and II, and the manner in which the Security Council has employed R2P exclusively in its

Pillars I and II forms. R2P has been used in Security Council Resolutions to disavow the Council's responsibility by emphasising that the resolution of the particular crises under discussion – such as Sri Lanka, Sudan, Yemen, Libya and Syria – is the preserve of the host state (Loiselle 2013; Hehir 2015). R2P is, therefore, employed as a means by which the host state is identified as the sole locus of liability.

That Pillar III remains highly contested and largely ignored by states is not an especially contentious claim (Glanville 2012, p. 28; Evans 2016, p. 2); UN Secretary General Ban Ki-Moon noted 'a lack in both the political will and cohesion of the international community' in this area (2015, p. 12) while UN Special Adviser on R2P Jennifer Welsh observed that there remained 'substantive contestation' over Pillar III (2013, p. 385). Hostility to Pillar III certainly increased in the wake of the 2011 intervention in Libya as the intervening coalition were deemed to have abused the mandate provided for the intervention; as Kofi Annan admitted, 'the way the "responsibility to protect" was used in Libya caused a problem for the concept' (Nougayrède 2012; see also, Garwood-Gowers 2013, p. 310, Thakur 2013; Morris 2013).

There is, therefore, scant evidence that consensus on Pillar III is building, despite the increased invocation of R2P. Illustrative of R2P's steady metamorphosis towards an exclusive emphasis on Pillars I and II is, as noted by Jeremy Moses in his chapter, the recent increase in appeals for Pillar III to be formally jettisoned from R2P so as to remove any lingering source of contention surrounding the concept (Morris 2013; Gallagher 2015a). Without an operable Pillar III – which constitutes the means by which R2P is enforced – affirming support for Pillars I and II imposes minimal constraints on states, as indeed Bellamy declared in an address to the General Assembly in 2012; he noted 'without the use of force in the RtoP toolkit, the international community would effectively need to rely on the perpetrators to deliver protection' (Bellamy 2012). As with any norm or law that lacks an effective means by which it is enforced, R2P stripped of Pillar III enables it to be cynically affirmed and instrumentally implemented, as discussed in the following section.

An instrumental consensus?

The literature on norms identifies purported norms that do not meet the criteria for recognition as a norm, former norms that have lost support/relevance, and established norms that remain contested (Acharya 2004; Wiener 2004; Sandholtz 2008; Krook and True 2010, p. 104). R2P is evidence of an additional type of relatively underappreciated norm, however, namely an established norm that is often applied in ways that actually run counter to its original ethos. As Diana Panke and Ulrich Petersohn warn:

> [S]trategic rational actors can save some compliance costs in violating the vague aspects of a norm or parts of its applicatory scope while still pretending to obey the norm as a whole. This reduces the risk of being accused of and

punished for norm violations and fosters a slow, step-by-step curbing of the norm instead of a speedy degeneration.

(2011, pp. 724–725)

Therefore, while Bellamy claims that R2P commands 'genuine and resilient international consensus' (2015, p. 2), there is a strategic logic behind the Security Council and certain states affirming R2P. The ascendency of R2P to the status of a norm does not, therefore, necessarily constitute a significant or inherently positive development.

The circumscribed consensus on the meaning of R2P noted above renders it largely impotent; expressing support for this particular interpretation of the concept imposes neither meaningful costs for violation, nor significant constraints on action. Expressing rhetorical support for R2P does not necessitate a change in the state's 'organisational culture' identified by Legro as crucial to the efficacy of a norm (1997, p. 33). While states have affirmed R2P, they have not necessarily implemented domestic changes so as to institutionalise a new set of interests reflected in their commitment to R2P; the three internal 'structures' – ideational, material and institutional – that determine the implementation of a norm have in crucial respects remained unchanged and thus the seminal step from R2P as an accepted (weakly) regulative norm to an embedded constitutive norm is lacking and there thus exists an 'institutionalization-implementation gap' (Betts and Orchard 2014, p. 12).

Not only does R2P not significantly alter the cost/benefit calculation of states with respect to committing or halting atrocity crimes, it constitutes a norm that states can co-opt as well as circumvent; at times invoking R2P has enabled states, and bodies such as the Security Council, to support principles and engage in behaviour inimical to the spirit of the norm without incurring significant punitive redress. R2P is particularly vulnerable to mendacious invocation as it is inherently malleable; while the routine affirmation of Pillars I and II has been widely heralded, these tenets of R2P are sufficiently vague so as to be instrumentally applied in a vast array of ways. The absence of clear prescriptions and independent oversight and enforcement, means invoking these elements of R2P is essentially cost-free. This is evidenced by the fact that many states routinely cited as engaged in systematic human rights violations have been comfortable with iterating support for R2P, appointing 'R2P Focal Points', and joining coalitions such as 'The Group of Friends of R2P'. Certain states thus use R2P to cultivate a particular image internationally and present themselves domestically as integrated into the international human rights regime.

Indicatively, Bahrain described R2P as 'the supreme goal' at the very time it was facing sustained international criticism for its internal human rights record (Bahrain 2012). Sudan likewise declared R2P to be 'a sublime principle to which we all aspire' despite its own risible record of respect for human rights (Sudan 2009). Therefore, when states such as Bahrain, Sudan, Iran and North Korea issue statements affirming R2P, and Qatar, Angola, and the Democratic Republic of

Congo appoint an R2P Focal Point, while at the same time engaging in practices wholly at odds with the ethos of this norm, we may reasonably conclude that R2P is being used strategically to send a 'signal' and thus illustrative of 'the strategic role of deception in public statements' (Kowert and Legro 1996, p. 484; see also, Goldsmith and Posner 2002, p. 123; Adler and Pouliot 2011, p. 17).

Invoking R2P is, therefore, often a means to further strategic aims, and to encourage the norm to evolve in a way that coheres with a pre-existing preference for sovereign inviolability, rather than a genuine commitment to the protection of human rights (Achayra 2011, p. 96). Welsh, indeed, has noted that many states use R2P as a way to preserve 'legal egalitarianism' whereby Paragraphs 138 and 139 of the World Summit Outcome Document have been interpreted to reiterate the principles of sovereign inviolability and sovereign equality, as well as enhance the primacy of the state in protecting its citizens and resolving intrastate crises; in other words as a means by which to reject external interference (2013, p. 394).

Likewise, the Security Council's use of R2P – the other keystone in the evidence cited to prove R2P's efficacy – evidences a particular trend that suggests R2P is being used instrumentally. Only five of the 53 Security Council Resolutions that refer to R2P acknowledge the existence of Pillar III.[1] The rest refer to R2P only in the context of the host state's responsibility; R2P is thus employed invariably to 'remind' the state in question that it must solve the problem under consideration. This suggests, therefore, that the Security Council uses R2P exclusively as a means by which to *evade* responsibility while appearing to be 'seized' of the matter, as per UN diplomatic parlance.

The R2P norm has, therefore, arguably suffered 'co-optation' (Goldsmith and Posner 2002, p. 104) and the fact that it is invoked 'habitually' (Bellamy 2015, p. 161) is in many cases a function of its hollow nature and malleability; Gareth Evans, indeed, admits that the support of certain states for R2P is just 'cosmetics' (2016, p. 2). The process by which R2P has been moulded and framed thus coheres with Mona Lena Krook and Jacqui True's analysis of norms that challenges more traditional constructivist accounts of the role of norms in positively shaping discourse and ultimately influencing policy. Debate, they argue, conducted in a context of power asymmetries, shapes a norm's meaning with power ultimately, 'determining what can and cannot be said' (Krook and True 2010, p. 108). R2P is not, of course, the first phrase or norm to be cynically invoked; the long history of norm co-optation should, however, temper the enthusiasm surrounding the perceived significance of R2P's increased invocation (Wiener 2008; Krook and True 2010, p. 104).

Therefore, while R2P is certainly a widely affirmed and invoked norm, rather than this constituting evidence of its advocates having 'won the battle of ideas', this is a function of R2P's malleability and the absence of any costs associated with its affirmation; R2P is popular not because it has convinced states to change their ways, but precisely because it demands negligible change and actually, in certain contexts, enables its proponents to behave in ways inimical to its original ethos.

Norms and existential crises

History shows that states will occasionally, and wilfully, violate a norm if they perceive that it is in their interests to do so in order to preserve a more pressing norm that coheres more directly with their interests; as Panke and Petershohn warn, when states 'experience a mismatch between their preferences, beliefs or identities, on the one hand, and an international norm, on the other hand [they] develop an interest in violating a norm' (2011, p. 734). The extent to which states will violate a norm is, of course, dependent upon the nature of the punitive redress they face for so doing.

For states that have accepted R2P superficially, an internal threat of an existential gravity can quickly create an imperative to act in a manner that directly violates the affirmed R2P norm (Panke and Petershon 2011, p. 734). In the absence of countervailing internalisation of R2P, the imperative to violently tackle this 'threat' – to engage in what Welsh terms 'an existential battle' (2013, p. 386) – far outweighs any perceived need to abide by R2P.

The impulse to commit mass atrocities domestically is largely unique to a particular type of state, namely those governed oppressively by a regime that considers the trappings of state power to be essential to their survival. Such groups have few qualms about incurring costs associated with norm violation, namely rhetorical censure from a 'jury of their peers' (Sandholtz 2008, p. 107; see also, Harff 2009). As R2P lacks coercive enforcement capacity – due to the contestation surrounding Pillar III – violating the R2P norm, therefore, (potentially) only results in 'shame' (Evans 2015) and 'social exclusion' (Bellamy 2015, p. 61). Those states most likely to engage in mass atrocities are, however, least susceptible to being influenced by this type of societal shaming, particularly if they have a set of powerful allies unconcerned about their domestic human rights record.

As the decision to engage in atrocity crimes is impelled by a sense of existential crisis that trumps norm compliance, this means that atrocity-crime prevention and cessation places great emphasis on the operationalisation of the external dimension of R2P, namely Pillar III. Too often the norm encouraging an external response has been trumped, however, by a more pressing imperative to support an ally or secure interests (Chesterman 2003, p. 54; Deng 2010, pp. 86–87; Buchanan and Keohane 2011, p. 47; Welsh 2013). Post R2P, the P5 have chosen to ignore the plight of people suffering within other states because the oppressive state is an ally (Murray and Hehir 2012, p. 392; Bloomfield 2016, p. 325). This has manifest with respect to the international reaction – particularly that of the Security Council – to a number of cases in the past ten years such as Bahrain, Sudan, Israel, Sri Lanka, North Korea, and Syria. Victims of systemic human rights violations are, therefore, prey to geopolitics, as they were prior to the establishment of R2P (Chesterman 2011; Hehir 2013).

Therefore, so long as Pillar III remains dormant, the response of the 'international community' is predicated on the political will of states and thus censure is inherently political.[2] Repressive governments know this and, therefore, commit atrocity crimes because they calculate that they will be shielded from robust external censure by those external actors with an interest in perpetuating their existence. These dynamics can be readily identified in practice with respect to how Syria and Bahrain responded to internal movements calling for reform; in both cases the governments considered domestic opponents to constitute an existential threat; though they knew that deploying extreme violence against these groups was illegal – and certainly a violation of their commitment to R2P – and would incur some degree of external censure, they calculated that the costs associated with engaging in oppression were bearable given that their respective allies among the P5 would shield them from robust external sanction. Additionally, external actors approached both cases with the same thought process; while the nature of the oppression, and the scale of the mass atrocities ensured the violence would catalyse pressure to act, resisting this pressure, though not cost-free, was deemed the preferable, prudent course to take in light of the perceived costs of acting.

Therefore, while the idea that R2P is as yet imperfect but making 'progress' is premised on the increased willing of states to affirm Pillars I and II, the absence of support for Pillar III must temper these claims; it is this aspect of R2P alone that can potentially change the cost/benefit calculations of those states likely to engage in intra-state crises. So long as support for the R2P norm is exclusively for Pillars I and II, the concept is impotent in cases where engaging in mass atrocity crimes is perceived of as a matter of existential gravity, as it invariably is. R2P is, therefore, ineffective precisely in those cases where it is needed most and in the absence of evidence of existing or emerging consensus on Pillar III, this predicament will continue.

R2P and the 'three biases'

While R2P emerged from within a movement in the 1990s that sought to diminish the inviolability of state sovereignty and devolve power to actors below and above the state, it has become an inherently conservative project that constitutes an affirmation of the status quo. Rather than challenge the legal rights of states or call for the reform of the international legal system, ICISS sought to work within the existing system and explicitly rejected the idea of reform (International Commission on Intervention and State Sovereignty 2001, p. 49). While the 2005 World Summit was heralded by many as a breakthrough, it did not change international law in any way or alter the powers of any of the international institutions. Supporters of R2P readily accept this but have argued that as a norm R2P can influence state behaviour without legal recognition or an objective, automatic means by which violations can be addressed/punished. The focus of R2P's advocates, therefore, has always been on lobbying states to voluntarily change their behaviour, rather than calling for substantive reform, which has invariably been dismissed as unrealistic (Evans 2008, p. 137; Bellamy 2015, p. 74; Stanley Foundation 2015, p. 1).[3]

In the context of this affirmation of the status quo, R2P's supporters have found it necessary to argue that the existing system *has* been responsive to R2P's agenda; this has created an imperative to, paradoxically, defend the very system and the practices therein that impelled R2P in the first place. The premise that R2P is making 'tremendous progress' (Adams 2015b), has often involved advancing a narrative of success that involves uncritically accepting what states say; this narrative hails rhetorical support from states and the Security Council despite the evidence that concomitant action is often lacking. This has been particularly evident with respect to the 'success' of campaigns such as 'Restrain the Veto', and the 'Focal Points' initiative (Evans 2015; Van Oosterom 2015; Gifkins 2016; Global Centre for R2P 2016b). While these campaigns have attracted sustained support, there is little evidence that this numerical support has had a tangible effect on improving the conditions of those suffering systemic intra-state oppression. Both campaigns circumvent potential conflict with states by avoiding proposing either institutional reform or innovative legal obligations; state support for these campaigns, therefore, involves little more than proffering rhetorical support. Yet, the emphasis has often been on quantity rather than quality as evidenced by the heralding of success and progress on the basis of numerical support; indicatively in his short address to the General Assembly on the theme 'Ten Years of the Responsibility to Project' Simon Adams noted that there were now R2P Focal Points in '51 countries', that the Group of Friends of R2P had made 'tremendous strides' as it now had '50 UN members', and the 'Code of Conduct' is 'now supported by over 110 member states' (Adams 2016).

Additionally, some of R2P's proponents have emerged as vocal supporters of the existing system, including the veto power of the P5 (Davies and Bellamy 2014; Cinq-Mars 2015). Perhaps most curiously, at times proponents of the concept have defended non-intervention in the face of mass atrocities such as in Darfur, Sri Lanka and most notably Syria as prudent and/or still evidence of R2P's efficacy because the decision *not* to respond was at least framed in terms that evoked R2P (Evans 2008, p. 145; Bellamy 2009, p. 145; Thakur 2009; Glanville 2016).

Another feature of R2P's success narrative is the claim that a number of cases of successful external intervention – in both diplomatic and military form – illustrate R2P's efficacy; R2P is presented as having demonstrated its real-world influence in cases such as the Côte d'Ivoire (Evans 2016, p. 3), Kenya (Adams 2015a), Kyrgyzstan (Luck 2015, p. 4), Libya (Bellamy 2015, p. 94), and the Central African Republic (Weiss 2014, p. 7). Yet, the evidence presented to support the claims that these cases evidence R2P's efficacy is both inherently correlative and tenuous. It has been argued, for example, that even if R2P was never mentioned during the international response to these cases, its influence can be identified in the use of 'implicit signifiers' of R2P; words and phrases – which in many cases actually predate R2P – that ostensibly 'invoke' R2P without actually employing the term (Dunne and Gelber 2014, p. 335). This clearly strains credulity. Additionally, R2P is held to have influenced a number of broader initiatives – such as the rise of 'Protection of Civilians' mandates in UN Peacekeeping – which again do not mention the term but are nonetheless said to evidence of R2P's progressive impact (Evans 2015), despite the fact that – as Catherine Jones notes in her chapter – they predate, and are markedly different from, R2P (Breakey 2012, p. 74; Hopgood 2014).

The defence of R2P, therefore, coheres with Legro's analysis of the 'three biases' prevalent among proponents of a norm's efficacy; so as to perpetuate the norm's alleged influence, analyses presented by norm entrepreneurs evidence 'a neglect of alternative explanations, particularly ideational ones, for the effects attributed to norms'. The fact that a particular norm is held by observers to be a catalyst for state behaviour leads, he notes, to these observers exaggerating the influence of this norm and 'spuriously crediting international norms with consequences . . . that are better explained by other types of factors' (Legro 1997, p. 34; see also, Bloomfield 2016, p. 316).

Conclusion

From an anthropological or social-psychological perspective, the determination to maintain an image of R2P as effective, dynamic and a force that has 'begun to change the world' would no doubt serve as an interesting case study on groupthink, collective delusions and/or denialism. Yet, the myth of R2P as effective and dynamic is more than just a curious insight into human behaviour; in fact it is ultimately quite damaging. With R2P touted as 'the only show in town for those serious about preventing future Kosovos and future Rwandas' (Bellamy 2006, p. 15), it has subsumed thousands of scholars into a restricted and inherently conservative paradigm. Thus, research has been conducted on preventing and responding to intra-state mass atrocities within defined parameters; chief among them being that reform of the international system is impossible and should not be entertained or advocated. Unfortunately, this has meant that the domi-nant framework within which research on how to improve the manner in which states and the international community protect human rights is conducted, is premised on an underlying assumption that by definition means that the product of this research will continually advocate the perpetuation of the existing systemic architecture, despite this being the principle cause of the problem. This continual refusal to alter the underlying normative assumptions and methodological strictures calls to mind the definition of insanity as attributed to Einstein: 'doing the same thing over and over again and expecting different results.'

Notes

1 Only, it must be said, insofar as they mention Paragraph 139.
2 This is not, of course, to suggest that law enforcement can ever be totally apolitical; the origins, function and execution of law, in whatever context, is to some extent political (Koskenniemi 2001; Charlesworth and Kennedy 2009; Orford 2011, p. 139). Yet, the explicitly, and constitutionally enshrined, political means by which international law is enforced has particularly profound implications for the protection and promotion of human rights (White 2004, p. 666; Hurd 2007, p. 191).
3 Notable exceptions being Weiss 2009, Roff 2013, Herro 2015, and on a more speculative level, Welsh 2013.

References

Acharya, A 2004, 'How Ideas Spread: Whose Norms Matter? Norm Localization and Institutional Change in Asian Regionalism', *International Organization*, vol. 58, no. 2, pp. 239–275.

Acharya, A 2011, 'Norm Subsidiarity and Regional Orders: Sovereignty, Regionalism, and Rule-making in the Third World', *International Studies Quarterly*, vol. 55, no. 1, pp. 95–123.

Acharya, A 2013, 'The R2P and Norm Diffusion: Towards a Framework of Norm Circulation', *Global Responsibility to Protect*, vol. 5, no. 1, pp. 466–479.

Adams, S 2015a, 'R2P at Ten', *E-International Relations*, 29 March. Available from: www.e-ir.info/2015/03/29/r2p-at-10/. [9 December 2016].

Adams, S 2015b, 'The Responsibility to Protect: Ten Years On', *OpenCanada*, 8 May. Available from: www.opencanada.org/features/the-responsibility-to-protect-10-years-on/. [9 December 2016].

Adams, S 2016, 'Statement by Dr. Simon Adams at the Thematic Discussion in the UN General Assembly on "Ten years of the Responsibility to Protect: From Commitment to Implementation"', 26 February. Available from: www.globalr2p.org/media/files/2016-february-adams-gcr2p-statement-pga-event-1.pdf. [9 December 2016].

Adler, E and Pouliot, V 2011, 'International Practices', *International Theory*, vol. 3, no. 1, pp. 1–36.

Axworthy, L and Rock, A 2009, 'R2P: A New and Unfinished Agenda', *Global Responsibility to Protect*, vol. 1, no. 1.

Badescu, C 2010, *Humanitarian Intervention and the Responsibility to Protect*, Routledge, London.

Bahrain 2012, 'Statement of the Kingdom of Bahrain at the Sixty-Seventh Session of the UN General Assembly', 27 September. Available from: http://gadebate.un.org/sites/default/files/gastatements/67/BH_en.pdf. [9 December 2016].

Bellamy, A 2006, 'The Responsibility to Protect after the 2005 World Summit', Policy Brief No. 1, Carnegie Council on Ethics and International Affairs.

Bellamy, A 2009, *Responsibility to Protect: The Global Effort to End Mass Atrocities*, Polity, London.

Bellamy, A 2012, 'Remarks to the General Assembly Informal Interactive Dialogue on the Responsibility to Protect', New York, 5 September. Available from: http://responsibilitytoprotect.org/Alex%20Bellamy.pdf. [9 December 2016].

Bellamy, A 2014, 'From Tripoli to Damascus? Lesson Learning and the Implementation of the Responsibility to Protect', *International Politics*, vol. 51, no. 1, pp. 23–44.

Bellamy, A 2015, *The Responsibility to Protect: A Defence*, Oxford University Press, Oxford.

Betts, A and Orchard, P 2014, 'Introduction: The Normative Institutionalization-Implementation Gap' in A Betts and P Orchard, (eds), *Implementation and World Politics: How International Norms Change Politics*, pp. 1–28. Oxford University Press, Oxford.

Bloomfield, A 2016, 'Norm Antipreneurs and Theorising Resistance to Normative Change', *Review of International Studies*, vol. 42, no. 2, pp. 310–333.

Bloomfield, A and Scott, S 2016, *Norm Antipreneurs and the Politics of Resistance to Global Normative Change*, Routledge, Oxon.

Breakey, H 2012, 'The Responsibility to Protect and the Protection of Civilians in Armed Conflict: Overlap and Contrast' in A Francis, V Popovski and C Sampford, (eds), *Norms of Protection: Responsibility to Protect, Protection of Civilians and their Interaction*, pp. 62–81. United Nations University Press, Tokyo.

Buchanan, A and Keohane, R 2011, 'Precommitment Regimes for Intervention: Supplementing the Security Council', *Ethics and International Affairs*, vol. 25, no. 1, pp. 41–63.
Bull, H 1995, *The Anarchical Society*, Macmillan, Basingstoke.
Charlesworth, H and Kennedy, D 2009, 'Afterword' in A Orford, (ed.), *International Law and its Others*, pp. 401–408. Cambridge University Press, Cambridge.
Chayes, A and Chayes, A 1993, 'On Compliance', *International Organization*, vol. 47, no. 2, pp. 175–205.
Checkel, J 1998, 'The Constructivist Turn in International Relations Theory', *World Politics*, vol. 50, no. 2, pp. 324–348.
Chesterman, S 2003, 'Hard Cases Make Bad Law' in A Lang, (ed.), *Just Intervention*, pp. 46–61. Georgetown University Press, Washington D.C.
Chesterman, S 2011, ' "Leading from Behind": The Responsibility to Protect, the Obama Doctrine, and Humanitarian Intervention after Libya', *Ethics and International Affairs*, vol. 25, pp. 279–285.
Cinq-Mars, E 2015, 'In Support of R2P: No Need to Reinvent the Wheel', *OpenCanada*, 18 March. Available from: www.opencanada.org/features/in-support-of-r2p-no-need-to-reinvent-the-wheel/. [9 December 2016].
Davies, S and Bellamy, A 2014, 'Don't be Too Quick to Condemn the UN Security Council Power of Veto', *E-International Relations*, 12 August. Available from: https://theconversation.com/dont-be-too-quick-to-condemn-the-un-security-council-power-of-veto-29980. [9 December 2016].
Deitelhoff, N and Zimmermann, L 2013, 'Things We Lost in the Fire: How Different Types of Contestation Affect the Validity of International Norms', Peace Research Institute Frankfurt, Working Paper 18.
Deng, F 2010, 'JISB Interview: The Responsibility to Protect', *Journal of Intervention and Statebuilding*, vol. 4, no. 1, pp. 83–89.
Dunne, T 1998, *Inventing International Society*, St Martin's Press, New York.
Dunne, T and Gelber, K 2014, 'Arguing Matters: The Responsibility to Protect and the Case of Libya', *Global Responsibility to Protect*, vol. 6, no. 3, pp. 326–349.
Evans, G 2008, *The Responsibility to Protect: Ending Mass Atrocity Crimes Once and For All*, Brookings Institution Press, Washington DC.
Evans, G 2009, 'From an Idea to an International Norm' in R Cooper and J Kohler, (eds), *Responsibility to Protect: The Global Moral Compact for the 21st Century*, pp. 15–30. Palgrave Macmillan, Hampshire and New York.
Evans, G 2015, 'R2P: Looking Back, Looking Forward', Keynote Address, Phnom Penh, Cambodia, 26 February. Available from: www.gevans.org/speeches/speech568.html. [9 December 2016].
Evans, G 2016, 'R2P: The Next Ten Years' in A Bellamy and T Dunne, (eds), *Oxford Handbook of the Responsibility to Protect*, pp. 913–931. Oxford University Press, Oxford.
Finnemore, M and Sikkink, K 1998, 'International Norm Dynamics and Political Change', *International Organizations*, vol. 52, no. 4, pp. 887–917.
Franck, T 1990, *The Power of Legitimacy Among Nations*, Oxford University Press, Oxford.
Gallagher, A 2015a, 'The Promise of Pillar II: Analysing International Assistance Under the Responsibility to Protect', *International Affairs*, vol. 91, no. 6, pp. 1259–1275.
Gallagher, A 2015b, 'The Responsibility to Protect Ten Years on from the World Summit: A Call to Manage Expectations', *Global Responsibility to Protect*, vol. 7, no. 3, pp. 254–274.
Garwood-Gowers, A 2013, 'The BRICS and the Responsibility to Protect: Lessons from the Libyan and Syrian Crises' in V Sancin and MK Dine, (eds), *Responsibility to Protect in Theory and Practice*, pp. 291–315. GV Založba, Ljubljana.

Gholiagha, S 2015, '"To Prevent Future Kosovos and Future Rwandas." A Critical Constructivist View of the Responsibility to Protect', *The International Journal of Human Rights*, vol. 19, no. 8, pp. 1074–1097.

Gifkins, J 2016, 'R2P in the UN Security Council: Darfur, Libya and Beyond', *Cooperation and Conflict*, vol. 51, no. 2, pp. 148–165.

Glanville, L 2012, 'The Responsibility to Protect Beyond Borders', *Human Rights Law Review*, vol. 12, no. 1, pp. 1–32.

Glanville, L 2016, 'Does R2P matter? Interpreting the impact of a norm', *Cooperation and Conflict*, vol. 51, no. 2, pp. 184–199.

Global Centre for R2P 2016a, 'R2P Focal Points'. Available from: www.globalr2p.org/our_work/global_network_of_r2p_focal_points. [9 December 2016].

Global Centre for R2P 2017, 'UN Security Council Resolutions Referencing R2P'. Available from: www.globalr2p.org/resources/335. [1 February 2017].

Goldsmith, JL and Posner, EA 2002, 'Introduction', *Journal of Legal Studies*, XXXI, S1–S4.

Habermas, J 1992, *Faktizität und Geltung: Beiträge zur Diskurstheorie des Rechts und des demokratischen Rechtsstaats*, Suhrkamp Verlag, Frankfurt.

Harff, B 2009, 'How to Use Risk Assessment and Early Warning in the Prevention and De-escalation of Genocide and Other Mass Atrocities', *Global Responsibility to Protect*, vol. 1, no. 4, pp. 506–531.

Hehir, A 2013, 'The Permanence of Inconsistency: Libya, the Security Council and The Responsibility to Protect', *International Security*, vol. 38, no. 1, pp. 137–159.

Hehir, A 2015, 'Assessing the Influence of the Responsibility to Protect on the UN Security Council during the Arab Spring', *Cooperation and Conflict*, vol. 51, no. 2, pp. 166–183.

Herro, A 2015, *UN Emergency Peace Service and the Responsibility to Protect*, Routledge, London.

Hofmann, G 2015, 'Ten Years R2P – What Doesn't Kill a Norm Only Makes It Stronger?', Peace Research Institute Frankfurt, Report 133.

Hopgood, S 2014, 'The Last Rites for Humanitarian Intervention: Darfur, Sri Lanka and R2P', *Global Responsibility to Protect*, vol. 6, no. 2, pp. 181–205.

Hurd, I 2007, *After Anarchy*, Princeton University Press, Princeton, NJ.

International Commission on Intervention and State Sovereignty 2001, *The Responsibility to Protect*, International Development Research Centre, Ottawa.

Katzenstein, P 1996, 'Introduction: Alternative Perspectives on National Security' in P Katzenstein, (ed.), *The Culture of National Security*, pp. 1–32. Columbia Press, New York.

Kelley, J 2008, 'Assessing the Complex Evolution of Norms: The Rise of International Election Monitoring', *International Organization*, vol. 62, no. 2, pp. 221–255.

Kersten, M 2015, 'The Responsibility to Protect Doctrine is Faltering. Here's Why', *The Washington Post*, 8 December. Available from: www.washingtonpost.com/news/monkey-cage/wp/2015/12/08/the-responsibility-to-protect-doctrine-is-failing-heres-why/. [9 December 2016].

Ki-Moon, Ban 2015, 'A Vital and Enduring Commitment: Implementing the Responsibility to Protect', UN Secretary General Report, A/69/981, 13 July.

Klotz, A 1995, 'Norms Reconstituting Interests: Global Racial Equality and US Sanctions Against South Africa', *International Organization*, vol. 49, no. 3, pp. 451–478.

Koskenniemi, M 2001, *The Gentle Civilizer of Nations*, Cambridge University Press, Cambridge.

Kowert, P and Legro, J 1996, 'Norms, Identity and Their Limits' in P Katzenstein, (ed.), *The Culture of National Security*, pp. 451–497, Columbia Press, New York.

Krook, ML and True, J 2010, 'Rethinking the Life Cycles of International Norms: The United Nations and the Global Promotion of Gender Equality', *European Journal of International Relations*, vol. 18, no. 1, pp. 103–127.

Labonte, M 2013, *Human Rights and Humanitarian Norms, Strategic Framing, and Intervention*, Routledge, London.
Legro, J 1997, 'Which Norms Matter?', *International Organisation*, vol. 51, no. 1, pp. 31–63.
Loiselle, M-E 2013, 'The Normative Status of the Responsibility to Protect', *Global Responsibility to Protect*, vol. 5, no. 3, pp. 317–341.
Luck, E 2015, 'The Responsibility to Protect at Ten: The Challenges Ahead', Stanley Foundation, Policy Brief, May.
March, J and Olsen, J 1989, *Rediscovering Institutions*, Free Press, New York.
Morris, J 2013, 'Libya and Syria: R2P and the Spectre of the Swinging Pendulum', *International Affairs*, vol. 89, no. 5, pp. 1265–1283.
Murray, RW and Hehir, A 2012, 'Intervention in the Emerging Multipolar System: Why R2P will Miss the Unipolar Moment', *Journal of Intervention and Statebuilding*, vol. 6, no. 4, pp. 387–406.
Nougayrède, N 2012, 'Interview with Kofi Annan: "On Syria, It's Obvious, We Haven't Succeeded"' *Le Monde*, 7 July. Available from: www.lemonde.fr/proche-orient/article/2012/07/07/kofi-annan-sur-la-syrie-a-l-evidence-nous-n-avons-pas-reussi_1730658_3218.html. [9 December 2016].
Orford, A 2011, *International Authority and the Responsibility to Protect*, Cambridge University Press, Cambridge.
Panke, D and Petersohn, U 2011, 'Why International Norms Disappear Sometimes', *European Journal of International Relations*, vol. 18, no. 4, pp. 719–742.
Quinton-Brown, P 2013, 'Mapping Dissent: The Responsibility to Protect and Its State Critics', *Global Responsibility to Protect*, vol. 5, no. 3, pp. 275–276.
Ramos-Horta, J 2015, 'Preventing Conflicts, Mediating the End of Wars, Building Durable Peace', Fifth Annual Gareth Evans Lecture, 8 October. Available from: www.globalr2p.org/media/files/gelramos-horta.pdf. [9 December 2016].
Risse, T 1999, 'International Norms and Domestic Change: Arguing and Communicative Behaviour in the Human Rights Era', *Politics and Society*, vol. 27, no. 4, pp. 529–559.
Roff, H 2013, *Global Justice, Kant and the Responsibility to Protect: A Provisional Duty*, Routledge, London.
Ruggie, J 1993, 'Territoriality and Beyond: Problematizing Modernity in International Relations', *International Organization*, vol. 47, no. 1, pp. 139–174.
Sandholtz, W 2008, 'Dynamics of International Norm Change', *European Journal of International Relations*, vol. 14, no. 1, pp. 101–131.
Sandholtz, W and Stiles, K 2009, *International Norms and Cycles of Change*, Oxford University Press, Oxford.
Slaughter, A-M 2011, 'A Day to Celebrate, but Hard Work Ahead', *Foreign Policy*, 18 March. Available from: www.foreignpolicy.com/articles/2011/03/18/does_the_world_belong_in_libyas_war?page=0,7. [9 December 2016].
Stanley Foundation 2015, 'The Responsibility to Protect at Ten: Perspectives and Opportunities', November. Available from: www.stanleyfoundation.org/resources.cfm?id=1581. [9 December 2016].
Sudan 2009, 'Statement by Sudan on the Protection of Civilians in Armed Conflict', 11 November. Available from: http://responsibilitytoprotect.org/Sudan(1).pdf. [9 December 2016].
Thakur, R 2009, 'West Shouldn't Fault Sri Lankan Government Tactics', *Daily Yomiuri*, 12 June 2009.
Thakur, R 2013, 'R2P after Libya and Syria: Engaging Emerging Powers', *Washington Quarterly*, vol. 36, no. 2, pp. 61–76.
Van Kersbergen, K and Verbeek, B 2007, 'The Politics of International Norms', *European Journal of International Relations*, vol. 13, no. 2, pp. 217–238.

Van Oosterom, K 2015, 'Statement on Behalf of The Group of Friends on the Responsibility to Protect at the UN General Assembly Informal Interactive on the Responsibility to Protect', 8 September. Available from: http://responsibilitytoprotect.org/Group%20of%20friends.pdf. [9 December 2016].

Weiss, T 2009, *What's Wrong with the United Nations and How to Fix It*, Polity, Cambridge.

Weiss, T 2011, 'R2P Alive and Well after Libya', *Ethics and International Affairs*, vol. 25, no. 3, pp. 287–292.

Weiss, T 2014, 'Military Humanitarianism: Syria hasn't killed it', *The Washington Quarterly*, vol. 37, no. 1, pp. 7–20.

Welsh, J 2013, 'Norm Contestation and the Responsibility to Protect', *Global Responsibility to Protect*, vol. 5, no. 4, pp. 365–396.

Welsh, J 2014, 'Implementing the Responsibility to Protect: Catalyzing Debate and Building Capacity' in A Betts and P Orchard, (eds), *Implementation and World Politics: How International Norms Change Politics*, pp. 124–243. Oxford University Press, Oxford.

Wendt, A 1999, *A Social Theory of International Politics*, Cambridge University Press, Cambridge.

White, N 2004, 'The Will and Authority of the Security Council after Iraq', *Leiden Journal of International Law*, vol. 17, no. 4, pp. 645–672.

Wiener, A 2004, 'Contested Compliance: Interventions on the Normative Structure of World Politics', *European Journal of International Relations*, vol. 10, no. 2, pp. 189–234.

Wiener, A 2008, *The Invisible Constitution of Politics: Contested Norms and International Encounters*, Cambridge University Press, Cambridge.

Wiener, A 2009, 'Enacting Meaning-in-use: Qualitative Research on Norms and International Relations', *Review of International Studies*, vol. 35, no. 1, pp. 175–193.

11

GUNS VS TROOPS

The ethics of supplying arms[1]

James Pattison

Introduction

At the time of writing (early 2016) it seems that Western states are less likely to wage major wars in the future. This is for (at least) four reasons. First, despite several ongoing conflicts, the world is generally becoming more peaceful. There are fewer mass atrocities and conflicts for which to wage war in response.[2] Second, the United States (US) and United Kingdom's (UK) misadventures in Iraq and Afghanistan have severely diminished any public appetite for large-scale war or humanitarian intervention. The significant public opposition to the mooted humanitarian intervention in Syria against Assad in 2013 indicates that any Western leader is likely to have to go against public opinion.[3] Third, in the wake of the financial crisis and neoliberal austerity measures, there have been significant cuts to military expenditure, further reducing the ability of Western powers to undertake large-scale military operations abroad. Fourth, in the future it will be more difficult to secure international support for major wars and military interventions, most notably from the UN Security Council, which is an important factor in their legitimacy and ultimately effectiveness (Pattison 2010). It is widely expected that the BRICS – Brazil, Russia, India, China, and South Africa – will rise in global influence and there will be a relative decrease in the power of the US and Europe. The BRICS are notoriously much more noninterventionist, at least in their rhetoric, and often define their foreign policy agendas in opposition to Western interventionism.[4] It seems likely, then, that any potential Western interventions will have to navigate carefully the positions of the BRICS and, if they oppose the intervention, potentially endure significant reputational and other political costs.

Although less likely to engage in direct military intervention, major Western powers will still, of course, attempt to secure their foreign policy goals – including the tackling of violations of human rights beyond their borders – by other means. Some of these measures have already been subject to ethical analysis, namely, the use of force short of war, such as targeted strikes and drone warfare. But the focus on the options to tackle the mass violations of basic human rights – such as in debates about the Responsibility to Protect (R2P) – has still been on direct military intervention; the alternatives to direct military intervention have not been sufficiently explored. These alternatives raise several important ethical issues and include the use of economic sanctions, diplomatic criticism, and various forms of humanitarian, financial, and military assistance.[5] In this chapter, I will focus particularly on one form of military assistance: the supply of military equipment to insurgents.

The ethical issues surrounding the supply of military equipment to insurgents in order to tackle human rights violations has become particularly pertinent in the wake of the Arab Spring. In response to the uprisings in Libya in 2011, several states, including France, Qatar, and the UK, supplied lethal and nonlethal weapons to the rebel groups fighting the incumbent regime (Corten and Koutroulis 2013, p. 90). In response to the uprisings in Syria, states provided arms to the various belligerents fighting the civil war. The supplying of arms became one of the central political issues. Various rebel factions were supplied arms by, among others, Qatar, Saudi Arabia, the UK, Turkey and France, and the Assad regime was provided with weapons by Russia and Iran (BBC 2013).

I recently considered the general permissibility of arming rebel groups elsewhere (see Pattison 2015a).[6] I have argued that arming rebels is, on the one hand, exceptionally permissible because it can help rebel groups to pursue legitimate ends, such as the protection of individual human rights and self-determination, but, on the other, is generally impermissible. This is because (i) it can be very difficult to determine precisely who the rebels are and whether they are fighting with regard to the principles of *jus ad bellum* and *jus in bello* and, if they were to get in power, whether they would be likely to be better than the current government. The arming of rebels can (ii) significantly escalate hostilities when, in response, other parties in the conflict also seek arms or intensify their response by clamping further down on any opposition groups. In addition, (iii) it is difficult to ensure not only that the weapons are delivered to or stay in the possession of the seemingly legitimate rebels.

In this chapter, I want to go beyond the question of the permissibility of arming rebels to consider two further issues. First, how does the case for providing arms to rebel groups in order to tackle human rights violations compare morally to humanitarian intervention? Second, are the current international laws on providing arms to rebel groups morally judicious? I will argue that providing arms to rebel groups in order to help protect human rights is even more dangerous than engaging in direct military intervention and offers potentially fewer countervailing benefits, even if there is some minor principled reason in favour of it. Nevertheless, I will also argue that the current international laws on providing arms *are* unfair to rebels. But rather than weakening the law, the chapter will argue that the laws on providing arms should be even more restrictive for the provision of arms to *states*.

Before beginning, a quick clarification is required: arming rebels should be (and in policy circles *is*) seen as an alternative to war and direct military intervention.

To start with, it is an alternative to states waging wars and directly intervening militarily in other states. That is, even if there is already a civil war going on in which the rebels are participating, arming rebels avoids a further war – an *inter*state war – such as between the external party and the repressive state. Indeed, during the public debate on Syria,[7] the sending of arms was widely viewed as an alternative to war by the West against Assad. It was defended by those more optimistic that it would help to remove Assad and therefore remove any purported need for direct Western military intervention. In addition, it is worth noting that, although this chapter will focus largely on civil wars, the rebels may not be engaged in a civil war, but instead in low-intensity conflict. The support for them in this enterprise may be sufficient to achieve the foreign policy goals of the supplying state. In short, the rebels need not be engaged in intra-state *war*. For instance, the airdrops of weapons by the UK to the French Resistance, which opposed the Vichy Regime and Nazi occupation during World War II, helped to disrupt the occupation, facilitate the escape of Allied forces caught behind enemy lines, and provide intelligence for the Allied invasion.

Notwithstanding, although the arming of rebels is sometimes an alternative to war and direct military intervention, it is sometimes carried out *alongside* war and direct military intervention. For instance, not only did the West arm the Libyan rebels, it also intervened militarily in support of them. Arming rebels is therefore a *separate* option to engaging in war and direct military intervention, but may be undertaken *alongside* these other options as well, just as other notable alternatives to war, such as economic sanctions, targeted killings, and strong diplomatic rebuke, are sometimes used as alternatives and are sometimes undertaken alongside war and direct military intervention.

Arming rebels and direct military intervention

First, let us consider how arming rebels compares to direct military intervention. For instance, in response to the mass atrocities and civil war in Syria, and before the emergence of Islamic State, would it have been better to arm the Free Syrian Army or to intervene militarily? And, as the West seems less likely to engage in major wars and interventions in the future, should it fill this void by supplying arms or should it attempt to retain some notable capacity to intervene, such as by increasing the pooling of resources between states?

In what follows, I will consider four potential principled reasons why arming rebels might appear to be preferable. These reasons largely stem from a clear and obvious difference to direct military intervention, which largely explains its popularity as a foreign policy option for states supplying arms to rebels in Syria, Libya, Ukraine, the Balkans, and beyond: the arming of rebels does not involve sending troops to fight beyond the borders of the state.

First, does it matter that sending arms is a lot cheaper and does not risk one's soldiers coming home in body bags? I think that this provides *some*, *small* reason to prefer arming rebels. This is patent if there would be *overall* less unjust harm to innocents, that is, when the harms of arming rebels would be lower than the costs of sending soldiers for both the sending state and for those subject to the potential intervention (and third parties, such as neighbouring states). For instance, arming rebels may, perhaps only exceptionally, be less costly since direct military intervention would result in the intervening state being dragged into a lengthy, bloody international war.

But I want to consider beyond this point if it may be preferable to arm rebels even when the direct military intervention by the external party would result in overall *less* harm than arming rebels. Suppose, for example, that there are two ways that France could address a brutal regime in Guinea that is engaged in mass atrocities. On the one hand, it could intervene militarily, risking the lives of soldiers at great expense. This would be more effective overall at tackling the mass atrocities. On the other, it could supply military hardware to a rebel movement, at much cheaper cost and not risk the lives of French soldiers. This option would still be likely to tackle the mass atrocities, but not as quickly. In the meantime, some innocents in Guinea would die. Which option should France choose? The supplying of arms *might* be preferable (depending on the overall number of lives saved). This is because of the (albeit limited) special obligations that France has to favour the interests of its citizens. That is, as is widely accepted, states have fiduciary obligations to promote the interests of their citizens, even if this will not be directly optimal overall in advancing human rights worldwide. As such, providing weapons to rebel groups may be a morally justifiable form of risk transfer in that it transfers risks to noncitizens – i.e. rebels – letting them carry the burdens of fighting rather than citizens.

However, I think that this provides only a minor reason in favour of arming rebels. Although states should give greater weight to the interests of their citizens, they still need to factor in the effects on the interests of individuals beyond their borders. More specifically, one should not endorse what Allen Buchanan (1999) calls the 'discretionary association view' of the state – in short, that the state must concern itself *exclusively* with the interests of its citizens.[8] Rather, one should hold instead only the view that the *primary* role of the state is to promote the interests of its citizens. On this more moderate view, states still possess some duties to those beyond their borders, including the duty to undertake direct military intervention in certain circumstances, even if it will be costly for its citizens (Buchanan 1999). Moreover, the amount of additional weight that they may give is small: they cannot permissibly give *much* greater weight to the interests of their own citizens compared to the interests of those beyond their state. Accordingly, partiality tips the balance only in borderline cases, such as the France case above, where the arming of rebels will be similarly proportionate (in agent-neutral terms) to direct military intervention.

A second potential argument focuses on humanitarian intervention and runs as follows. Rebels more clearly consent to fight in their own defence than intervening soldiers who may not agree to fight in humanitarian interventions. This is because (i) humanitarian intervention involves the coercion of those fighting, since, it is claimed, soldiers only agree to sign up for national defence (Cook 2000) and (ii) a rebellion is more likely to be fought by volunteers. Thus, considerations of individual autonomy render it preferable to arm rebels than to intervene. This is because, although (as I have argued elsewhere in Pattison 2014) it is all-things-considered permissible to force some to fight when there is no other option, it would be better *not* to force individuals to fight and instead look to the alternatives to doing so, such as arming rebels.

Is this argument plausible? It is, of course, a contingent matter whether rebel forces are made up of conscripts or volunteers. Some clearly do involve coercion (e.g. Liberia and Uganda), but others (such as the African National Congress in South Africa) are based on voluntary participation (Eck 2014). This is in part because of the costs of coercion for the rebels. These include the costs of policing and tackling attrition, the negative effects for the success of the rebellion due to desertion on the battlefield, and the alienation of the civilian population (Eck 2014).

However, it is also the case that wars and humanitarian interventions are often based on volunteers: soldiers can expect when they sign up that their state will engage in humanitarian interventions. Indeed, enlistment documents typically do not distinguish between the types of wars that those enlisting will be required to fight. Hence, there does not seem to be sufficient basis for a general presumption in favour of arming rebels because of the individual autonomy of those fighting.

Nevertheless, it is certainly possible that a humanitarian intervention may involve conscription and that a rebellion will not. Perhaps more likely is that, even if enlistment documents do typically allow for humanitarian intervention, there may still be particular individuals who do not wish to fight. Such documents can also be vague about what exactly it is to which individual soldiers agree. By contrast, *certain* rebels more clearly consent since they take up arms for a specific fight – the war against their state – than regular soldiers who may or may not expect to fight wars of other defence when they sign up. In such cases, considerations of individual autonomy render it preferable to arm rebel groups. This is because, although it is all-things-considered permissible to force some to fight when there is no other option, it would be better *not* to force individuals to fight by looking at alternatives to doing so, such as arming rebels. Yet, given that rebels may oftentimes be conscripted, there does not seem to be sufficient basis for a general presumption in favour of arming rebels because of the individual autonomy of those fighting.

Third, does it matter that the rebel soldiers benefit from the action against their state? The thought is this: arming rebels in order to help protect human rights is preferable to intervening directly because the rebels are potential beneficiaries of the action. That is, they may benefit, for instance, from the overthrow of their repressive government. For example, if successful, providing weapons could mean that the Free Syrian Army will benefit from a stable, human rights-respecting government instead of the brutal Assad regime. By contrast, intervening soldiers are much less likely to benefit in this way. By arming rebels, rather than intervening, states transfer risks to those who may benefit from these risks being undertaken.

This does not provide a weighty (or likely) reason in favour of arming rebels. This is because, obviously, benefiting does not depend on anything about individual responsibility for the conflict that means that it is acceptable to impose *significant* costs on the rebels who 'benefit'. Furthermore, the rebels being 'benefited' in this context might still be significantly disadvantaged, such as being under an authoritarian leader (e.g. through no fault of their own, they have already had to endure years of rule by Assad). Although their situation may improve, it will have often started at a very low level (e.g. subject to poverty and human rights abuses). Those who have not been benefited by the overthrow of their authoritarian government (e.g. British, American, and French soldiers) may often be far better off. In fact, if we hold that many of those who bear the burdens of mass atrocities or an authoritarian leader are not morally responsible for this situation, then, given that these individuals already bear the costs of the mass atrocities or their authoritarian leader, it may seem fairer that *others* should bear the costs of tackling the situation.

To be sure, being benefited may have some moral relevance when those benefited already have their just entitlement. For example, it might be relevant when rebels are generally much better off than the regular soldiers from other states, when the latter are extremely poor, subject to various abuses in their home state, and so on. However, it seems generally that rebels will be in an even worse situation. Therefore, although it is conceivable that being benefited may provide a reason to prefer arming rebels, it is unlikely to be relevant in practice.

A fourth potential reason in favour of arming rebels is that it more fairly shares the duties to promote the enjoyment of human rights. It is only a limited number of states that can launch humanitarian interventions to protect the enjoyment of human rights in cases of mass atrocities. This is because only a few states (e.g. the US, France, and the UK) have sufficient air- or sea-lift capacity. Thus, when humanitarian interventions are required, a significant burden will fall on a limited number of states that are able to wage just humanitarian interventions. If these states have already waged a significant number of just interventions already, they could not be reasonably asked to bear any further costs in tackling mass atrocities. Other states should bear these costs. Yet other states are not able to do so since they are not sufficiently capable militarily. By contrast, the argument runs, the arming of rebels better shares the costs of tackling mass atrocities so that they are not borne by only a few states. In particular, states that are not capable of waging war can still play a significant role in fulfilling their duties to tackle mass atrocities by the arming of rebel groups. Even if these states do not possess the arms themselves to transfer, they can purchase arms from states that do, or develop these weapons themselves, in order to supply them to rebel groups.[9]

Yet, this reason seems unlikely to apply. Even if a few states carry more of the burden of warfighting, they can still share some of the burden by having the soldiers of other states carry out the frontline duties. In fact, this is already the predominant practice with recent direct military interventions. That is, direct military interventions have typically become 'hybridised', with major Western states providing logistical support to non-Western troops on the ground (Bellamy and Williams 2009).

More fundamentally, even though a few states may have to bear the greater burdens of fighting wars, this is not problematic since the unfairness of bearing the burdens of fighting wars or direct military interventions should not be viewed in isolation. The more militarily capable states – such as the US, France, and the UK – typically do very well out of the current global political and economic system. It therefore is fairer that, as major beneficiaries of a system that has some major injustices, they should bear much of the costs of tackling the current injustice. Moreover, there is a plausible case for holding that these states in fact owe reparative duties to tackle the injustice because of their prior violations of human rights, such as by sustaining the unjust global economic system and by propping up illegitimate actors. Concern about unfairness to major military powers is therefore a weak reason to favour arming rebels. Worries about unfairness therefore seems unlikely to provide a reason to favour arming rebels since militarily capable states could still be legitimately required to fight wars or direct military interventions.

The upshot is this: the principled reasons for preferring arming rebels to direct military intervention are either unlikely to apply or not very weighty. The most notable principled reason in favour of arming rebels for human rights purposes concerns limited partiality towards fellow soldiers, but the import of this concern seems relevant only for borderline cases. More important is the (i) likely efficacy of supplying arms to rebel groups, in terms of helping them to achieve just goals, such as tackling the conflict or removing an oppressive regime. Also crucial is, of course, (ii) whether there are likely to be negative effects of arming rebels in terms of harms to innocents, such as from rogue rebels who target civilians, escalation of the conflict, and the diffusion of arms. It seems that (i) the efficacy of supplying arms is generally very questionable, in large part because any arms supplied are likely to be matched by arms supplied to the state opposing the rebels (Moore 2012), and (ii) the likely negative effects (in terms of harms to innocents) will be more pronounced than those of direct military intervention. These effects will often be worse because intervening forces can exert greater control over the military forces that they deploy than the arms that they supply. By contrast, supplying arms to rebel groups puts undue hope on the prospect of rebels fighting justly and destroying the weapons at the end of the conflict. Ultimately, then, providing arms to rebel groups is even more dangerous than engaging in direct military intervention and offers potentially fewer countervailing benefits, even if there is some minor principled reason in favour of it.[10]

International law and arming rebels

Having compared the ethics of arming rebels to military intervention, let us now consider the morality of arming of rebels under current international law.

The arming of rebels is widely viewed as generally illegal according to international law. This is because, first, the arming of rebels is illegal when the rebels may use the weapons supplied to disregard the rules of international humanitarian law (IHL), as in the cases of Syria and Libya (Corten and Koutroulis 2013; Ruys 2014). This is based on a customary norm to 'ensure respect' for IHL. This is supported by the Arms Trade Treaty (ATT), which in Article 6 (3) asserts that a state cannot authorise the transfer of arms if it has knowledge that the arms would be used to breach IHL; although not yet ratified, the ATT provides clear *opinio juris* of current customary international law (Ruys 2014, pp. 28–29).

Second, arming rebels violates Article 2 (4) of the UN Charter (the prohibition on the use of force) since supplying arms is widely viewed as a 'threat to use of force', and violates the related Article 2 (7) (the principle of nonintervention) (Akande 2013; Ruys 2014, p. 32; Schmitt 2014). There are potential exceptions, but these are unlikely to apply in the case of arming rebels. One exception is if the UN Security Council authorises the supply of arms (e.g. with a resolution under Chapter VII) (Corten and Koutroulis 2013, p. 90; Schmitt 2014). But this is, of course, contingent on UN Security Council authorisation being forthcoming, which it may not be (e.g. in Syria). On the contrary, the Council may explicitly deny the legality of supplying arms in an arms embargo. Another potential exception is if states consent to the arming of groups within their borders. The supplying of arms might not then contravene the prohibition on the use of force or the principle of nonintervention (Ruys 2014, p. 40). But, obviously, states are highly unlikely to give their consent to the arming of opposing rebel forces. Perhaps a seemingly more plausible exception is if the opposing rebel forces were recognised as the new *de jure* government; states could then legally assist the former rebels (now, the 'government' forces) in their conflict against the 'rebels' (the former government forces). Yet such a view contravenes the widespread understanding of recognition as requiring that the government exercise effective control over most of the state's territory (Ruys 2014, pp. 37–38; Schmitt 2014, p. 154).[11] Moreover, such a view would have serious legal repercussions for understandings of recognition more generally since almost any party may be recognised and then consent to intervention by another state, thereby massively weakening the prohibition on the use of force and the principle of nonintervention (Ruys 2014, p. 39).

There is an apparent, general unfairness in international law since it is illegal to arm rebels but is legal to arm the opposing state forces. This is because states can invite intervention, which does not undermine the prohibition on the use of force or the duty of nonintervention (Ruys 2014, p. 40).[12] To be sure, there are two exceptions to the general (legal) permissibility of arming states. First, transfers to governments are not permitted when there is a substantial risk that the arms will be used to violate IHL (Ruys 2014, p. 45). Second, UN arms embargoes legally oblige states not to supply arms to the entire territory of embargoed states. Indeed, arms embargoes are often imposed on rebel groups *and* on government forces, such as in the cases of the Democratic Republic of Congo, Iraq, Liberia, Rwanda, Sierra Leone and Somalia (Holtom 2012, p. 10).

How should we judge such apparent unfairness? On the one hand, we may think that, if it can be exceptionally permissible to arm rebels, the law should *not* prohibit arming rebels. Let us call this the 'Less Restrictive Option': the law should allow for the arming of rebels. This is because the current legal regime is problematic since it massively favours states, such as the Assad regime. Those subject to grave violations of their basic human rights by their states are denied access to the means to address these violations. In similar vein, John Bolton (then US Undersecretary for Arms Control and International Security) argued, in his 2001 plenary address to the UN Conference of Action on the Illicit Trade of Small Arms and Light Weapons that:

> [w]e do not support measures limiting trade in [small arms/light weapons] olely to governments. This proposal, we believe, is both conceptually and practically flawed ... Perhaps most important, this proposal would preclude assistance to an oppressed non-state group defending itself from a genocidal government. Distinctions between governments and non-governments are irrelevant in determining responsible and irresponsible end-users of arms.[13]

Similarly, the discussions in 1998 about the Canadian-sponsored effort to develop a 'Global Convention Prohibiting the International Transfer of Military Small Arms and Light Weapons to Non-State Actors' faced opposition from states and NGOs 'because it would ban arms transfers to [nonstate actors] in cases where armed opposition against an illegitimate or repressive government was deemed "the only option"' (Holtom 2012, p. 7).

Conversely, we might think that there should be an absolute prohibition on the arming of rebel groups, but not states. Let us call this the 'Statist Option'. Why can states be armed? One might hold that there are Hobbesian (moral) reasons for maintaining that governments – and not rebels – should be able to obtain military supplies. This is to uphold a monopoly on the use of force so that there can be some degree of stability within the state, which is ultimately necessary for legitimate governance and to reduce the overall levels of conflict within both the state and the international system (e.g. so that armed rebels do not destabilise neighbouring states). The apparent unfairness in international law is therefore necessary for international order and internal legitimacy.

Alternatively, one might hold that *both* rebels and governments should be precluded from being armed. We might call this the 'Highly Restrictive Option'. To that extent, Tom Ruys argues that, in the case of civil wars,

> considering the fact that third-State weapon supplies often tend to prolong the duration of a civil war and complicate the achievement of a political solution, it is much to be desired for arms transfers to both parties in the actual civil war to be treated in identical fashion, and, more specifically, to be equally prohibited under international law ... The perception that international law is far more permissive vis-à-vis support (armed or other) on the side of the State authorities, even in situations of civil war, seems

fundamentally irreconcilable with the right of people to choose their own political future without outside interference.

(2014, p. 44)

In addition to the worries about illegitimate governments strengthening their regime, similar worries about the proportionality of supplying arms to rebels also *to some degree* apply to the arming of states. Just as when rebels are supplied arms, governments are also likely to misuse the arms and harm innocent civilians. Arming states is also likely to escalate the conflict, since other agents will provide arms to the rebel groups in response (see Moore 2012, pp. 335–336). The weapons are also likely to be present in the society long after the conflict, as they, for instance, are stolen from government stockpiles (see Jackson 2010). Accordingly, the likely efficacy of supplying arms to governments, in terms of helping them to achieve just goals, is generally questionable, and there will be pronounced negative effects.

There is a fourth option: the 'More Restrictive Option'. This holds that rebels and *some* governments should be precluded from being armed. That is, it adds that there should be a prohibition on arming *certain* states, that is, states that are likely to violate the human rights of their citizens. To have legal force, this blacklist could – as a nonideal but currently optimal measure – be endorsed by the UN Security Council (even if some notable states are not listed). To start with, then, it would resemble the legal status quo, acting in a similar manner to UN arms embargoes (or regional arms embargoes, such as by the OSCE and ECOWAS). Nevertheless, it could develop so that many more states are blacklisted and in the end that all states need import licences in order to purchase arms legally. There could be a supranational, independent licensing body that would provide licences only for states that are not likely to misuse the arms and that would keep tight control of them – in essence, a strengthened, more robust and far less permissive version of the current end-user certification system. There would be a well-resourced body to monitor the enforcement of the licensing regime (e.g. to protect against fake licences) and robust political, economic, or criminal sanctions for those who violated its rules by, for instance, exporting to those who do not possess a licence.[14]

Although space precludes fleshing out this option more here, it seems to be the most favourable. It accepts the concerns about arming states but does not fully preclude doing so, which could render it too hard for legitimate states to maintain their justified monopoly on force. This is because states would be reliant simply on the weapons that they can produce themselves, which leaves them vulnerable to rebels who obtain major conventional weapons through the black market. Yet it also accepts, along with the Highly Restrictive Option, that there are serious worries with providing arms to states, as well as to rebels.

How should this view (or the Statist Option or the Highly Restrictive Option) on the illegality of supplying arms be reconciled, if one holds that arming rebels can be exceptionally permissible (if generally problematic)?[15] I suggest that the occasional permissibility of such instances should be viewed as illegal but legitimate. That is, it should be viewed as similar to the occasional instances of humanitarian intervention that lack clear state consent or UN Security Council authorisation, such as, famously, NATO's intervention in Kosovo in 1999. (The Independent International Commission on Kosovo concluded that NATO's action was 'legitimate, but not legal, given existing international law' (2000, p. 189). What this means is that, when arming rebels is all-things-considered morally justifiable, those supplying arms should not be subject to the various reputational and other political costs associated with action that contravene international law. In short, those justifiably but illegally arming rebels should make a plea of mitigation (i.e. present the case for their action). Various other actors in the international community (states, NGOs, the media, etc.) can have what Thomas Franck (2006) calls a 'jurying' function in order to assess whether the plea is plausible and so whether the state supplying arms should be subject to international opprobrium and to other sanctions.[16]

The law therefore does not need to reflect *fully* the applied morality of the issue of arming rebels. It is unlikely that the law could be specified sufficiently so that all the morally permissible cases of arming rebels are legal and, conversely, all the morally impermissible cases are illegal. Too fine-grained distinctions would need to be made that may undermine the generality of international law or may require impartial and very well-informed judgments on rebel groups' fidelity to the principles of *jus ad bellum* and *jus in bello*, and on the likely impact of the arming of the rebels by outside parties. Even if such institutions are feasible in the longer term, in the short term something such as the blacklist approach and relying on pleas of mitigation in other cases seems to be all that could be achieved.

Conclusion

Thus, although arming rebels may occasionally be permissible, this should not be reflected by changes in international law. Instead, the law should be amended to retain the prohibition on arming rebels and be more restrictive for arming states. In the meantime, permissible cases of arming rebels should be seen as similar to permissible cases of direct unilateral military intervention without UN Security Council authorisation and states' consent. That is, it should be viewed as illegal but legitimate.

Accordingly, in the face of decreased ability to undertake wars and interventions, major Western powers should not provide arms to rebel groups instead in order to tackle human rights violations. Rather, they should seek alternative, more peaceful means, such as naming and shaming, arms embargoes, and targeted financial sanctions.[17] And, if there is still, on occasion, a choice between undertaking direct military intervention and arming rebels for human rights purposes, it seems more likely that the former – direct military intervention – will be the better option.

Notes

1 Parts of this chapter were presented to audiences in Birmingham, Brittany, Dublin, Frankfurt, Manchester Metropolitan University, the University of Manchester, the University of Oxford and the University of Sheffield. I would like to thank the participants for their comments and questions. I would also like to thank Ned Dobos, Toni Erskine, Cécile Fabre, Christopher Finlay, Mark Reiff, Don Scheid, Michael Skerker, Jean-Baptiste Jeangène Vilmer, and the editors of this volume for their very helpful written comments. This chapter was written while holding a research fellowship from the Arts and Humanities Research Council (AHRC) for the project, 'The Ethics of the Alternatives to War' (AH/L003783/1). I would like to thank the AHRC for their support.

2 This is a central premise of Pinker (2011). I should note here that this 'declinist thesis' is somewhat controversial. The counters of the debate are spelt out by Gleditsch (2013), who notes that it is widely accepted (even among critics) that there has been a decline in war and other forms of violence. According to Gleditsch, the main controversies surround (1) what causes this phenomenon and (2) whether there will continue to be a decline, in the light of both climate change and the potentially significant changes to geopolitics if and when the relative power of the West decreases. Indeed, 2014 saw a clear spike in the death rate, although Goldstein and Pinker (2016) – the most well-known defenders of the declinist thesis – point to seemingly positive trends in early 2016 (at the time of writing) and argue that 'virtually all the war in the world is now confined to an arc stretching from Nigeria to Pakistan'.

3 For instance, an Opinium/Observer poll found that the UK public opposed action against Assad in September 2013. www.theguardian.com/politics/2013/aug/31/poll-british-military-action-syria. There was, however, more public support for the action against ISIS, but this was not a humanitarian intervention. For instance, in December 2015, a CNN/ORC Poll found that there was support for a ground war against ISIS. http://edition.cnn.com/2015/12/06/politics/isis-obama-poll/

4 To be clear, I do not think that this scepticism should be overstated. A degree of support for occasional humanitarian interventions will remain as the relevant norms and doctrines continue to influence, and occasional interventions will be likely.

5 I address this lacuna in Pattison (under contract).

6 This is available to download for free on www.jamespattison.co.uk.

7 See, for instance, Vilmer (2012).

8 Note that Buchanan (in my view, persuasively) rejects this view.

9 Reasons of fairness also may provide a reason to arm rebels compared to not doing so. That is, the rebels have already had to take on the costs of *fighting* injustice. It is unfair that they should also have to bear the costs of supplying the arms, such as purchasing them from the black market.

10 It might also be held that causal remoteness provides to prefer arming rebels to engaging in direct military intervention since the former is more causally remote. When arming the rebels, the supplying state is not the agent that *commits* the foreseeable killing of innocents, unlike when engaged in direct military intervention. In other words, being complicit in a wrongdoing might be thought to be better than directly committing the wrongdoing oneself. Notwithstanding, it seems that this does not provide a weighty reason in favour of arming rebels. For instance, if France is considering (i) arming a rebel group which would harm 100 innocents or (ii) intervening militarily which would harm 99 innocents, it seems that it should do the latter, despite the causal remoteness of the former.

11 It is worth noting here that the recognition of the Syrian opposition by various states was only political, rather than formal, legal, recognition (Ruys 2014, p. 37; Schmitt 2014, p. 154).

12 This seems to be true even in the case of civil wars, which, interestingly, the lack of strong international criticism over the arming of Assad provides an important precedent

in establishing that governmental forces can be legally supplied arms in civil wars (Ruys 2014, p. 14).
13 Also see Holtom (2012, p. 8).
14 Even these measures may struggle because of the growth of the illicit global arms network and because dual-use technology is increasingly important but often treated as innocuous; there may therefore need to be a more holistic approach, including moratoria on arms imports, a global levy on arms transfers, and better instruments to prosecute defence firms that breach international law (Cooper 2006).
15 As I argue in Pattison (2015a).
16 To be sure, if there are several, regular instances of the illegal arming the rebels where the international community does not repudiate the supplier, there may develop a new exception to the general prohibition on doing so based on customary international law, although it would also need to be accompanied by relevant *opinio juris*. On the ethics of illegal legal reform, see, more generally, Buchanan (2001).
17 See Pattison (2015b).

References

Akande, D 2013, 'Would It Be Lawful for European (or Other) States to Provide Arms to the Syrian Opposition?', *EJIL: Talk!*, 17 January. Available from: www.ejiltalk.org/would-it-be-lawful-for-european-or-other-states-to-provide-arms-to-the-syrian-opposition. [13 December 2016].

BBC 2013, 'Who is Supplying Weapons to the Warring Sides in Syria?', *BBC News*, 14 June.

Bellamy, A and Williams, P 2009, 'The West and Contemporary Peace Operations', *Journal of Peace Research*, vol. 46, no. 1, pp. 39–57.

Bolton, J 2001, 'Plenary Address to the UN Conference on the Illicit Trade in Small Arms and Light Weapons', UN Conference on the Illicit Trade in Small Arms and Light Weapons in all its Aspects, 9 July, New York. Available from: http://2001-2009.state.gov/t/us/rm/janjuly/4038.htm. [13 December 2016].

Buchanan, A 1999, 'The Internal Legitimacy of Humanitarian Intervention', *Journal of Political Philosophy*, vol. 7, no. 1, pp. 71–87.

Buchanan, A 2001, 'From Nuremburg to Kosovo: The Morality of Illegal International Legal Reform', *Ethics*, vol. 111, no. 4, pp. 673–705.

Cook, M 2000, ' "Immaculate War": Constraints on Humanitarian Intervention', *Ethics & International Affairs*, vol. 14, no. 1, pp. 55–65.

Cooper, N 2006, 'What's the Point of Arms Transfer Controls?', *Contemporary Security Policy*, vol. 27, no. 1, pp. 118–137.

Corten, O and Koutroulis, V 2013, 'The Illegality of Military Support to Rebels in the Libyan War: Aspects of *Jus Contra Bellum* and *Jus in Bello*', *Journal of Conflict & Security Law*, vol. 18, no. 1, pp. 59–93.

Eck, C 2014, 'Coercion in Rebel Recruitment', *Security Studies*, vol. 23, no. 2, pp. 364–398.

Franck, T 2006, 'Legality and Legitimacy in Humanitarian Intervention' in T Nardin and MS Williams, (eds), *NOMOS XLVII: Humanitarian Intervention*, pp. 143–157, New York University Press, New York.

Gleditsch, NP 2013, 'The Decline of War: The Main Issues', *International Studies Review*, vol. 15, no. 3, pp. 397–399.

Goldstein, JS and Pinker, S 2016, 'The Decline of War and Violence', *Boston Globe*, 15 April.

Holtom, P 2012, *Prohibiting Arms Transfers to Non-state Actors and the Arms Trade Treaty*, United Nations Institute for Disarmament Research, Geneva.

Independent International Commission on Kosovo 2000, *The Kosovo Report*, Oxford University Press, Oxford.

Jackson, T 2010, 'From under Their Noses: Rebel Groups' Arms Acquisition and the Importance of Leakages from States Stockpiles', *International Studies Perspectives*, vol. 11, no. 2, pp. 131–47.

Moore, M 2012, 'Selling to Both Sides: The Effects of Major Conventional Weapons Transfers on Civil War Severity and Duration', *International Interactions*, vol. 38, no. 3, pp. 325–347.

Pattison, J 2010, *Humanitarian Intervention and the Responsibility to Protect: Who Should Intervene*, Oxford University Press, Oxford.

Pattison, J 2014, *The Morality of Private War: The Challenge of Private Military and Security Companies*, Oxford University Press, Oxford.

Pattison, J 2015a, 'The Ethics of Arming Rebels', *Ethics & International Affairs*, vol. 29, no. 4, pp. 455–471.

Pattison, J 2015b, 'The Ethics of Diplomatic Criticism: The Responsibility to Protect, Just War Theory and Presumptive Last Resort', *European Journal of International Relations*, vol. 21, no. 4, pp. 935–957.

Pattison, J (under contract), *Just and Unjust Alternatives to War*, Oxford University Press, Oxford.

Pinker S 2011, *The Better Angels of Our Nature: A History of Violence and Humanity*, Penguin, London.

Ruys, T 2014, 'Of Arms, Funding and "Non-lethal Assistance": Issues Surrounding Third-State Intervention in the Syrian Civil War', *Chinese Journal of International Law*, vol. 13, no. 1, pp. 13–53.

Schmitt, M 2014, 'Legitimacy versus Legality Redux: Arming the Syrian Rebels', *Journal of National Security Law & Policy*, vol. 7, no. 1, pp. 139–159.

Vilmer J-B J, 2012, 'Il Faut Armer Les Rebelles Syriens', *Le Monde*, 7 December.

12

THE LIMITS OF R2P AND THE CASE FOR PACIFISM

Jeremy Moses

Introduction

The relative successes and failures of the Responsibility to Protect (R2P) can, it seems, be endlessly debated. Has the R2P project succeeded in reshaping our understanding of sovereignty? Has it honed the conflict prevention skills of the international community? Has it now become an embedded norm of international relations? Did it play a part in the resolution of the Kenyan political crisis in 2008? Was it a prime motivation for the Libyan intervention in 2011 and, if so, was that a positive or a negative thing? Do the cases of Syria and Yemen demonstrate the failure of the project and the emptiness of the norm? All of these questions, and more, have been keenly contested in the academic and journalistic literature on the R2P, with very little ground given on any side to the exhortations of those opposing.

In an attempt to open up some new ground in this apparently intractable debate, I will seek to raise significant questions regarding the attempt to develop norms that both allow for and seek to constrain the use of force in international relations. For while much recent R2P scholarship has tended to focus on the relatively uncontroversial effort to prevent conflicts from reaching a critical stage, the problem of using force in order to intervene in a crisis situation remains the most difficult and contentious problem associated with the doctrine. In short, I will argue that the use of force, whether for ostensibly universal, humanitarian purposes or for specific and narrow national interests, cannot ever be adequately encapsulated in a normative framework. It is precisely this foundational problem that illustrates the relative weakness of the 'norm entrepreneur' and generates the repeated disappointments and endless arguments over the validity of using force for humanitarian purposes, as well as inducing futile attempts to re-shape the normative project to avoid further disappointment. As such, I will argue, if the R2P wishes to succeed as a normative programme aimed at the reduction of the amount of extreme violence in the world, its adherents will need to eschew the sovereign trappings of military force and adopt a more consistently non-violent approach to the resolution of political conflict.

I will develop this argument in three parts. The first will provide an overview of the normative theory that undergirds the promotion of the R2P and the various attempts that have been made to sharpen and refine this theory in response to the disappointments of the past 15 years. The second part will then seek to establish the argument that the deployment of interventionist force for humanitarian purposes, as a necessarily violent political act, cannot be logically grounded in normative principles, insofar as all such violence necessarily takes place in an exceptional condition in which 'normality' has already been suspended. It is this fundamental problem that has generated the repeated failures of the R2P to come to terms with the always ambiguous outcomes of the application of force for humanitarian purposes, a problem again made obvious in a variety of recent cases, most notably Libya, Syria and Yemen. A potential corrective to this flaw will be briefly and tentatively advanced in part four, where I will argue that R2P advocates can only extricate themselves from the problems of inconsistency, hypocrisy, and the associated accusations of failure if they abandon the potential resort to force from their normative project and adopt a non-violent or perhaps pacifist position that, in recognising the limits of force, also recognises its own limitations and promotes only those principles that aim toward prevention and non-violent resolution of political conflicts.

Normative thought and the responsibility to protect

It has become conventional to discuss the R2P in terms of a normative project. The very premises of the concept lie in the quasi-anti-foundationalist belief that the structures of international politics – indeed, the structures of human life in general – are not pre-given or inevitable, but are developed through the interaction of ideas and power. The preferred approach of advocates of the R2P tends to be constructed upon the foundation of the normative theory developed by Martha Finnemore, Kathryn Sikkink and Thomas Risse (among others) in the 1990s, focusing primarily on the role of 'norm entrepreneurs' in promoting the R2P, the processes by which the norm has been 'diffused' and attempts to measure its place in the 'norm life-cycle' (Finnemore and Sikkink 1998; Risse 1999; Risse *et al.*, 1999).

From this point of view, the R2P norm is conventionally seen as having emerged through the initial work of the 'norm entrepreneurs' attached to the International Commission on Intervention and State Sovereignty (ICISS) and the culmination of their year-long endeavours: *The Responsibility to Protect* report of 2001. The conventional story of R2P then continues through to the 2005 United Nations (UN) World Summit Outcomes Document, which is regarded as having confirmed the acceptance of the norm on a global scale, albeit in a modified form from that presented by ICISS in 2001. As Jennifer Welsh summarises it:

This picture would suggest, following the life-cycle model of norms set out by Finnemore and Sikkink, that R2P has successfully passed through the stages of 'norm emergence' (during which entrepreneurs such as ICISS lobbied states and key individuals to promote R2P) and 'institutionalization' (during which the norm's meaning was clarified by the SOD), and has now entered the phase of norm 'cascade' and 'diffusion', during which states and other actors will begin to consistently act on the norm's precepts.

(Welsh 2013, p. 378)

Yet the picture is not, of course, as simple as this, as Welsh herself acknowledges. The reality is that while there has been an extraordinary amount published and said about the R2P since its inception in 2001, frustration remains among advocates over the perceived inability, as UN Secretary-General Ban Ki-moon put it, to turn 'the authoritative and enduring words of the 2005 World Summit Outcome into doctrine, policy and, most importantly, deeds' (UN General Assembly 2009, p. 28). What is particularly lacking, for many advocates and critics alike, is a mechanism for ensuring the consistent application of R2P principles in response to the perpetration of mass atrocities that amount to genocide, war crimes, ethnic cleansing and crimes against humanity. From frustrations over the failure to induce decisive action in the Sudanese civil war (Bellamy 2005; Williams and Bellamy 2005; Piiparinen 2007; Matthews 2008; Barber 2009), to debates about the success or failure of UN Security Council action in Libya in 2011 (Adams 2011; Pattison 2011; Rieff 2011; Weiss 2011; Welsh 2011; Çubukçu 2013; Hehir 2013; Hehir and Murray 2013; Loiselle 2013; Machnouk 2014; Dunne and Gelber 2014), and to the concerns held by many over the lack of traction that the R2P has had in the Syrian civil war (Zifcak 2012; Garwood-Gowers 2013; Nuruzzaman 2013), questions emerge as to why there is so much difficulty in bringing about a consistent application of R2P principles in extreme crises.

For a number of advocates of the R2P, the difficulties of selectivity and inconsistency in application of the R2P are, unsurprisingly, not seen as being indicative of its failure as a normative project. From this point of view, the problem is not with the normative content of the R2P, but with the challenges of implementing the norm (Weiss 2011). The sense that the normative project has stalled at the point of implementation has led to a variety of responses from both advocates and critics of the R2P. Some, such as Welsh, call for a more limited understanding of what R2P represents. For Welsh, R2P must be understood as being 'particularly susceptible to contestation, given its inherently indeterminate nature', pointing toward a more modest vision for R2P 'as a responsibility to *consider* a real or imminent crisis involving mass atrocity crimes – what in legal literature is sometimes called a 'duty of conduct' (Welsh 2013, p. 368, emphasis in original). Others propose modified theories of norm diffusion, embracing apparent failures and setbacks as evidence of healthy norm development (Badescu and Weiss 2010; Widmaier and Glanville 2015; Glanville 2016). Recent years have also seen growth in proposals for greater inclusion of non-Western thought as an antidote to accusations of imperialism, led by Amitav Acharya's work on 'norm localisation' (2013, 2015; Thakur 2016). Finally, from a more critical (yet still clearly normative) perspective, scholars such as Aidan Hehir (2010, 2011, 2012, 2013) and Theresa Reinold (2011, 2012) have advanced arguments in favour of firmer legal duties of human protection, on the grounds that 'international law and more robust international legal institutions ... hold the only hope for solving this problem' (Hehir 2012).

In addition to these general trends in the R2P-related literature, a good deal of energy continues to be expended in the attempt to correct perceived misunderstandings of the core concepts of R2P, as these misunderstandings are seen as responsible for inhibiting the implementation of the norm. As Gareth Evans has argued:

> Why is there so much continuing resistance to a principle that so many accept as an important breakthrough, capable of resolving an age old debate in a practical and principled way? A good part of the answer seems to lie in some serious misunderstandings which continue to exist about the intended scope and limits of the responsibility to protect norm.
>
> (Evans 2008, p. 55)

This theme is continued in Ramesh Thakur's (2016) review article entitled 'The Responsibility to Protect at 15', particularly in his angry insistence that the continued use of the term 'humanitarian intervention' as a synonym for R2P 'is due to intellectual hubris, laziness or incompetence' on the part of scholars who make this mistake (Thakur 2016, p. 418).

It is here, I would argue, that we can identify a stark inconsistency in the very foundations of the normative theories that lie at the foundations of the R2P. Both Evans and Thakur, as a co-chair and commissioner on the ICISS panel respectively, are undoubtedly viewed as key R2P norm entrepreneurs, yet their ongoing denunciations of the 'misunderstandings' of the 'scope and limits' of the R2P indicate a somewhat skewed understanding of normativity itself. For if it is indeed the case that many still see 'humanitarian intervention' and 'R2P' as closely related, if not interchangeable, then that itself must be the product of a normative process, as such meanings can only be constructed in a social context. To rail against the association of humanitarian intervention and R2P (see also Glanville 2013), therefore, is to suggest at one and the same time that the R2P norm entrepreneurs have moved us away from thinking about 'humanitarian intervention' and that no alternative definitional movement is possible, a move that requires self-contradiction in order to make sense. Normative theory, dependent as it is on an anti-foundationalist epistemology, cannot logically lead to claims about right and wrong interpretations or definitions, as this flies in the face of its own basic commitments. Thus, if many people (scholars and practitioners alike) still believe that humanitarian intervention and R2P are closely associated and perhaps even synonymous, then that speaks to the normative status of the R2P in the present.

A norm entrepreneur may wish to deny that as a part of their campaign for a particular reading of their ideas, but it is entirely disingenuous and self-contradictory to claim that that preference represents any kind of concrete reality that all must accept. This apparent confusion over the implications of normative thought is not purely theoretical. It runs parallel with – and, in my view, is related to – confusion in the attempt to apply the principles consistently to real-world cases, as I will explain further below.

While the majority of the authors mentioned above, among many others (Arbour 2008; Knight 2011; Shawki 2011; Contarino *et al.* 2012; Karlsrud 2013; Labonte 2013; Loiselle 2013; Brockmeier *et al.* 2014; Negron-Gonzales and Contarino 2014; Brosig and Zähringer 2015; Kurtz and Rotmann 2016), have attempted to introduce certain modifications into the basic propositions offered by Finnemore, Sikkink, Risse and other influential normative theorists, they still operate within the basic assumption that norms (including binding international legal duties at the 'hardest' end of the spectrum) can and do provide the keys to unlocking the problem of military intervention and the role that R2P might play in it. Despite the various critical angles that have been taken on the R2P, it appears that the instrumental effectiveness of norms in international politics now appears to be taken for granted and no longer requires justification in itself.

In remaining within the confines of normative theory and holding to the expectation that the R2P, or a firm new set of international legal norms, can and will change the way in which states understand their sovereignty and broaden the scope of responsibility among the international community, the possibility that norms may not be able to produce such outcomes is rarely confronted. Might it be that the power of norms and the norm entrepreneurs that promote them has been vastly over-inflated? Could there be elements of human conduct, most notably the extreme, violent situation of war, that cannot be effectively contained within a normative frame? And if it is indeed the case that normative transformation is incapable of fundamentally altering the problems associated with sovereign power in international relations, what options does that leave for those who want to work toward the construction of a more peaceful world? These are the questions to be addressed in the remainder of this chapter.

The limits of norms in times of crisis

While there has been a significant turn toward the preventative dimensions of R2P over the past decade, the problem of when a 'timely and decisive response' becomes necessary and what form such a response should take remains as the most difficult and contested issue surrounding R2P. These questions and contentions, I will argue, are the inevitable outcome of any attempt to apply normative principles to situations of violent political crisis, as any situation that calls forth the possibility of 'timely and decisive response' from the international community will invariably be. We are, therefore, immediately confronted by questions around the applicability of normative principles in a context in which the very existence or threat of extreme violence always already represents a breakdown of normative principles. It is here that we encounter the boundaries of norms and exceptions, leading in turn to considerations of the meaning and manifestations of politics and sovereignty – in short, questions of power – in the context of the universal humanitarian values of R2P.

Such questions over the logic of applications of normative thought in the context of relations among sovereign powers tend to be raised from within realist international relations theory and find their clearest expression in Carl Schmitt's critique of liberal normativity and just war theory (Schmitt 1996, 2003, 2007; Slomp 2006, 2009). As Mika Luoma-Aho argues, Schmitt maintained that 'political life cannot be regulated by legal norms, because societies encounter crises that must be resolved by the use of political authority' and consequently 'the nature of the state that emerged as a result of Schmitt's polemics against normativism was decisionist: the will of the sovereign stands above the law of the land' (Luoma-Aho 2007, p. 38). As I have argued elsewhere (Moses 2013, 2014), this depiction of politics requires a very precise understanding of the sovereign as the final, decisive actor in a crisis situation. This, for Schmitt, is the hallmark of any sovereign power and an inescapable dimension of all political life (Schmitt 1985, 1996). Most importantly, this expression of sovereign power above and beyond the law is not limited to the internal politics of states, but is also observable in relations among states. In this sense, any state or group of states that maintains the capacity to exert decisive power over the internal politics of another state is essentially assuming sovereignty over that state. Thus, the R2P, while claiming to have redefined sovereignty in terms of responsibility, reaches a point of decisive sovereign action – essentially unaccountable to any higher authority – when military intervention occurs.

While advocates of R2P have sought to place a redefinition of sovereignty at the centre of their normative project, the emergence of decision in a crisis remains an essential element of all humanitarian crises that the international community seeks to engage with. The very use of the phrase 'timely and decisive response' in pillar three of the R2P points to this fact, as does the explicit location of that decisive power in the UN Security Council. In this case, then, the formal sovereignty of the UN Security Council, and specifically of the permanent five (P5) members with their veto power, is manifest in the capacity to decide what constitutes a crisis and what should be done to remedy the situation. The reluctance of these states to be bound by specific duties and thresholds related to R2P and the structural impossibility of holding any of the P5 to account were they to commit mass atrocities against their own populations, speaks precisely to this sovereign authority and suggests that the redefinition of sovereignty proposed by the norm entrepreneurs of the R2P is far from having its desired effect.

Roland Paris (2014), in his account of the structural problems of the R2P in practice, touches upon may of the symptoms that arise out of this basic problem, demonstrating that military interventions associated with the norm are inevitably beset by 'mixed motives', 'the counterfactual problem', 'the conspicuous harm problem', 'the end-state problem' and 'the inconsistency problem'. None of these problems, he argues, can be overcome through normative refinement. Yet rather than identifying these as structural problems specific to R2P, I would argue that these are structural problems that would attach to any attempt to regulate the conduct of military intervention in general, insofar as these are always situations of crisis in which normative standards of any kind cannot have consistent traction. Paris is, therefore, quite correct in suggesting that these structural problems cannot be resolved, but he does not explicitly recognise this as a problem for *any* attempt to normatively manipulate situations of war. War-fighting, from this point of view, can never be contained or captured by normative principle because war itself occurs as a consequence of the inability of norms to prevent exceptional cases of political conflict. As Schmitt (1985, p. 12) bluntly puts it, 'the norm is destroyed in the exception', a point that connects directly with the claim that 'there is no trans-cultural or trans-historical notion of justice that can be invoked to claim that a war has *justa causa*' (Slomp 2009, p. 99). This is not to say that norms will never exert any influence over the conduct of each combatant in a war situation, but they cannot effectively adjudicate the legitimacy or justness of one side or the other in the absence of a sovereign entity that is capable of taking such a decision. The very existence of the phenomenon of war is, in short, evidence of a breakdown in normativity; war, as exception, exceeds the norm and cannot find justification on moral grounds.

This issue is strikingly illustrated by Thakur's defence of the Sri Lankan government's actions against the Tamil Tigers in 2009. While many have made the case that the Sri Lankan military acted in ways that breached fundamental human rights (The Secretary-General's Internal Review Panel 2012) and should have called forth a timely and decisive response under 'pillar three' of the R2P (Kingsbury 2011), Thakur suggests that such calls may have been misguided, as:

> [G]iven the nature of the conflict as a civil war and the particular brutality of the Tigers, the government [of Sri Lanka] would have been just as entitled to seek international help under R2P in order to discharge its responsibility to protect all people in its territorial jurisdiction.
>
> (Thakur 2016, p. 424)

Similar claims could, of course, be made in relation to Milosevic in Kosovo, Bashir in Sudan, Gaddafi in Libya, and Assad in Syria. All have faced domestic insurgencies that have sought to destabilise their respective *de jure* states and all have responded with extreme force to suppress those insurgencies. Unsurprisingly, all claimed (and in Assad's case, continue to claim) that they were acting in the best interests of their citizenry. In such a context, choices as to which party should be supported and which confronted by intervention under R2P are inescapably political choices, not purely ethical or moral ones.

Russia's decision to militarily intervene in Syria represents a further example of the impossibility of an objective or apolitical determination as to when intervention is necessary and which side in a violent conflict should be supported. While Russia has repeatedly been portrayed as an obstruction to the implementation of R2P in Syria, it can just as easily be argued that intervention on behalf of the Assad regime and against the extremist forces of the Al-Nusra Front and Islamic State is the best (and most legally justifiable) option for the protection of the Syrian population (Averre and Davies 2015). Most R2P advocates have, however, been reluctant to embrace such a claim, preferring instead to argue that non-intervention in Syria is the best alternative given the low prospects for success. Such a position is even presented by Wesley Widmaier and Luke Glanville as an example of the benefits of the ambiguity of the norm. Hence:

> While some have asserted that the failure of the USA and the broader international community to act with force in Syria as it did in Libya demonstrates the imprecision and therefore ineffectiveness of the R2P norm, we suggest that it is indicative of this ambiguous aspect of the norm working exactly as it should, by demanding international engagement with the occurrence of mass atrocities without locking states into undertaking a military intervention that would likely do more harm than good.
>
> (Widmaier and Glanville 2015)

Nevertheless, two separate coalitions are now militarily intervening in the conflict, on the basis of a mix of self-interest, security, and humanitarian concern. Neither the Russian- nor US-led interventions have been authorised by the UN Security Council, yet the possibility of either power being effectively restrained or sanctioned for their actions is practically zero and both continue, in any case, to maintain that they are acting legally (Narwani 2015). Both have been applauded for achieving apparently humanitarian outcomes (such as the defeats of Islamic State in Kobani and Palmyra) and castigated for killing civilians and further degrading public infrastructure. So while Libya illustrates the structural deficiencies of R2P in action, Syria shows how the messy and unpredictable realities of war can render the norm irrelevant, as does the relatively muted debate on the ongoing humanitarian crisis in Yemen.

The implication of this reading of political crisis in relation to R2P is that no normative principle can effectively encapsulate the political interests and contextual constraints or provide the political judgement required to decide on when forceful intervention for human protection purposes should take place or how it should be conducted. All political violence, to put it differently, can be legitimated as being in support of 'the people' or 'civilians', either by parties engaged in civil wars, or by their allies and supporters. Between these competing claims, only those powerful enough to make a decision (as to whether intervention is required and on whose behalf it should be carried out, for example) can provide an answer, and every answer must necessarily be understood as political rather than ethical or normative (Brown 2013, p. 425; Morris 2015, p. 207). The ultimate outcome of this is that any hope or expectation that R2P might act as a restraint on the great powers in their consideration of military intervention is misplaced. The great powers, as a consequence of their *de facto* and formal legal sovereignty under the UN Charter, effectively face no constraint other than consideration of their own gains and losses when deciding when intervention should take place. In such a context, moral justifications for intervention under R2P can serve only as enabling tools for the justification of force by those powers.

This is why, moreover, proposals for the improvement of the R2P norm, such as those outlined in the preceding section, or Brazil's 'Responsibility While Protecting', cannot lead anywhere helpful: the sovereign authority of the P5 within the UN Security Council leads to a situation where even if intervening powers were found, through a process of stricter monitoring and reporting, to be acting beyond their mandate, no power exists that can prevent such abuse from continuing, due to the political and legal standing of the intervening powers. What we end up with is the expectation of a new norm of sovereignty being expressed through what are clearly sovereign acts of military intervention in the classical realist sense. At precisely the moment at which military intervention occurs, therefore, a fundamental contradiction arises in the theory and practice of the R2P. This is a contradiction that produces inconsistent and sometimes perverse outcomes, as cases such as Sri Lanka, Libya, Syria and Yemen, among others, clearly illustrate. Claims about the successful redefinition of sovereignty as a normative breakthrough are, therefore, both misguided and misleading. No norm, by definition, can consistently control the absolute freedom of decision exercised by sovereign powers in these exceptional moments. R2P, in these complex contexts, can only offer false impressions of what the world is and what the potential is for fixing it. Even the suggestions, advanced by Reinold and Hehir, of binding obligations of humanitarian intervention under international law fall prey to this basic difficulty of international politics, as the long history of unpunished breaches of the UN Charter demonstrates.

Violent humanitarian crises are always exceptional situations, and it is in the exception that norms, whether weak or strong, ambiguous or clear, find their limit and the sovereign is left to decide. If this basic structural limit cannot be overcome or nullified by normative activism, what choices remain? Some advocates of R2P or more binding legal obligations might suggest that to turn away from attempts to regulate preventive military intervention will lead to even worse outcomes, as unconstrained powers intervene at will and without any normative tethers on the conduct of their wars. From this point of view trying is enough, even if it does not always produce the best outcome. In opposition to this, I will argue that the major failing of the R2P and related attempts to legally regulate humanitarian intervention labour under the false expectation that the use of force can be derived from morality and can deliver moral outcomes. While it would represent a major departure from the initial concerns of R2P as it emerged from the ICISS process, the only morally consistent position to take if the worst violence and inconsistency associated with the norm is to be avoided is to eschew the recourse to force altogether and adopt a consistent pacifist position.

Toward a pacifist R2P?

Despite the challenges facing any attempt to apply normative principles to the chaos of political violence, there is a continuing insistence that the R2P is effectively empty without the potential resort to force. As the 2009 UN report on *Implementing the Responsibility to Protect* put it, 'no strategy for fulfilling the responsibility to protect would be complete without the possibility of collective enforcement measures, including through sanctions or coercive military action in extreme cases' (UN General Assembly 2009, pp. 24–25). Likewise, even following his exposure of the perennial shortcomings of military interventions under R2P, Paris maintains that 'R2P would almost certainly be dismissed as a hollow doctrine if it did not allow for the possibility of military action as a last resort' (Paris 2014, p. 578). There are perhaps many good reasons for this insistence on the need for forceful measures as part of the R2P norm, not least of which would be the fact that ICISS was established in order to work through the challenges posed by the military intervention in Kosovo in 1999 and come up with a workable solution that would allow for such action in the future. Others might argue that without the possibility of force, the norm would lack the teeth required to influence violent actors in international politics. Still others could maintain that the accommodation of forceful measures is simply the only realistic way of approaching the challenge of mass atrocities in the contemporary world. As I have argued above, however, the attempt to apply normative restraint to exceptional situations is doomed to fail, meaning that the debates over the legitimacy of R2P and its complicity with great power violence will never be overcome while it remains in its current form.

A commitment to pacifist or non-violent principles would draw the sting out of many critiques of R2P and would allow for the kind of morally consistent advocacy that is not currently available while a militarised response remains available. Such an approach affirms and calls for an extension of the recent work of Jonathan Graubart (2015) and Justin Morris (2015), who have both called for a move away from the interventionist dimension of R2P. As Graubart (2015, p. 218) argues:

> [B]y being deprived of the R2P justification . . . states will face greater normative hurdles for employing force. Similarly, eliminating R2P's military intervention component will modestly affect internal debates – both in policy circles and among the broader public – by giving one less rhetorical lever for interventionists.

Likewise, Morris has argued for the 'excision' of the R2P's 'non-consensual, coercive military aspects', on the grounds that this move 'would reassure those states that harbour genuine concerns over the association of R2P with forcible intervention', 'will deprive those who cite such fears as a cloak for ulterior reasons for wanting to prevent intervention of a means of rationalising and justifying their stance' and will 'preserve and cement those aspects of the R2P which enjoy more widespread support' such as early warning and conflict prevention (Morris 2015,

p. 201). Yet while I would fully endorse the conclusions that Morris reaches in relation to the need to sever the military dimension from R2P in order to salvage its positive features, I am more hesitant about his argument that '[a] shared understanding of sovereignty as responsibility will remain at its heart' (Morris 2015, p. 212), as it is precisely the theoretical weakness of this redefinition of sovereignty that produces the problems associated with the use of force in the first place. Recognition that there are dimensions of state sovereignty that cannot be conveniently defined away in this manner is the first step to rethinking the problems surrounding the application of force for humanitarian purposes.

Responding to these problems with a commitment to non-violence can, I would argue, be viewed as being strong, in the sense that it refuses to provide moral legitimation to the acts of powerful states, represents a moral rebuke to those who continue to believe in the utility of military force, and denies the opportunities for 'abuse' that have been such a consistent problem since R2P's inception. Yet such an approach also requires a good dose of humility, in that it represents an acknowledgement of the relative powerlessness of norm entrepreneurs in the context of a militarised world in which the stark realities of sovereign power have not been overcome. Thus, while many would consider such a proposal to be profoundly unrealistic and defeatist, it could as easily be seen as encompassing 'a more cautious position, wary of what may follow from intervening in conflicts where the capacity of external actors to understand what is happening is inevitably incomplete' (Hobson 2016, p. 454). It also accords with the pragmatism and hesitancy of realist thought in relation to the regulation of warfare, as well as avoiding the theoretical and practical traps surrounding any attempt to invoke universal principles in support of war. In short, a pacifist revision of R2P would allow the activists and norm entrepreneurs associated with it to avoid the pitfalls of engagement with militarised politics; for, as Max Weber famously put it:

> he who lets himself in for politics, that is, for power and force as means, contracts with diabolical powers and for his action it is not true that good can follow only from good and evil only from evil, but that often the opposite is true. Anyone who fails to see this is, indeed, a political infant.
> (Weber 1994, pp. 122–123)

The basic point here is that there is more downside than upside for R2P advocates in the attempt to engage with the 'diabolical powers' that are always present in situations of extreme political violence.

In place of the endless and irresolvable debates over the legitimacy of using force for humanitarian ends, R2P advocates and others who share their interests in a more peaceful world could get 'back to building the norm of peace, toward creating a general norm of nonviolence' (O'Connell 2010, pp. 48–49). Or as Catherine Lutz puts it in James Der Derian's film *Human Terrain* (2010), the question should be 'How do you make war less likely rather than more humane?', as '[w]hen you start with that question, then you proceed to some very different conclusions about where we should put our research efforts.' This would mean a deepening of the already-evident trend toward research and advocacy on conflict prevention and peacebuilding, which represents the most interesting, practically feasible, and potentially valuable element of the R2P. Focusing on prevention is itself beset by political and structural challenges (Hehir 2015; Welsh 2015) and is not going to lead to a situation where the problem of mass atrocities and military interventions goes away. It will, however, mean that the work of developing preventative strategies and other measures for the reduction of political violence can proceed without being weighed down with accusations of hypocrisy and imperialism (Graubart 2015) when interventionist powers unleash their arsenals on necessarily weaker target states, invariably killing civilians and destroying vital infrastructure in the process.

Conclusion

For those who wish to see a continuation of the use of force for ostensibly humanitarian purposes, it is becoming more and more difficult to present such uses of force as anything other than deeply compromised by the violent political realities in which they seek to have an impact. Moves are currently afoot to provide further weaponry and training to the nascent government in Libya, this time to defeat the burgeoning power of Islamic State that found fertile ground in the country in the wake of the UN-backed, NATO-led intervention of 2011 (Wintour 2016). Such an effort will undoubtedly require an enormously costly development of aerial and ground force and, if failure is to be avoided on this occasion, a commitment of force and resources lasting decades will likely be needed to ensure that the territory of Libya can be effectively pacified. Meanwhile, in Yemen, the Saudi-led coalition has been aerially bombarding the country for over a year in a mission that they have premised at least partially on R2P principles (Alhaidar 2015). The universal, humanitarian values of the R2P cannot be separated from, nor reconciled with the death and destruction that has occurred and will continue to occur in places such as Libya and Yemen. As I have argued in this paper, this is an outcome of the fact that no norm premised upon universal values can be effectively reconciled with the political causes, conduct and consequences of war, no matter how well-intentioned.

Finally, it should be emphasised that none of these conclusions can or should be read in absolute terms. It is probably the case that there are times where humanitarian norms inspire military responses, or where military action is voluntarily limited as a consequence of ethical principles. It may well be true, though it is always impossible to prove (Paris 2014, pp. 574–575), that the use of force has, in some cases, led to better human rights outcomes than would have otherwise been possible. What norms cannot do, however, is govern such outcomes or make them into duties in the absence of a sovereign entity that can uphold such principles and punish breaches. In the absence of an absolute guarantee of right or wrong, the norm entrepreneur or activist is faced with the question as to what norms might do the least harm. My argument here is that the military dimension of R2P is far more likely to act as an enabling device in the interests of the greatest powers within international politics than it is to promote effective protection of civilians or restraint in the use of force. This claim is backed by the challenging practical issues attached to the R2P, as outlined above, and also by the theoretical claim that no further normative development is possible in the context of the extreme crisis, precisely because such crises are indications of an exceptional, extra-normative situation. Given these challenges and limitations, exploration of non-violent alternatives should be a priority for those interested in extending the preventive dimensions of the R2P.

References

Acharya, A 2013, 'The R2P and Norm Diffusion: Towards A Framework of Norm Circulation,' *Global Responsibility to Protect*, vol. 5, no. 4, pp. 466–479.

Acharya, A 2015, 'The Responsibility to Protect and a Theory of Norm Circulation' in R Thakur and W Maley, (eds), *Theorising the Responsibility to Protect*, pp. 59–78. Cambridge University Press, Cambridge.

Adams, S 2011, 'R2P and the Libya Mission', *Los Angeles Times*, 28 September.

Alhaidar, S 2015, 'Our Goal is to Protect Civilians: Al-Assiri', *Arab News*, 4 June. Available from: www.arabnews.com/saudi-arabia/news/756646. [4 June 2015].

Arbour, L 2008, 'The Responsibility to Protect as a duty of Care in International Law and Practice', *Review of International Studies*, vol. 34, no. 3, pp. 445–458.

Averre, D and Davies, L 2015, 'Russia, Humanitarian Intervention and the Responsibility to Protect: The Case of Syria', *International Affairs*, vol. 91, no. 4, pp. 813–834.

Badescu, C and Weiss, T 2010, 'Misrepresenting R2P and Advancing Norms: An Alternative Spiral', *International Studies Perspectives*, vol. 11, no. 4, pp. 354–374.

Barber, R 2009, 'Reflections on the Peacekeeping Failure in Darfur: Is There Any Substance to the "Responsibility to Protect"?', *Journal of International Peacekeeping*, vol. 13, no. 3–4, pp. 294–326.

Bellamy, AJ 2005, 'Responsibility to Protect or Trojan Horse? The Crisis in Darfur and Humanitarian Intervention After Iraq', *Ethics and International Affairs*, vol. 19, no. 2, pp. 31–55.

Brockmeier, S, Kurtz, G and Junk, J 2014, 'Emerging Norm and Rhetorical Tool: Europe and a Responsibility to Protect', *Conflict, Security and Development*, vol. 14, no. 4, pp. 429–460.

Brosig, M and Zähringer, N 2015, 'Norm Evolution a Matter of Conformity and Contestedness: South Africa and the Responsibility to Protect', *Global Responsibility to Protect*, vol. 7, no. 3–4, pp. 350–375.

Brown, C 2013, 'The Antipolitical Theory of Responsibility to Protect', *Global Responsibility to Protect*, vol. 5, no. 4, pp. 423–442.

Contarino, M, Negrón-Gonzales, M and Mason, KT 2012, 'The International Criminal Court and Consolidation of the Responsibility to Protect as an International Norm', *Global Responsibility to Protect*, vol. 4, no. 3, pp. 275–308.

Çubukçu, A 2013, 'The Responsibility to Protect: Libya and the Problem of Transnational Solidarity', *Journal of Human Rights*, vol. 12, no. 1, pp. 40–58.

Der Derian, J, Udris, D and Udris, M 2010, *Human Terrain: War Becomes Academic*, Bullfrog Films.

Dunne, T and Gelber, K 2014, 'Arguing Matters: The Responsibility to Protect and the Case of Libya', *Global Responsibility to Protect*, vol. 6, no. 3, pp. 326–349.
Evans, G 2008, *The Responsibility to Protect: Ending Mass Atrocity Crimes Once and for All*, Brookings Institution Press, Washington, DC.
Finnemore, M and Sikkink, K 1998, 'International Norm Dynamics and Political Change', *International Organization*, vol. 52, no. 4, pp. 887–917.
Garwood-Gowers, A 2013, 'The Responsibility to Protect and the Arab Spring: Libya as the Exception, Syria as the Norm?', *University of New South Wales Law Journal*, vol. 36, no. 2, pp. 594–618.
Glanville, L 2013, 'In Defense of the Responsibility to Protect', *Journal of Religious Ethics*, vol. 41, no. 1, pp. 169–182.
Glanville, L 2016, 'Does R2P Matter? Interpreting the Impact of a Norm', *Cooperation and Conflict*, vol. 51, no. 2, pp. 184–199.
Graubart, J 2015, 'War Is Not the Answer: the Responsibility to Protect and Military Intervention' in R Thakur and W Maley, (eds), *Theorising the Responsibility to Protect*, pp. 200–220. Cambridge University Press, Cambridge.
Hehir, A 2010, 'The Responsibility to Protect: "Sound and Fury Signifying Nothing"?', *International Relations*, vol. 24, no. 2, pp. 218–239.
Hehir, A 2011, 'The Responsibility to Protect in International Political Discourse: Encouraging Statement of Intent or Illusory Platitudes?', *The International Journal of Human Rights*, vol. 15, no. 8, pp. 1331–1348.
Hehir, A 2012, *The Responsibility to Protect: Rhetoric, Reality and the Future of Humanitarian Intervention*, Palgrave, Houndmills.
Hehir, A 2013, 'The Permanence of Inconsistency: Libya, the Security Council, and the Responsibility to Protect', *International Security*, vol. 38, no. 1, pp. 137–159.
Hehir, A 2015, 'The Viability of the "Responsibility to Prevent" ', *Politics and Governance*, vol. 3, no. 3, pp. 85–97.
Hehir, A and Murray, R, (eds), 2013, *Libya, the Responsibility to Protect and the Future of Humanitarian Intervention*, Palgrave Macmillan, Houndmills.
Hobson, C 2016, 'Responding to Failure: The Responsibility to Protect after Libya', *Millennium – Journal of International Studies*, vol. 44, no. 3, pp. 433–454.
International Commission on Intervention and State Sovereignty (2001) *The Responsibility to Protect*, Ottawa: International Development Research Centre.
Karlsrud, J 2013, 'Responsibility to Protect and Theorising Normative Change in International Organisations: From Weber to the Sociology of Professions', *Global Responsibility to Protect*, vol. 5, no. 1, pp. 3–27.
Kingsbury, D 2011, *Sri Lanka and the Responsibility to Protect: Politics, Ethnicity and Genocide*, Routledge, New York.
Knight, WA 2011, 'The Development of the Responsibility to Protect – From Evolving Norm to Practice', *Global Responsibility to Protect*, vol. 3, no. 1, pp. 3–36.
Kurtz, G and Rotmann, P 2016, 'The Evolution of Norms of Protection: Major Powers Debate the Responsibility to Protect', *Global Society*, vol. 30, no. 1, pp. 3–20.
Labonte, M 2013, *Human Rights and Humanitarian Norms, Strategic Framing, and Intervention: Lessons for the Responsibility to Protect*, Routledge, Oxford.
Loiselle, M-E 2013, 'The Normative Status of the Responsibility to Protect after Libya', *Global Responsibility to Protect*, vol. 5, no. 3, pp. 317–341.
Luoma-Aho, M 2007, 'Geopolitics and Grosspolitics: From Carl Schmitt to E. H. Carr and James Burnham', in L Odysseos and F Petito, (eds), *The International Political Thought of Carl Schmitt: Terror, Liberal War and the Crisis of Global Order*, pp. 36–55. Routledge, Oxford.

Machnouk, SE 2014, 'The Responsibility to Protect After Libya', *Kennedy School Review*, vol. 14, p. 88.
Matthews, MW 2008, 'Tracking the Emergence of a New International Norm: The Responsibility to Protect and the Crisis in Darfur', *Boston College International and Comparative Law Review*, vol. 31, no. 1, p. 137.
Morris, J 2015, 'The Responsibility to Protect and the Use of Force: Remaking the Procrustean Bed?', *Cooperation and Conflict*, vol. 51, no. 2, pp. 200–215.
Moses, J 2013, 'Sovereignty as Irresponsibility? A Realist Critique of the Responsibility to Protect', *Review of International Studies*, vol. 39, no. 1, pp. 113–135.
Moses, J 2014, *Sovereignty and Responsibility: Power, Norms, and Intervention in International Relations*, Palgrave Macmillan, Houndmills.
Narwani, S 2015, 'Breaking International Law in Syria', *RT*, 25 November. Available from: www.rt.com/op-edge/323396-unsc-isis-syria-us/. [25 November 2015].
Negron-Gonzales, M and Contarino, M 2014, 'Local Norms Matter: Understanding National Responses to the Responsibility to Protect', *Global Governance*, vol. 20, no. 2, pp. 255–276.
Nuruzzaman, M 2013, 'The "Responsibility to Protect" Doctrine: Revived in Libya, Buried in Syria', *Insight Turkey*, vol. 15, no. 2, pp. 57–66.
O'Connell, ME 2010, 'Responsibility to Peace: A Critique of R2P', *Journal of Intervention and Statebuilding*, vol. 4, no. 1, p. 39.
Paris, R 2014, 'The "Responsibility to Protect" and the Structural Problems of Preventive Humanitarian Intervention', *International Peacekeeping*, vol. 21, no. 5, pp. 569–603.
Pattison, J 2011, 'The Ethics of Humanitarian Intervention in Libya', *Ethics and International Affairs*, vol. 25, no. 3, pp. 271–278.
Piiparinen, T 2007, 'The lessons of Darfur for the future of humanitarian intervention', *Global Governance*, vol. 13, no. 3, pp. 365–390.
Reinold, T 2011, 'The United States and the Responsibility to Protect: Impediment, Bystander, or Norm Leader?', *Global Responsibility to Protect*, vol. 3, no. 1, pp. 61–87.
Reinold, T 2012, *Sovereignty and the Responsibility to Protect: The Power of Norms and the Norms of the Powerful*, Routledge, New York.
Rieff, D 2011, 'We Have No Idea What We Are Doing in Libya', *The New Republic*.
Risse, T 1999, 'International Norms and Domestic Change: Arguing and Communicative Behaviour in the Human Rights Era', *Politics and Society*, vol. 27, no. 4, pp. 529–559.
Risse, T, Sikkink, K and Ropp, C, (eds), 1999, *The Power of Human Rights: International Norms and Domestic Change*, Cambridge University Press, Cambridge.
Schmitt, C 1985, *Political Theology: Four Chapters on the Concept of Sovereignty*, The MIT Press, Cambridge, MA.
Schmitt, C 1996, *The Concept of the Political*, Translated from Der Begriff des Politischen [2nd edn 1934], MIT Press, Cambridge, MA and London.
Schmitt, C 2003, *The Nomos of the Earth*, Telos Press, New York.
Schmitt, C 2007, *Theory of the Partisan*, Telos Press, New York.
Shawki, N 2011, 'Responsibility to Protect: The Evolution of an International Norm', *Global Responsibility to Protect*, vol. 3, no. 2, pp. 172–196.
Slomp, G 2006, 'Carl Schmitt's Five Arguments against the Idea of Just War', *Cambridge Review of International Affairs*, vol. 19, no. 3, pp. 435–447.
Slomp, G 2009, *Carl Schmitt and the Politics of Hostility, Violence and Terror*, Palgrave Macmillan, Basingstoke.
Thakur, R 2016, 'The Responsibility to Protect at 15', *International Affairs*, vol. 92, no. 2, pp. 415–434.

The Secretary-General's Internal Review Panel 2012, *Report of the Secretary-General's Internal Review Panel on United Nations Action in Sri Lanka*, The United Nations, New York.

United Nations General Assembly 2009, *Implementing the Responsibility to Protect: Report of the Secretary-General*, The United Nations, New York.

Weber, M 1994, 'The Profession and Vocation of Politics' in P Lassman and R Speirs, (eds), *Weber: Political Writings*, pp. 309–369. Cambridge University Press, Cambridge.

Weiss, T 2011, 'RtoP Alive and Well after Libya', *Ethics and International Affairs*, vol. 25, no. 3, pp. 287–292.

Welsh, JM 2011, 'Civilian Protection in Libya: Putting Coercion and Controversy Back into RtoP', *Ethics and International Affairs*, vol. 25, no. 3, pp. 255–262.

Welsh, JM 2013, 'Norm Contestation and the Responsibility to Protect', *Global Responsibility to Protect*, vol. 5, no. 4, pp. 365–396.

Welsh, JM 2015, 'The Responsibility to Prevent: Assessing the Gap between Rhetoric and Reality', *Cooperation and Conflict,* vol. 51, no. 2, pp. 216–232.

Widmaier, WW and Glanville, L 2015, 'The Benefits of Norm Ambiguity: Constructing the Responsibility to Protect across Rwanda, Iraq and Libya', *Contemporary Politics*, vol. 21, no. 4, pp. 367–383.

Williams, PD and Bellamy, AJ 2005, 'The Responsibility To Protect and the Crisis in Darfur', *Security Dialogue*, vol. 36, no. 1, pp. 27–47.

Wintour, P 2016, 'World powers prepared to arm UN-backed Libyan government', *The Guardian*, 16 May. Available from: www.theguardian.com/world/2016/may/16/world-powers-prepared-arm-un-backed-libyan-government. [17 May 2016].

Zifcak, S 2012, 'The Responsibility to Protect after Libya and Syria', *Melbourne Journal of International Law*, vol. 13, no. 1, pp. 59–93.

13
THE RESPONSIBILITY TO PROTECT

A long view

Justin Morris

Introduction

How are we to judge the success (or otherwise) of the United Nations (UN)? The difficulties associated with performing this task are rooted in the UN's institutional size and diversity and the breadth and complexity of the roles that it seeks to perform. At the most fundamental level we might deem the UN to have been a success because, unlike its predecessor the League of Nations, its years of operation have, so far at least, been witness to an absence of the kind of great power conflict that, twice before in the twentieth century, wrought untold destruction and misery on humankind. Any such assessment smacks, of course, of the great methodological sin of confusing correlation with causation, but more significantly, in a world in which Great Power conflict seems a distant prospect but the dangers of terrorist threats, intra-state conflict and humanitarian crises are all too evident, it might also be deemed problematic because it premises the measurement of UN success against a criterion that few would deem particularly appropriate. Consequently, to a far greater degree the organisation's contemporary reputational standing rises and falls in accordance with its ability to respond effectively to conflicts that are local rather than global; today the UN is judged in large part in light of the adequacy of its responses to the Somalias, Rwandas, Kosovos and (most currently) the Syrias of international politics, and in these contexts the verdicts tend so often to be damning.

At first sight the drawing of such conclusions may seem wholly appropriate. The incongruity of a situation in which the UN boldly proclaims the 'Responsibility to Protect' (R2P) people from mass atrocity crimes, while at the same time the world's media alert us to the horrors of conflicts such as that which currently engulfs Syria and the consequent 'unchecked slide' into an unparalleled 'era . . . of global forced displacement' is striking (UN High Commissioner for Refugees 2015, p. 3). But hand-wringing and condemnation offer little attempts to answer the question:

why has the UN – and here we must look at both the institution and the 193 sovereign states that constitute its membership – so often failed to respond adequately when faced with crises that result in catastrophic levels of human suffering?

This is, of course, the proverbial million-dollar question that has given rise to a vast array of diplomatic and academic comment on the huge assortment of factors that stifle the UN's attempts to deliver relief to those who fall victim to the ravages of conflict. Invariably these endeavours adopt a largely twenty-first-century perspective, sometimes developing a narrative that has its historical roots in the UN's humanitarian efforts of the 1990s, but nevertheless focusing more extensively on issues such as the work of the International Commission on State Sovereignty and Intervention (ICISS), the UN's adoption of the R2P in 2005, and the impact that, to a debateable degree, the concept has had on institutional and state practice. In contrast this chapter turns its attention to events that preceded the R2P's adoption by 60 years. Drawing primarily on the official record of the United Nations Conference on International Organization (UNCIO) at which the UN Charter was adopted, it examines the extent to which decisions made at the time of the UN's creation parallel key decisions made at the time of the UN's adoption of R2P, and it considers what this mirroring tells us about attitudes to R2P and about the UN more generally.

The chapter begins by examining the debate that culminated in the agreement that the organisation would not attempt to 'penetrate directly into the domestic life' (UNCIO 1945, vol. 6, p. 508) of member states. It then briefly considers how this decision and its underpinning rationales continued, over the following decades, to affect the UN's attempts to overcome this Charter limitation. The chapter then considers the advent of R2P and two particular issues of deliberation, namely criteria for intervention and the exclusivity of United Nations Security Council (UNSC) authority, both of which resemble quite remarkably the discussions that took place in San Francisco 60 years earlier. The analysis provided shows the UN to be a creature largely of the Great Powers. This was emphatically so in the more deferential days of its founding, but it also remains the case today, especially when questions relating to the use of force are concerned. The chapter therefore illustrates the fact that the UN remains what it always was and what, indeed, it was designed to be, namely an arena for acting out and (hopefully) managing the politics of the Great Powers. Where this allows for the palliation of the gross human wrongs that all too often characterise intrastate conflict and that the R2P was intended to address, the greater good is undoubtedly served, but as the chapter will show, to judge the success or failure of the UN primarily in terms of its ability to deliver such redress is to fundamentally misunderstand the purpose for which the organisation was created in the first place.

The UN and the principle of non-intervention

In his 2011 report on R2P the UN Secretary General (UNSG) Ban Ki-Moon sought to locate the concept within the broader historical evolution of the UN, asserting that the notion that '[s]overeignty endows the State with international and domestic responsibilities, including for the protection of populations on its territory ... is not a new or radical idea' but rather one that was clearly acknowledged at the time of the organisation's establishment in 1945. According to Ban, at this time:

> the drafting committee in San Francisco, referring to the domestic jurisdiction clause of Article 2(7), declared that if fundamental freedoms and rights are 'grievously outraged so as to create conditions which threaten peace or to obstruct the application of the provisions of the Charter, then they cease to be the sole concern of each State'.
>
> (Ban 2011)

In fact the statement cited by the UNSG was made in relation to what was to become Article 1(3) of the Charter (UNCIO 1945, vol. 6, p. 705), but more significant is the reception that the notion received once it was forwarded by the drafting committee to its parent commission for approval. At this point it was agreed that where domestic human rights violations have repercussions for international peace and security they cease to be a matter of domestic concern, but crucially this acceptance constituted the limit of the argument; other than in a loose, aspirational sense, internal behaviour that did not have international implications was not to be considered a matter for the UN. This point was made clear when the commission considered a proposal from the Panamanian delegation that Article 1(3) be amended to refer to the 'promotion and *protection* of human rights' (emphasis added) rather than 'promotion and encouragement of respect for human rights' (UNCIO 1945, vol. 6, p. 324–325). The commission, led by the US and UK delegates, rejected the amendment on the basis first, that it 'would raise the question as to whether or not the Organization should actively impose human rights and freedoms within individual countries', which in the commission's view it should not, and second, that 'it would lead many peoples of the world to expect more of the Organization than it could successfully accomplish' (UNCIO 1945, vol. 6, p. 325).

The cautious approach to the issue of human rights displayed at San Francisco, most especially by the Four Sponsoring Governments (i.e. the USA, USSR, UK and China), was also evident in the manner in which the Conference dealt with the Charter's non-intervention principle. Ultimately adopted as Article 2(7), disbarring UN intervention 'in matters which are essentially within the domestic jurisdiction of any state',[1] this provision was initially intended to apply only to UNSC actions relating to the pacific settlement of disputes. But following the adoption of an amendment proposed by the sponsors, the provision was extracted from the section of the Charter relating to pacific settlement of disputes and transplanted into the section that sets out the UN's guiding purposes and principles, dramatically widening its scope to encompass all aspects of UN activity, excluding UNSC enforcement action (UNCIO 1945, vol. 12, pp. 9, 127, 181). This was necessary, they argued, because during the course of the conference there had been a significant 'broadening of the scope of the Organization' to include social, economic and humanitarian issues, and while this was 'a great advance', it had nevertheless to be made clear that 'the Organization would deal with the governments of member states [and would neither] penetrate directly into the[ir] domestic life . . . [nor] go behind the[m] . . . in order to impose its desires' (UNCIO 1998, vol. 6, pp. 507–509).

The broadening of the scope of the UN's non-intervention principle was, however, not the only change to which it was subject at San Francisco. The Sponsoring Governments also succeeded in ensuring that what constituted a matter of 'domestic jurisdiction' was to be decided by the UNSC – in which they would dominate – rather than by reference to principles of international law, over which the newly created International Court of Justice (ICJ) would have power of determination. In the so-called Dumbarton Oaks Proposals (DOPs), which the Sponsoring Governments had drawn up to serve as the basis for negotiation at UNCIO (Russell 1958; Hilderbrand 1990), the clause had originally mirrored the equivalent provision of the Covenant of the League of Nations (Article 15(8)), excluding organisational involvement in 'situations or disputes arising out of matters which by international law are solely within the domestic jurisdiction of the state concerned' (Russell 1958, p. 1024). But simultaneous with its Charter relocation the clause was completely rewritten, with the phrase 'matters which by international law' being replaced by an undefined reference to 'matters which are essentially within the domestic jurisdiction of any state' (UNCIO 1945, vol. 12, p. 181).

Speaking on behalf of the Sponsoring Governments, John Foster Dulles argued that this rewording reflected the fact that the issue of domestic jurisdiction was a 'basic principle, and not . . . a technical and legalistic formula designed to deal with the settlement of disputes by the security council' (UNCIO 1945, vol. 6, p. 507), but debate over the matter suggests that many national delegations viewed the change as a retrograde step. A Greek amendment to the Sponsoring Governments' proposal, requiring that questions over domestic jurisdiction be referred to the ICJ garnered majority support within the deliberating committee, but by a margin that was insufficient to satisfy the two-thirds majority rule that governed such votes (UNCIO 1945, vol. 6, pp. 509–510). A similar fate befell a Belgian proposal to reinstate a reference to international law into the non-intervention clause, and at the close of the discussion the Sponsoring Governments' newly worded proposal carried the day (UNCIO 1945, vol. 6, pp. 511–513).

The above analysis highlights three particular points of shared concern among the Sponsoring Governments, and especially the 'Big Three', the UK, USA and USSR. The first of these was a reluctance to see the UN subjected to what they perceived to be overly intrusive legal constraint, whether in the form of specific references to international law, or oversight by the ICJ. As the Panamanian delegate to the conference exclaimed, this disinclination was evident from the time at which the DOPs were first circulated, with, 'many thinking persons . . .

astonished to note that the phrase "international law" did not appear one single time in the two chapters on Purposes and Principles of the Organization; [and] that in the whole document it appeared only once' (UNCIO 1945, vol. 6, p. 79). Yet the Sponsoring Governments, which had spent such time and effort negotiating the terms of the draft proposals, sought very deliberately to build an organisation that would be primarily political and strategic, rather than legal, in nature. Keen to avoid the fate of the League of Nations, where technical arguments over what constituted a 'resort to war in disregard of [Article 16 of the League] Covenant' (Carr 1967, pp. 167–179) were deemed to have stymied the organisation's effectiveness, they aimed to maintain maximum diplomatic room to manoeuvre. Hence at the Sponsoring Governments' instigation, the relevant deliberating committee 'put aside a proposal which would have obligated the Council to aid any party submitting to judicial settlement ... believ[ing] that ... it unduly restricted the Council's freedom of action' (UNCIO 1945, vol. 11, p. 16). Similarly, they opposed and ultimately defeated the proposal, supported by a number of delegations, that the term 'aggression' be defined within the Charter, their prevailing argument being that 'the progress of the techniques of modern warfare renders difficult the definition of all cases of aggression' (UNCIO 1945, vol. 11, p. 17), and consequently 'prior definition would be difficult, whereas recognition of an act after it had been committed would be simple.' Accordingly, the Sponsoring Governments argued, 'the safest course would be to give the council discretion to decide when an act of aggression had been performed' (UNCIO 1945, vol. 12, p. 342).

The Sponsoring Governments' second – and intimately related – aim was to ensure that the UN would revolve around and cement their global managerial role as Great Powers (Morris 2013). Hence the line of argument set out above was applied most assiduously to the UNSC, empowered as it was to be with the most intrusive and potentially dictatorial powers of any of the UN's organs, and destined to be dominated by the Great Powers. Nowhere is this sentiment captured more clearly than in a statement of Harold Stassen, a key member of the US delegation, when he declared that:

> It is our view that the people of the world wish to establish a Security Council, that is, a policeman who will say, when anyone starts to fight, 'stop fighting'. Period. . . . That is the function of a policeman, and it must be just that short and that abrupt; that is, unless at that place we would add any more, then we would say 'Stop fighting unless you claim international law is on your side'. That would lead to a weakening and a confusion in our interpretation.
>
> (UNCIO 1945, vol. 6, p. 29)

The third of the Sponsoring Governments' concerns related more specifically to the issue of domestic affairs and human rights, and in particular to a recognition that while such issues were ones over which they had notably discordant views, they nevertheless had between them to agree on an approach that could ultimately be incorporated into the UN framework. The limited common ground that was eventually agreed upon among the Sponsoring Governments in this regard was that 'since wars usually start over poverty or social dissatisfaction, the U.N. should make every effort to improve living standards worldwide' (Schlesinger 2003, pp. 240–241). But beyond this there was little that tied the Great Powers together, with the ideological chasm between the UK and US on the one hand, and the USSR on the other, being further complicated by the issue of colonialism which saw the UK as the odd ball among the Big Three (Morris 2013).

From the outset the UK and US 'viewed arrangements for social and economic cooperation as integral parts of any world organization', but the Soviets initially acknowledged only that it 'might be desirable to establish a separate organization ... "not connected with the inter-national security organization", to carry out [such] objectives' (Hilderbrand 1990, p. 86). As the Big Three debated the matter throughout the course of the Dumbarton Oaks conference there appeared to be hope for optimism, as Soviet Ambassador Gromyko intimated to the lead US negotiator, Under Secretary of State Edward Stettinius, that he would be able to concede ground on the inclusion of provisions for economic and social issues within the Charter provided progress could be made on what was ultimately the 'crux of the problem' dividing the Great Powers, namely the voting procedure for the UNSC (Campbell and Herring 1975, pp. 128–129). Such hopes seemed, however, to have been dashed when the Americans changed their position by arguing for the inclusion of a hitherto absent reference to human rights in the 'Principles' section of the Charter (Hilderbrand 1990, p. 91). This proposal served only to unite the UK and USSR in opposition; for the British such a step was unacceptable on the grounds that it 'would give rise to the possibility that the organization might engage in criticism of the internal organization of member states' (which for the British raised concerns over colonial matters), while the Soviets argued that 'reference to human rights and basic freedom is not germane to the main tasks of an international security organization' (Department of State 1966, vol. 1, p. 789). This opposition was intensified by the obligatory terms in which the Americans phrased their proposed addition to the Charter:

> It is the duty of each member of the Organization to see to it that conditions prevailing within its jurisdiction do not endanger international peace and security and, to this end, to respect the human rights and fundamental freedoms of all its people and to govern in accordance with the principles of humanity and justice. Subject to the performance of this duty the Organization should refrain from intervention in the internal affairs of any of its members.
>
> (Department of State 1966, vol. 1, p. 829, n. 23)

Faced with British and Soviet resistance the US yielded ground, withdrawing their proposal and instead settling for a single, non-obligatory reference to human rights under which it was proposed that 'the Organization should . . . promote respect for human rights' under Chapter IX of the DOPs relating to 'Arrangements for International Economic and Social Cooperation'. On the basis of this compromise the Big Three established ground for agreement; what was to ultimately become the Charter of the United Nations would include a section on economic and social issues (see Chapters IX and X), but no obligatory reference to human rights would be included in the document either here or elsewhere.[2]

This might, at first sight, appear something of a diplomatic climb-down for the US given the undeniable timidity of the agreed addition to the DOPs. The agreement might similarly seem undeserving either of Franklin Roosevelt's 'surprise', expressed to Stettinius, 'that the Soviets had yielded' to it, or of his associated proclamation that 'the inclusion of the human rights sentence was extremely vital' (Department of State 1966, vol. 1, p. 842). But the satisfaction displayed highlights the incredibly precarious line that US negotiators were forced to tread, for not only did they have to deal with British and Soviet opposition, they also had to keep a watchful eye on the still powerful forces of conservatism and isolationism that continued to typify much of US Congressional foreign policy thinking. Determined to rid the US of the 'suicidal consequences' (Department of State 1963, vol. 1, p. 592) of such a mindset and to debunk once and forever the 'folly and lack of vision' (Hoopes and Brinkley 1997, p. 59; see also Divine 1971) on which it was premised, the President and those to whom he entrusted the formulation of US UN-policy would doubtless have been bolder in their approach had they not had to stand Janus-faced, watching both their Great Power allies *and* domestic power-brokers suspicious, for example, 'of a prospective world body investigating the racial and immigration policies of the United States' (Hilderbrand 1990, p. 91). In this context it was the concentration of power in a UNSC in which the US held the power of veto that provided the ultimate rebuttal to Congressional Opposition, as US Secretary of State Cordell Hull pointed out to key US Senators when he stressed that 'the veto power is chiefly for the benefit of the United States' (Hull 1948, p. 1662). But so precariously balanced was the US domestic political situation that it was necessary to ensure that matters such as human rights, which might serve to poison a steadily growing and carefully nurtured congressional consensus, be referred to in as dilute a form as possible.

Overcoming the limitation of non-intervention

The preceding discussion demonstrates just how fraught an issue human rights was for the Great Powers as they negotiated the content of what was to become the Charter of the United Nations. The diplomacy of the San Francisco Conference may have ensured that the Charter came ultimately to include far more numerous references to the matter than had the DOPs on which it was based, but the continuingly tremulous terms in which these were proclaimed bear testament to the predominantly statist vision that delegates had for the organisation. The legacy with which this leaves us, as Ian Hurd has observed, is a UN:

built around the idea that a threat to international peace and security is the concern of everyone, but the domestic affairs of a state are the concern of no one except the state itself . . . [and consequently] there is no international legal category of a "threat to domestic peace and security" which . . . serve[s] as the counterpart to the idea of a "threat to international peace and security."
(2012, p. 36)

Yet as Hurd also notes, 'the Security Council has over its history employed a series of devices to overcome this limitation' (2012, p. 36) and what is striking from an historical perspective is that such manoeuvrings were not unanticipated back in 1945. Such foresight is evident, for example, in the debate over domestic jurisdiction and the question of whether this should be cited in the Charter with direct reference to international law, where leading US delegation member John Foster Dulles advocated an approach based on 'simple and broad principles' while stressing that what constituted such jurisdiction would inevitably be 'subject to evolution' (UNCIO 1945, vol. 6, p. 508). Of course Dulles advanced this position and claimed that 'future generations would be thankful to the men at San Francisco' for it (UNCIO 1945, vol. 6, p. 508), safe in the knowledge that when it really mattered, namely in the UNSC, the US would be able to veto an evolutionary step with which it did not agree. But his position, along with the fact that it was eventually accepted by other delegates at the conference, indicates an expectation that the Charter's terms, through state and institutional practice (if less so through formal amendment), would at least to some extent be malleable in nature.

A detailed account of this process of change is beyond the scope of this chapter, and exhaustive chronicles have, in any case, been deftly provided elsewhere (Wheeler 2000; Welsh 2004; Evans 2008; Bellamy 2009, 2015; Hehir 2010a, 2012). Suffice to say here that the process has been long, uneven and tortuous. It began in the organisation's very first year of existence (Higgins 1963, p. 78), but despite this and the potential impetus of a plethora of intra-state conflicts and crises in which thousands (and sometimes millions) died, throughout the Cold War the UN and its member states showed little appetite for re-striking the balance between human and state rights. The widespread prevalence of human rights abuses and episodic mass killing that characterised much of this period may have contradicted the standard setting, welfare promoting instruments[3] to which the vast majority of states pledged fidelity at the time, but the Charter's non-intervention principle was generally perceived to be the superior prevailing norm and it was interpreted in near absolutist terms.

In the post-Cold War world such geostrategic rationales, which for almost half a century had impeded moves towards a more liberal view of the principle of non-intervention, seemed less compelling. Many states undoubtedly continued to harbour serious normative reservations over any moves that diluted the sovereign prerogatives of states, but in the context of a global distribution of power that so heavily favoured the pro-interventionary states of the West, such views became increasingly difficult to voice or sustain. Consequently, the 1990s witnessed an unparalleled period of UNSC activism aimed at addressing intra-state crises involving human suffering on a catastrophic scale. It is, therefore, somewhat ironic that, in the broader context of the glacially slow progress that the UN had previously made toward providing an effective palliative for the victims of the grossest of humanitarian violations, the UNSC's reputational standing during the final decade of the twentieth century should be shaped by two cases in which it failed to act, rather than by recognition of its significant steps towards repudiating the organisation's hitherto unyielding adherence to absolutist notions of sovereignty. With greater historical perspective the cases in question, namely Rwanda (where faced with an act of genocide the UN failed to act because none of its key members felt sufficiently interested to do so) and Kosovo (where continued and more robust UNSC involvement was blocked by discord among the Permanent Five [P5]), appear not simply as new chapters in an ongoing catalogue of humanitarian ineptitude, but rather as parametral markers of a rebalancing of human and state rights in which the UN has long been engaged.

In a similar vein, the fact that reflection on the UN's performance in Rwanda and Kosovo provided the most immediate impetus for the process that eventually gave rise to R2P reminds us of the need to see this concept not as a revolutionary leap in UN practice, but rather as an evolutionary step in this longer term process of reassessing the institution's role and priorities (Morris 2015). Debate continues over just how large and significant a step R2P's adoption is for the UN and for those whose misfortune it is to fall victim to the perils of the most abhorrent excesses of pernicious state behaviour; should it be viewed as 'much ado about nothing' (Reinold 2010, p. 55), essentially 'sound and fury signifying nothing' (Hehir 2010b, p. 218), or as 'the most dramatic normative development of our time' (Thakur and Weiss 2009, p. 22) which constitutes the 'end of the argument . . . [in] the debate over stopping genocide' (Evans 2011). But it does at least appear to signal an in principle acceptance that the UN and its members can no longer simply turn a blind eye to gross human rights violations.

For Alex Bellamy, one of the stalwarts of R2P analysis and advocacy, the concept, 'although far from perfect', is unique in UN history for offering a 'genuine and resilient international consensus' that 'offers the best chance to build an international community that is less tolerant of mass atrocities and more predisposed to preventing them' (Bellamy 2015, p. 1). Yet wherever one stands on the wider questions of R2P's efficacy, it is evident that such consensus and community become stretched to breaking point in those most extreme of cases where military force offers the only viable means by which violations of human rights can be stopped. Such cases are, of course, at one extreme end of the spectrum of situations that the R2P seeks to address,[4] but equally they command a level of diplomatic, media and public attention that gives them particular notoriety. Hence they inevitably play a disproportionately (some might say distortingly) large part in shaping perceptions of R2P and of the UN more generally. Moreover, whereas at UNCIO Great Power divisions over human rights were contained through diplomatic compromise, in relation to this aspect of the R2P such agreement has often proven unattainable, with splits between the more interventionary-inclined US, UK and France on the one hand, and Russia and China on the other (Newman 2013; Kurowska 2014; Liu and Zhang 2014) being a source of open, often acrimonious discord within the chamber. The fact that the position of the latter two P5 members resonates with rising powers such as India and Brazil (Rotmann et al. 2014) may have significantly detrimental implications for the concept's longer term prospects (Welsh 2010), but more immediately their concerns have led to the very type of Security Council stalemate that R2P was initially designed to alleviate.

It is in the particular context of the potential use of force that R2P struggles most to emerge from the shadows cast by the decisions of 1945. Some of these shadows are immediately identifiable, as Syria shows for example in relation to the P5 power of veto. This was originally intended to operate as 'a deliberately created weak point in the line, designed to . . . interrupt the flow of power whenever circumstances make the continued operation of the circuit dangerous' (Claude 1962, p. 160), but in practice it has proved a more sensitive trigger than initially planned (UNCIO 1945, vol. 11, pp. 130–133; also Claude 1984, pp. 141–162), thus thwarting many attempts to provide humanitarian assistance.[5] Similarly, for those who believe that effective provision of humanitarian relief can only be transformed from aspiration to reality if the UN itself is subjected to significant institutional change (Pattison 2010; Hehir 2012), or less radically if the working methods of its most powerful body, the UNSC, are amended (Blätter and Williams 2011; Morris and Wheeler 2015), the obstacles to reform put in place at UNCIO are an all too clear impediment. But these are just symptoms of a more pervasive issue, namely the relationship between the UN and its Great Power members. This is revealed by the presence of two further shadows – first the determination on the part of the P5 to act unencumbered by criteria, and second the omnipotent position of the UNSC at the centre of the UN system – cast in San Francisco and recast at the 2005 World Summit, and so it is to these that we now turn.

The shadows of San Francisco

The culmination of the work of the ICISS, its report *The Responsibility to Protect*, has at its heart two interrelated propositions. First, that 'State sovereignty implies responsibility, and the primary responsibility for the protection of its people lies with the state itself', and second, that 'where a population is suffering serious harm . . . and the state in question is unwilling or unable to halt or avert it, the principle of non-intervention yields to the international responsibility to protect' (ICISS 2001, XI). As earlier discussion has shown, the notion that 'sovereignty implies responsibility' was far from alien to those who negotiated the terms of the UN Charter, but the need to maintain Great Power unity during that process led to a dilution of terminology that in turn allowed subsequent UN practice to convert sovereignty from an implication of responsibility into an entitlement to immunity. ICISS aimed to recalibrate the UN's normative compass, but acutely aware of the sensitivities surrounding matters of human rights and state sovereignty, it sought also to ensure that where these two issues came into starkest conflict, namely in those cases where use of force appeared to offer the only means of stopping mass atrocity crimes, the UN's ability to authorise such action would not fall victim to the UNSC's voting procedures.

With this goal in mind, the Commission recommended two particular measures designed to enhance the UN's responsive capabilities. First, its report sought to enumerate criteria that could be applied in order to determine the circumstances in which the 'exceptional and extraordinary measure' of 'military intervention for human protection purposes' would be 'warranted' (ICISS 2001, vol. 1, 4. 14–4. 18). Such criteria, combined with a proposal that P5 states should not cast their veto over situations where these criteria were met, where no vital interests were at stake, and where there was a Council majority in favour of intervention, combined to form a so-called Code of Conduct that was seen by ICISS as being key to R2P's success. This idea was subsequently endorsed and adopted by the UNSG's 'High-level Panel on Threats, Challenges and Change' (HLP), the panel of experts convened by Kofi Annan to consider questions of UN reform (United Nations 2004), which viewed it as a means of addressing the twin scourges of humanitarian intervention. As Ramesh Thakur notes, in the view of the HLP, 'criteria would make the Security Council ... more responsive to outbreaks of humanitarian atrocities ... [while simultaneously making] it more difficult for "coalitions of the willing" to appropriate the language of humanitarianism for geopolitical and unilateral interventions' (2005, p. 283). Among many African states – a crucial constituency given their status as the most commonly intervened in by members of the UN – the criteria proposal resonated powerfully as a means of bringing greater legitimacy to UNSC action, but as Bellamy has explained:

> the US, China and Russia opposed them – although for very different reasons: the US, because it believed that criteria would limit its freedom of action; the others, because they feared that criteria might be abused and might legitimise interventions not authorised by the Security Council.
>
> (2009, p. 84)

Such Great Power opposition was crucial in ensuring that, when R2P came ultimately to be endorsed by the UN, criteria for intervention (along with any references to veto restriction (Morris and Wheeler 2015)) were notable by their absence.

The negotiations over criteria for intervention and the ultimate fate that befell the proposal mirrors in many ways the debates at UNCIO over the proposal that acts of aggression that warranted a Council response should be explicitly defined and detailed in the Charter. In the more general context of the Sponsoring Governments' reluctance to have their actions fettered by references to international law, this has already been considered above, but given its parallels with the debate over R2P criteria it warrants a brief reprise at this point. At San Francisco a number of states supported a Bolivian proposal that the DOPs be amended to include a definition of aggression (UNCIO 1945, vol. 3, p. 579) on the grounds that 'the Council's work would be facilitated if a definite list [of acts constituting aggression] were written in the Charter' since this would 'provide for automatic Council action in these cases' (UNCIO 1945, vol. 12, p. 341). But the proposal was successfully rebutted by opponents, led by the US and UK, on the grounds first, that 'mak[ing] Council action automatic would be dangerous for it might force premature application of sanctions' (UNCIO 1945, vol. 12, p. 342), and second, that it 'might endanger the Council's free discretion' and was therefore 'in contradiction . . . with the general spirit of the Charter' (UNCIO 1945, vol. 11, p. 18). The parallels are clear: 60 years might separate UNCIO from the World Summit of 2005, but the passage of time has done little to diminish the determination of the Great Powers to ensure that their role within the UN remains largely unencumbered by the criteria or definitions that others might seek to impose on their actions.

The privileges of the P5 are, of course, at their most pronounced within the confines of the UNSC, and so the second of the ICISS proposals designed to maximise the ability of the UN to respond to humanitarian catastrophes, namely that the United Nations General Assembly (UNGA) or regional organisations be considered as potential (if limited) alternative sources of authority when Council action was prevented by the casting of a veto (ICISS 2001, vol. 1, 6. 30–6. 31), was always destined to be highly contested. For the US and UK a general reluctance to see P5 prerogatives eroded was, to some extent, counterbalanced by their greater predisposition towards intervention and the consequent desire to hold open the possibility of action even in situations in which a UNSC mandate could not be secured. But most particularly in the aftermath of conflict in Iraq, few other states wished to countenance such a proposal, with UNSC veto-bearing Russia and China among the most influential opponents. The debate over authority was one of many serious bones of contention among delegates at the 2005 World Summit, and as negotiations became increasingly fraught and acrimonious, the whole R2P project looked at times to be seriously imperilled (Bellamy 2009, pp. 83–91). It was ultimately resolved through the time-honoured tradition of employing 'intentional ambiguity' (Byers 2004); the paragraphs of the Summit Outcome document relating to R2P stressed the exclusive role of the UNSC in authorising coercive action (United Nations 2005, para. 139), but elsewhere the document simply reiterated the mantra that states must not use force 'in any manner inconsistent with the Charter' (United Nations 2005, para. 77). As such, as Bellamy notes, UN members remained able under the terms of the document to avail themselves of the argument that, since human rights *are* consistent with the Charter, action taken to protect them does not violate the Charter's prohibitions (2009, p. 91; also Gray 2008, pp. 30–55).

This particular episode provides us with another parallel between the World Summit of 2005 and UNCIO, for as discussed above, a very similar drafting device was employed at the latter when the Sponsoring Governments found themselves split over the issue of human rights and the prominence they should be afforded in the Charter. But the two instances are also characterised by a more substantive similarity, because at San Francisco just as at the World Summit, the exclusivity of the UNSC in matters relating to the use of force was also debated, and the outcome was much the same. Proposals, for example, that 'as the forum of world public opinion' the UNGA should be entitled 'on its own initiative' to make recommendations regarding issues of international peace and security that were being dealt with by the Security Council (UNCIO 1945, vol. 9, p. 33) or that it 'should have the power to supervise the activities of the Security Council and to approve them' or not (UNCIO 1945, vol. 11, p. 113) were successfully opposed by the Sponsoring Governments on the grounds that they 'might obstruct the smooth working between the General Assembly and the Security Council' and would lead to 'the authority of the Security Council be[ing] weakened (UNCIO 1945, vol. 5, p. 509; see also Russell 1958, pp. 750–776). Likewise a proposal, particularly though not exclusively favoured by many Latin American delegates at UNCIO, that regional bodies should have greater leeway to resort to or authorise force without the Council's prior permission (UNCIO 1945, vol. 1, p. 364 and vol. 12, p. 568) was similarly rejected on the basis of the need to 'forestall any essential conflict between those organizations and the Security Council' (UNCIO 1945, vol. 11, p. 235; also Russell 1958, pp. 688–712).[6]

The resemblance that the debates and outcomes of the 2005 World Summit negotiations over R2P bear to those of San Francisco illustrate well the difficulties inherent in attempts to progress an agenda that challenges the statist, Great Power oriented logics that characterise the UN and, indeed, international politics more generally. In the immediate aftermath of the Second World War such reasoning might have been inevitable – the gratitude and sense of indebtedness that the lesser powers owed to the Great Powers is palpable within the record of proceedings of UNCIO – but it is striking, and no doubt disheartening for advocates of R2P, to see just how powerful it remained some 60 years later. That the sentiment of R2P might at first distract our gaze from this fact is understandable, especially given the volume of comment that the concept has attracted, but we will be deluding ourselves if we believe that the shadows of San Francisco and all that they represent no longer colour the international landscape.

Conclusion

Nothing in the preceding discussion is intended to suggest that the delegates who gathered at the 2005 World Summit were consciously mirroring the positions adopted by those who had met in San Francisco 60 years earlier, or that they were fully conversant with the actual debates recorded in the 22 volumes of the UNCIO proceedings. Explicit references to the reasoning of 1945 have recently been made in R2P-related debates, most significantly by the UK, Russia and China when they sought to defend their great power privileges (Morris and Wheeler 2015), but the continuing potency of UNCIO's foundational logics of statism and Great Power dominance is evident as much in the manner that it prevails implicitly as in direct citation. The realisation of R2P's full potential is dependent on a significant diminution in the institutional sway that these logics hold among the UN membership today, but the parallels between UNCIO and the 2005 World Summit suggest that they remain deeply ingrained.

For some this is no bad thing; as scholars such as Robert Jackson (2000) have argued, the pluralism that is entrenched in the UN Charter is not without its merits, and in this sense the darkness of the shadows cast by UNCIO might more appropriately be thought of as the comforting shade that plurality provides not just to ruling elites, but also to populations fearful of social and cultural homogenisation. The questionable efficacy of intervention for humanitarian purposes might give further grounds for questioning the solidarist line of argument on which such action is premised (Wheeler 2000), but wherever one stands on the debate between these two positions, what is clear is that neither statist attitudes and policies nor the influence of the Great Power can simply be wished away.

Hurd has noted how attempts to broaden the scope of UN activity to include intervention in domestic affairs:

> erase the distinction between domestic and international matters on which the Charter was premised, [in turn] ... enabl[ing] us to pretend that international human rights law is what we would hope it could be rather than what it actually is.
>
> (2012, p. 36)

Extending this argument further, so too might we be tempted to pretend that the UN itself is what we would hope it could be rather than what it actually is, but whenever we are so tempted we should recall the words of E.H. Carr and his cautionary account of the perils of adopting an approach in which 'wishing prevails over thinking' (1946, p. 8). This is not to advocate a counsel of despair. R2P does constitute a normative advance in the UN's attempts to address the gross abuse of human rights at least in the sense that it places a significant impediment before those states that might otherwise be inclined to argue that human rights are the sole preserve of sovereigns (Morris 2016). But it cannot wholly overwrite the powerful and deeply entrenched precepts that underpinned the organisation's conception, gestation, birth and subsequent development. Indeed, those very phases of R2P's own existence confirm this, as the parallels between the conferences of 1945 and 2005 and subsequent events show.

The P5 states proved willing to countenance, negotiate over and eventually support the version of R2P agreed upon in 2005. For the western Great Powers the concept's underlying principles always chimed powerfully, and whatever reservations they may have harboured, for all five the individual, collective and institutional reputational costs alone would have been so dauntingly high – especially in the more permissive circumstances of the post-Cold War era where grounds for such dissention are less apparent – as to make opposition an untenable course of action. Since its adoption the Council's permanent members have also cited the concept and the rebalancing of state and human rights that it enshrines when they have deemed it appropriate to do so, although they have sometimes done so with notably varying enthusiasm, emphasis and intent. But as the preceding analysis has shown, what ultimately makes R2P acceptable to the P5 is the fact that, as adopted in 2005, the concept leaves intact the fundamentals of the UN as understood and agreed in 1945, including the constitutional privileges of the UNSC's permanent members, especially in relation to the authorisation of the use of force. Consequently, while R2P's precise import today remains a matter of contention, there is little to suggest that its alchemic properties are sufficient to transform the fundamental nature of the UN itself, and this in turn means that the organisation's ability to bring succour to those most deserving of it remains tightly circumscribed. However unpalatable this may be – especially when our TV screens are filled with the horrors of conflicts such as that which currently afflicts Syria – it needs to be understood before judgements about the success or failure of the United Nations are made.

Notes

1. Article 2(7) states: 'Nothing contained in the present Charter shall authorize the United Nations to intervene in matters which are essentially within the domestic jurisdiction of any state or shall require the Members to submit such matters to settlement under the present Charter; but this principle shall not prejudice the application of enforcement measures under Chapter VII.'
2. The Charter contains seven references to human rights: three in Chapters IX and X (see Articles 55(c), 62(1) and 68); in the Preamble; in Article 1(3) relating to the Purposes of the UN; in Article 13(1)(b), relating to the Functions and Powers of the UNGA; and in Article 76(c) relating to the International Trusteeship System.
3. The Universal Declaration of Human Rights and the Genocide Convention, both passed in 1948, and the International Covenants on Civil and Political Rights and on Economic, Social and Cultural Rights adopted in 1966 are key in this regard.
4. On the weighting of the prevention and protection aspects of the R2P, see UN Doc. A/63/677 of 12 January 2009 and Bellamy 2010.
5. For a discussion of the veto in relation to R2P, see Morris and Wheeler, 2015.
6. Article 53(1) of the UN Charter states that 'no enforcement action shall be taken under regional arrangements or by regional agencies without the authorization of the Security Council', and while the UNSC has on occasions effectively provided retrospective authorisation (e.g. over ECOMOG interventions is Liberia in 1992 (Levitt 1998) and Sierra Leone in 1997 (Berger 2001)) such Council mandates are far from guaranteed and as such the basic tenet of Article 53 continues to apply.

References

Ban, K 2011, *Report of the Secretary-General: The Role of Regional and Sub-regional Arrangements in Implementing the Responsibility to Protect*, UN Doc. A/65/877–S/2011/393.

Bellamy, AJ 2009, *The Responsibility to Protect: The Global Effort to End Mass Atrocities*, Polity, Cambridge.

Bellamy, AJ 2010, 'The Responsibility to Protect – Five Years On', *Ethics and International Affairs*, vol. 24, no. 2, pp. 143–169.

Bellamy, AJ 2015, *The Responsibility to Protect: A Defense*, Oxford University Press, Oxford.

Berger, LF 2001, 'State Practice Evidence of the Humanitarian Intervention Doctrine: The ECOWAS Intervention in Sierra Leone', *Indiana International and Comparative Law Review*, vol. 11, no. 3, pp. 605–632.

Blätter, A and Williams, P 2011, 'The Responsibility Not To Veto', *Global Responsibility to Protect*, vol. 3, no. 3, pp. 301–322.

Byers, M 2004, 'Agreeing to Disagree: Security Council Resolution 1441 and Intentional Ambiguity', *Global Governance*, vol. 10, no. 2, pp. 165–86.

Campbell, TM and Herring, GC, (eds), 1975, *The Diaries of Edward R. Stettinius, Jr., 1943–1946*, New Viewpoints, New York.

Carr, EH 1946, *The Twenty Years' Crisis 1919–1939*, Macmillan, London.

Carr, EH 1967, *International Relations Between the Two World Wars (1919–1939)*, Macmillan, London.

Claude, IL 1962, *Power and International Relations*, Random House, New York.

Claude, IL 1984, *Swords into Plowshares: The Problems and Progress of International Organization*, McGraw-Hill, New York.

Department of State 1963, *Foreign Relations of the United States: Diplomatic Papers 1943, Volume 1*, Government Printing Office, Washington, DC.

Department of State 1966, *Foreign Relations of the United States: Diplomatic Papers 1944, Volume 1*, Government Printing Office, Washington, DC.

Divine, RA 1971, *Second Chance: The Triumph of Internationalism in America During World War II*, Atheneum, New York.

Evans, G 2008, *The Responsibility to Protect: Ending Mass Atrocity Crimes Once and For All*, Brookings, Washington, DC.

Evans, G 2011, 'End of the Argument: How We Won the Debate over Stopping Genocide', *Foreign Policy*, 28 November. Available from: www.foreignpolicy.com/articles/2011/11/28/gareth_evans_end_of_the_argument. [23 September 2014].

Gray, C 2008, *International Law and the Use of Force*, 3rd edn, Oxford University Press, Oxford.

Hehir, A 2010a, *Humanitarian Intervention: An Introduction*, Palgrave Macmillan, Basingstoke.

Hehir, A 2010b, 'The Responsibility to Protect: "Sound and Fury Signifying Nothing"?', *International Relations*, vol. 24, no. 2, pp. 218–239.

Hehir, A 2012, *The Responsibility to Protect: Rhetoric, Reality and the Future of Humanitarian Intervention*, Palgrave Macmillan, Basingstoke.

Higgins, R 1963, *The Development of International Law through the Political Organs of the United Nations*, Oxford University Press, London.

Hilderbrand, RC 1990, *Dumbarton Oaks: The Origins of the United Nations and the Search for Postwar Security*, University of North Carolina Press, Chapel Hill, NC.

Hoopes, T and Brinkley, D 1997, *FDR and the Creation of the U.N.*, Yale University Press, New Haven, CT.

Hull, C 1948, *The Memoirs of Cordell Hull*, Hodder & Stoughton, London.

Hurd, I 2012, 'The Selectively Expansive UN Security Council: Domestic Threats to Peace and Security', *Proceedings of the Annual Meeting (American Society of International Law)* vol. 106, pp. 35–38. Available from: www.jstor.org/stable/10.5305/procannmeetasil.106.0035?seq=1#page_scan_tab_contents. [14 December 2016].

ICISS 2001, *Report of the International Commission on Intervention and State Sovereignty: The Responsibility to Protect*, International Development Research Centre, Ottawa.

Jackson, R 2000, *The Global Covenant: Human Conduct in a World of States*, Oxford University Press, Oxford.

Kurowska, X 2014, 'Multipolarity as Resistance to liberal norms: Russia's position on responsibility to protect', *Conflict, Security and Development*, vol. 14, no. 4, pp. 489–508.

Levitt, J 1998, 'Humanitarian Intervention by Regional Actors in Internal Conflicts: The Cases of ECOWAS in Liberia and Sierra Leone', *Temple International and Comparative Law Journal*, vol. 12, no. 2, pp. 333–375.

Liu, T and Zhang, H 2014, 'Debates in China about the Responsibility to Protect as a Developing International Norm: A General Assessment', *Conflict, Security and Development*, vol. 14, no. 4, pp. 403–427.

Morris, J 2013, 'From "Peace by Dictation" to International Organisation: Great Power Responsibility and the Creation of the United Nations', *International History Review*, vol. 35, no. 3, pp. 511–533.

Morris, J 2015, 'The Responsibility to Protect and the Great Powers: The Tensions of Dual Responsibility', *Global Responsibility to Protect*, vol. 7, no. 3–4, pp. 401–424.

Morris, J 2016, 'The Responsibility to Protect and the Use of Force: Remaking the Procrustean Bed?', *Cooperation and Conflict*, vol. 51, no. 2, pp. 200–215.

Morris, J and Wheeler, NJ 2015, 'The Responsibility Not to Veto: A Responsibility Too Far?' in A Bellamy and T Dunne, (eds), *Oxford Handbook on the Responsibility to Protect*, pp. 227–246. Oxford University Press, Oxford.

Newman, E 2013, 'R2P: Implications for World Order', *Global Responsibility to Protect*, vol. 5, no. 3, pp. 235–259.

Pattison, J (2010), *Humanitarian Intervention and the Responsibility to Protect: Who Should Intervene?* Oxford University Press, Oxford.

Reinold, T 2010, 'The Responsibility to Protect – Much Ado About Nothing?', *Review of International Studies*, vol. 36, Special Issue, pp. 55–78.

Rotmann, P, Kurtz, G and Brockmeier, S 2014, 'Major Powers and the Contested Evolution of a Responsibility to Protect', *Conflict, Security and Development*, vol. 14, no. 4, pp. 355–377.

Russell, RB 1958, *A History of The United Nations Charter: The Role of the United States 1940–1945*, Brookings Institute, Washington, DC.

Schlesinger, SC 2003, *Act of Creation: The Founding of the United Nations*, Westview Press, Boulder, CO.

Thakur, R 2005, 'A Shared Responsibility for a More Secure World', *Global Governance*, vol. 11, no. 3, pp. 281–289.

Thakur, R and Weiss, TG 2009, 'R2P: From Idea to Norm – and Action?', *Global Responsibility to Protect*, vol. 1, no. 1, pp. 22–53.

United Nations Confernce on International Organisation 1945, *Documents of the United Nations Conference on International Organisation*, Volumes 1–22, Hein, Buffalo, New York.

United Nations High Commissioner for Refugees 2015, *World at War: UNHCR Global Trends – Forced Displacement in 2014*. Available from www.unhcr.org/556725e69.pdf. [28 October 2015].

United Nations 2004, *A more secure world: Our shared responsibility – Report of the Secretary-General's High-level Panel on Threats, Challenges and Change*.

United Nations 2005, *2005 World Summit Outcome*, A/Res/60/1 of 24 October.

Welsh, JM, (ed.), 2004, *Humanitarian Intervention and International Relations*, Oxford University Press, Oxford.

Welsh, JM 2010, 'Implementing the "Responsibility to Protect": Where Expectations Meet Reality', *Ethics and International Affairs*, vol. 24, no. 4, pp. 415–430.

Wheeler, NJ 2000, *Saving Strangers: Humanitarian Intervention in International Society*, Oxford University Press, Oxford.

CONCLUSION

The future of human rights protection

Robert W. Murray

> But the responsibility to protect also demands more. It calls upon every member of the international community to speak out whenever and wherever atrocity crimes are being committed, or are imminent. As a statement of political commitment, it is designed to galvanize collective action to prevent and respond to atrocity crimes—at the national, regional and international levels—and to raise the political costs of failing to act in the face of genocide, war crimes, ethnic cleansing and crimes against humanity. In order to meet this commitment, it asks Member States to prioritize the protection of vulnerable populations over narrow national interests, to work tirelessly to overcome political divisions and make concrete investments in stronger capacities for prevention and response. In short, the responsibility to protect demands sustained political leadership.
>
> (Ki–Moon 2016, p. 18)

In his July 2016 report on the Responsibility to Protect (R2P), UN Secretary-General Ban Ki-moon argued for a series of steps that international society should focus on to mobilise collective action on the R2P. Arguing in favour of a universal approach to R2P implementation, Ban emphasized four areas that the UN should focus on in order to better address atrocity crimes through R2P – effective and coordinated preventative strategies, timely and decisive responses, prevention of atrocity crime recurrence, and renewed institutional capacity, with particular emphasis on the UN's role and obligation to oversee R2P efficacy which he argues will be achieved given that 'the United Nations is undergoing a series of transformations to make the Organization fit to meet the challenges of protection' (Ki-Moon 2016, p. 17).

As the contributors to this volume note, while there has been some progress made in efforts to protect civilian populations from horrific crimes, there remains a significant gap between the discourse surrounding human rights protection and enforcement. This volume has effectively begged two questions that continue to plague international society's efforts to protect human rights in the twenty-first century – *why* are greater strides not being made in protection efforts, and *how* can the society of states improve its porous record in acting to prevent and/or to halt atrocity crimes? Summarizing the ideas presented in this book, there are five key variables to highlight in an effort to start answering these questions and to contemplating a way forward.

1) States do not recognise a responsibility to protect that is divorced from their direct national interests

From the outset, the normative framework of R2P seemed to operate in contradiction to one of the fundamental realities of international politics – that states make decisions based on their national interests. In its initial version of R2P in 2001, the ICISS sought to redefine sovereignty as conditional in nature and to emphasise aspects of common global interest, yet states have not embraced the idea of acting in the name of human security nor has R2P become part of their national interests. The ICISS report provides guidelines as to how states might consider tenets of R2P as part of an evolving global landscape and the need to redefine national interests, focusing on mobilising domestic political will and overcoming partisanship related to human rights protection, regional refugee flows, economic security, and states wanting to be seen as good international citizens (ICISS 2016, pp. 71–72). Even, as Heinze notes, the liberalism at the heart of interventionism and R2P is not consistently embraced by liberal states, and previous intervention experiences have done more to scare states from wanting to act than they have shown a framework for action to be followed in the future.

Beyond structural or societal theoretical questions raised in my chapter, Jarvis examines an even more fundamental issue when contemplating why states have yet to wed national interests with rights protection. According to Jarvis, the very definition of 'humanity' and international society's inability to properly define and understand what we mean by 'human' impacts how and why R2P and rights protection efforts continue to be debated and often lead to inaction on the part of states. In his chapter, Lang proposes a global constituent power as an effective means of overcoming the lack of progress on rights protection, while others such as Curran and Gilmore look to more practical means of overcoming issues by noting that while states may see interventionism as connected to their interests, they tend to only commit to piecemeal or short-term civilian protection missions. Pattison also notes that states have been more inclined towards intervention-by-proxy by selling arms to the belligerents.

In order for doctrines such as R2P to become effective tools of rights protection, there must be a clear commitment from states to not only use the language of R2P, but to accept a duty or obligation to act when faced with atrocity crimes. International society has used conventions, doctrines, statements and resolutions to identify this imperative, but thus far states have shown their reluctance to accept and adhere to a genuine *obligation* rather than just a vague *responsibility*. This lack of recognition of an obligation has prevented genuine efforts to protect civilians in some of the most egregious cases of rights abuse, and continues to serve as a vital barrier to progress on human rights protection.

2) International institutions comprising states have yet to find consistent and enforceable frameworks through which to protect populations facing humanitarian crisis

Given the reluctance states have shown to fulfil a duty to act in cases of rights abuse and humanitarian emergency, international organisations have yet to find success in compelling states to act when they simply choose not to. Debates surrounding intervention in the face of atrocity are rarely, if ever, isolated to a single state. Instead, debates about action in cases of humanitarian emergency are inextricably linked to assessing the role of international organisations in the twenty-first century.

The institutional elements of the human rights protection discussions are focused more around norms such as legitimacy, authority and enforcement than on whether an obligation exists to begin with. In most international organisations associated with human rights, the bureaucratic side of these institutions recognises and emphasises the universality of human rights, but not the imperative to act. However, in the decision-making bodies of organisations such as the UN, particularly the UN Security Council, where states comprise the membership, translating affirmations of support for human rights into action has proven both complex and difficult. Further complexity is added to the equation when focusing on the Security Council, as it remains the most prominent forum for great power politics; the ongoing use of the veto by the Permanent 5 members of the Council shows that self-interest is alive and well. These challenges have served to bring institutional legitimacy and purpose into question, and tend to lead to discussions about the need for reforms of the global governance architecture around human rights protection, though again, these proposed reforms fall to the whims of the states that make up the organisations.

As Morris notes, many of the challenges faced by international organisations have to do with their underlying structure and historical justification for formation. Morris explains that this is particularly poignant for the UN, which was founded on the idea of non-intervention and great power politics, and how these structural elements continue to affect debates about the criteria for intervention through the UN structure. The same would be true of regional organisations that have inherited much of the responsibility for intervention, such as NATO, whose foundational principle is that of collective defence, though a transformation into an international human rights protection force has demonstrated both successes and failures.

In light of these limitations and difficulties, those states who support human rights protection, as well as institutional bureaucracies, have been creative in trying to use various tactics to highlight the need to act in cases of humanitarian crisis. This has taken the form of publicly identifying those who do not act when faced with decisions on such matters and engaging in 'naming and shaming' as identified by Bloomfield, and in the UN's case, an increasing appetite for a return to traditional peacekeeping to focus more on a Protection of Civilians (POC) model rather than an R2P-based model, as noted by Keating, Jones and Staples. Ultimately, institutions are vital for the legitimacy of decisions made around rights protection given that unilateralism or coalitions of the willing have been destructive to the norms of interventionism and R2P in recent history. The issue remains, however, that institutions comprised of states are bound to be hamstrung by the self-interested approach to rights protection states have always displayed, regardless of how much naming and shaming takes place.

3) The responsibility to protect doctrine is not international law and is thus not obligatory

Among the primary obstacles to seeing a successful adoption of the R2P doctrine internationally is the fact that R2P is not part of the international legal framework, and thus states are able to implement the doctrine's tenets selectively or not at all. The various iterations of R2P, ranging from the 2001 ICISS version to the 2005 World Summit Outcome Document, and interpretations since, have all attempted to encourage states and institutions to adopt the doctrine, but there has been no progress on embedding R2P as a statute of international law in its own right. Further, the erosion of R2P's tenets between the ICISS version and the World Summit Outcome Document version saw R2P become simply a re-articulation of existing conventions on genocide, war crimes, crimes against humanity and ethnic cleansing, rather than as a transformational legal principle, which has served to allow states to skirt their responsibility in those four areas in the same way that they had prior to the 2005 World Summit.

The core of R2P is the redefinition of sovereignty, perhaps the most important principle of international law. R2P is not a doctrine of intervention according to the historical interpretation of sovereignty, sometimes referred to as 'Westphalian sovereignty', which enshrines the norm of non-intervention. Instead, what makes R2P such a pivotal aspect of debates over rights protection and interventionism is its effort to fundamentally reinvent sovereignty as a responsibility rather than a right. States are not seen as legally sovereign among the society of states, according to R2P, if they demonstrate an unwillingness or inability to effectively protect their people. In the cases where states are not adequately protecting their civilians, R2P's tenets dictate that the society of states bears an obligation to react, whether action is invited or not.

Without a new set of legal norms that entrenches R2P or another doctrine of human rights protection, there are significant questions surrounding whether norms alone can compel states to act in the name of responsibility. In his chapter, Moses confronts the limits of norms in crisis situations, and effectively demonstrates the impact this has on R2P's progress. Morris' chapter discusses the legitimacy granted to decisions made under the auspices of the UN Security Council and how this relates to international law, but rightly points out that R2P operates more as a means by which to find consensus at the UN level rather than as a legal principle. What is evident since the end of the Cold War, and since the advent of R2P, is that, as Jarvis claims, the rallying cry of a common humanity has simply been inadequate to effectively urge states into acting consistently on behalf of human rights.

Despite the progress made in normative terms by R2P, there remains a large gap between where the doctrine currently stands and actively protecting human rights. While R2P is a relatively young doctrine in the gaze of international history, this does not lessen the imperative to find effective solutions for action in the face of atrocity crimes. To date, states have not been willing to accept the transformational impact of R2P to their sovereignty, nor have they appeared interested in embedding R2P in international law. This lacuna will continue to allow for the perpetuation of inconsistency around the norm and brings into question any sort of claim surrounding a genuine 'responsibility'.

4) The problem is both conceptual and practical

When evaluating the successes and failures of civilian protection efforts and R2P, it is important to appreciate that the issues raised are both at a conceptual and practical level, and that both serve to prevent greater action in the face of human rights violation. In debates over the best approaches to overcome the existing obstacles to effective and consistent action in humanitarian crises, the authors in this volume have demonstrated there are a variety of theoretical and empirical issues that need to be addressed before real progress can be made. The chapters in this book probe many of these issues, including some of the most basic conceptual tenets of doctrines such as R2P, and beg questions worthy of examination if further value in such approaches to rights protection is to be seen as anything more than discursive tools.

Each contributor to this book raised a different conceptual issue with R2P and civilian protection, and these issues must be addressed before looking at better methods of implementing solutions to atrocity crimes in practice. Morris and Murray raise key questions about the role of great powers and the structure of the international system, and in particular, how this affects decision making by great powers both in their own right as well as through institutional arrangements such as the UN Security Council. Hehir, Bloomfield and Moses probe one of the most important aspects of debates surrounding R2P – the normative foundations of the doctrine – and question whether R2P is a norm at all, and how to better understand its flaws by questioning normative fundamentals and discourse. Heinze and Jarvis take a step back from discussions about human rights and pose a series of questions about what is meant by 'human', and the more fundamental term to right protection narratives, being the idea of a 'common humanity'. Building on the notion of a liberal concept of humanity, covered particularly by Heinze, Lang discusses whether the methods of interpretation about humanity's rights are appropriately conceived through constitutional theory and how this might better explain current limitations of the international human rights regime. Curran and Gilmore, Keating and Staples all provide novel insights into how international society contemplates POC, the selectivity of when the society of states decides to act, and how many aspects of the current POC model is flawed. Pattison's discussion around the ethics of outsourcing interventionism begs a number of questions regarding states' willingness to intervene and to what lengths they will go to not be held to a standard where they bear a duty to act.

The conceptual questions introduced in this volume highlight various areas associated with rights protection in practice. If the society of states cannot agree as to whether there is, in fact, a 'common humanity' or what is meant by 'human' and those worthy of the right of protection, how can there be a serious effort at creating legal frameworks around enforcing such dubious standards? If norms are not as advanced, binding or effective as many claim them to be regarding R2P and a globally recognised duty to act, how can there ever be an expectation of action when faced with a dire humanitarian crisis? Extending further, if states see an opportunity to move away from an R2P model and look to a model of civilian protection such as peacekeeping, does this delegitimise the entire purpose of emphasising a collective responsibility?

These are not light questions to consider, and each chapter has provided insight into various aspects of these debates. Looking forward to an age of greater uncertainty, the society of states must come to terms with a number of difficult questions, the most important of which is whether the lack of effectiveness and consistency of civilian protection and R2P efforts is a matter of will, or whether there are more fundamental conceptual issues at play that have yet to be resolved. Perhaps the worst thing that can happen is for states, institutions and intellectuals to sit back and proclaim success in the face of obvious and continuous failure. Enduring conceptual and practical challenges will be difficult to overcome as the future of the international human rights regime becomes more uncertain given the evolving international order.

5) The responsibility to protect doctrine has contributed significantly to awareness of humanitarian emergency and has become inextricably linked to efforts surrounding the protection of civilians

Despite the challenges and flaws of R2P demonstrated throughout this volume, each contributor notes that R2P represents a critically important variable in how states, institutions, non-governmental organisations and global citizens understand human rights and efforts at rights protection. R2P's most valuable contribution to date has been its ability to raise awareness of humanitarian crises and to force states to confront the harsh realities of their inaction and inability to consistently protect suffering populations. Within a relatively short span of time, R2P has become entrenched in rights discourse and cannot be divorced from how states and institutions approach POC. Though the contributors to this volume are sceptical of the effectiveness of R2P as an enforcement tool of protecting human rights, it is difficult to deny the role R2P plays in the global narrative surrounding rights protection. Advocates of R2P tend to point to two justifications for R2P's role in expanding discourse on humanitarian emergency. Some, such as Gareth Evans, point to the growth of the normative aspects of the doctrine, arguing:

> [I]t is certainly true to say that R2P has gained over the last decade much more worldwide normative traction than most observers had thought possible, and has done so in a way that remains unimaginable for the concept of 'humanitarian intervention' which it has now almost completely displaced.
>
> (Evans 2015)

Others such as Bellamy look to the so-called consensus surrounding R2P in global forums:

> R2P offers the best chance in our time to build an international community that is less tolerant of mass atrocities and more predisposed to preventing them. My optimism is based on the fact that R2P has achieved something that other projects aimed at eliminating genocide and mass atrocities have not: genuine and resilient international consensus.
>
> (Bellamy 2015, p. 1)

As such, it is reasonable to claim that R2P has contributed significantly to vast gains in global awareness of humanitarian crisis and the need to do more when faced with such horrific situations. How this awareness translates into substantive action is where the authors of this book take exception to claims of R2P success.

In the span of approximately 15 years, R2P has become synonymous with human rights, rights protection, and has been a dominant part of the international discourse surrounding how international society responds to atrocity crimes. What is equally as important to note, however, is the false conflation made between R2P and humanitarian intervention, which remain distinctly different concepts. The far-too-prevalent equation of intervention and R2P has been damaging to R2P, as states and many critics of the doctrine argue the true successes of R2P, such as awareness and prevention, are outweighed by an expectation to intervene in every case of human rights violation. Further, R2P tends to be evaluated by whether or not a response will see boots on the ground and troop deployment, even if other forms of intervention are being employed.

Given the examples explored above and in detail throughout this volume, it is evident there are significant challenges to addressing human rights in an age of increasing complexity and uncertainty. The problems with motivating states and institutions to act in cases of humanitarian emergency are neither new nor simple, but this realisation does not negate or lessen the need for the society of states to continue the discussion and to work towards finding consistent and meaningful ways to intervene on behalf of those who most need it. By far the most important and tangible issue to address is not to simply count the rhetorical uses of R2P or human rights language state leaders employ, but rather, there is a distinct need to find a way to compel states and institutions to recognise an obligation to act.

As the contributors to this book have shown, there are relatively few ways to demonstrate to states that they have a duty to act, and even fewer mechanisms to compel or punish them when faced with decisions regarding action. There are essentially three paths to moving states in this direction:

a) force states to act through a more robust system of international law that sees R2P as legally entrenched;
b) coerce states to act via appeals to national interest; or
c) increase efforts to name and shame when states do not act.

Unfortunately, none of these potential solutions is adequate on their own, and the greatest likelihood of success would be for all three to be employed by international society consistently. Even worse, two of these three mechanisms are already in place and have provided little to no movement in urging states to act, and states, particularly great powers, are simply not interested in binding themselves to a more forceful body of law that would force them to act when they typically have to bear a larger load in such missions.

The ongoing evolution of the international system and the society of states is unlikely to provide the ideal environment for legal and normative progress in the quest to better protect human rights, but much depends on the nature of the great powers dominating the discussion and their willingness to recognise rights and the protection of civilians as part of a strong international order. There is a possibility that rights protection can represent an important part of the emerging international order, if the great powers and other members of international society choose to make it one. The character of order, and the normative agenda that emerges as part of a new order, are negotiated between the great powers that dominate it, and reinforced by other states as the order develops. Convincing liberal states such as the US, UK and France that rights protection must become a prominent normative and actionable component of a new multipolar order is challenging enough, but believing that China and Russia, for instance, would agree to a normative framework inherently contrary to their national interests is quite another. The emerging age of uncertainty around human rights protection may provide some important advances in the prevention of atrocity crimes, but it is doubtful there will be substantive progress made on an international consensus around a responsibility to act that overcomes current challenges.

References

Bellamy, A 2015, *Responsibility to Protect: A Defense*, Oxford University Press, Oxford.

Evans, G 2015, 'Responsibility to Protect: Ten Years On', Talk, South African Institute of International Affairs, Pretoria.

International Commission on Intervention and State Sovereignty 2001, *The Responsibility to Protect*, International Development Research Centre, Ottawa.

Ki-moon, B 2016, 'Mobilizing Collective Action: The Next Decade of the Responsibility to Protect', A/70/999–S/2016/620. Available from: www.responsibilitytoprotect.org/SG%20Report%202016-%20Mobilizing%20collective%20action-%20the%20next%20decade%20of%20the%20responsibility%20to%20protect.pdf. [17 September 2016].

INDEX

Abbott, K.W. 93, 95
Acharya, A. 218
Afghanistan 133, 138
African Union 177
airpower use *see under* humanitarian intervention, Western, and UN peacekeeping
American Revolution 23, 28
Annan, Kofi 34, 133, 175, 177
Arab League 177
Arab Spring 202
Aristotle 22
arms' supply ethics: arms embargoes 208; benefit to rebel soldiers argument 205–206; cost/lives argument 203–204; direct military intervention alternative 201–203; duty/burden sharing argument 206–207; general illegality 207–8; highly restrictive option 209–11; humanitarian intervention argument 204–205; international law options 207–211; key issues/conclusion 202, 211; less restrictive option 208–209; permissibility of arming rebel groups 202; positive/negative effects 207; principled reasons for arming rebel groups 203–207; prohibition on use of force 208; statist option 209, 210–211
atrocity crimes *see under* failures of R2P

Bahrain 190
Ban Ki-moon 3–4, 41, 45–46, 111, 217, 232–233, 249
Bassiouni, C.M. 95

Beitz, C. 24
Bellamy, A.J. 73, 82, 92–94, 165, 166–7, 175, 186, 190, 239, 241, 255
Berkman, T. 134
bill of rights *see under* Wilson, James
Blair, Tony 128
Bolton, J. 209
Bosnian conflict 112, 126, 133
Brahimi Report 133
brand comparisons *see* policy brand comparisons, POC, and R2P
Brazil 156
Breakey, H. 93, 94–95, 99, 101
BRICS' global influence 201
Brown, C. 179
Brown, G.W. 21
Browning, C. 149
Brunnée, J. 168, 178
Bull, H. 73, 78, 80
Buzan, B. 76, 78

Carr, E.H. 78, 244
Cecil, R 100
Chatterjee-Miller, M. 179
China 115, 156, 176
Cohen, J. 21
Coleman, K.P. 104
complexity/contestation, in R2P norm: accepting assistance (ICE 3) 171–172; assignment problems 174–175; background 165; collective-permissive effect 176–177; conditional assistance 172; discursive spaces 167; entrenchment 166–169, 178–179;

incentivising compliance (ICE 4) 172–173; inconsistent application of rule 178; intended constitutive effects (ICEs) 165–166, 169; key issues/conclusions 165–166, 178–180; legal obligations 169; non-UN organisations' role 177; offering assistance (ICE 2) 171; Pillars I and II 169, 176, 177, 178; Pillar III responsibility 167–169, 177; as political norm 169; prohibiting mass atrocities (ICE 1) 170–171; proscriptive/prescriptive effects 168–169; punishments 168–169; reform options 179–180; Security Council role 176–177, 178, 179; self-permissive effect 173–174; sovereignty 179; supporting international community (ICE 5) 173–177; UN Secretariat role 175–6, 178
compliance theory of international law *see under* international protection uncertainties
conflict in Syria 3–4
Congo, Democratic Republic of 114
constitutionalization *see under* global constituent power
Cote d'Ivoire 114–115
Cronin, B. 93–94

Darfur genocide 78, 136
de Carvalho, B. 113
democratic systems *see under* Locke, John
Deng, F. 144–5
denial and fatalism as challenges: age of enforcement, post-Cold War 2; alternative approaches 6–7; conflict in Syria/refugee crisis 3–4; decline in global respect 2–3; fundamental principals re-thought 7–8; key issues/conclusion 1–2, 4–6, 12–13; new attitudes 2–4; protection of civilians (POC) 8–10; R2P (responsibility to protect) 2, 3, 4–7, 10–13
Doyle, M. 42
Dulles, J.F. 234, 238
Dunne, T. 97
Dworkin, R. 21

electoral focus *see under* Locke, John
English School approach *see under* post-American international society
Erskine, T. 171, 173, 177
European Union 21
Evans, G. 46, 218

failures of R2P: atrocity crimes 192–3; categories/complexities of norm 188; circumscribed consensus 188–9; co-option of concept 191; concept of norm 187–8; degeneration of ethos 186; domestic implementation 190–2; existential crises and norms 192–3; external intervention claims 194–5; R2P focal points 190, 191; instrumental consensus 189–92; key issues/conclusion 184–5, 195; official discourse 186; Pillars I, II, III 188–9, 190, 192, 193; questions about norm 187–93; reasons for failures 185–7; Security Council 190, 191; states' support 185; status as norm 186–7; status quo affirmation 194; support for R2P 185; three biases analysis 193–5; voluntary reform advocacy 193–4; weak regulative norm 184
Fassbender, B. 21
Feldman, I. 38
Finnemore, M. 216, 219
Francis, A. 101
Frank, J. 27–28
French Revolution 20, 23
Frost, M. 24

Gallagher, A. 5, 40, 44, 178
Geiβ, R. 96
Genocide Convention 40
Giddens, A. 168
Gifkins, J. 45
Glanville, L. 169
global constituent power: background 19; constituent moments 27–30; constituent power 20; constitutionalization 21; Enlightenment foundations 22–23; enumeration of rights 24–25; and human rights 22–25; international relations theorists 21–22; key issues/conclusion 19–20; legal pluralism 21; limiting/enabling principles 20–21; political theorists 21; protest movements 30–31; republican literature 22; rights 21; rule of law 20; self-determination 22–23; separation of powers 20; socio-economic equality 23; specific constitutional texts 21; state roles 24; theoretical approaches 21–22; versions of 23–24; and Wilson *see* Wilson, James; World Social Forum (WSF) 20, 28–30
Gloliagha, S. 167
Graubart, J. 224
Gromyko, A. 236

Guterres, António 3
Guzman, A.T. 97

Habermas, J. 21
Haiti 114
Hardt, M. 23
Hehir, A. 45, 169, 176, 178
hierarchical system *see under* Locke, John
Hohfeld, W. 21
Holt, V. 134
Hopgood, S. 41, 167
Hull, Cordell 237
human rights (R2P) protection: conceptual/practical issues 253–254; denial and fatalism *see* denial and fatalism as challenges; direct national interests of states 250–251; humanitarian emergency, awareness contribution 254–256; international institutions' frameworks 251–252; key variables 250–251; as non-international law 252–253
humanitarian emergency, awareness contribution *see under* human rights (R2P) protection
humanitarian intervention, Western, and UN peacekeeping: airpower use 129–130; armed intervention as exception 128–129; consent and legitimacy 136–137; ground troop deployment 129–130; increased military role 139; institutional limitations of peacekeepers 137; key issues/conclusion 127, 138–139; local forces 130–131; Obama doctrine 128, 129; personnel deployment 135–136; POC interventions 126, 133–138, 138–139; policy guidance 134–135; proximity of peacekeepers 136; public opinion 132–133; R2P concept 127–128, 137, 139; remote cosmopolitanism 131; risk transfer war 131–132; Security Council resolutions 129, 134; showpiece interventionism 127–133; significant constraints 132; subtle/showpiece interventions 126–7; Weinberger-Powell doctrine 132
humanity concept: background 34–35; critiques 38–39; dehumanisation 37; as dual concept 38; duality 38, 39; evaluation of R2P 45–46; genocide, response to 40–41; grounding of 36–40; humankind 37; humanness 36–37; ICISS report 41–42, 44, 47; key issues/conclusion 35–36, 46–47; language of

use 39; moral application 39–40; Pillar 3 engagement 45; R2P 34–6, 38, 40–7; rhetorical tool 38–9; states' obligations 41; World Summit Outcome Document (WSOD) 43–45, 47
Hurd, I. 237–238, 244

ICISS report 144, 185, 193, 216–217, 240
ICISS report *see under* humanity concept
Ikenberry, G. John 21
intended constitutive effects (ICEs) *see under* complexity/contestation, in R2P norm
International Committee of the Red Cross (ICRC) 2, 111–12
international humanitarian law (IHL) *see under* international protection uncertainties
international protection uncertainties: background 91; basic reciprocity 94; civilian targets 96; combatant POC 94–98, 105; compliance theory of international law 97; compliance/commitment issues in POC 102–104; consensus as social notion 93–94; dimensions of legislation 93; European engagement 104; failures of peacekeeping 99; host-state consent 102–103; individual criminal responsibility 96; international humanitarian law (IHL) 94–96; international norms 93; key issues/conclusion 91–92, 104–105; legal protections 93; normative concepts 103; peacekeeping POC 98–102, 104; PKO mandates 99–101; protection of civilians (POC) 92; R2P 91; reciprocal interests 97; sources of POC 92–94; UN peacekeepers 96
international relations theorists *see under* global constituent power
Iraq war 60; outcomes 62–63, 133, 138

Jackson, R. 77, 78–79, 80, 244
Jahn, B. 52, 64, 65

Kant, I. 21, 56–57
Kosovo intervention 59, 60–1, 126, 129, 211, 221, 239; outcomes 61–62, 64–65
Kratochwil, F. 167
Krook, M.L. 191
Kurtz, G. 43, 165, 179

Lebanon 114
Legro, J. 184, 187, 190, 195
liberal internationalism and interventions:

commitment to achieving goals 64–65; contradictions of liberalism *see under* Locke, John; current practice 58–65; key issues 52–53; legality issue/conclusions 58–59, 65–66; political institutions 63–64; post-Cold War/post 9/11 51–52; property rights 64; recent interventions 58; selectivity/motives/means 59–61; short-term/long-term outcomes 61–65

liberalism's contradictions *see under* Locke, John

Liberia 114

Libyan intervention 60–61, 129, 133, 221; outcomes 62, 63

Linklater, A. 73–4

Locke, John 52; democratic systems 56–58; electoral focus 57; hierarchical system 56; legality issue 59; liberal despotism 58; liberal states' intervention 55–56; liberalisms' contradictions 53–8; political project 53–4; pre-liberal principles 53; property rights 54; states' interests 54–55; universal human rights 54–56

Luck, E. 145, 166

Luoma-Aho, M. 220

McCormack, T. 132
MacDonald, M. 73
Maley, W. 95
Malloch-Brown, M. 128
Maurer, Peter 3
MONUSCO intervention 100, 103
Morris, J. 166, 179, 224–225
Murthy, C.S.R. 43

Nasu, H. 98
Negri, A. 23
Newman, E. 165, 167

Obama doctrine *see under* humanitarian intervention, Western, and UN peacekeeping

Orford, A. 169

pacificism case and R2P norm: application of norm 217–218; commitment to non-violence 224–226; conflict prevention/peacebuilding 225–226; crisis decision limits to norms 219–223; foundational problem 215; great power restraint 222–223; key issues/conclusion 215–216, 226–227; non-absolute approach 226–227; and normative theory 216–219; perceived misunderstandings 218–219; realist international relations theory 220; selectivity/inconsistency in R2P application 216–218; sovereignty issues 220; war as normativity breakdown 220–221

Panke, D. 167, 189–190, 192
Papamichail, A. 167
Paris, R. 220–221, 224
Partis-Jennings, H. 167
Pattison, J. 174

peacekeeping *see* humanitarian intervention, Western, and UN peacekeeping

Petersohn, U. 167, 189–90

policy brand comparisons, POC, and R2P: architects of brands 152–154; audience for brands 148–150; circulation of brand 154–156; commercialisation of politics/policies 147; creation of brands 148; creation/implementation politics 153–154; cultural/philosophical/liguistic/ethical divides 149–150; documents/literature 155–156; as dual concepts 143–144, 157; familiarity with brands 156–157; General Assembly debates 154–155; and international politics 146–151; key issues/conclusion 144, 157; localisation of brands 156; nation branding 149; origins/evolution of policies 144–146; POC, origins/evolution of policies 145–146; product/brand disconnect 146–147; R2P, origins/evolution of policies 144–145; resolution data 151–152, 155; success indicators/criteria for brands 150–151, 152–157; as synonyms 143, 146

political theorists *see under* global constituent power

Popovski, V. 101

post-American international society: common interests 73–74; English School approach 72, 80, 84–85; institutions 76, 81–82; intervention 81–83; key issues/conclusion 71–72, 83–85; multipolar questions 71–72; pluralist approach 73, 77–80; post-Cold War order 72–81; R2P emergence 71, 72, 75, 78–82*passim*, 83–84; rules 75–76; Security Council reliance 82–83; solidarist approach 73–77, 80–81

protection of civilians (POC), international protection *see under* international protection uncertainties

protection of civilians (POC), and UN peacekeeping: conflict toll on civilians 110; Conventions' violations 111–112; host country responsibility 115; international humanitarian law 110–111; key issues/conclusion 111, 123; panel of experts 117; performance of mandates 116–117, 120–121; POC mandates 113–115; policy reviews/guidelines 117–119; security sector reform 122; spending on UNPKO 121; UN resolutions 112–114; UNPKO (peacekeeping operations) 114–122; use of force 116, 121–122
protest movements *see under* global constituent power
Provost, R. 94, 96, 103
Pu, X. 179
public opinion *see under* humanitarian intervention, Western, and UN peacekeeping

R2P (responsibility to protect): denial and fatalism as challenges 2, 3, 4–7, 10–13; humanitarian intervention, Western, and UN peacekeeping 127–8, 137, 139; humanity concept 34–6, 38, 40–7; international protection uncertainties 91; origins/evolution of policies 144–5; post-American international society, emergence 71, 72, 75, 78–82*passim*, 83–4; United Nations and intervention 232, 239–40, 241–5, *see also* complexity/contestation, in R2P norm; failures of R2P; human rights (R2P) protection; pacificism case and R2P norm; policy brand comparisons, POC, and R2P
Ralph, J. 128
Ramos-Horta, J. 101, 186
realist international relations theory *see under* pacificism case and R2P norm
refugee crisis 3–4
representative government, importance *see under* Wilson, James
republican literature *see under* global constituent power
Reus-Smit, C. 24
rights *see under* global constituent power
rights bearing citizen *see under* Wilson, James
risk transfer war *see under* humanitarian intervention, Western, and UN peacekeeping
Risse, T. 168, 216, 219

Robertson, G. 38
Roosevelt, Franklin 237
Roth, K 2
Rotmann, P. 165, 179
Ruggie, J.G. 167
rule of law *see under* global constituent power
Russia 115, 176, 221–222
Ruys, T. 209
Rwanda genocide 60, 78, 112, 126, 133, 239

San Francisco Conference *see under* United Nations and intervention
Schmitt, C. 38, 220, 221
Schnabel, A. 179–180
Security Council *see under* R2P failures
Security Council: reliance *see under* post-American international society; role *see under* complexity/contestation, in R2P norm
self-determination *see under* global constituent power
Sending, O.J. 113
separation of powers *see under* global constituent power
Shaftsbury, Earl of 54
Shaw, M. 131
Sierra Leone 112, 114
Sieyes, E.J. 20
Sikkink, K. 216, 219
socio-economic equality *see under* global constituent power
Soffer, J. 104
Somalia intervention 59–60, 126
South Sudan 114, 135–136
Sri Lanka 221
Stahn, C. 43
Stassen, H. 235
Stettinius, E. 236, 237
Syrian Civil War 97, 129, 130–131, 155, 203, 221–222

Tan, K-C 174–175
Thakur, R. 35, 101, 145, 180, 218, 221, 241
Thornhill, C. 23
Ticktin, M. 38
Toope, S.J. 168–169, 178
True, J. 191

UK humanitarian intervention 128
UN Charter 21, 34
United Nations and intervention: background 231–2; Cold War

geostrategies 238; criteria for intervention discussions 241–242; economic and social issues 236–237; Great Powers 232, 235–236, 237, 242, 244; historical development of non-intervention principle 232–237; human rights approaches 233–234; key issues/conclusion 243–245, 323; local conflicts 231; overcoming non-intervention limitation 237–240; post-Cold War 238–239; R2P impact 232, 239–240, 241–245; San Francisco Conference 233–234, 237, 238, 240–243; Security Council 235, 238, 242–243; sovereignty and responsibility 240–241; sponsoring governments' concerns 234–6, 241

UN peacekeeping *see* humanitarian intervention, Western, and UN peacekeeping

Vincent, A. 24

Weber, Max 225
Weinberger-Powell doctrine 132
Weinert, M. 36
Welsh, J. 41–42, 166, 191, 217
Wheeler, N. 75
Wiener, A. 22
Williams, P.D. 92, 94
Wilson, James 19, 21, 28; and bill of rights 26; critique of British Parliament 25; defence of rights 27; representative government, importance 25–26; rights bearing citizen 26
World Social Forum (WSF) 20, 28–30
World Summit Outcome Document (WSOD) *see under* humanity concept

Zehfuss, M. 35